Irris Makler is an award-wi
reporting from the Middle E
of broadcasters, including C
she worked for the ABC f................................... as its
Moscow correspondent. There she covered breaking news like
the sinking of the *Kursk* submarine and the ongoing war in
Chechnya, as well as unforgettable stories like The Reindeer
Serenade, following an orchestra to the Arctic circle, where
they played Mozart for nomads and their reindeer.

Irris began her career at BBC TV in London, where she
specialised in investigative programs, including a series on
medical negligence and the BBC's major current affairs
program, *Panorama*. There, an investigation into the case of
the Guildford Four won the Royal Television Society Award.
Irris also worked for independent TV in the UK.

Our Woman in Kabul

IRRIS MAKLER

BANTAM BOOKS
SYDNEY • AUCKLAND • TORONTO • NEW YORK • LONDON

OUR WOMAN IN KABUL
A BANTAM BOOK

First published in Australia and New Zealand in 2003
by Bantam

Copyright © Irris Makler, 2003

National Library of Australia
Cataloguing-in-Publication Entry

  Makler, Irris.
  Our woman in Kabul.

  ISBN 1 86325 386 6.

  1. Makler, Irris. 2. Afghanistan – Politics and government – 2001–.
  3. Afghanistan – History – 2001–. 4. Women – Legal status, laws, etc. –
  Afghanistan. 5. Women – Afghanistan – Social conditions.
  6. Women journalists – Australia. 7. Women journalists –
  Afghanistan. I. Title.

  958.1046

Transworld Publishers,
a division of Random House Australia Pty Ltd
20 Alfred Street, Milsons Point, NSW 2061
http://www.randomhouse.com.au

Random House New Zealand Limited
18 Poland Road, Glenfield, Auckland

Transworld Publishers,
a division of The Random House Group Ltd
61-63 Uxbridge Road, London W5 5SA

Random House Inc
1540 Broadway, New York, New York 10036

Cover design by Darian Causby/Highway 51
Cover photograph by Jonathan Mossek
Typeset in 11/13.5 Sabon by Midland Typesetters, Maryborough, Victoria
Printed and bound by Griffin Press, Netley, South Australia

10 9 8 7 6 5 4 3 2 1

Contents

Notes on Spellings

As there is no standard method of transliteration from Dari and Russian to English, I have used, for the most part, the simplest spelling of a word or name that comes closest to denoting its sound. However, for names of authors who publish in English translation, I have used their spelling, and for names that have appeared in newspapers and websites, I have adopted the most common spellings, which have become 'accepted' and are now recognised by people.

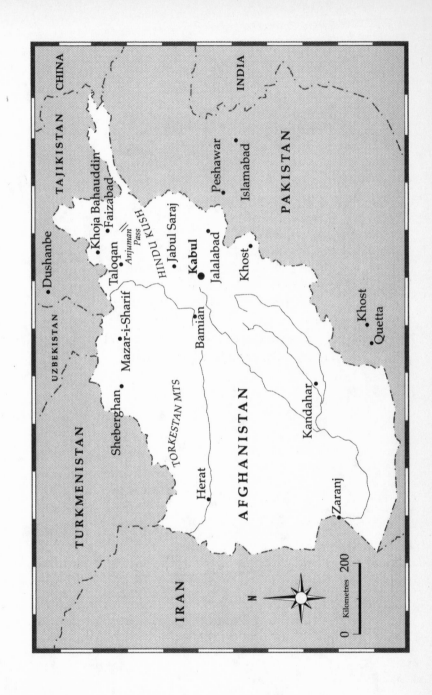

Acknowledgements

First and foremost I have to thank my colleagues in the field – in such a hostile environment, we were reliant on each other. I would especially like to thank my friends from BBC Moscow, who helped me make it in and out of Afghanistan, and the boys from American network NBC, who hauled me across the Hindu Kush, the country's most rugged mountain range, and found a way for us out of Kabul.

I also have to thank my friends Greg Bearup, Margaret Coker and Craig Nelson, and Karen Coleman and Andrew Salgo, for their invaluable help and support, across continents.

For Davo and AI, my inspiration and anchor,
who convinced me to write

Prologue

KABUL, NOVEMBER 2001

This is the best Kabul has to offer – a huge empty house with blocked toilets and a bomb in the kitchen. We don't know about the bomb when we move in, of course, and initially the owner pretends he doesn't either. But afterwards he says he told us all about it, like it was a feature of the house: there's your downstairs toilet, your double garage, your concierge, and your guided missile in the pantry. He's indignant when we want to move out. Welcome to Kabul.

I guess he hasn't had many hard-currency tenants. The Taliban fled six days ago – abandoning the capital they vowed to defend to the last man and the last breath. After weeks of US bombing, the leaders left their weapons stashes behind, loaded their families into their cars – the white Toyotas paid for by Osama bin Laden – and simply took off. While we journalists were heading towards Kabul, they were driving away from it. The highway south was clogged with escaping Taliban Toyotas, snaking all the way back to Kabul, their tail lights a red chain along the dark road. The rare Afghan traffic jam lasted all night.

We drove along a road pocked with bomb craters and the wrecks of tanks into a grimy city where the thin air smelt of petrol, dust and dung.

1

Kabul is a mountain-encrusted jewel, home to one million euphoric, wary, war-weary people. There are restaurants and streetlights and paved roads and a sewerage system. This is the Big Smoke.

There is some traffic, and absurdly overdressed traffic police in elaborate braided uniforms, like costumes from a 1930s Fascist opera. They look as if they should be directing Lamborghinis and Maseratis, but many of them stand at empty crossings. There are more bicycles than cars on the roads and bike repair shops everywhere. In fact, there is every type of repair shop – tyres, washing machines, fridges. This is the opposite of our throw-away society.

The only exception seems to be the 'instant ageing' of rugs – new carpets are thrown onto the road for cars to drive over, to give them the patina that only years of life or two weeks under traffic can produce. I felt a pang when we drove over our first rug, but once the process was explained, I considered we were contributing to the revival of the Afghan economy.

It wasn't easy to find somewhere to stay in a city destroyed by twenty-two years of war, but the American networks came to the rescue. When friends from NBC TV offerered me a spot on their floor in the best house in the best suburb in Kabul, where Taliban mullahs lived until six days ago, I accepted gratefully. Covering this war has been about surviving by helping each other out of tight spots. I'm a freelance journalist, though, without the resources of a big news organisation behind me, so I'm not sure what I offered them in return.

'You give us contacts, flexibility, gossip,' said an NBC reporter kindly, 'and all delivered in that irresistible, incomprehensible accent.'

'Nah, she's like one of those small birds that lives on the backs of hippos,' said an NBC satellite engineer as we walked through a gate into our new home.

In a way they were both right. Single white female in a war zone. Australian accent recommended but not essential.

We gingerly pushed open the doors of a large two-storey house. They squeaked, a forlorn Afghan sound, the closest thing to music during Taliban times. The air was stale and musty, as if the house had just been opened for the first time in months. There was no furniture, except for an old Russian fridge in the kitchen, and a 1970s washing machine in the bathroom. We were impressed to see carpets on the floor, and two toilets, both blocked. There was the possibility that they would be unblocked. Kabul was all about possibilities now.

This was a classy place to unroll my sleeping bag. Nine of us would share the house, eight NBC guys and me. It belonged to a local businessman whose family was in Pakistan. Many now lived like this, separated for safety's sake. He said he was not Taliban, and we chose to believe him.

After four days on the road, with no opportunity to wash, my first shower was luxurious. This was not the cold river water delivered by donkey that we'd become used to every-where else in Afghanistan. It was warm water that came out of a tap, warmly, lazily into a bath, and then swirled down a drain. I watched it, amazed. I was even more amazed at the mud and dust pouring off me. I'd never been so filthy.

I looked around my bedroom with delight. In Afghan terms there was a luxurious amount of space, since I only had one roommate, a young Russian sound recordist called Pasha. He had tweaked our new tin stove so the room was warm and smoke-free. Things had looked grim when it was installed – there was a small explosion, leaving an ugly black stain on the wall – but Pasha sorted it out. He even gave me a container of yoghurt, something I hadn't tasted in weeks. I was too tired to ask where he obtained such a luxury item. Instead, I offered him some pistachio nuts and, for the first time in almost a week, fell asleep smiling and clean.

Now, on our first morning in Kabul, we are standing in the kitchen wondering if we can boil water. Our kettle is nowhere to be seen. Will the stove work? The electricity's on so we may be able to coax it into action. *Where is that kettle?* I am spreading a cracker with apple jelly from an NBC pre-packaged meal, when a stranger saunters in, pokes his head round the corner, turns back to us and says in a broad Australian accent, 'Youse guys better get out of here.'

We look at him in surprise.

He gestures over his shoulder with his thumb: 'Unexploded bomb in there.'

I shake my head in disbelief. 'Who are you?'

The tall, laconic Aussie is Ross Chamberlain, Deputy Director of the United Nations Mine Action Program in Afghanistan. He was called here to investigate a reported bomb, and without too much investigation, he's found one.

I go to the pantry to take a peak, and recoil.

There, partly buried, is a huge American missile, as sleek as a shark, thirty centimetres wide and as tall as I am. It turned in flight and landed tail first, which will make it more difficult to defuse. In the ceiling is the surprisingly small neat hole it made on entry. It is just possible to see the sky, and Pasha takes a photo. His English is excellent, but one thing confuses him.

'Irris – on the side it says: MADE IN USA, 5–0–0–L–B–S. What does that mean?'

'It means it's a 500-pound bomb.'

We'd been sleeping directly above it. And there'd been that explosion in our room as we tried out our new tin stove. It adds a certain zing to the morning. Actually, it cheers me up. I'd been feeling tired and flat after our dangerous drive across the mountains from northern Afghanistan, but the bomb puts a stop to all that. You can't feel sorry for yourself and lucky to be alive at the same time. That's the upside to danger.

In the kitchen, Ross Chamberlain sets down his laptop, and scrolls through 'Bombs in Afghanistan' in much the same way that other people might call up 'Birds of Britain'. His job is to identify the bomb so it can be defused. The NBC guys agree that it's just as well Ross is Australian. An American official would not be so relaxed about announcing a 'major potential personal danger to citizens of the US of A'. It would be much more high octane and we'd be marched out in double quick time. Ross sets the tone and none of us panics.

'Our bomb' – as we come to think of it – was dropped by the US on 12 November, the night the Taliban leaders began packing up their families and fleeing. It was one of five dropped in a precision bombing attack on this residential area, identified by Washington as a Taliban 'command and control' centre. But many of the bombs that hit the city that night either missed their targets or failed to explode, or both, apparently due to a malfunction in their computer guidance system. 'It's 2001, these things are meant to go off,' Ross Chamberlain says. 'But it seems there were more misses than hits in Kabul.'

We tiptoe around the house, packing up our gear. I check that there's nothing left in the bedroom, and see the stain on the wall where the tin stove exploded. I am grateful that it's all there – the stove, the room, me.

We are back to square one, but at least it's daylight. You always feel more hopeful in the morning. After nearly two months in Afghanistan, this is starting to seem normal. Crowded interiors, dangerous exteriors. Chaos, dirt, sleeping bags, eight men and me. The bomb in the kitchen is the only wild card.

There are some personal compensations to this strange life. For once, the odds are in the gals' favour. The guys calculate it down to the last percentage point. 'It's official – there are 10.7 men for every woman. I'll never score,' one bloke tells me despondently. You have to feel sorry for them. All these Errol Flynn adventure types stuck in the Islamic state of Afghanistan, where there are no women, not even the pro-stitutes who are a fixture in every war zone. *It'll be Vietnam with snow and no hookers,* an old Central Asia hand warns gloomily at the start of the conflict.

So we are it. And there are almost none of us. But oppor-tunity – well, that's another matter. Until now we have been sleeping six to a room in sleeping bags on the floor, with Islamic warriors patrolling the compounds where we live. So there hasn't been all that much we could get up to, no matter how good the odds. 'I meet an interesting man I could sleep with every half hour. How often does that happen? Never! And I can't do anything,' a friend wails. It's like being a teenager at some strange religious summer camp – with bombs dropping.

As a result, sex is a hot topic of conversation, though it still takes second place to talking about food. One reporter who's back from the front is telling me the latest, until he suddenly smiles and says, 'Let's stop all this war talk, and get back to flirting.' Fighting and Flirting. Sometimes I feel I'm covering a war while taking part in an episode of Bridget Jones in Afghanistan.

But even Bridget knows when she's gotta get going, so we finish packing and leave the NBC house as quickly as we can.

At the bottom of our street, we drive past a boy selling balloons. They shimmer in the autumn sun, jaunty and hopeful. I'm spellbound by such a simple symbol of happiness and glad I'm alive to see him. The bomb highlights how much we perplex each other, the Western journalists and the Afghan locals.

It turns out that one of the translators NBC employs found the bomb yesterday evening, soon after we moved in, but he decided not to tell anyone till the morning, 'when we could do something about it'. While we think we could have done something about it last night, like sleeping in our cars, he thinks that if the bomb explodes while we are in the house, *Inshallah*, it's the will of Allah.

Allah didn't want us to die, we tell each other happily, as we drive away from the bomb and into the centre of town, all smiles. Kabul is an ancient metropolis, polluted, unfriendly, and vital. It ignores you, like big cities do. It has its own life to live. Since the retreat of the Taliban, that life is changing, re-forming, like a frozen river cracking apart at the end of winter. It's a confusing, thrilling, dangerous time to be here.

The city sits in the lower reaches of the Hindu Kush, one of the highest capitals in the world. The air at this altitude is thin, making it difficult to walk here. The city's demanding hills, or even the stairs inside a building, can easily wipe you out.

The altitude also starts to affect your vision. It's a trick of the thin air, and the lack of industry. The clear, bright light makes every image more intense, as if you have put on glasses that are too strong. The grand mountains surrounding the city appear closer than they are. You feel you can reach out and touch the tawny peaks, dusted with snow like icing sugar on muffins.

We drive to the bazaar, a crowded, dirty open-air market. Although we should be finding somewhere new to live, we get out to look. People push by, apparently in a hurry. Small boys sell toilet paper, two sheets at a time. Wooden barrows with vegetables, herbs, nuts and spices sit next to clothes stalls heaped with Western jeans and T-shirts imported from Pakistan. There are mounds of cumin and coriander and a red spice the colour of dried blood. I wonder what it tastes like. There are piles of sticky sweets and sugary biscuits, and small stalls frying savoury pancakes, even though it is the holy month of Ramadan, when Muslims fast between dawn and dusk.

There are suitcases, aluminium pots and pans, buckets and all kinds of kitchen utensils, as well as Western soap in grubby packets, hair clips, hand cream and make-up, laid out on stalls in neat rows. You can buy karaoke dolls, blonde ones wearing elaborate beautifully sewn Western clothes, dancing and singing to Madonna, and dark ones, wearing even more elaborate Pakistani saris, dancing and singing to Madonna. They're both material girls. But the batteries to make them jive aren't easy to find.

Local metal workers, spotting a niche market, are making satellite dishes by hand. The journalists need them, to report back to the rest of the world, and then the locals want them, to catch cable TV. The dishes are made of scrap metal, covered with the brand names of canned goods. Functional Pop Art objects with Afghan chic.

'Change money?' The age-old question of every bazaar the world over. There are two types of currency here, 'up-money' and 'down-money'. The notes are almost identical – in fact, I never really learn to tell them apart. Having just come from northern Afghanistan, I have up-money, which down here in Kabul is only worth half its value. I'm sure if I took down-money up north, the same thing would happen.

'Look, there are lots of burqas shopping,' says an NBC journalist. I'm not the only woman in the market, but I am the only one whose face you can see. Afghan women are just smudges of colour, hidden under burqas, head to foot cloaks that cover the entire body and face, with only a small mesh screen at eye level.

The burqa is hot, uncomfortable and constricting, limiting vision and breathing, turning women from human beings into bird shapes, identical and anonymous. But in the context of Islamic women's garb, the burqa's eccentricity is its colour. Most Islamic garments designed to cover women are black, though none is as all-enveloping as the burqa. As if to compensate, the burqa is startlingly bright. Most are blue. A white burqa denotes wealth as they are harder to keep clean and indicate that the wearer can afford more than one, and perhaps even has someone to do her washing.

After six weeks in Afghanistan, I still haven't adjusted to the sight of a woman covered in this way, robbed of her individuality and of the chance of a smile from a stranger in the street. Or even a friend. That most basic human contact – a meeting of eyes – is denied to women here.

The possibility of being recognised, a sense that you belong in the public sphere, that there is a space for you here, too – that if you see someone you know, you can stop to chat – all disappear with that swish of fabric, as it comes down, suffocating and separating. Most women say they will remove their burqas when times improve. Despite the flight of the Taliban, they don't feel that time has yet come. My hair is covered by a scarf, and I'm wearing long-sleeved loose clothes, but I receive menacing looks. I can see why women feel safer hidden away.

Osama bin Laden still gazes up at you from sweet stalls. You can buy 'Super Osama bin Laden Kulfa Balls', coconut treats with a picture of bin Laden on the packet, surrounded by tanks, jets and cruise missiles. It seems that bin Laden – like a Teletubby in the West – could be counted on to shift merchandise here.

But now bin Laden bon-bons are making way for postcards of glamorous Indian movie stars. They are pinned up on boards in colourful rows, like butterflies. Other than the occasional journalist, these are the only women's faces to be seen. Teenage boys stand around them in groups.

Even alcohol is becoming available. 'Is Madam looking for something special?' they ask meaningfully at a grocer's stocked with Pakistani goods past their use-by date. If Madam is, then for an extortionate price, a bottle wrapped in newspaper materialises from under the counter. Like a conjurer's trick they remove the paper to reveal – Gordon's gin. The north was dry. Madam swoons and pays up.

We see more food here than in the rest of the drought-stricken country, and excitedly show each other chocolate and crackers and tinned tuna. But there is also more unmanageable poverty. Children black with grease work as mechanics. Six-year-olds bent double push heavy carts, small right angles to their loads. There are shoeshine boys and chimney sweeps, barefoot and filthy, like in Dickens' England. They only sound like children when they laugh. The rest of the time they are small adults, the prime breadwinners for their families, scrabbling to survive in this brutal marketplace.

There are also beggars, of course. The most aggressive are women in filthy burqas, sticking out scaly hands with chipped nail polish. They swarm outside the best restaurant in Kabul, once the Taliban's favourite. Some women also lie on the edge of the road, their burqas spread in the mud like wilting flowers, begging money from passing drivers. It's a heart-rending sight, but at least they can get out of the way if they have to – the bravest beggars are the legless men who perch in the middle of the road. I am horrified when I see the first one, and then realise there are more heads bobbing up along the road, like a row of human cabbages, risking their lives and their truncated bodies in the hope that someone will throw some money out of a car window. This is what injured war victims do in Kabul instead of collecting social security. It's a dire symbol of the city's poverty and collapse.

But Kabul does not elicit pity. It's a tough city, and Kabulis are resilient survivors. They seem happy but watchful, aware that liberation is precarious and could be snatched away at any moment, and that what comes next might be worse than all they have endured so far.

As we drive out of the bazaar, I find I am also excited and wary. So much is unknown – including whether we will find somewhere safe to stay tonight. A truck full of Northern Alliance soldiers hurtles past. The men are dusty and their weapons are slung over their shoulders at a rakish victor's angle. We catch up with them and stop them. According to promises made to Washington, they are not meant to be inside the city. They tell us they are clearing remaining pockets of Taliban resistors, and have found al-Qaeda training camps and weapons stashes. The truck takes off with a crunch of its gears, some soldiers firing into the air. We drive over an Afghan rug back into town. History is waiting for us.

Chapter 1

MOSCOW, 11 SEPTEMBER 2001

I was one of the first journalists into Afghanistan during the conflict, but my ten weeks here started almost accidentally. Like many big journeys, it began with a series of small apparently unrelated steps . . .

I was reporting in Moscow when the world tilted on its axis on 11 September 2001. I had been there for almost two years, first as the TV and radio correspondent for Australia's public broadcaster, the ABC, who posted me there, and then as a freelance journalist. When I explain to Russians that I didn't pick Russia, it picked me, they understand immediately. It fits with their concept of *sudba*, fate.

Moscow is a grand world capital where everything is a struggle – language, politics, money, environment, weather. The heart of what one American President dubbed the 'evil empire' is only four hours' flight from London, but it is another world. Onion domes, snowflakes, fur coats, gothic skyscrapers, delicate ballerinas, senseless drunks, crumbling Soviet nuclear reactors, restored czarist palaces – Russia catapults between extremes. 'We are the barbarians,' said a man from Tartarstan, one of the many nationalities that make up the Russian Federation, as he offered me flowers and chocolates one day. 'We have to be – we are the bulwark against Asia.'

It is fascinating to report from this society in transition, sliding from Communism, to gangster capitalism, to – where next? 'We are destroying in freedom what we built in slavery,' a scientist explained morosely. There are so many other paradoxes: anarchy and bureaucracy, sentimentality and cruelty, passion and apathy, Communist modesty and New Russian ostentation. There is no more May Day Parade – instead Geri Halliwell was the headline act for Moscow's birthday celebrations, while a poster advertising the musical *42nd Street* promised 'Brodvei' in Moscow. A statue of Lenin, striding towards world domination, loomed over a square where a white stretch limo was stuck in traffic. Reconciling all these contradictions, or accepting that they cannot be reconciled, is part of the job of a correspondent in Russia.

On September 11, I was reporting for a number of American broadcasters, including National Public Radio and Voice of America. VOA is the overseas propaganda arm of the United States government. Born under President Franklin Roosevelt during World War II, it came into its own during the Cold War, when antagonism between Russia and the US was at its height. Russians tuned into VOA for two things they didn't receive from their own government – information and jazz, both curtailed under Communism. One legacy of these years of conflict is that for some reason phone lines to the Moscow bureau always drop out at crucial moments. Another is that when you say you file for Voice of America everyone presumes you are a spy. You can't convince them otherwise, even if you have an Australian accent. 'Great cover!' they enthuse.

That Tuesday I was going to an American State Department press conference about the latest round of talks between Washington and Moscow on a new US nuclear missile shield. I caught the metro into town. The metro is one of the jewels of Moscow – clean, cheap, efficient and beautiful. Some stations are like art galleries, with grand marble halls and chandeliers. Built during Soviet times as 'palaces for the people', each station is unique, decorated with paintings, murals or statues, usually depicting happy peasants welcoming the Soviet liberators, or heroes of Soviet labour building a Better Future. But by the time I was living there Tomorrow belonged to the Mafia.

When I emerged in the town centre, it was a balmy autumn day. I walked down Tverskaya, Moscow's busy main street, crossing eight chaotic lanes of traffic. Tverskaya runs from Red Square at one end – with the Kremlin and the rococo, ravishing onion domes of St Basil's church – to the huge wedding cake of Belorussky train station at the other. It is said that Communist dictator Joseph Stalin widened all the streets in the heart of Moscow to reinforce the irrelevance of the individual, and to make sure that if he needed them, tanks could fit comfortably. These days, Stalin's vast sandstone edifices have street-level stores full of ritzy Western labels: Hugo Boss. Dolce & Gabbana. Benetton.

I passed the statue of Pushkin, Russia's national poet, a traditional meeting place for Muscovites. After I moved to Moscow, a bomb tore apart the metro underpass at that spot, another of the long list of unsolved crimes blamed on Chechen terrorists. Every time I passed it, I had to blink away the images of smoke and noise and blood-covered people stumbling out from below ground, a scene from Dante's *Inferno* in the heart of Moscow. That Tuesday there were just ordinary crowds of shoppers and dreamers.

I was heading for the Marriott Hotel, where the State Department was holding its press conference. The sunshine magnified all smells – of carbon monoxide and leaded petrol, of hotdogs cooking at the street corner, and beer and vodka spilt on the footpath. I was revelling in the sun's warmth, and willing its rays to hold back the fierce Russian winter.

At the press conference I heard the first sketchy reports of the attacks on the World Trade Center. Not from the State Department, but from other journalists. These reports were shocking but garbled, and I didn't understand the scope of the attack. My first reaction was as a journalist – I needed to get back to the bureau to see what the American media was reporting. Could the terrorists really have hit the Pentagon – that symbol of US military might? It didn't seem credible. And were there more attacks planned?

I rushed to catch the metro back to VOA, and on the escalators deep beneath Moscow, I had time for more personal reactions. I was shocked by the terrible audacity of turning innocent people into a weapon and killing them in order to destroy a target. It was a sinister milestone, changing the nature of warfare. As I stepped off one escalator and onto the next, two musicians were playing Vivaldi. 'Oh, what beautiful violin,' said the woman on the step in front of me, holding her hand over her heart. The haunting notes followed us onto the train, seeming to mourn a tragedy the performers didn't yet know about.

A drunk snored opposite me as a beggar in a wheelchair was pushed into the carriage. He was a soldier who had lost both legs in battle, a veteran of Russia's war in Afghanistan in the 1980s. He still wore his uniform, neatly pressed, the empty pants folded and pinned at the thigh. His medals shone. For some reason of all the beggars, the injured veterans upset me the most. He had to compete with people selling pens, batteries and magazines. They stepped onto the train and addressed us, *Dear Passengers*, projecting loudly and clearly, as they had been taught in the Communist youth groups. The soldier – half a soldier – rolled silently by. Most people averted their gaze. Only kind-hearted pensioners ever donated anything to the injured veterans, and there were none aboard. I gave him some money. A young woman bought a pen.

After thirty interminable minutes the train reached my stop and I ran all the way to Voice of America. The VOA bureau is located in a depressing, expensive suburb, away from the grandeur of central Moscow. It is on the sixteenth floor of a huge Soviet tower block, with views of freeways and other identical tower blocks beyond. I raced in and turned on the TV, but the cable connection had dropped out so there were no English-language services available. I switched to Russian television, which was running American coverage dubbed into Russian, and quickly realised I had underestimated the scale of events. I found myself numb with shock. I actually didn't believe what I was seeing, and was aware that I didn't understand it, that this event was too large to comprehend immediately. Nevertheless, I watched the horrifying images of the planes smashing into the World Trade Center, and the twin towers collapsing, over and over again, as if the repetition would help make sense of it.

Tearing myself away from the TV, I covered Russia's response to the unfolding events for an American audience. It was swift and passionate. People were sobbing in front of the American embassy in Moscow, where they gathered to pile candles, flowers and icons.

'Our hearts are with them,' one old woman said, adding a beautiful Russian icon of Jesus, black-eyed with a flat gold face, to the sea of tributes at the embassy gates. 'I know what it's like, I was buried under rubble during World War II, but I knew they could rescue me.'

'This is terrible, I have been to the World Trade Center. It could have been me,' said a young man holding back tears. 'I have friends in New York, I don't know if they are safe.'

They were standing at the same spot where Muscovites had last gathered to protest the NATO-led bombing of Belgrade. This was the first of many signs that the September 11 attacks were a watershed, which would redraw the geo-political map and alter the balance of alliances.

The political reaction from the Kremlin was also immediate and supportive. President Vladimir Putin expressed horror, extending sympathy to the American people. He emphasised, self-servingly, that Russia understood the need to fight terrorism because it was involved in its own battle with terrorists, fighting Islamic rebels in Chechnya.

Within days, Washington launched a War Against Terror, with the aims of toppling the Taliban in Afghanistan, capturing Osama bin Laden and destroying the al-Qaeda network.

Journalists anaesthetise themselves against the terrible things they see by keeping busy, and I veered between shock and trying to figure out where I should go to best cover this breaking story. Like most foreign correspondents, I wanted to get as close to the action as possible. This is one of those incomprehensible things people born with the journalist gene have to do. My curiosity overcomes my fear. I want to be there when history is being written. I want to see it, feel it, touch it for myself.

And in purely practical terms, no one was taking any of the usual stories we filed from this region anyway. There was only one foreign story in the world and this was it. In any case Moscow correspondents generally cover Central Asia, the former Soviet satellite states sandwiched between Russia and Afghanistan. Of all 'the Stans', Tajikistan, which lies to the

14

north of Afghanistan, appeared to be the best starting point because it bordered the only part of the country controlled by the opposition to the Taliban. I reasoned that US troops would have to come in from the north since access was impossible from Iran in the west and problematic from Pakistan in the south and east.

Tajikistan was the place to go.

But before I went anywhere, I had to finish some overdue work for BBC radio. It was strange to be editing a frothy piece on Russian cooking while the drums were beating for war, but I completed the assignment and went to the BBC's Moscow bureau on Monday 17 September to send the story to London.

The BBC bureau is in the Slavyanskaya Hotel, a 'New Russian' venture unimaginable in Soviet times. It has Western decor, reworked in the ornate Russian style to service long-legged prostitutes and black-leather clad *biznyessmen*. Their beefy guards wear holsters and earpieces, and loiter near the restaurants and specialty shops, looking menacing. Smile at them and they reach for their guns.

I decided not to take the lift, preferring to climb past these regulars – *Make exercise a part of your day* – musing about the hotel's American owner Paul Tatum, a man who thought he could do business in the new Russia. Tatum was involved in a struggle for ownership of the hotel during the mid-1990s, and lived holed up in his suite for months because there was a contract out on his life.

The first time he left the hotel he was shot. He'd barely made it out of the gates when he copped eleven rounds from an AK-47 at close range. In that classic Moscow underworld touch, his bodyguards did nothing to protect him, though they did take him to hospital afterwards. He was dead on arrival. The blood he'd left on the snow was soon covered by a new flurry. Like so many crimes in Moscow, Paul Tatum's murder remains unsolved.

I was distracted from this grisly story when I reached the BBC's office and had to battle to feed my story to London – always a mysteriously trying process from their studio, where the equipment only seemed to work intermittently.

Afterwards, I went to see BBC reporter Jacky Rowland, one of the close community of foreign journalists in Moscow.

On screen she is formidably fluent, self-assured and serious, but off screen it is her ready laugh and her mischievousness that strike you immediately.

Sinking into a seat opposite her I suggested that we should go to Tajikistan.

'Yes,' she replied in her cool blonde way, 'we're going tomorrow. We've chartered a plane. The bureau chief paid for it on his credit card and he's very chuffed! Do you want a seat?'

'Tomorrow?' I gulped. I'd been hoping for a bit of a discussion of regional politics, and didn't expect it to become so practical so quickly.

'Tomorrow?' I repeated. 'Can I get back to you?'

'You'd better be quick – seats are going like hotcakes.'

So I put my name down and left the building mulling over the logistics of leaving Moscow for Central Asia in fifteen hours' time. The charter would be expensive, almost three times the cost of an ordinary flight, and I had very little time to contact all the broadcasters I worked for, check on visas, pack, get cash – never an easy business at short notice in Moscow – and learn some more about Tajikistan.

I learned one crucial fact that helped me make my decision: the ordinary Tajik Air flights were booked solid for the next ten days with Tajik market gardeners bringing the autumn harvest of tomatoes and melons to Moscow. You probably could get a seat if you paid a bribe, but it was unlikely to be cheap (like with the melons, prices were market driven) and it was certain to be time consuming. To reach Tajikistan simply and quickly, it seemed a charter flight was the best bet.

So I'm going. At 1 a.m. I'm still up, talking to colleagues who've been to Tajikistan, and downloading facts from the Internet. That's the extent of my preparation. I don't even have time to buy a book on Central Asia. Five hours later my taxi arrives. It's a wheezing, beaten-up yellow Lada belonging to a Russian sports coach called Alexei who moonlights as a driver, when his car's working and he can fit it in with his sports schedule. I've known Alexei for about a year, and 6 a.m. suits him better than it suits me. He is cheerful until he hears where I'm going.

'But why are you going there – a woman? On your own?' Alexei moans. 'I wouldn't go to Tajikistan on my own and I'm a man. It's not safe. Why are you doing it? *Why? Why?*'

Alexei could get a third job in a Greek Chorus, vocalising 'your worst fears'.

He wails at me before I've had a chance to wake up, and I don't have a good enough answer – certainly not in my basic Russian – so the trip to the airport takes on a funereal air, with Alexei shaking his head and repeating '*Why? Why?*' reproachfully every so often. Alexei has that peculiarly Russian terror of the provinces of their former Empire.

We arrive at Moscow's Vnukovo airport at 8 a.m. on Tuesday 18 September. This small airport services flights to Central Asia, and it already feels more Asian than Russian. There are almost no blonde wide-cheeked Slavs, instead it's teeming with smaller darker Tajiks and Azeris. Since the airport has no seats, people sit on their bags, or squat on their haunches as they wait.

Alexei says goodbye as if he'll never see me again, so it's a relief when I find my BBC friends. We perch on our luggage like the locals, too tired and grumpy to be anxious. Jacky Rowland shows me her one indispensable bit of war-zone kit – a proper full-sized pillow. 'I'm wearing a green jacket for my live shots – Islamic green,' she jokes.

It turns out I'm lucky to still have my seat as the Moscow press corps fought hard for places on the BBC plane. In the end there are around fifty of us: journalists, producers and camera crews from the BBC, the English newspapers, and European and American broadcasters. Having made an effort to get here early, we are forced to sit and wait for hours.

We are told that 'the Minister' hasn't given permission for us to land in Tajikistan. So we call. He's in a meeting. Then another meeting. Then lunch. A BBC correspondent based in Tajikistan shakes her head, muttering darkly that this is a bad sign.

We sit outside in the sunshine of a Moscow Indian summer and eat stale caviar sandwiches. While we're there, a German journalist comes up and asks, 'Is English your natif langvidge?'

I say, yes, rather sharply, it is what we speak in Australia, and he beams.

'Good, zen you can do ze "lives" for the Deutsche Welle English service. I am very content to find you.'

This chance meeting with Christoph Wanner, a Moscow correspondent for German public TV channel Deutsche Welle, sets me up with a huge amount of work, and when fortune smiles like that I regard it as a reward for taking risks. I choose to see it as a blessing on this decision to go to Tajikistan, and it improves my mood as we wait.

I fall asleep on a patch of grass in the sun, and when a BBC engineer wakes me up it's 3 p.m. The Minister has given us the green light. We board the plane, the first of its type we've seen, with leather couches and armchairs, French-polished walnut inlaid tables, and DVD players with a stock of in-flight porn. We conclude this is how Russia's oil barons traverse the country. Someone examines the couches for semen stains before we sit down. Swivelling in a leather armchair, an English journalist announces that in future, he's always flying BBC.

High on anticipation, flying into the heart of the biggest story in the world, the four-hour trip whizzes by. The girls swap war stories, and two tough blokes from the British broadsheets do some male bonding, discussing their divorces.

It's night when we land in the Tajik capital Dushanbe. We walk across the tarmac, which smells of fuel and some indefinable Asian spice, and Passport Control let us in without local visas because we have Russian multi-entry visas. An NBC producer is not so lucky. They want to exclude him because he is smooth shaven in his passport photo, but has a goatee now. 'No, no, I don't want to shave off my beard,' I hear him remonstrating, as I walk out into the warm Central Asian night. After some spirited arguing, he emerges with his facial hair intact.

Dushanbe is a dusty, gracious, tree-lined city of half a million people. It has Soviet buildings, the legacy of decades of Russian rule, but they are softened by pastel colours and Asiatic decorations. Unlike in Moscow, where every edifice is gargantuan, designed to dwarf the individual, these buildings are more human scale. But there is a regulation oversized Presidential palace, a vast Stalinist structure with armed guards, stage lighting, and fountains gushing in its forecourt, despite the worst drought in seventy years.

There are almost no cars on the road and the few that chug by are old and drab. An ancient grey trolley bus putters along the empty main street, sparks flying from its overhead wires. This is how Communist cities used to look before the collapse of the Soviet Union – from Prague in the West to Vladivostok, eleven time zones away across Siberia. In fact, Vladivostok still looks pretty much like this today – only there are more cars.

The buildings loom over empty streets in a series of appealing pastels, trimmed with white. This is a well-maintained city. Despite its poverty, there is even a casino – that symbol of post-Communist success – but we barely have time to drink this all in because we have to find somewhere to sleep.

If every war has its hotel, in Dushanbe it's the Hotel Tajikistan. There are two other 'first class' hotels, but the Tajikistan, at 22 Communist Youth Street, has the longest waiting list, and is the base of operations for three major news broadcasters. It is also the main TV feed point for satellite dishes belonging to the European Broadcasting Union, Reuters, and the TV arm of the Associated Press wire service, APTN.

A gloomy 1960s Soviet building in regulation dreary grey, with terrible food and without working telephones, the Tajikistan is an unlikely winner. Every time you want to file a story you have to go down to the front desk and watch a good-natured Tajik woman do battle with an ancient PABX telephone system. Only one call in four gets through and she often shakes her head apologetically and asks you to come back later. Needless to say, our Moscow cell phones don't work here, though advertising leaflets promise, 'The footprint will extend to Tajikistan next year!' Since some quirk of the phone system means it's equally difficult for our news desks to ring in to us, we hire brick-sized fifteen-year-old mobile phones, paying usurious rates and counting ourselves lucky because there are soon none left – the journalists have hired every last cell phone in Dushanbe. All ten of them.

The hotel has long corridors with worn red carpet disappearing into the distance. It seems to stretch forever, reminding me that the definition of infinity is the point where two

19

parallel lines meet. Will it ever reach the next corridor? On my first night it seems that infinity is probably here in Tajikistan, at the end of a distant corridor, as far as possible from the only (rarely working) lift.

But to reach infinity, you have to pass by the keeper of the keys, that old Soviet stalwart, the Floor Lady. The *dezhurnaya* was once a powerful figure – spying on you, informing the authorities, and doling out unobtainable products like soap, in return for the right gift, of course. She still hands out soap and towels and she still spies on you, but it's all less vital now the Soviet Union has collapsed.

The *dezhurnayas* are Russian and Tajik women with hard lives, spending the night on sofas behind their shabby desks, minding our keys – and our business. The floor lady's desk is strategically placed opposite the lift, and she doesn't like it if you use the stairs because it makes it harder for her to keep an eye on you. Whichever floor you go to, before you even open your mouth, the *dezhurnaya* looks at you and pipes up, 'No – he's out. He's been out for a while.' She's usually been observing you so closely she can pick it in one, but if it turns out she's made a mistake, and you're looking for someone else, she says dismissively, 'Oh, *that one*. No, he's not in his room either. I haven't seen him *all day*.'

The *dezhurnayas* also know how to drive a hard bargain, lording it over weaker women with a flash of their former power. The hookers who stream into the hotel when we arrive aren't going to be allowed onto the floor without a fight. 'This is an illegal activity,' one *dezhurnaya* huffs to me in pretended anger. 'It shouldn't be allowed.' In the end, the hookers have to pay the *dezhurnayas* as well as their pimps and the bar, leaving the girl who did the work with less than half the money – about US$8.

Watched closely by the *dezhurnaya*, I make my way to my gloomy room and fall into one of the two single beds. Being freelance means that after two days spent travelling and organising, tomorrow I'll have to start earning money to pay for the hotel room and the flight. But like Scarlett O'Hara, I'll think about that in the morning.

Chapter 2

DUSHANBE, 19 SEPTEMBER 2001

I am run off my feet. There turns out to be a lot of interest in Tajikistan's potential as a base for American troops, and as a haven in the looming refugee crisis.

During the day we accumulate material, attending press conferences and conducting interviews with politicians, aid workers and refugees. At night we file our stories and any live updates from the roof of the Hotel Tajikistan, where the European Broadcasting Union has its feed point. The European Broadcasting Union, EBU for short, was formed when Europe's TV stations banded together to share the cost of satellite equipment.

I meet the boys from EBU Moscow all over the world – from Chernobyl to Chechnya – at every disaster and war in our region. The Moscow bureau is run by a band of charming, efficient multilingual Belgians. Bruno Beeckman worked at EBU Moscow for most of the 1990s, and he's back from Geneva for this conflict. To hear him switch effortlessly from Russian to English and then to any of the five other languages he speaks fluently is actually dazzling. 'It's my only talent,' he says modestly, and then goes on to organise complex satellite operations in difficult remote locations. It's a pleasure to run into him and Joris Wauman here. I feel safe as soon as I see them.

After my fortuitous meeting at the airport, I am filing to the English service of German TV Deutsche Welle. There appears to be an endless appetite for analysis of Russia's role in any future conflict, since Tajikistan's border with Afghanistan is still patrolled by Russian troops as well as Tajik troops – ten years after Tajikistan became independent from the Soviet Union. There is also avid interest in what appears at this stage to be the central question for any ground war: Russia's attitude towards American troops landing here in Russia's traditional sphere of influence. Will Vladimir Putin prove he is a 'man the West can do business with', as Margaret Thatcher memorably described Mikhail Gorbachev?

I also file on what the representatives of the Northern Alliance – the opposition to the Taliban – have to say about their willingness to fight a ground war and to co-operate with the US. My satellite feeds are sandwiched in between European reports – Dutch, Slovakian, Slovenian – which are being filed back to the same time zones. I climb through a window and hop down onto the roof of the hotel. After the first day, someone thoughtfully places a TV packing case there so that we don't fall. EBU has set up a generator and satellite dish at the far corner where the signal is best. They also have a remote communications centre in a tent nearby, with phones, TV monitors, lights, and sometimes even coffee. They ferry all this equipment with them wherever they go, setting it up and connecting it to the rest of the world – if necessary from a field in the middle of nowhere. I head towards the tent. The generator hums like a lawnmower and the satellite crew trade jokes in every language.

No matter how many times I do it, I've never been able to quite comprehend that this ten-minute feed, with all the worry about whether Berlin has the right number, and whether they can hear you properly, and if the presenter is ready, and whether there's a problem with the tape, will actually be seen on cable TV around the world. It all feels like a much smaller affair, relevant only to the two or three people on the spot here. Perhaps it's because I just speak to a camera, and can only hear the interviewer in my earpiece – on a good day, when everything's working. On a bad day, I don't even hear them properly. It seems part of the absurdity of television that I speak to someone I can't see, but the rest of the world can see me.

I also always have to remind myself that no one back home knows or cares what we've been through to get to a feed point and to file a story. They just expect to look up from their dinner and see the reporter filing coolly and authoritatively in their news bulletin. Fluency is all. Then comes the ability to look unflustered, no matter what crises are occurring around you, and it seems that maybe only third on the list is actually knowing what you are talking about. That is also part of the absurdity of television.

For a year 12,000 refugees who have fled the fighting in northern Afghanistan have been huddled on two sandy islands in the Pyang River, which marks the border between Tajikistan and Afghanistan. Most are women and children, and their lives on the islands are desperate. There's no water or sanitation. They have almost nothing to eat except grass and dwindling supplies of flour.

There are no trees on the islands. People don't have tents or even plastic sheeting. They dig holes and construct coverings made of reeds for shelter. People live in holes, like animals. Even in summer, dozens die, sleeping outdoors at night.

One nine-member family fled Avul, a village in northern Afghanistan, carrying only one pot and several shabby blankets. The youngest of the five children is a little over a year old. He has no nappies and is wrapped in his mother's dress. Few families here have warm clothes and most children have no shoes. Many have frostbite scars.

Aid workers say conditions here are worse than in other refugee camps around Afghanistan. It is almost impossible to grow vegetables or fruit on the sandy islands. In the past the refugees had some flour, and ate cooked grass to survive. But the drought has removed even that desperate option. This summer their main source of food has dried up. Many are now starving, and only a recent food drop funded by Iran has saved more from dying.

Water is also a problem. The refugees have dug shallow wells, but sand quickly seeps into the holes. What little water they collect in this way is salty and muddy, and as there is no sanitation, the groundwater is becoming contaminated.

As a result, people are sick all the time, racked by epidemics. Last winter it was typhoid fever. This summer, malaria. Women are anaemic. Children suffer from scurvy. Diarrhoea is rife and families bury babies every day. Mothers sit by simple graves and sob.

But despite the appalling conditions, the refugees fear the idea of returning home. They are ethnic Tajiks, and the Taliban – from the rival Pashtun tribe – have conquered their villages after bitter fighting. They say if they go home, the Taliban will kill them. Alleviating their situation on the islands is complicated, however, by the presence of Northern Alliance soldiers. Many aid agencies haven't been allowed onto the islands because they can't treat combatants, although they need to reach the women and children who live with the armed men.

Now, though the islands are becoming over-crowded and provision of aid is complex, Tajikistan has closed its doors to these refugees. Tajikistan had previously granted asylum to some Afghans, but faced with the possibility of a flood of refugees if conditions inside Afghanistan worsen, it has sealed its borders shut.

'Our country is still recovering from a five-year civil war,' says Deputy Prime Minister Saidamir Zuhurov. 'We are not in a position to provide shelter and fair living conditions even to our own refugees. To admit the Afghan refugees we will need billions of dollars for food, housing and medical services.'

Another official is more blunt. 'A rich country like Australia won't have them – why should we, who are so poor that we cannot even feed our own people?'

When I ask people on the street in Dushanbe what they think of the policy of closing Tajikistan's border to these refugees, many of whom are Tajiks, I am surprised at the numbers who are against it. 'We should let them in, after all they are Tajiks, and they are suffering.'

Iranian film-maker Mohsen Makhmalbaf has worked in Afghanistan for two decades, making powerful, evocative movies, intimate, intense and unforgettable. He is Iran's most celebrated film-maker and was a political prisoner under the Shah.

When filming in Tajikistan in 1999 Makhmalbaf witnessed

24

a terrible scene where tens of thousands of starving Afghans, who had reached the border on foot, were turned away. He describes it in a lecture, later reprinted in an Iranian magazine. An Iranian journalist gives me a copy in Dushanbe.

'It looked like doomsday. The war-stricken and hungry children had run for miles and miles barefoot. Later on, the same fleeing crowd was attacked by Tajiks, and was also refused asylum in Tajikistan. In the thousands, they died in a no-man's land between Afghanistan and Tajikistan . . . These scenes are never shown in the media anywhere in the world.'

Makhmalbaf's most recent film set in Afghanistan is *Kandahar*. It deals with the impact of war and chaos on the lives of ordinary people, through the story of a woman trying to return from the West to Taliban-controlled Afghanistan. She wants to see her sister, who was left behind by their fleeing family because she stepped on a land mine. Her sister had been warned to avoid mines, but they are often brightly coloured to make them attractive to children. After fifteen years as an amputee, surviving without family in Afghanistan, the sister has lost the will to live.

Afghan suffering haunts the Iranian film-maker. When he describes the Taliban's destruction of the ancient statues of Buddha at Bamian, he reaches a bitter conclusion: '[It] was not demolished by anybody; it crumbled out of shame. Out of shame for the world's ignorance towards Afghanistan. It broke down knowing its greatness didn't do any good.'

He concludes bleakly that the destruction was all in vain – the Buddha shattered to inform the world of Afghanistan's poverty and oppression, but the world only saw the demolition of the statue.

'A Chinese proverb says: You point your finger at the moon, the fool stares at your finger. Nobody saw the dying nation the Buddha was pointing to.'

Mohammed Barbar is an Afghan refugee who made it into Tajikistan five years ago. A diffident man in his mid-thirties, Mohammed runs a radio program and a centre in Dushanbe where Afghan refugees learn English and computer skills. It is in a small, dusty, single-storey building not far from the Hotel Tajikistan.

Twenty pupils, ranging from young children to women in their thirties, are squashed into tiny desks and chairs in a makeshift classroom. None of the women or girls wears a headscarf. They are reading from an American textbook about a fire in the Ritz Hotel. It seems an odd text post-September 11. They stumble as they read, in thick accents. I record the lesson and ask them why they are here.

'We escaped because there was a bloody war in our country and girls could not study,' eleven-year-old Nasrine says in English.

'We want to learn English so we can migrate to the West and improve our lives,' says Setareh, a beautiful fifteen-year-old whose name means star.

The boys are more reticent. They have to be pushed to answer, and falteringly repeat what the girls have said. 'Please don't ask me anything too political,' Mohammed begs before I interview him. 'My family is still in Afghanistan and I fear for their safety. I don't want them to be punished or to suffer because of this.'

Mohammed says he works hard here in Tajikistan. 'Life is difficult everywhere. I am setting up an educational NGO [non-government organisation], and organising funding. We've set up this school, and we feel ourselves happy because we help our nationals, who are homeless, and we provide jobs, especially for the women.'

But he remains worried about the people left behind in Afghanistan.

'They need schools, not more destruction. The best way to fight terrorism is to build schools and train people. Those who want to become terrorists do it because they don't know much about life. We must train the people. We must tell them, "Life is important, for you. Don't kill."'

After the interview, Mohammed invites me to come home with him for lunch. I accept and we walk in the warm sunshine down a quiet street, under large overhanging trees. We reach a sky-blue block of flats six storeys high. The cheery paint can't hide the Soviet dreariness that characterises identical apartment blocks from here to the Arctic.

We climb four flights of stairs to a simple apartment with very little furniture. Everyone removes their shoes at the door

26

and sits on the floor to eat. Mohammed's flat is a drop-in centre for the local community. At lunch there is a former professor of architecture from Kabul University who speaks English, as well as two older women who speak Dari, and two young men who speak some Russian. A waxy, patterned table-cloth is spread on the floor. They serve naan bread and some tomatoes, cut into wedges. The food is simple, the quantities small. The cook, Genia, a talkative blonde Russian woman in her fifties, brings a bowl of *lapsha* – meat soup with noodles. How poor must she be, this woman from the colonial super-power, sent out here to settle the far reach of the Empire, to be a cook for the most recently arrived refugees in Dushanbe?

'Yes, times are very difficult,' Genia says, sighing. She has five children and her husband doesn't contribute to the family's upkeep. She flicks the skin under her chin with her middle finger, the evocative Russian shorthand for drunkenness. 'Well, what with the drink . . .'

Before the collapse of the Soviet Union, she worked in one of the countless bureaucratic jobs that allowed Moscow to maintain the myth of full employment. She now receives a pension, and when she tells me how much it is I am incredulous – it works out to US$3.50 a month.

'It is very little, it is too little,' she agrees, which is why she does the cooking and cleaning here and for other families. But she remains optimistic. 'You know, others get less than me,' she says a moment later. 'I was a high-ranking office worker. Some women only get two dollars a month, or even one dollar fifty.'

Dushanbe is a city of monuments. In 1929 it was renamed Stalinabad, when the dusty town of thirteen streets was invested by Moscow with the status of a city and turned into the capital of the Soviet Republic of Tajikistan. Stalin arbitrarily created the five Central Asian republics by drawing lines on a map. The new state of Tajikistan, for example, consigned half of the Tajik people to the state next door, Uzbekistan, which also netted the most famous Tajik landmarks – the fabled Silk Road towns of Samarkand and Bukhara.

It was only in 1961, eight years after Stalin's death and long after the formal process of 'de-Stalinisation' had been carried out in the rest of the Soviet Union, that the Tajiks dared to change the name of their capital. They played it safe. No local heroes were invoked. Instead they reverted to the city's original name, 'Dushanbe'. It means Monday.

Soviet war memorials still gaze down on the city – white plinths topped with laurel wreaths. In the city centre there is what looks like an ancient triumphal stone arch, painted red and topped with a garish gold crown. It turns out to be less than five years old and is a monument to the first Tajik Emperor, the national hero Somoni. Since the collapse of Communism, the tenth-century emperor has replaced the Soviet idols and everything is named after him – restaurants, websites, even the local currency.

There are also many monuments to Tajikistan's President, the former Communist boss Emomali Rakhmonov. 'Ah, your standard Central Asian tyranny,' one of my Russian colleagues murmurs. It is incredible what Russians feel they have to be superior about.

President Rakhmonov appears in posters and murals plastered and painted over walls throughout the country. Posters of Emperor Somoni, represented as a winged beast with a human face, are everywhere, too – but this mythical creature is painted with President Rakhmonov's face. People explain sheepishly that it's legitimate because no one knows exactly what Somoni looked like. I consider buying a rug featuring Somoni, with President Rakhmonov's features staring out forcefully from between his wings, but I decide that it's one of those gifts that won't travel.

Even the traditional teahouse – or *chaikhana* – has been turned into a monument called the Rohat. Purpose built in the centre of town by the Soviets in the 1950s as a 'representation of Tajik culture', the Rohat is four floors high, as tall as the Presidential palace which is down the street. Beautiful yellow columns hold up the ceiling that soars thirty metres high. The airy room, so vast it echoes, is open on two sides. Its two walls are decorated with sweeping murals, pale blues and greens swirled with yellow. The murals continue on the ceiling, diagrams of colour like a Cubist Sistine chapel. A teahouse of such grandeur is irresistible.

All the tables are on the ground floor, but the best seats in the house are the raised benches in the windows. Waitresses wear traditional dress. Their teeth gleam gold when they smile. The food is plain and doesn't really suit the setting. A man stands at a barbecue outside grilling lamb, and the restaurant serves meat noodle soup as well as vodka in the Russian manner – *'Fifty grams or 100 grams?'* – and of course tea.

Dushanbe's twin city is Boulder, Colorado, and the people of Tajikistan have built a teahouse on a smaller scale in downtown Boulder. I can't see much evidence of Boulder in Dushanbe.

One of my favourite spots for a working lunch in Dushanbe is more simple. In a small lane outside the city's only Internet 'café' – a bare office with two computers – there is an improvised roadside restaurant. A man and his wife put out plastic tables and chairs and a small kerosene burner, near a drainage ditch under some trees. From ten o'clock every morning, except Friday, they cook on the spot for Dushanbe's taxi drivers and anyone else who might want some home-made *plov*, the national dish of rice, chickpea, carrot and meat stew. The smell is appetising but as I'm a vegetarian I ask for a portion without meat. They look astounded and give me extra tomato salad to make up for it, along with some delicious naan bread that is the local specialty.

The whole meal costs forty US cents, and I sit under the umbrella of trees, drinking green tea and writing my script on the sun-dappled table. I have transcribed the interview with Mohammed Barbar, and the refugees in the English class, and now I am writing up the story. I enjoy the relaxed form of Islam in Tajikistan. No one appears bothered by me. Men greet each other in the warm Muslim way, hugging one another close and touching their hands to their hearts. Some wear patterned skullcaps, others wear Western clothes, and all seem happy to speak to a Western woman.

Women in Dushanbe also choose what they wear – either Western clothes or the traditional Tajik dress of brightly coloured and patterned smocks over crushed velvet pants in contrasting colours. Since their headscarves are another hue again, they are modest but riotously colourful. They have striking, square faces, with thick painted-on eyebrows and dark red lipstick. They look like the Mexican artist Frida

Kahlo and their clothes look like Latin American murals.

But the important thing, in the context of a Muslim country right next door to Afghanistan, is that you can see their faces. Women talk and smile and are part of the life of the city. There are no head to foot coverings here. The Soviets banned the veil in Tajikistan in the 1920s, but even in the 1960s it was not forgotten. The writer and famous foreign correspondent Ryszard Kapuscinski, who came here in the 1960s, observed that women in the countryside turned their backs as he drove past and hid their faces in their hands. As he succinctly put it, 'The veil was gone, but the reflex remained.' In 1963, Rochat Nabijeva was the first Tajik woman to receive a university degree. Her thesis was on the struggle to abolish the veil. During the 1920s, many women who dared to bare their faces were killed – some publicly executed. Sitting in the sun, with the woman who cooked the *plov* smiling at me, all that seems very distant.

The ease here is partly the result of a civil war which ended in 1997. Former Communists, funded by Russia, fought assorted Islamic groups, including Islamic militants. After seven years of bitter fighting that cost more than 50,000 lives, the ex-Communists won. But the war took its toll on Tajikistan, leaving it the poorest of the former Central Asian Republics – which is saying something.

Now, after years of severe drought, relief agencies estimate that half of Tajikistan's six million people face possible famine this winter. But it's still not as poor or as backward as Afghanistan.

The journalists who've come to Dushanbe are scrambling to get into Afghanistan.

To get our visas we make our pilgrimage to the Afghan embassy run by the opposition to the Taliban, the Northern Alliance. Although it rules only between five and ten per cent of the country, the Northern Alliance is still the internationally recognised government of Afghanistan, holding the country's chair in the United Nations. Only two countries recognise the Taliban as the legitimate government of Afghanistan: Pakistan and Saudi Arabia.

But over the past year the Alliance's fortunes have been

waning. It has been beaten back even within its stronghold in the north of the country, as officials concede at their embassy on Pushkin Street, just around the corner from the Hotel Tajikistan. September 11 has altered many factors, and it is crunch time for the Northern Alliance. How they handle this crisis will make or break them, as officials in Dushanbe are aware. However, the Alliance has been crippled by the assassination of its Defence Minister, the charismatic Ahmed Shah Massoud. He was killed by two Arab suicide bombers posing as journalists two days before the attacks on the World Trade Center. The Northern Alliance accuses Osama bin Laden of organising Massoud's murder and condemns the terror attacks in the United States, calling on the Taliban to give up Osama bin Laden to the United Nations. The Northern Alliance says everything must be done to save Afghanistan from possible US attacks.

Positioning itself as an ally for Washington in the War Against Terror, the Northern Alliance says it is prepared to discuss military action against the Taliban. But despite having a fighting force on the ground in Afghanistan, with a consistent history of opposition to the Taliban, the Alliance says it has not yet been approached by the US regarding any military action. In Dushanbe, the Northern Alliance's military attaché, Saleh Mohammed Registani, says the Alliance would be prepared to launch military action on behalf of the United States.

We report this offer, but Northern Alliance officials tell us accusingly that Washington has remained silent. 'Why does Washington talk to Pakistan and not to us? They created the Taliban.'

They are looking to us for a response, as if we are spokespeople for the US government.

Journalists meet daily at the Afghan embassy, sitting under trees as we wait to be admitted for meetings with Afghan consular officials. Some of the journalists are friendly, others frenzied. Their news desks want them *inside* Afghanistan, and they want them there *now*. They don't want to hear why it's difficult to get in. Their despondency is catching.

Everyone smokes and gossips, exchanging rumours as we wait to see the Afghan officials. One rumour doing the rounds is that CNN paid US$15,000 to hire a Northern Alliance helicopter to take them and their satellite gear into the Panjshir Valley, the spot the Northern Alliance holds nearest Kabul. The waiting is endless, and while most people are friendly, many are competitive with their main rivals – the American TV networks look over their shoulders at each other, and reporters from the British papers keep a wary eye on other British hacks. The *Sunday Times*' Moscow correspondent is being given a hard time because the *Daily Telegraph*'s Moscow man is already inside Afghanistan. 'He was at Massoud's funeral. The Tele ran it on page one and I've been getting my arse kicked every day since,' says our man in Dushanbe, exhaling gloomily.

Here in Central Asia it's all 'face' – you have to meet officials and then meet them again, and more often than not pay a small fee before you are granted any favours. An English journalist I meet summarises it neatly: 'I like the Tajik bureaucracy – the prices are modest, the service flexible.'

At the Afghan embassy, our contact is Amroullah Saleh. He's clean shaven, wears Western clothes and speaks four languages, including French and English. He is their very savvy media flack – in fact, he's the best person I've encountered in this role anywhere in the world. It's almost mysterious that he is so sophisticated, and the only hint he gives of being an Islamic Holy Warrior comes when he tells us that he spent six months in Moscow as a student. Back then he had a long beard and looked like a mullah, and was frequently stopped by the police. 'I tried to keep them talking so that I could improve my Russian. I didn't have much chance to talk,' he says with a wry smile.

Amroullah Saleh says the Northern Alliance will make some of its military helicopters available for us. But they can't always fly, he warns, due to the weather. If it's cloudy in the Panjshir, they can't land. They have no navigational equipment and rely on the pilot's vision to co-ordinate landings. Visibility is crucial. And sometimes the Northern Alliance will need the four helicopters it has here for ferrying military supplies, not journalists. There is also the requirement for approval by the

Tajik government. So it is not yet a done deal. All the journalists gathered around him nod.

'But having said all this, the Northern Alliance wants reporters on the ground – it's in our interests – and we will do our best to help you get there.'

Pointing to a map, Amroullah Saleh shows us where they can take us, indicating the Panjshir Valley or, failing that, to a small speck in the far north, not named on any map, called Khoja Bahauddin. From there, we could drive down to the Panjshir, or perhaps catch another chopper.

One journalist points to another spot on the map and asks whether we could fly there. Amroullah Saleh looks uncomfortable for an instant. 'No, not any more – that's now under Taliban control.' Noticing my sleeveless top he adds that once we are inside Afghanistan we will have to respect local feeling and wear more modest clothing.

Before we can go to Afghanistan, however, we need to have our name on The List. In classic Central Asian style, there are two Lists, one at the Tajik Foreign Ministry and one at the Afghan embassy, with two sets of fees. Modest amounts of US$30 and US$50 respectively, which later climb to hundreds of dollars as the number of journalists swells.

People devote days to commuting between the two buildings, befriending different staff to make sure they're on both lists. I am not so driven. I feel myself being carried on the tide of my colleagues' energy towards Afghanistan, but I don't have a producer able to queue at both places for me and I'm too busy filing to give it my full attention. While there is the possibility of America landing ground troops here, there is huge interest in this story from broadcasters all over the world.

So, in between filing, I troop to the Tajik Foreign Ministry, a vast apricot-coloured Soviet building with outsized white columns, marble stairs and wooden doors five metres high. Inside it's all grand vistas and high ceilings, with most of the space wasted on long corridors, leaving only small, poky offices for people to actually work in. Despite a smart paint job, the Foreign Ministry is undergoing a *remont*, the all-purpose Russian word for repair and renovation, used to cover a variety of situations including 'closed for *remont*', which usually means that a business will never reopen.

The Foreign Ministry doesn't dare to scale down its operations with the prospect of so much hard currency to be earned. So, despite the fact we can't use the main doors or the grand marble stairs, we scramble in via scaffolding on a side door to conduct the endless administration and payments required to obtain two documents – a Tajik press pass and a Tajik double-entry visa. Both are only valid for four weeks, so the whole rigmarole will have to be repeated again in a month's time, by which time prices will no doubt have tripled.

The Afghan officials tell us that on Thursday 20 September, when the lists held at the Tajik Foreign Ministry and Afghan embassy will be complete, they will post up the Final Final List of people able to travel to Afghanistan, on a noticeboard outside the Afghan embassy in Pushkin Street.

'Please be here at 8 a.m. on Thursday, ready to travel,' says Amroullah Saleh.

I file till late on Wednesday night and, with no anticipation of being on both lists, I turn up at the Afghan embassy at 11 a.m., without my bags and without having checked out. A Russian colleague runs up to me.

'What are you doing, where have you been? You're on Chopper Number 3.'

I can't believe it or comprehend it, although it's true that one person is easier to fit in than a group of six, and the Northern Alliance is trying to send as broad a selection of journalists as possible into Afghanistan. Voice of America is also a name they know and respect, because it broadcasts in local languages into Afghanistan. Radio is an important medium in a country where many people have no electricity and no television.

But I suffer a moment of real uncertainty. There are other journalists here, in torment because they are not on the list or because only two or three from a team of six have been allowed to go. People are gathered around Amroullah Saleh, arguing with him.

Here I am, in a box seat, not sure what to do next. I look at the neatly typed list stuck on the embassy wall. I'm the only female freelance journalist on this chopper, heading for a lawless country, which the US is about to carpet bomb.

Until this moment the enormity of that has not hit me.

I didn't expect to have to make a decision about Afghanistan so soon. My name in black and white on the list calls my bluff. I will be going to a dangerous location without the protection of a big organisation if anything goes wrong – without a chopper to medivac me out if I'm wounded, without an office to campaign on my behalf or pay a ransom if I'm kidnapped.

I call a friend in Moscow to ask her advice. Lygia O'Riordan is the conductor of an orchestra, and she's tough, but generally errs on the side of caution. I tell her all my doubts, ending my litany with 'I have a bad feeling about this.'

'Is it a bad feeling like when I didn't go back to Ireland to see my mother, the last time before she died?'

'No, it's not that kind of bad feeling.'

'Then get on that chopper.'

So I check out of the Hotel Tajikistan and go to the local market to buy provisions for Afghanistan. There an old Tajik man is selling Russian *piroshki*, pastries filled with meat or potatoes, and I stop to ask for one without meat. The man tears a page out of an old book, wraps the pastry in it and hands it to me. My oily page contains Lenin's ideas about revolution, written in 1905. I ask the *piroshki* man which book he is using. 'No, no, don't worry, we have many like this,' he assures me, showing me an old Communist history book. He is more interested in why I don't eat meat. Is it a religious prohibition? Or a national one? Is there no meat in Australia?

I buy fresh apples and tinned food. Since I arrived so late, my colleague Christoph from Deutsche Welle says he will buy me a sleeping bag when he gets one for himself, a kind offer that saves me time. I rush back to the Afghan embassy and settle down to wait. Another suave official, who wears a different Western suit every day, solves the mystery of how I come to be on The List. 'I put you there,' he says. 'I made sure you were on both lists, because I so enjoyed our conversations in Russian.'

We'd chatted each day at the gate but I never even knew his name. Makes eighteen months of lessons worthwhile, I guess. Store that one up to tell my Russian teacher, if I ever come back alive.

There's a rustle among the waiting journalists. We are to move to the airport, a hopeful sign. But we sit there for the afternoon, and no choppers fly.

We drive despondently to the Hotel Tajikistan and check back in. I file till late about Russian troop movements near the Afghan border. News is also breaking that Washington is making its first overture to the Northern Alliance. At a press conference, jubilant Northern Alliance defence spokesman Saleh Mohammed Registani, is asked exactly what this means.

'Before we have no tanks, and now we have. Before we have no air force and no missiles and now we have air support and missiles. We had ground forces, but now we have air support.' He smiles. 'I think that's what it means, don't you?'

Thank you Mr Registani, that's a grab.

Pressed about a timetable for the US attacks, he says, 'I don't agree that it should be soon. We need a little bit of time to understand the situation. The Taliban have changed their places, they live with civilians. We can't attack the new targets until we find their new positions.'

In the morning we check out again, going directly to the airport to wait again in the dust. Cars and journalists and bags are spilled everywhere. It's strangely festive, like a picnic, except without food or water or toilets. One of the taxi drivers has his tape recorder blaring. Frank Sinatra sings 'I Did it my Way' over and over again, an ironic counterpoint to people stuck waiting for someone else to tell them what to do. Everyone is smiling at the incongruity of that velvet American voice in the middle of a dusty field in Dushanbe.

Morbidly, we compare statistics about helicopter crashes, one of the biggest dangers we face here. The helicopters are ageing and poorly maintained. If we're going to die, says a reporter who has been to Afghanistan many times, that's the most likely cause of death.

In the background Frank is crooning about the end being near and facing the final curtain.

Then one chopper takes off, followed by a fixed-wing aircraft, flying to Faizabad in the north-east of the Panjshir Valley. I wave goodbye to new friends. After nine hours, Chopper Number 3 is ready to take off. Now it's our turn to wave goodbye and we heave our bags onto a creaky old Russian military helicopter. Our passports are stamped. We're on our way to Afghanistan. Nothing can stop us now. Until our bags are thrown back into the dirt.

No reason is given. It appears the Russian Security Service had approved everything, the problem was with the Tajik Security Service, which everyone here still calls by its old name, the KGB.

'Try again tomorrow,' says Amroullah Saleh, 'the Tajik KGB changed their minds at the last minute. We don't know why.'

So much officialdom in Central Asia works this way, but all your doubts rise up to confront you while you wait idly in the dust. I find myself thinking that perhaps I shouldn't really be going on this mad venture alone to Afghanistan. One of the Russian producers tells me that Amroullah Saleh looked her straight in the eye and told her she shouldn't go. She never wanted to, and now she isn't. Results depend on determination. I decide I have only one more day of this in me.

At 4 p.m. the next day, with one hour of light left, Chopper Number 3 finally takes off. It is less than two weeks after the September 11 attacks, and all my doubts evaporate as we judder up above the bare brown mountains of the Hindu Kush. Another stroke of luck is that we are in a much safer chopper – this was the personal helicopter of Ahmed Shah Massoud, the military leader assassinated fifteen days ago. Massoud was the most charismatic of the Islamic resistance heroes, the bravest of the anti-Soviet fighters, and his death has almost destroyed the Northern Alliance. His picture is on the door to the pilot's cabin, an iconic shot of the handsome Massoud kneeling in prayer, wearing his *pakul*, a Tajik woollen beret, his gun by his side. Halfway though the flight a translator turns to me and says, 'Irris, did you know you are sitting in Massoud's armchair?'

I'm on my way to Afghanistan.

Chapter 3

AFGHANISTAN, 24 SEPTEMBER 2001

The helicopter flies over the stunning barren mountains that mark the border between Tajikistan and Afghanistan. After an hour we circle Khoja Bahauddin, a desolate village perched on a desert basin, ringed by refugee camps. From the air it looks biblical. Things don't improve when we land.

Houses are made of mud brick, surrounded by mud-brick walls. There are no paved roads, no running water, no sanitation and no electricity. Camels and donkeys carry water and firewood. Everything is dun-coloured: the walls, the paths, the animals. Women and children provide the only splashes of colour, but the women are distant presences. Covered from head to foot in brightly coloured burqas, they always seem to be disappearing around earthen corners just in front of you. They see the world through a tiny mesh screen in their veils.

I feel I have gone back in time. Biblical names flood back to me. This is how I imagine Ur of the Chaldees, or Tyre of the Phoenicians. If it weren't for the Russian jeeps clattering along the sand – and the Kalashnikovs – this could be an Old Testament town. The New Testament is too new for Khoja Bahauddin.

We throw our bags onto a pick-up truck and are driven up the hill. There really are no roads, we just take off bouncing across a field. Hanging on tight soon becomes a reflex in vehicles here. We turn into a compound which is the Northern Alliance 'Foreign Ministry' – a very grand name for a low building with six rooms where they are putting up journalists until they find guesthouses for us. The offices are already bulging – women sleeping in one room, men in all the others. Work is done outside in an open corridor, and I fight for a spot near a pillar, on a step above a thousand cigarette butts. I'm thrilled to see my BBC friends who arrived yesterday. A friendly face is important when you've travelled by time machine hundreds of years into the past.

We embrace and questions tumble out.

'Are you free to move about and cover stories here?'

'What do you do for electricity?'

And that most important journalistic enquiry:

'What are the toilets like?'

The news is bad – there are no telephones, and the BBC satellite dish is working intermittently. They do have a beautiful 'live' spot on the roof though. 'It's a cooking live shot,' one American cameraman says – slang for he really likes it. There is only occasional electricity because the Northern Alliance generator is already starting to falter under the pressure of so many users, so it's better to have your own generator. Yes, the Northern Alliance will do interviews. Yes, there are translators here – they know the local language, Dari, a relative of Persian, and some English, though the best translators know Dari and Russian. But translators and drivers are expensive: US$100 per day each – more than they would cost in Moscow. If you want to be out every day you have to find US$1400 a week. That's almost all the cash I have with me.

And one other very important thing the BBC tells me: if you're nice to Abdul, an eighteen-year-old who looks thirty, and has a wicked laugh, he will bring tea. Green tea. *Choi sahbs*. The BBC girls have also learnt the word for sugar, but I don't bother since I don't like sweet tea. It seems this is the best way to drink water, which is only safe if it's boiled. Some people are boiling water and then filtering it and drinking that. Water purifying tablets make water taste putrid.

I grab a weak green tea. My ten litres of water won't last long in this heat.

Christoph Wanner from Deutsche Welle was on another

chopper, and he – and more importantly the satellite phone we are sharing – is nowhere to be seen. I can't believe that I have come to a place with no communications at all without my own satellite phone. Once again it's the BBC to the rescue. They have a deal under which they provide equipment for some broadcasters I file for, such as Irish radio RTE. This first night everyone – Deutsche Welle, RTE, Voice of America – wants a piece on my impressions of Afghanistan. I also file about the Northern Alliance, the morale and the state of military preparedness of this force that may yet be America's ally on the ground.

I have international telecommunications support from an unexpected source – the Northern Alliance. They have a satellite phone that will receive calls. You can ring into it, but you can't call out. They let me give out their number. It is true that if I'm not there to connect things up, there is no guarantee their phone will always be on, or charged – but it is a fantastic help. Later, when there are literally hundreds of journalists here, no one can believe that Northern Alliance officials would take calls and come looking for 'Irris from VOA'.

The operation in Khoja Bahauddin is still small and personal and we know all the Northern Alliance officials by name. Zubair runs the compound. The former medical student is twenty-seven years old, with that local trait of looking at least ten years older. He has been in charge for just two weeks – since the assassination of military leader Ahmed Shah Massoud. Massoud's second-in-command, Suhail, was also killed in the same suicide bombing.

'So now I am the one,' Zubair tells me in disbelief.

Ahmed Shah Massoud was assassinated here, in this compound, two days before the attacks on the Pentagon and the World Trade Center. He invited in journalists just like us – but they turned out to be terrorists. They were two Tunisian Arabs, travelling under Belgian passports. Some around Massoud were suspicious of them from the start because they had come in through Taliban lines. They came as guests of senior Northern Alliance leader Abdul Rusul Sayyaf, who had fought with Osama bin Laden against the Soviets. He says he was also fooled by the two men.

Massoud had been the target of a number of assassination

attempts by bin Laden and the Taliban for more than a year, and he was often on the move, sleeping in a different location each night. But he let the two suicide bombers stay here at the compound. They were his guests, living among his security chiefs and bodyguards. For five weeks they did what we do here: they went to the front lines and interviewed soldiers. They travelled to the Panjshir Valley to see the Kabul front. They hung out with the guys. But they were waiting.

The assassination occurred about three weeks later than planned. Three interview times were set, but postponed for a variety of reasons, including Massoud needing to be at a battle near Kabul. The suicide bombers were becoming increasingly impatient, especially as they were in the Panjshir Valley while an important meeting was underway where all the Northern Alliance leaders, including Massoud, were in one room at one time. They begged to be allowed to film. 'We just need one shot.'

They were refused until finally, on 9 September, Massoud had time for them. His killers walked across the Foreign Ministry compound to his home, and set up their gear. The cameraman had Semtex strapped to his body but Massoud's bodyguards didn't check them, or their equipment. They would have detected it easily.

Massoud sat down for the interview, shaking hands with his assassins first. After one question, the terrorist ignited the Semtex, killing himself, Massoud and Suhail. But the second terrorist, the 'reporter', survived. He picked up a camera and nonchalantly walked out. He had reached the street outside by the time Massoud's bodyguards captured him, running barefoot. They had removed their shoes to sit indoors and simply sprinted across the gravel from the blackened room, in shock. The guards locked the surviving attacker in a room, but he escaped through a window and stole a gun. Before he could scramble very far, they shot him.

Everyone here is still coming to terms with the seismic shock of Massoud's loss. I am watching the making of a martyr. The feelings are heartfelt. Everywhere, warriors are in tears at the mention of his name. 'I have lost my eyes,' one says, looking at the ground, suddenly bereft.

When they get to know you better, some men suggest in whispers that Ahmed Shah Massoud chose to die. Tearful

41

warriors tell us earnestly that on a visit to France five months before he was assassinated, Massoud – like Martin Luther King – predicted his own death. It was Massoud's first official visit to the West, and he was addressing the European Court in Strasbourg, positioning himself internationally as the alternative Afghan leader. But in reality he knew that the Taliban front lines were only twelve kilometres from his house, and little more than a handful of troops, and a river, kept them from attacking Khoja Bahauddin. One view was that his victories were behind him. Ousted from Kabul in 1996, then from his regional headquarters here in the north in 1999, perhaps he feared that the Northern Alliance was on the verge of disintegration. Perhaps it was easier to shake the assassins' hands, sit down for a last interview, and choose death.

Perhaps.

But the bodyguards never satisfactorily explain the lapse in security that led to the assassination. They say that Massoud didn't want the two checked. However, the only person who could confirm that is now dead. Another count against this fatalistic assessment is that earlier in 2001, it was Massoud who drew other warlords, including Rashid Dostum and Ismail Khan, back into the fight against the Taliban. Until his death, the Lion of the Panjshir – *Shir-e-Panjshir* – remained the lynchpin of the anti-Taliban forces. He was the true heart of the coalition of disparate groups and warlords that make up the Northern Alliance.

Massoud was also the Afghan leader whose reputation best survived two decades of war, despite persistent allegations of corruption and cronyism and the human rights abuses that occurred when he was Defence Minister in Kabul in the early 1990s. His Jamiat-i-Islami faction, like the others, had rained rockets down on civilian areas of Kabul, causing massive destruction. Tens of thousands of people died in the bombardments or fled the city.

But over time, Massoud came to embody the myth of the charismatic warrior. He was magnetic, compelling and – it must be said – extremely sexy. Photographers turned him into the poster boy of Fundamentalism, the David Beckham of Islamic warriors. A French photographer wearing a local scarf and a *pakul*, a Tajik woollen cap, sighs, 'Women always found

Massoud attractive. I just accept it.' He's right. Massoud was an irresistibly romantic figure – the beautiful careworn Tajik face under its *pakul*, the sensitive warrior, funny and media savvy. He had women and men swooning. Even hard-bitten war reporters wrote gushing pieces about the true warrior, backed into a corner, outnumbered and outgunned, but never outclassed.

The Northern Alliance blames Osama bin Laden for Massoud's death, an assessment confirmed by Western intelligence sources. They say that before carrying out the terror attacks in the US, bin Laden neutralised opposition within Afghanistan, perhaps to reward the Taliban leaders for their support of al-Qaeda. The Northern Alliance goes further, arguing that Massoud's assassination was a signal to Mohammed Atta and his men to carry out the World Trade Center attacks. 'Now, with Massoud dead, it was safe for them to go ahead.'

For Zubair in Khoja Bahauddin, the tragedy has personal implications. He was in Pakistan with his new bride of three months when Massoud was assassinated, and has had to leave her behind to run this HQ. We remove our shoes to sit in his office. Unlike most Afghan rooms which have only mats around the walls, here there is fake antique furniture, ornate and out of place, like furniture reserved for special guests in a rarely used English sitting room. But one aspect of the decor is very typically Afghan: the walls are bare. The only decoration is posters of the stunningly photogenic Massoud.

I ask Zubair if this is a good life. He looks around helplessly. 'It's a life.'

What would improve it?

'Peace,' he answers automatically.

Mohammed, another Northern Alliance official, chimes in: 'Why didn't journalists protest when Ahmed Shah Massoud was murdered by journalists? It is your job to do this. The people here will not understand – they will be very angry with you,' he says furiously.

'Massoud's assassination was a terrible event,' I reply carefully, surprised by his vehemence, 'but his murderers weren't journalists, they were terrorists.'

'Yes, but why didn't journalists all over the world protest? You must understand that the people here will be suspicious of you – they will blame you for the death of Massoud.'

Great. As if it's not difficult enough to work here, people think we have murdered their national hero.

The European Broadcasting Union, EBU, is one of the first groups to come into Afghanistan overland, hauling more than two tonnes of gear by road rather than waiting for the chance of a chopper and a plane both becoming available at the same time. Once the Northern Alliance persuades the Russians to open the road, this is how most people will reach Afghanistan, but Joris Wauman from EBU is one of the first foreign journalists to present his passport at the Afghan border crossing at the Pyang River, and he has a hard time.

He tells them his nationality, Belgian, and is thrown face first onto the ground. There are three Kalashnikovs in his back, the bayonet of one in his neck.

He lies very still, with no idea what is going on. Luckily for him, there is a Russian journalist who speaks some Dari going through at the same time. It seems that the men who murdered Massoud entered Afghanistan using Belgian passports. The Russian journalist explains to the Afghan border guards that not every Belgian is a terrorist, and that Joris certainly is not one.

After some consultations, they reluctantly remove their Kalashnikovs from Joris' back, and let him up.

When Joris tells me this story he is still shaken. We can't afford any misunderstandings so close to Massoud's death.

'Tomorrow there will be a memorial here for Ahmed Shah Massoud,' says Zubair, looking overwhelmed again.

The generator splutters and dies, plunging the Foreign Ministry office into darkness. It feels very late, though it's only nine o'clock. It's time to go to sleep, but where? There is no more floor space in the women's room.

'We will take you to another guesthouse. It will cost only a small amount. Ten dollars every night,' says Zubair.

Together with eight other journalists I'm driven to an empty house across the other side of town. The drive is terrifying because it is my first experience of the enveloping, crushing darkness of night here, the night of the desert, the night of history, the night the ancients used to fear. I understand that fear now. The only light making a pathetic attempt to pierce the utter blackness is the beam of our jeep's headlights.

44

The car has a poster of Massoud slap bang in the middle of its windscreen, making it more difficult to see out; this and a black flag that is tied to the aerial appear to be obligatory on all vehicles here. After fifteen minutes of driving we suddenly career to a stop in front of a mud-brick wall. We bang on a door in the wall but no one comes. Our driver doesn't speak English. We look at him and bang again. A short, sleepy man finally answers, holding a lamp, and after an exchange with our driver in Dari he motions us to come with him. Clutching our bags, we stoop to pass through the door and follow his flickering light across the courtyard.

As I try not to stumble and to stay within this small arc of candlelight, I'm aware that here even finding your room at night has the feel of an ancient ritual. It seems absurd, unbelievable, that only two hours ago I was filing to Berlin, Dublin and Washington, via a satellite hovering in the night sky. Instinctively I look up. The stars shine down so brightly that I feel if I look hard, I should be able to see that satellite winking at me. In the darkness, the stars are your guides. Here, I understand why they were once worshipped as gods.

We are taken to two rooms with carpets on the floor and mats around the walls. We respect the Northern Alliance request that men and women sleep separately. In practice it means the men are squashed into one room, while the only other female journalist and I can luxuriate on the floor by ourselves.

I decide to check out the bathroom. Lighting my way with a kerosene lamp, I gingerly open the door. The light flickers about a bare concrete room, revealing a tin drum full of water, which I discover is delivered daily by donkey. There's a tin pitcher for removing water from the drum, and a hook on the door on which you can hang your clothes, although it doesn't really lock, which makes me nervous. But all in all, not too bad.

Then I go outside to the toilet. Here, as everywhere in Afghanistan, it becomes the bane of my life. A mud outhouse, without a door, with a slit in the mud floor, above a two metre drop. It has a pungent smell which makes you gag, tearing at your throat, acidic and goaty. 'Hold your nose and learn to squat,' Jacky Rowland from the BBC advises. Both essentials that I never really master.

From this first moment I learn we are all in it together. With the helpfulness that is to sustain us throughout our time 'in country', a Dutch journalist says 'You'll need this,' and offers me his headlamp. I feel ridiculous – a coal miner going to do her business, but he's right. You can't squat, aim and hold a torch and toilet paper all at once.

Food. Water. Medicine. Generators. Satellite phones. Information. Costs. Toilet paper. We will share everything in Afghanistan. While of course there are selfish, greedy journalists here, too, and I will see fist fights over access to a toilet, even access to a roof where a live broadcast is to be filmed, my essential experience of this hostile environment is that everyone pitches in together, so that we can all file – and survive.

The next morning we're up with the light as there are no curtains on the windows. We're stiff from our first night on the floor, and have to get dressed with men standing outside our windows staring at us. Like the toilets, this never gets any easier.

The man we met briefly by candlelight last night, Qasim, is funny and calm. We have no common language, but communicate well. He brings us pots of tea and the Afghan breakfast of bread – tasteless, dusty brown 'pitta' bread – and UHT cream, which they pour into a bowl. The Dutch journalist offers me cheese – 'Edam, it's good' – and I contribute apples from the market in Dushanbe.

We go out into the town. Khoja Bahauddin boasts one of the most dismal town squares I've ever seen. It is dominated by a huge stretch of gravel, shining whitely under the merciless sun, surrounded on four sides by unkempt wooden shacks which sell a very limited variety of packaged food, string and toilet paper. Both the shacks and the goods are covered in the dust that swirls in the square, making your eyes smart and your skin chafe.

A man walks by carrying a rooster. A Russian jeep squeals past, throwing up more dust. A donkey defecates at my feet. The shacks appear to be battened down, preparing to withstand something. When I experience my first dust storm here I will appreciate that it's actually a testimony to the determination of these people that the wooden structures remain

46

standing. But now, cauterised by the shock of the new, everything appears grey.

It is also relentlessly harsh. Roads are built by crews who break rocks with sledgehammers to make gravel. On market days, people walk from distant villages – some even cross Taliban lines – to buy livestock. Horses, camels and donkeys are auctioned in a mud-brick enclosure behind the main square. Then the animals are herded home, back across the desert and across the front lines.

On this first day, surrounded by jostling crowds of turbaned men, I also fail to see that there *are* plants in the square. They are so small and stunted and covered in dust that it is only on later visits I realise they are rose bushes – and then only when a man throws a bucket of dirty water over a small grey bush as I walk past, and for a moment a pink rose emerges. It's a tribute to the resilience of the flower and the people that it grows here, in the desert, during the worst drought in seventy years.

This town, which looks as old and decrepit as time, is in fact new.

'We built it three years ago, when Khoja Bahauddin was upgraded from a village to a town,' Mehibullah, a pharmacist, tells me proudly. He speaks to me in Russian, which he learnt studying pharmacy in Prague in the 1980s. I just stop myself from saying *And you ended up here?* Prague boasts what is arguably the most beautiful medieval square in Europe, grand buildings from the 1300s painted an exquisite array of gelato colours, and maintained even during Communist times. The contrast to this ugly, filthy, desolate square is so painful it's almost comical. Afghanistan was never conquered, but its history is directed by the swirls and eddies of Empire. Mehibullah reaped some of the benefits of the Soviet occupation. Education. Travel. Career Opportunities. He sighs with me for the changes in his life.

Like many of the people here, Mehibullah is a refugee from the Taliban. He took flight with his family when the Taliban conquered Taloqan just over a year ago.

'We had to run away, they beat us because we were Tajiks,' he says.

Refugees have swelled the population of this town, so that it is somewhere between 3000 and 35,000. Somewhere. No one seems to have a more reliable figure. Like so many facts in Afghanistan, this appears to be about the range of accuracy journalists can pin down.

Mehibullah possesses that other very Afghan trait – overwhelming hospitality. He wants me to come to visit his wife and family, an hour's drive away by motorbike. I explain that I can't come because today I have to cover the memorial service for Ahmed Shah Massoud. 'Another day, you must come to my home another day. I will tell my wife,' he insists.

Everywhere, people offer me meals and clothes. Girls take off their headbands to give to me. Even in refugee camps where people are starving, they offer me their precious bread, baked with the first flour they've seen in months. I am overwhelmed.

This hospitality has another side, too. The people are so innately generous, they can't understand why we don't give them our possessions. Give me your scarf, your camera, your shoes. 'My shoes? I only have one pair, you can't have my shoes,' I protest.

'But I need your shoes,' the girl replies with unimpeachable logic.

I notice that when my male colleagues are approached for something by an Afghan man with a gun, they find it harder to explain why they won't give it to him. But keeping your sense of humour is essential – petulance won't get you anywhere, and actually the man isn't using the gun as leverage, it's just an extension of him, like his arm, so you *can* reject his request. It's about approach. Men approach each other differently. Maybe it's like asking for directions – there are just some things men can't do.

Despite the warmth of the welcome, there's no doubt that this influx of Western journalists is confusing to the people of Khoja Bahauddin. Many of them have never seen a Westerner before. Tourists don't come here. Even people from Kabul can go their whole lives without coming here. Russian soldiers ten years ago and some Western aid workers are the extent of it. And now, here we are – in droves. We've come because of the attacks on the World Trade Center and the Pentagon. But two weeks on, many people in Afghanistan still don't know about them. At a barbershop in the square, some men are waiting to have their beards trimmed. Out of seven men only one, twenty-eight-year-old Nasr, has heard about the September 11 attacks, though he hasn't seen any pictures of the two planes crashing into the tallest towers in New York and their spectacular collapse.

'No. We don't have television and our newspapers don't have pictures,' he says.

Under the Taliban there has been no television broadcasting, and anyway most people don't have electricity, so they couldn't power their televisions even if there was anything to watch. There are only a few two-page newspapers such as *Shariat*, *Heevad* and *Anise*, produced in the south. They have text but no pictures.

For information, you listen to the radio, if you have one. Many people are pleased I file for Voice of America. They point me out to each other as the reporter from *Sa'aday Amrika*. A stranger runs up to me in the square to ask me the frequency for the Dari service. I can't help him.

But if you don't have a radio, there is always the town crier, the *jatchi*. Abdulmommen, the *jatchi* in Khoja Bahauddin, wears a striped turban and carries a megaphone. 'If a donkey is lost, then the owner comes to me and I describe it throughout the town,' he says. 'Then, when with the help of God the donkey is found, the owner pays me money.'

Abdulmommen says he is not familiar with stealth bombers or cruise missiles. He knows more about Russian weaponry, and could easily make announcements concerning Kalashnikovs or Katyusha rockets. But like the international TV networks, Abdulmommen finds there isn't much money in news. In the afternoons, he works as a bricklayer.

The *jatchi* is also the public face of justice. When a crime is committed, the suspect is tied to a donkey and paraded through the town. The town crier walks by his side, describing the man's crimes, and asking him to repent. Journalists standing in the square watch as Abdulmommen accompanies one suspect, trussed backwards onto the donkey. The man's face is dabbed with black oil, and he is bleeding where he has been hit. It's a busy day and there's a crowd in the square. They all get in on the act. Bystanders hit the suspect, and so does Abdulmommen. The man is crying.

'He repented, so we did not send him to gaol,' says Abdulmommen, 'He was a pickpocket, you know.' He pauses for emphasis. 'I saw him stealing in the rice bazaar myself.' God knows what they would dish out to someone who had committed a serious crime.

A huge group of turbaned men crowd around to listen to this interview. It passes for entertainment in a place with no modern distractions such as movies or computer games. Abdulmommen does the entire interview through his megaphone. I think he's playing to the crowd, but an American cameraman says this is probably how he talks to his wife as well. 'HI HONEY. WHAT'S FOR DINNER?'

It seems Abdulmommen enjoys being interviewed – he is patient with my questions and with the lengthy process of translation backwards and forwards. The crowd is certainly fascinated, and sorry when it is over.

What do people do for entertainment when I'm not here to provide it? They listen to a storyteller or *mado*.

The *mado* stands in front of a dusty building on the outskirts of the bazaar at an appointed time every day. A group of men sits around him. He is a bearded man in his forties, and he starts by singing in a pleasant, earthy baritone. His song has the hypnotic quality of a chant, and the men listen raptly, some swaying in time. Then he narrates the story he's been chanting, often a traditional Islamic tale. Today, it's a parable about love and sacrifice.

'The Prophet Esau comes upon a man crying by a fresh grave, and asks him why he is sad,' the *mado* begins. '"My beautiful young wife has died," the man replies, "and I am inconsolable." The Prophet offers to bring her back to life, but says there will be a price – the man will have to give up half his own life. He agrees, and Esau brings the beautiful young woman back from the dead. She climbs out of her grave and stands beside her husband. He is overjoyed to see her and takes her hand. But now he is an old man.'

After he tells this story, the *mado* collects money from his audience. Before he does, he offers a blessing, referring to current events.

'May God bring peace to Afghanistan,' he says, 'and may God kill every terrorist.'

It's only at the end that I realise there wasn't a single woman there to listen to this parable about love – or to receive the *mado*'s blessing. Like so much of life in northern Afghanistan, public entertainment is for men only.

We bewilder people here, with our state-of-the-art satellite equipment, and our hourly deadlines. It's not just because they have only the haziest idea of the significance of the attacks on the World Trade Center, it's because they have an utterly different sense of time.

We try to explain to a translator why it is important to be punctual.

'In the West time is precious, it is like gold.'

'Here time is like stone.'

Time is like stone, and life is basic. You shit where you stand. You die where you fall.

The cemeteries are a collection of mounds, like ants' nests. None has an identifying mark that would let you distinguish the grave of your loved one from any other. In fact, if you didn't know what they were, graveyards would be almost indistinguishable from the surrounding desert.

These are the most basic funerary markings I have seen anywhere in the world

I look out onto a large cemetery every day. It lies behind the Foreign Ministry, and I see it from the roof when I climb up the rickety bamboo ladder to do my live shots. Sometimes children play there. It makes me reflective as I wait my turn at the BBC's camera. Death never feels far away in northern Afghanistan.

And it isn't. More than ten per cent of the country's population have died over the past two decades of war. The chaos has meant there has been no rigorous collection of statistics, so figures are approximate. Afghanistan had a population of twenty million in 1992. During the past twenty years, including the war against the Russian occupation, about 2.5 million Afghans have died, killed in fighting, famine, or from lack of medical facilities. Those who survive have shortened life spans – the average male life expectancy is only 41.5 years.

Afghanistan also has the largest refugee population in the world, with more than six million people living in camps outside the country, in Pakistan and India, and a huge population of internal migrants as well, fleeing battles or moving in search of food and water. Thousands now live in camps here where we are.

The advent of the Taliban made life even more difficult for the long-suffering population. Although more than fifty per cent of people were dependent on aid agencies for provision of food, water and medical supplies, the Taliban had an ideological reluctance to accept international aid. After they came to power across the south and centre of the country, they harassed the non-government organisations and the United Nations until in July 1998 they forced them to leave Kabul.

This had an immediate impact on the poor of the capital, especially women and children. As the city's stretched water distribution suffered, people waved empty bottles and buckets at Taliban jeeps. However, the Taliban remained unconcerned. 'We Muslims believe that Almighty God will feed everybody one way or another. If the foreign NGOs leave, then that is their decision,' said Planning Minister Qari Din Mohammed.

The Taliban clearly did not see it as their job to step in and provide water and food for the population they had conquered at gunpoint. More people suffered and died, and climbed these treacherous mountains to escape the Taliban, living in desolate refugee camps in Khoja Bahauddin, rather than in their own homes under Taliban rule.

This backwater is an unlikely centre of government. The Northern Alliance retreated to Khoja Bahauddin in August 2000, when the Taliban overran their regional headquarters in the nearby town of Taloqan. This retreat is a sign of how gravely weakened the Northern Alliance is. It cannot hold onto its stronghold here in the north, and has been beaten back into pockets of the country, covering less than ten per cent of Afghanistan.

The Taliban front lines are about twelve kilometres from here. President Burhanuddin Rabbani and the Alliance's new Defence Minister, General Mohammed Fahim, come to this exposed point on 25 September for Massoud's memorial service. It is being held in the main mosque – a low white building, entirely without charm. It could be an office. There is no minaret or any of the gracious fluid lines that characterise mosques all over the world. Like so much in Khoja Bahauddin, it is utilitarian, and no more.

The mosque is close to the Foreign Ministry compound, but I don't feel safe walking to it on my own. I feel conspicuous despite my loose clothes and headscarf. It's noon on a scorching day and local feelings are bubbling over. The mosque is full, with thousands of mourners spilling over into the dust outside. Standing in the burning sun, they listen to their leaders.

There's a call and response, with the men shouting *nad* – death – to Osama bin Laden, to Taliban leader Mullah Omar, to Pakistan, and to the Pakistani security service, the ISI. That yields the biggest shout of *nad*. There are hundreds of fighters among the mourners, here to remember their charismatic military leader and to prepare themselves for the war ahead. They listen to eulogies about Ahmed Shah Massoud from his successor, General Fahim, and from President Rabbani, political leader of the Northern Alliance.

With one eye on the Western reporters, President Rabbani says that the September 11 attacks are the bell waking the world to the threat of the Taliban. He proclaims that the death of Massoud has not weakened the Northern Alliance – that now with the prospect of international help it's even stronger.

Stirring stuff, if you can get near it. We are told that as women we can't attend the ceremony in the mosque. There are probably fifteen female reporters at this stage – and ten times as many men. I ask whether it might be possible to be outside in the yard, not in the mosque itself, so that I can pick up audio for a radio report. The Northern Alliance officials agree, but after only a few moments in the yard it's obvious that it is not possible. The crowd is hot, restive and angry. One man points at me furiously. Remembering that many of these men believe that Western journalists murdered Massoud, I retreat back outside the fence. A crowd can turn so easily and it doesn't feel like this one needs much prompting. Even in this position I'm not sure I'm safe – and the quality of the sound I record from here is unusable.

But we get around it. Female journalists watch and listen from the fence. A translator tells us what's being said, and our male colleagues, who are inside the mosque, let us use the material they record. I file for Berlin and Dublin on President Rabbani's comments at the memorial service, and the state of Northern Alliance preparations for war.

Back at home, no one cares that it was hard; you're only judged by what's on the screen and, if you're a woman, by your hair. I have never done a TV story – no matter where from, no matter how dangerous – where people haven't commented on how I look. You'd think you could rely on your mother to worry about you in a war zone – but even she will say 'I liked your hair' before she says 'What were you doing in that dangerous place?' It's forced me to the conclusion that probably the most important thing I do for any story is put on my lippy. Another of the surreal factors in doing this job in dusty, dirty, dangerous Afghanistan.

Chapter 4

The crowd in the square is ten deep, and the flames leap above their turbans, leaking acrid black smoke. We have to push our way forward since we're late. A soldier in uniform is pouring kerosene over sacks lying on the gravel inside the square. He sets them alight, and more clouds of noxious smoke billow towards us. The onlookers cover their faces with scarves. They should – this is pure heroin burning in front of them.

In the week of Massoud's funeral, the region's military commander, Quazi Kobir, destroys 300 kilograms of heroin he says was captured from the Taliban. He exhibits stamps from the bags that contained the heroin, saying they indicate the drugs were produced by the Taliban, and destined for Pakistan. It is a very hot day and the cloying, pharmaceutical smell of the burning narcotic tears at the back of our throats, making us dizzy and nauseous. The only person in the square seated to watch the proceedings, Commander Kobir answers questions from croaky-voiced, teary reporters. He says that the Northern Alliance is fighting the Taliban on all fronts, and the struggle against narcotic smuggling is part of that war. 'It is part of our Islamic duty to clamp down on narcotics.'

According to CIA figures, more than seventy per cent of the world's heroin is produced from Afghan opium. Opium poppies flourish in the country's southern desert region – as well as in northern provinces like Badakshan – and have done so since the time of Alexander the Great. Unlike wheat, they require little water and are ideally suited to the country's arid valleys.

In 2000 the Taliban said they were ending opium production, and ripped up the poppy fields. They took journalists along, and the pictures went all around the world. But even though the ban was enforced at gunpoint in some villages, it may have been no more than a publicity stunt. The previous two years had been bumper crops – 4600 tonnes of heroin were produced here in 1999 alone – giving the Taliban such huge stockpiles that a temporary cessation would make little difference to world supply. Authorities in neighbouring Tajikistan say there has been no decrease in opium trafficked at the border. The opium bazaar in the Taliban stronghold of Kandahar never closed, even during the poppy ban.

In a country with almost no industry of any type, it's estimated that up to half of the population are involved in the narcotic trade. For example, even war widows, prevented by the Taliban from holding any other jobs, work as couriers. Smugglers often take members of the courier's family hostage to ensure delivery and payment.

I report the burning of the heroin, although it has the feel of a public relations exercise, and a disgruntled local later whispers to me that we didn't ask the right questions, and that local Northern Alliance commanders *are* involved in drug trafficking. I am never able to confirm the extent of Northern Alliance involvement in this region, but it is clear that across the country it is not only the Taliban who are involved in opium production.

The Islamic warriors fighting against the Soviet invaders, the Mujaheddin, got into the business in the 1980s to fund their 'holy war' against Russia. That includes many of these same Mujaheddin from the Northern Alliance who now have an Islamic duty to put a stop to it.

According to British research, the Northern Alliance has been as closely associated with narcotics as the Taliban. Dr Mark Galeotti, the Director of the Russian & Eurasian Organised Crime Research Unit at Keele University in

England, argues, 'The Taliban regime largely confined itself to taking a ten to twenty per cent levy on opium harvests, heroin production, and drug shipments, earning it a minimum of US$40–45 million annually. By contrast, the Northern Alliance – or at least key figures in it – actively engaged in the production, sale and trafficking of opium for factional and personal gain. Unofficial estimates from the Tajik authorities suggest that supplies this year have been fairly evenly split between the Northern Alliance and the Taliban, even though the Taliban controlled four times as much land before November.'

This is confirmed by UN research, which has found that most of the opiates crossing Tajikistan have come from Northern Alliance-controlled territory, and also that on Tajikistan's major smuggling routes, seizures of heroin out-number those of opium. To European researchers, this suggests that laboratories in Alliance-controlled areas are successfully refining opium into the more potent, compact final product. A study for the International Crisis Group concludes that 'Ahmed Shah Massoud may have publicly opposed the drugs trade, just as Taliban leader Mullah Omar did, but weapons and troops are paid for by individual commanders. There is no doubt drugs have funded all factions.'

Even an active front line does not prevent the trade from continuing. An aid worker says that last year, when he was helping distribute wheat to refugees near the front line on the Kokcha River, close to Khoja Bahauddin, he saw donkeys ferrying opium between the Taliban and Northern Alliance sides. He tells an American writer that the commanders arranged the exchanges by radio.

'Some of them had friendly contacts, even though they were fighting one another.'

The Northern Alliance city of Faizabad, nine hours' drive from here, is reportedly a centre for opium production and smuggling. German TV journalists who are in Faizabad try to buy some heroin from a local chemist. They go in, cameras rolling.

'Heroin? Yes. How much do you want?' the chemist asks.

'Oh, two or three kilos,' the journalist replies, for laughs, playing to the camera.

The chemist brings up a box from under his counter, filled with white powder. Using a plastic scoop he starts to measure out two kilos of heroin into a bag. The journalist can't believe his eyes.

In Dushanbe, Afghan officials told us we should bring water to Afghanistan, but that we didn't have to bring food. However, if you're a vegetarian like me, that was not entirely accurate advice. After a breakfast of dusty bread and UHT cream, lunch and dinner are the same: rice cooked in goat fat, and beans stewed with potatoes in goat fat, and goat shashlik on skewers (I don't eat that bit). There's also more of the dusty bread. And so it goes every day. In fact, it doesn't matter who you are, even meat eaters quickly get bored. And plenty of people get sick.

I have a cast-iron stomach, and don't usually get sick anywhere I travel, no matter how remote the location or how dodgy the food – or how many of the rest of the crew are felled. But finally the bugs in that goat fat wear me down, and I get giardia. I think it's that and not something floating in the water, because after I've suffered for two days and dosed myself with Gastrolyte and antibiotics, and emerged pleasingly thinner, I can never eat that rice again. Just the thought of it makes me want to vomit. Even now.

So I find myself eating meat for the first time in twenty years. Goat, of course. What else is there? Shashliked on skewers, it's somehow more bearable than the goat fat, oozing all over the rice and potatoes. Mostly, I eat chocolate and apples. Swiss chocolate (a box of Toblerone left behind by a departing journalist) and local apples, once I've carefully rinsed off all the dust. For breakfast I often have Russian instant porridge, which the Canadians from the Moscow bureau of CBC have brought. It comes in sachets and you add boiling water. I ask CBC's Russian producer, Tanya, if she wants me to wash my plastic plate, and she looks horrified. 'Things aren't that bad yet.' Recycling hasn't permeated the Russian consciousness. But when Tanya finally leaves she tells her friends that Afghanistan was 'worse than Chechnya'.

Another Just Add Boiling Water staple here is instant noodles, and sometimes the NBC boys share their MREs –

'meals ready to eat' – which they have shipped in from the United States. But they are soon sick of these, too. There are five vacuum-packed alternatives, and even the tastiest soon become boring. 'Oh no, not cheese tortellini. I've had this for three days in a row. It's almost inedible, you know.' I hear the cheese tortellini wail over and over.

Those same five meals quickly become as predictable as the rice, beans and goat. But at least they won't make you sick.

The dust is becoming more pervasive. It is as fine as cake flour but gritty, and it is in our eyes and ears and throats. We are only ever clean for approximately five minutes a day – straight after washing. After that it's as if we hadn't washed in a week. Most worryingly, the dust is clogging up our equipment. Some people's cameras and laptops seize up, and radio gear simply dies.

Today the air seems to be opaque, and is swirling in stinging gusts in the square. I look at the two English reporters with whom I am out doing interviews. Their hair is stiff with dust, their faces grey with dust, and they are wearing their local scarves wrapped around their mouths, so that they don't breathe too much dust down into their lungs. I'm glad I can't see myself. After less than ten days, we look like locals.

I don't recognise the beginnings of a dust storm because I've never experienced anything like it before. After a twenty-four-hour build-up, in which the sky turns a sulphurous yellow and you feel that the end of the world is near, a colossal wind begins to howl. It seems to pick up half the desert, which has nothing to hold it down after years of drought, and blows it back in the faces of the long-suffering population. People walk along bowed against the wind, their scarves wound around their faces, women carrying children. Soon the town is empty, sand swirling through it in hot gusts.

The storm's force is frightening. Heavy satellite dishes worth thousands of dollars and rated for 150 kilometre per hour winds are knocked over. Journalists living in tents come indoors and take refuge in our rooms.

We secure the satellite equipment as best we can, and then just lock the doors, break out the contraband vodka, and drink. You can't work, you can hardly breathe, even indoors. 'Dust stopped play,' says Jacky Rowland from the BBC.

The next morning everything inside is covered in a thick coating of fine powder, including our sleeping bags. Waking up I feel like I'm gazing at a collection of mummies in the British Museum, until one of the mummies sits up, taps a pool of sand off his glasses, and puts them on his nose.

'Do you think it's over?' he croaks.

We go out to assess the damage. The European Broadcasting Union guys are there, covered in dust, dismantling their gear. They closed down their operation for twenty-four hours because their set-up was in a tent outside. They are planning to move to a safer location. Indoors. 'Not making that mistake again!' While they're packing, Joris from EBU finds something in the sand. He is certain it is a piece from the camera wired with Semtex that killed Ahmed Shah Massoud. But he doesn't keep this gruesome memento because he is Belgian and if he is found with it he'd be killed, no questions asked. He still remembers the feel of those Kalashnikovs in his back at the border coming in.

I look around. The air is no longer yellow. It is grey and heavy, but quiet. Locals say this phase lasts for another two days. 'Wear your scarf like this – it's safer for your breathing,' they say, gesturing to me to wrap my scarf around my face.

I wonder if there's any point in washing, or if the water is also full of sand.

After the dust storm I decide I need new clothes. I'm ready to become an Afghan fashion victim. I can't keep up with all the washing and I'm inspired by Jacky Rowland from the BBC, who's had an Afghan man's pyjama suit made up and looks fab.

'Their clothes are much better for this weather, they're very cool,' she says.

You can buy them 'off the rack', which the boys do after Jacky leads the way, wearing her local clobber on camera. But Jacky advises me to have the full Khoja Bahauddin experience and go to the tailor, the *chayati*, to have a suit made.

'Here's what you do, you buy fabric – you need metres and metres of it, because of the way they make the pants – then you go across to the tailor. I'll take you to both.'

I trot behind her across the square. There is something magnificent about Jacky, striding ahead in her blue Afghan pyjama suit with designer sunglasses and a white scarf wrapped around her blonde hair. Watching her sweep in and out of these dusty shacks, choosing between bolts of blue cloth, specifying amounts of fabric and frowning over the cost, puts me in mind of the British Raj.

Under her direction, I buy enough fabric for one suit and one shirt – three metres for US$4 – and we walk back across the blisteringly hot white gravel to the tailors' shacks. There are five or six in this Savile Row, and Jacky looks for the one with a hand-painted sign of a sewing machine above it.

'Here. This is it.' Jacky strides in. 'Nasr from the Foreign Ministry came with me and I just pointed to what he was wearing and said I wanted one exactly the same. They were a bit scandalised that it was men's clothes, but I was firm and they did it.'

The tailor is by now used to crazy Western women wanting to wear men's suits, and he measures me up through my clothes – placing his tape measure across my shoulders, down my arms, and from my shoulders down to my knees. The shack is open on two sides and a crowd gathers, fascinated. I point to a friend's shirt, and say I want one just the same. The delighted crowd settles in for the next instalment. After he measures me again, the tailor sets a price – at US$2, labour costs less than the fabric. He can have them ready in three days.

When I come back, the shirt isn't anything like my friend's, which the tailor was meant to be copying, but the pantaloon suit is perfect. It is in two pieces – a long overshirt, which reaches to the knees, and pyjama pants, which look large enough for an elephant. One size fits all, twice. They give you a white cotton belt to thread through a seam at the waist. It's the only way to hold up such gargantuan pants.

Jacky does the threading for me as it's very fiddly and she is better at it. While she does it she tells me what it was like freelancing from Belgrade during the NATO bombing, which was more dangerous than here because it was a built-up environment. After explaining that she likes 'roughty toughty' stories like this one, she says, 'Here, make a knot in it straight away, or you'll have to do it again.'

Once it's all fixed, and I can wear it, I'm a convert. The pyjama suit is absolutely the best thing in this environment – loose-fitting, modest and cool. The Afghan translators and drivers beam when they see me.

'Irris! You are wearing Afghan clothes! *Now* you look beautiful.'

The BBC sends in correspondent Caroline Wyatt, a dear friend from Moscow. When she sees us in our Afghan gear she says despairingly, 'You've all gone native!' She is the first person to be impressed with Khoja Bahauddin. 'I just remember what it was like in Buj in India after the earthquake where there was absolutely nothing and we had to sleep outside on the ground without even a blanket . . . this isn't that bad.'

It's official – Afghanistan is one step above the epicentre of an earthquake . . .

The house where Massoud was assassinated is here in another section of the Foreign Ministry.

He designed it himself and had it built on the spot with the best view in Khoja Bahauddin – over the river and across to the fields that provide the only greenery in the area. At night, particularly, when the stars seem to tumble down brightly to this vista, gleaming above the river, it is very peaceful. You can almost forget that just down the road in front of you, twelve kilometres away, is the Taliban front line.

As the number of journalists grows, Zubair decides to open up Massoud's house. Khoja Bahauddin is bursting at the seams. Every available room in every available house has been turned over to journalists, and more and more are arriving every day, with new arrivals forced to sleep outside in corridors. It had to reach crisis point before the Northern Alliance would consider handing over Massoud's house to the foreigners. Not all of the house will be open, however. The room where he was assassinated will remain closed. All eight windows in the room thirty metres square are blown out and blackened. I am stunned by the force of the explosion, feeling some echo of it whenever I walk by or sit on the balcony, overlooking the river below.

Zubair sets one room aside for women because it has an indoor toilet, and because the Northern Alliance doesn't want men and women to live together. I like the idea. I feel a bond with Massoud since I flew into Afghanistan in his helicopter, sitting in his armchair. But it is strange to live in the shadow of a legend. His personal bodyguards, some nine soldiers from the Panjshir Valley, also live in the house. Some of them come up to us as we are moving our bags in.

'We are the bodyguard of Massoud,' they announce. They don't yet use the past tense.

'Well, you didn't do a very good job, did you?' Jacky Rowland and I say to each other. Most of the women in the women's room are from the BBC. When the BBC finds its own house, further up the hill, they move out, leaving only me and two European journalists, one from Holland and one from Finland. American network NBC does a deal with Zubair and takes over Massoud's house, which becomes the main base for its operations in northern Afghanistan.

NBC has an all-male crew, but they invite the 'left-over' women to stay. In addition, they seem to have inherited Massoud's bodyguards with the house. The guards relate better to the NBC boys than to us – chess becomes their primary shared sport. NBC employs the nephew of one of the soldiers to clean up for them. Though he is earning unimaginable sums of US dollars, he is surly and doesn't do much work. He thinks it's enough to be the nephew of the clan chief. And maybe it is, like with other important clans the world over. Maybe a young Kennedy wouldn't make a great waiter, either. He doesn't last – in the end NBC fires him.

After two weeks, the number of journalists increases dramatically again. Journalists are now sleeping on concrete balconies, and even on gravel. There is still only one bathroom and one toilet in the Foreign Ministry compound, and as conditions deteriorate so do people's tempers. Fights over access to the shower are becoming more common. The Foreign Ministry compound is becoming like a journalist refugee camp – and just like with the refugees, new journalists keep pouring in.

We suggest to Zubair that he should put Massoud's bodyguards to work and dig a second toilet to prevent the outbreak of disease. He agrees, but nothing is ever done.

There is one other bathroom, of course, inside Massoud's house, but since NBC are paying to supply it with water, they don't want everyone else using it. Particularly since some of the others who do use it leave it so filthy it is truly disgusting, even for here. Life in shared houses is never easy, but trust me, you don't want to clean up after someone else with diarrhoea.

This leads to so much acrimony that I think that CBS have missed a trick by not setting an episode of *Survivor* here. It would have everything: war, reality TV, plus you'd be able to evict people from the compound with a clear conscience. Many journalists are behaving so appallingly the audience wouldn't care that they have nowhere else to sleep, and that once they're out, there's a real chance they'd be attacked by the wild dogs who roam in packs.

An exasperated Iranian producer warns anyone who wants to go out walking at night: 'Man, you can't go outside, the dogs will eat you.'

Despite the daily battle to survive, and to produce good work in such conditions, our lives are telescoped and becoming simpler. Strangely, the dust storm acts like rain, and after it finally passes, the air feels clearer.

One morning I am sitting on a wooden chair in a patch of gravel near Massoud's house. My laptop is plugged into NBC's power supply and I am writing a story. The sun is warm on my back, it's not too dusty, and the boys are playing Jimi Hendrix. As the sounds of the 1960s float out over the valley, I'm aware I am happy. It takes so little to make me happy now. Just the absence of dust, a sunny day, and a power source.

Producer Tom Baer interrupts this reverie. 'You should do your washing,' he booms enthusiastically. You always know when Tom Baer's around because he starts impromptu addresses in his deep voice: 'Men! Men, not since the dark days of Pearl Harbor . . .'

We usually send our laundry out to local families, but Tom has decided to do his own washing this morning, and persuades me to stop writing, hop up and do mine, too. 'Look, we've got Persil . . .' he says temptingly, showing me where he has set up three tin buckets, one for washing, one for rinsing and one with fresh water. In Dushanbe the washing powder was called Barf, so Persil is irresistible.

Tom is a legendary NBC figure, a huge bear of a man and a fabulous raconteur, of the type who thrive in television, one of the reasons I love this medium. Tom leaves every war zone in a helicopter, yelling 'NBC is leaving the building.' The stories of where the insanity of war meets the insanity of TV newsgathering are unsurpassable.

And I love how we sit around and tell these stories, on the floor in one of the bedrooms, passing around a water bottle in which someone has hidden gin, so that the Northern Alliance won't see it on their spot-check visits. They must be getting suspicious as they've started turning up 'Just to see what you're up to' almost every night. We are in one of the bedrooms, talking and laughing, when they poke their heads in, looking disapproving. It's like being at boarding school. The laughter stops and everybody looks uncomfortable, as East meets West, and we wait to face war. Together.

The Northern Alliance also keeps tabs on how we portray them to their Western allies by presenting us with a pool of translators to use when working here. Not only do they set a very high fee – twenty per cent of which goes to the Foreign Ministry – they also have our translators write a daily report on what we do. The Foreign Ministry doesn't like it when we use translators that they don't supply, but soon the sheer number of journalists makes their attempts at control unmanageable.

However, there are two sets of people the Foreign Ministry can monitor – and that's the BBC and me, because they can hear our reports on the foreign-language services of Voice of America and the BBC on their short-wave radios. The first time Zubair comes to shout at me about a mistake in a report I'm shocked – well, actually I think he's joking, he's so stern: 'In that report about the burning of the heroin, you made two mistakes, TWO VERY SERIOUS MISTAKES.'

'What mistakes did I make?'

'The first is that you referred to the local commander as Qasim Kobir, and his name is Quazi Kobir.'

I apologise and explain that I must have misheard the translator since I asked him twice if I had the pronunciation right.

But Zubair is not mollified. In fact, he works himself up into a magnificent rage.

'And you also didn't say it was heroin. That's bad, it's very bad.'

The other Foreign Ministry staff stand around Zubair nodding angrily.

'Yes I did, Zubair, that was in the lead – you weren't listening to the whole thing, were you?'

He stalks off and I realise that the whole point of this exercise is to let me know that he is listening. Another kind of theatre of war.

Rummaging through the NBC food store later, I find two gleaming cooking pots, hidden under cartons of instant noodles, and tins of pressed meat, grey, wobbly and vile smelling, imported from Russia, which only Russians will ever eat.

'You've got pots!' I say triumphantly to Nate, the cockney sound recordist. Nate is already auditioning for 'Apocalypse Now, the Afghan Generation', wearing a bandana and listening to The Doors while he lies outside working on his tan.

'Wanna cook for me, darlin'?' he calls out as Jim Morrison sings about being down so goddam long that it looks like up to him.

'Maybe . . .' I start rummaging in earnest and find olive oil, pasta, tomato paste and tinned soups that don't look too disgusting. I am so starved of vegetables that I fantasise about cooking every fresh vegetable I can find in the market. Not that there are many.

It's a slow news day, and I walk up to the bazaar. The vendors are sitting on sacks in the dirt, with their vegetables heaped in front of them. By this time in the afternoon everything is covered in the dust of the day. There are onions, garlic, chillies, potatoes, tomatoes, some yellowish carrots, and turnips. Not a great range and all the vegetables are scrawny and stunted with the strain of trying to grow in this drought-stricken earth. It won't be the best stew in the world, but I won't let anything deter me.

I point to the onions and ask how much they cost. The veggie man tells me and I write the amount down in my book just to make sure I have understood. I show him, he nods and measures the onions out on a flat tin plate linked with a piece of twine to another similar plate: a very rudimentary set of scales. Do I want one small rock's worth?

I gesture that I want more. A large rock's worth?

I look, and decide I might need more again. The crowd of about forty men and children that has gathered draws its breath. 'She wants more.' The children fight to get in closer and see what I am buying, almost pushing me over. 'STOP!' I say loudly in Dari, 'CHALAS!' The adults pull the children back, laughing good-naturedly. 'She said "Chalas",' they say to each other.

I turn back to the veggie man. We agree an amount – one large rock and one small rock's worth – and four small children fight to provide me with a plastic bag, almost knocking me over again. They make their living selling bags here in the dirt. The veggie man takes a bag from one filthy child, and chases them away.

Then we start all over again for the other vegetables. After this lengthy process, watched attentively by the crowd, there comes the difficult moment of paying the bill. I ask the total, but I am not sure I understand what I am told. Sometimes these stallholders can write and sometimes they can't, and I don't want to embarrass him by asking. I know from previous experience that I won't have to, because always at this exact moment a man emerges from the crowd with a calculator and shows me the amount on that. Sometimes he even knows some English, enough to say the numbers.

The man materialises, on cue. I pull out the agreed sum, and as I pay the crowd murmurs its pleasure that the transaction went so well. I walk off carrying my purchases and they all come with me, prepared to enjoy my next fascinating adventure. It takes five minutes for them to disperse when they realise that I am only walking back to the Foreign Ministry compound.

I carry my bags full of vegetables into Massoud's house and discuss with the NBC producer whether I can use their two-ringed hotplate to cook. He is thrilled and, it turns out, so is everyone else. From the second I sit down to chop onions, every person who passes takes a keen interest in the proceedings.

I am almost defeated when I realise that despite all my planning I hadn't thought of a knife. There isn't a usable cooking knife anywhere. Three men whip out their pocket-knives. While the knife on a Leatherman is not an ideal kitchen tool, it is so familiar and pleasant to be peeling and chopping onions that I don't mind. But one of the locals hired by NBC to do their 'housework' is affronted. Am I trying to show him up? This is his job. He indicates that he will do it. I say that no, I am happy. He takes my knife and begins to chop, I take it back, and so it goes until I can't bear his baleful looks, and relent. I find him a pocketknife and let him chop, too, but he soon forgets that he is only the kitchen hand. He calls a translator over to tell me that I don't need so much garlic.

'I only use so much garlic with ten kilos of meat.'

'Well, I use this much garlic with two kilos of vegetables. If you insist on helping, shut up and chop.'

It's wonderful how direct you can be with someone who doesn't understand English.

The aroma of onions, garlic and chilli frying in olive oil is so delicious and homely that it brings every man in NBC to my side. They stand by me, inhaling.

'I'm so happy you're doing this,' says the cameraman.

Nate, the sound recordist, can't let him get away with that. 'I don't know, I think it could do with some goat.'

Zubair from the Northern Alliance comes by. Even he seems happy that I'm cooking. 'You should invite me,' he says smiling. I tell him I will be happy to bring him a dish, if it turns out to be edible.

Suddenly it becomes everyone's meal, and I have to cook up more pasta when I realise how many hungry people are here tonight. Everyone makes a contribution to this magical thing, a home-cooked meal. They come to stand by the pot, to stir and to find more ingredients that should be added to the sauce. What began as a whim five hours earlier is now a communal enterprise, much grander and lovelier than anything I envisaged. And tasting quite different by the end, too. I'd never have put in salami if one new arrival hadn't brought his secret stash and begged me to use it. It's not a bad addition.

Someone sets the table, gaffer-taping white paper onto the wooden workbench to make a tablecloth. Someone finds wine. Someone else finds candles. The satellite engineer rigs up his laptop and some speakers so we have music. When the table is set on Massoud's balcony, it is simply beautiful. The meal is lovely and funny and convivial, my own dusty Afghan version of Babette's Feast.

As we smile for a photo, 'Dateline' reporter Dennis Murphy leans in and says, 'You see, women civilise men.'

Perhaps that's part of the problem in Afghanistan, where men isolate themselves from women.

In the end I don't invite Zubair because I know there will be alcohol at the table. The next day he calls in the NBC producers and carpets them. He tells them this is an Islamic state, bound by Islamic rules, and that if there is ever a repeat of this performance – including women, but especially alcohol – the entire NBC contingent will be deported from Afghanistan and will never be allowed to return. When I was first here, Russian crews living in the Foreign Ministry compound were drunk every night, leaving their empty vodka bottles right next door to Zubair's office without any complaints. Maybe we should have invited Zubair after all.

Chapter 5

'You're a woman. On your own. In Afghanistan. That's strange. I mean it's magical, but strange,' says a friend from NBC, smiling, as he walks with me across the square and past the slaughterhouse in Khoja Bahauddin. Freshly skinned sheep and goats are loaded for delivery onto the backs of small boys. They heave the warm, raw carcasses, almost the same size as they are, onto their shoulders, and run past us into town.

'It's strange because what happens if something bad happens to you? If something bad happens to me then NBC will look after me, but if something happens to you – who's going to medivac you out of here?'

Well, the answer is of course that no one is going to medivac me out of here. That's part of the freelance equation – you get yourself in, you get yourself out, and you file for more than one organisation to help pay your way. Some of them help you to defray expenses, but basically you are on your own. Suddenly I find myself carrying thousands of dollars in cash, when in my ordinary life I don't like to keep more than fifty dollars in my wallet. And it's one thing walking around with ten thousand dollars of your employer's cash on you – it is quite another level of vulnerability when it's your own money. 'It's not magical – it's mad,' I say frankly, 'but it's not as if I planned all this. It's my first big story as a freelance journalist. I'm used to working within a large news organisation with its equipment and facilities available to me, and I find being out here on my own strange, too.'

The other aspect that I find unusual is something more fundamental to me, and that is being a woman. There are very few of us here, as reporters or aid workers. Men outnumber women by a factor of ten to one, as the blokes have calculated despairingly. The BBC is one organisation that has sent a large number of women to Afghanistan. But most haven't. NBC, for example, has sent none – and won't send any until after the fall of Kabul.

And local women are almost invisible, hidden beneath burqas. Even places where you usually see women – like the market – are closed to women here, by order of the local military commander Quazi Kobir, who has his own strict interpretation of Islam. In Afghanistan, women are notable by their absence.

When I can't bear this strange excision any more and decide I must interview some of them, it proves by far the most difficult story I do – much harder than covering the war, or the politics. This absence also has a strange impact on me as journalist. Like all Western women here, I'm followed by a crowd of men wherever I go. Until they come with me, none of my male colleagues can believe what it is like for me just to go shopping. 'It's like travelling with Madonna,' says one NBC producer. Another colleague, who can't bear the crowds that turn out to watch me buy apples, grabs my camera and snaps five shots along the assembled men, for a panoramic view – as if they were a vista or a beauty spot. At the time I'm so inured to being followed that I think he's crazy. Now, joining up the five photographs, I can't believe it myself.

I am modestly dressed in loose-fitting clothes, with my hair covered by a scarf, and dark sunglasses obscuring my eyes. But some of my face is visible and this is so astonishing that men gather simply to stare, as if I were a creature from outer space. In the market, leaning over to look at a rug, I look over my shoulder and find 100 turbaned men leaning over with me. When I decide to buy the rug, and realise that I don't have enough local money, I go to the moneychangers.

71

I walk across the square and my troops walk with me. Someone who sees me from a distance says it looks as if I've started a small cult. When I reach the moneychangers, they haul me inside and bolt the door so I can take US bills out of my money belt without being watched. I lean against the door. After a calming cup of green tea with the moneychangers, who are playing chess on the floor and happy to chat, I take the brick of 'up-money' that my dollars have bought and I brave the square again. By now the old crowd has mostly dispersed, but a new one gathers in the time it takes me to walk back across to the market, and they gravely observe the purchase of the rug. After all that, I hope my sister likes it.

Perhaps I shouldn't go out on my own, and in the beginning I didn't. But I have been here for so long now that I can't always be with a male Afghan chaperon. First of all they're very expensive, and the downside to being freelance is that I simply can't afford one fulltime. But the other more practical point is it makes no difference. The men stare and follow no matter whom you are with and in which language he tells them to go away.

An English print journalist has the same translator for two months. He even picks up some of her expressions. 'I told them, "Don't stare at her, it's not a show, she's not a monkey,"' he recounts to her proudly. For all the difference it makes.

So although my male colleagues look after me far more than I have ever experienced in any other environment, I feel isolated. Whenever I meet another female reporter I'm thrilled. And I'm yearning to meet the local women, even more isolated under their burqas. 'They don't want to meet you,' the Northern Alliance officials tell me. But when I am out walking on my own, the women often stop and hold out their hands, as if to greet me, making their burqas balloon out around them. I sense that they want to make contact with me and feel they can because I am on my own – as they often are. It's hard to tell exactly, though, with someone you can't see.

Then the Northern Alliance nominates one woman who is willing to talk to us – Farahnaz Nazir, an Afghan health worker employed by international aid agency Médecins Sans Frontières (MSF). She received a university education during

Soviet times and speaks Russian and English, as well as four local languages.

She is the only woman in Khoja Bahauddin who chooses not to wear the burqa, though she does cover her hair with a scarf at all times.

'I was not brought up with it, I don't think it is a part of Islam,' she says.

Farahnaz has an attractive habit of adjusting her scarf each time it slips back, to modestly cover her hair while she speaks. She is a beautiful woman in her late thirties, and so elegant that it is difficult to believe that she has spent the day in this hot, dusty village and the refugee camp where she works.

Her life story is a typically Afghan one of relocation and flight, moving her family over and over again, often just ahead of Taliban troops. She spent five years in Pakistan, returning to Afghanistan in 1999 after the Taliban conquered most of the country. 'Yes, everyone is asking, why would you leave a peaceful life to come back into Afghanistan at such a time? But when I studied the impact of Taliban policies on women, I thought that this was the time to return, to protest against the violence against women and children, to help women have some voice, someone who could explain her plight to the outside world. Because no one was talking on behalf of women.'

Farahnaz's friends in the Afghan community in Pakistan tried to dissuade her – but she was determined. 'My only thought was to help, I didn't think about the personal cost.'

This is the second time that Farahnaz has returned to Afghanistan when others were fleeing. The first was in 1989, as the fighting was becoming more bitter and Russia was about to pull out of Afghanistan. Farahnaz and her husband were studying in the Ukraine, and had just graduated. Many of their Afghan classmates were worried about the political instability and did not return. 'They said "It will be more wars" and they stayed behind. But I was thinking, we are engineers, Afghanistan needs us.'

This time, Farahnaz persuaded her husband to return so that she could campaign for women's rights, by promising that they would stay out of Kabul and the south of the country where the Taliban were strongest.

Your husband sounds like a remarkable man, I tell her.

'You don't know how remarkable,' Farahnaz says.

He travelled ahead with her two children. She had to travel alone through Taliban-controlled areas to reach the north. 'Kabul was like a city of the dead. There were no people in the streets. It was terrible.'

Farahnaz found a driver who would take her even though she was a woman on her own. 'I asked him "Are you Talib?" and he said "No". And he said he would let me travel without a burqa, but he told me when I had to put it on and when I had to lie down on the back seat because it wasn't safe.'

She and her family settled in the northern town of Taloqan, and when it fell thirteen months ago, they went further north, eventually arriving in Khoja Bahauddin. She is an engineer by training, but now works in the area of female health. 'It's where the greatest challenges are – the statistics in our country are so bad, so depressing.' Afghan women have high rates of anaemia, seventeen women in every thousand die in childbirth, and those that survive giving birth have much shorter life spans than women in the West. One in four of their children will die before their fifth birthday.

Farahnaz says that problems of women's health emanate from their position in society. 'Our society has a very small mind for women. They think woman is like material. They can sell, they can buy, they can beat, they can hit them,' she says.

Six months ago when she arrived in Khoja Bahauddin, Farahnaz tried to establish a Women's Association, to teach local women English and hygiene. At the start five women came – the only women she knew in the region.

'After four months we have 150 women, because every woman knows the necessity of freedom for living.'

The group received no funding of any kind.

'I teach English in the centre without any money, and chalk and such things we buy.' She catches my pained expression. 'Yes, it's very basic, I know, for us it's very difficult, nobody cares for us, but we try to care for ourselves.'

Farahnaz counts as one of her group's successes a campaign to reopen the local girls' school. They launched their school campaign on 8 March 2001, International Women's Day, when they also put forward a charter of women's rights. They condemned the destruction of the statues of Buddha at Bamian, and ended: 'We are courageous women living in extreme poverty facing a hard winter. Some of us are without shelter, adequate clothing, food or medicine. However, we take this small opportunity to celebrate International Women's Day and ask for all humanitarian souls to support the innocent women of this world.'

Farahnaz's success has led to trouble. She has received death threats, which made her redefine the group's aims.

'Because of that we become careful, we don't want to push women to die, because of that we become slowly by slowly,' she says.

I ask her if she takes those threats seriously.

'Yes, I take those threats seriously because I have children and a husband, and for them I'm afraid always.'

Farahnaz applied to the local authorities in Takhar province for permission to conduct more formal classes, teaching illiterate local women to read and write, as well as holding some baby health classes. Regional commander Quazi Kobir refused. He said he did not approve because in his view it was not appropriate or necessary for women to undertake further studies instead of their duties at home.

'We have an English centre, health education and we want to make a new school, but it was not permitted. The local authorities do not allow me. I explain that this is health education, it is not other things, and that it's good for women to know health education and to look after their babies, but nobody listened to me and they did not allow it.'

The Women's Association was limited to infrequent meetings in which the women could at least discuss their lives and any problems they might be experiencing. 'We see if we can solve these problems. This helps them always,' says Farahnaz. 'I know some intelligent, educated women who lose hope. They can't see any future for Afghan women, but I try to work with them so that we can have faith in our good future, and make a good future. We may have to take some risks, but we can hope for a good future for Afghan women.'

'Society is like a bird,' she explains poetically. 'It has two wings. And a bird cannot fly if one wing is broken.'

Farahnaz applied to the Northern Alliance, asking them to step in and try to influence local commander Quazi Kobir. Instead, they shut down the Women's Association. At their final meeting, Farahnaz read this statement to Suhail, Ahmed Shah Massoud's second-in-command.

'Should women forget the ideals of independence and freedom? Should we leave the determination of women's basic rights to cruel people? Should we give up leading Afghan women to freedom? Shall we silence the voice of Afghan women seeking freedom? . . . We women know that whenever fanatics face such questions, they feel shame, and react with hatred. They try to turn the page without answering. But deep down they know that closing their eyes will not solve problems but amplify them. You must know that Afghan women will sacrifice themselves for freedom; eventually our demands for freedom will get you by the throat.'

Suhail just smiled in response and said, 'You have become steel – but I can't do anything for you now.'

Instead Farahnaz established classes under the umbrella of MSF, as part of the clinics she runs for women in the refugee camps that ring Khoja Bahauddin.

'We start from the Koran, and now they're reading very well. We also give health education, and in this group no one is sick and nobody has thin babies. The babies are all fat and healthy, and the mothers take care very well.'

That must make them happy?

Farahnaz laughs. 'Yes, they all pray for us.'

For two hours each morning, in a tent at the refugee camp, women learn to read Arabic from a copy of the Koran. They write the intricate Arab characters in a large, battered book that the teacher keeps, as there are not enough exercise books to go around. In the afternoons they learn health and hygiene, mainly using pictures drawn on a cotton cloth. The teacher, a local woman whom Farahnaz has trained, shows the women how to keep food clean and free of flies and how to diagnose childhood illnesses.

But these achievements don't influence the regional commander. Farahnaz is still not permitted to hold similar classes for women in the town even though it is plain there is desire for such help. Some women subvert the commander's edict

76

by going to the refugee camp to take part in the classes there.

I tell Farahnaz that to do this story properly, I need to meet and interview some women from the group, at the very least to see and hear them doing some activities. She looks dubious. I ask about a women's sewing centre that she mentioned – could I perhaps go there?

'Cameras will be very threatening. It could be dangerous,' she replies.

Perhaps just a radio story then? A mini-disc is so much more unobtrusive. Farahnaz will have to ask. She explains how dangerous it is for her to meet me.

'So that some mullah will not be asking questions I came here today and did not invite you to my home. They could make difficulty for me. "Why did you have journalists in your home, why did you do interview without your husband being present?" It's too dangerous for me to conduct interview in my home. Maybe you can feel now how difficult it is for us, for women talking to journalists and others.'

Farahnaz says that she will check with the other women and come back in twenty-four hours to let me know.

But Farahnaz does not come back again the next day. A Northern Alliance official tells me she has reconsidered and any further interviews with her or any other women would be too dangerous. I try to contact Farahnaz myself, which is difficult in a place with no telephones. You have to turn up in person, during daylight hours, and hope the person you want to meet is there. I leave messages for her at the MSF office.

In the meantime, I try for a lateral solution. I plan to try the local girls' school for some audio for my report. Unlike in Taliban-controlled areas of the country, here girls are allowed to study until the age of fourteen. That is Northern Alliance policy. There are three state-funded schools in Khoja Bahauddin, one only ten minutes' walk from the Foreign Ministry office. After receiving permission to visit the school from the Foreign Ministry and the head teacher, I arrive in the dusty schoolyard as the bell is ringing.

Facilities are simple. The schoolyard has six mud-brick classrooms built around it. Each classroom has a blackboard and chalk, and rush mats on the floor. Girls aged from five to fifteen sit on the mats, doing their lessons. There are few books, not enough to go around. The younger girls are boisterous while the older girls are shy and won't meet my eyes. All are wearing headscarves. But these girls are the lucky ones – they're receiving an education. They study the Koran and Islamic religion, history, mathematics and geography. Some of the older children learn English. It's estimated that no more than fifteen per cent of women in Afghanistan can read and write. Since the Taliban came to power and closed girls' schools in the vast majority of the country they control, that low level of literacy is falling further.

The girls learn their tables the old-fashioned way, chanting and singing them out loud. Layers of sound mingle in the schoolyard, the chanting of the tables from one classroom, the singing of the alphabet from another. I remember vaguely doing a similar call and response in my maths classes, but it was already out of fashion by the time my younger sisters went to school.

The girls at this school know they are fortunate, and they have aspirations. Fourteen-year-old Nachitsa says she wants to continue her education.

'I want to study literature and maths,' she says, pulling her white scarf more tightly around her face, but speaking confidently. 'I want the war to come to an end and then I want more rights for women to study.'

Many of the other girls are too shy to speak, hiding their faces in their scarves.

This is the last year Nachitsa can study at this village school. To further her education she will have to be sent away to another city. It is a rare rural family that would have the commitment to their daughter's education, or the money, to do this, especially during wartime. They would need funds to send her away, and extended family with whom she could live, who would support her while she studied. They would also have to turn down offers of marriage, which start pouring in once a girl turns fourteen, the age of adulthood here. For some families the 'bride price' is the only income they have, and they sell their daughters into marriage at ever-earlier ages, before they have matured physically. In the south, desperate families sell young girls to wealthy foreign men who are in Afghanistan to fight with the Taliban and al-Qaeda.

The teachers at this school are women, which is an inspiration to the pupils. Most of the girls, when asked about possible careers, say 'teacher' or 'doctor' – the only two jobs they see women do. An English reporter who visits the school says he hopes one of the girls will say she wants to be an astronaut. Does he think these girls, sitting in the dust, learning without books, know what a space station is?

The school's head teacher is male. He is an old man with a white beard and kind eyes, and the contentment that comes from years in a job you love. 'I have been a teacher for thirty-two years. I am the father of these children, I want them to study their lessons and go to university.'

He gathers the girls at the end of the school day.

'Hurry home, children, don't take too long to get there, don't be too noisy along the way. Be kind and helpful to your mothers when you return to them.'

They listen attentively.

Despite all the constraints, he is proud of his pupils. 'Oh, these girls are very clever!' he says, then sighs as he concedes most will not be able to continue their education. Kabul University has been closed since 1992, the start of the Mujaheddin's fratricidal infighting. 'This is part of the price we pay for war,' he says. 'America should bomb the camps of the terrorists and destroy them – taking care not to harm the civilians, of course. Then there will be good grounds for the children to go to university and prepare for their education.'

The other main problem is resources. 'There is not much here,' he says, waving his hand at the small school. Staff salaries are low. He earns less than US$50 a year. Life is hard.

As I prepare to leave, I ask one of the teachers who stays behind to chat if I could visit her home. She hangs her head. In this most hospitable part of the world, that would not be appropriate.

'They are embarrassed,' my translator Mahmoud tells me as we leave. 'Their homes are so poor.'

I like this translator. He does not charge hundreds of dollars like the others, cognisant of the fact his English is actually quite poor. He also 'understands' the process. He lets people talk into the tape and then translates without talking over them.

He tries to translate what is *said* – a fundamental part of the job, which many never master. Some turn to you after an impassioned three-minute answer, full of hand waving, and foot stamping, and say, 'He says "yes".' Or worse, they start translating before the person has finished their answer.

'But he hasn't finished, he's still speaking,' I remonstrate.

'I know what he's going to say.'

Mahmoud is clever and fun to be with. As we leave the school I see a donkey delivering water. I want to record the distinctive sounds of its hoofs tapping on the gravel, as the water laps in the canisters on its back.

'You want interview with donkey?' he asks, indicating he is prepared to translate.

When I realise he is developing a bit of a crush on me, I dust off my trusty 'Moscow fiancé' and press him into action. A jealous fiancé is a boon for a woman on her own. As we trudge back from the school, Mahmoud tells me he will walk all the way across Russia to attend my marriage party. He pronounces it 'marr-i-age', which somehow makes it more touching. I promise I'll let him know when it is.

My British friends from the *Mirror* newspaper have a wonderful translator. Wahab is an older man, a former engineer who speaks excellent English. His English is so good he understands us when we speak quickly to each other. Not even our American colleagues can always do that. Wahab has a high-pitched laugh, which explodes out of him often, especially when the boys ask him how to translate their rude jokes – usually about penis size – into Dari.

Wahab is sensitive and intelligent and I like him straight away. And since the boys talk about sex a lot – they are from the British tabloid press after all – Wahab feels he can ask them about Western sexual habits.

'In your culture, do boys, you know, do it with donkeys?'

'No, we tend to stick to our own species,' one of the hacks shoots back, trying to disguise his distaste.

Then Wahab reveals that *he* has done it with a donkey, and the boys lose all control, unable to disguise their reactions. 'Oh, Wahab! Not with a donkey . . .'

Tabloid journalists shocked: shock!

He realises he's gone too far, and says quickly, defensively, 'I *was* fifteen at the time.'

Now that Wahab has four wives, he no longer needs donkeys, of course.

When we're away from Wahab it's all we talk about. I'd never believed the donkey stories before, even though I can see a lot of sexual energy is being sublimated into other pursuits in this strange, separated society, from which women have been virtually removed.

I joke to one of the boys that he can't fool me, I saw him eyeing up that sweet donkey we passed earlier, the one carrying firewood.

Completely deadpan, he replies in his broad Manchester accent, 'What, you mean Edith?'

That line cheers me up in several dark times.

But I look at donkeys and the small boys who tend them differently from now on.

We tell Wahab the story of Princess Diana, whom he has never heard of, and her marriage to Prince Charles. He follows the sad fairy tale of the young girl married to an older man who didn't love her, with great interest. When we reach the part about Diana's infidelity, Wahab has one question about Charles.

'Did he kill her?'

No, we say.

'Why not?'

Wahab watches one of the *Mirror* journalists talking with me, and after taking it in with his keen, kindly eye, he comes to have a private word. 'Have you heard of *Mut'a*?' he asks.

Mut'a is a Sunni Muslim practice that allows a man to take a temporary wife when he is travelling. The marriage is legal, and any offspring of such a marriage are legal. I am touched that Wahab is so concerned for me, particularly in this place where there is no opportunity for privacy, as we all sleep six to a room in sleeping bags. I pursue his suggestion.

'Wahab, can a woman do this while she travels – take a temporary husband?'

Wahab laughs. 'No, of course not.'

81

'And would a woman who did this find it easy to make another marriage after her temporary husband returned home to his proper wife?'

He laughs again. 'No, of course not.'

'So, Wahab, why are you telling me this? It seems to me that this *Mut'a* is designed to suit only the men.'

Later, I hear about a very glamorous magazine journalist who is propositioned by a warlord she is interviewing. He is bewitched by her – her face, her hair, the opportunity to sit and talk to her – everything about her is alluring. He asks her to marry him.

She declines.

'But I have 1500 Kalashnikovs.'

'Yes, but I am in a long-term relationship, I have a fiancé at home.'

'And how many Kalashnikovs does he have?' thunders the warlord.

The male journalists discuss how strange the absence of women is for them.

English journalist John Sweeney says he misses the smell of a woman.

One of his colleagues retorts, 'Yes, but does any woman miss the smell of John Sweeney?'

This excision of women from society is no easier for local men to bear. There are only so many donkeys you can chase. One of the translators, Safi, explains the rules of courtship to us. He has to decide if a woman interests him by looking at the only parts of her he can see: her hands, her wrists, and her ankles. If they are attractive – and he has become a careful judge – he asks his mother and sisters to go and visit the girl on his behalf. This places so much power in the hands of the women in his family! Perhaps this is where women exercise authority in this society.

If they come back and tell him that the girl is attractive, he will begin a correspondence, writing to the girl. Love letters? Not right away – it depends on what kind of response he gets. Of course, the invisible girl can see him, so if she likes him maybe she will write a steamy letter back.

By the time a chaperoned meeting is set up inside the girl's house, he has to be pretty sure that he wants to get married, otherwise there could be dishonour to the family, which could have lethal consequences. Safi has so far not seen the faces of any of the girls he has courted. Kind of like meeting in an Internet chat room, I find myself joking lamely, to overcome my sadness for him. Safi looks at me blankly.

Some men marry never having seen the faces of their brides. In the markets I notice that blocks of a white substance that looks like lard are on sale everywhere. Local women use it as hand cream. Hands have to stand in for a woman's face and hair. These blocks of fat are face cream, make-up, shampoo and hair gel all rolled into one. These blocks of fat make women beautiful.

'Ow!' A BBC producer is leaving the Foreign Ministry compound when one of the guards at the gate pinches her bottom. She is cross. They wouldn't dare do it to their own women, so they shouldn't do it to her. She turns around, marches back into the Foreign Ministry office, and complains.

'This is unacceptable. You've invited women to work here, and if we are to be working here we have to be respected, and we have to feel safe. We especially have to feel safe walking in and out of this compound.'

The Northern Alliance officials agree with the feisty BBC producer. They implement the rough justice the region is famous for. The guard is taken and immediately thrashed. Then he is made to stand all night with his hands above his head, holding heavy stones. At this point the BBC intercedes to plead for mercy. In this story, everyone is true to their national stereotypes.

The Northern Alliance officials are incensed. 'Mercy? Certainly not. We must be allowed to deal with this matter in our own way.'

In the morning, they sack the guard.

I suppose he was lucky they didn't kill him.

I'm back to square one for my radio story. In a piece about women, I still have no women's voices. I have girls at school and a hasty interview with Farahnaz, but I need more material. I go back to the Northern Alliance to make one more request for their help. I know that if they wanted me to do this story, it would happen in a flash. I find these Northern Alliance men, whom I actually like, very frustrating. They are polite, pleasant and often funny and cheeky. They are hospitable and helpful. But as with most men here, there is a double standard. I know that while they are cocooning their women and closing them out of society, they are also not averse to a little non-Islamic stimulation. How do I know this? Because I know the guy who hooked up their satellite TV.

A man can't have any secrets from his valet – or his satellite engineer.

The Foreign Ministry here has a TV, but when I first arrived it wasn't connected to any satellite dish. They could pick up only patchy local coverage – turgid Tajik television with its endless shots of President Rakhmonov, and scratchy Russian television with its endless Brazilian soaps ('How Maria cries!'), with a Russian male dubbing all the voices. Occasionally they also caught some broadcasts from Pakistan, which they hated because they hate Pakistan. And that's about it.

The Northern Alliance officials couldn't watch the major cable news channels and nor could they monitor the output of all the journalists they had on the ground here, which was clearly not satisfactory. Then they twigged that the people who could connect their TVs to the satellite – and probably wouldn't even charge them – were right under their noses. They asked NBC if Julian, their satellite engineer, could help. Julian was happy to. He hopped onto their roof and linked them up, and then asked them which channels they wanted him to program. It seems the Islamic warriors desired some adult entertainment for the long, lonely nights with only a generator for warmth. Yep, porn. The Northern Alliance's porn channel of choice is – Ultra Blue TV, a small European outfit, which leaves little to the imagination, in distinct contrast to the ultra blue burqas the Mujaheddin bury their women under.

The Foreign Ministry were so pleased with Julian's work that they insisted he connect up their other office, the Defence Ministry. He went there, climbed onto the roof, and looked down when he'd finished to find a forest of guns pointing at him. No one had informed General Fahim's personal guards that the satellite was being fixed, and they thought Julian was just another Western assassin. Once this little misunderstanding was cleared up, a slightly shaken Julian hopped down and programed in some channels for the Defence Ministry, including of course Ultra Blue.

A room full of mullahs, watching as he did this, gasped and covered their faces. Julian realised he'd made a mistake, blocked the porn channel and beat a hasty retreat. As he was leaving, the Defence Ministry boys took him aside, and just when he thought he was in real trouble, they asked him for the code – for unblocking Ultra Blue.

That's the trouble with modern life. You can't even rely on your religious fundamentalists for consistency.

As is often the way with journalism, the best things happen by chance.

I unlock my piece on women accidentally while visiting the local office of ACTED, a French aid agency. ACTED has stayed in Afghanistan since September 11, unlike other major aid agencies and the United Nations, who evacuated their staff following the attacks in the US. The Director of ACTED here in Khoja Bahauddin, Sebastian Miller, says he pulled his staff out for a couple of days, to the town of Faizabad. 'We did that just to see if there would be riots up here in the north, and then it became apparent that it was all unchanged, so we came back.' ACTED has been here ever since – and will remain throughout the air strikes.

'Would you like to see our women's centre?' he asks. I almost fall off my chair.

He makes a call and Manesha walks into my life. Manesha is the director of the ACTED women's sewing centre – the only women's centre in the region, and the only place in town where women are allowed to work outside the home. An attractive, lively woman in her thirties with an infectious laugh, Manesha trained as an economist during Soviet times and speaks Russian, so she is thrilled to find that I understand Russian too, and bypassing the ACTED translator she gabbles away to me.

'Yes, of course you must come to see us. Come now.'

When I explain that I don't have a translator with me she insists that I don't need one. 'No, you don't have to wait for a translator since we have a common language.'

85

I wince. I'm not confident enough of my Russian to conduct interviews. I am at that stage in learning a language where I understand an enormous amount, but can barely speak. I can see though that Manesha will be more comfortable talking to me directly than through a male translator, and it will therefore be a different dynamic. I have to do it.

We set out and Manesha disappears under her burqa. I feel as if I'm accompanying a blue ghost. The centre is in a compound five minutes away, across some pitted ground stinking of human excrement, just off the main square. Once we enter, Manesha shakes off her covering and walks into a crowded, noisy room where thirty women are sitting on the floor around a low table, working on old Singer sewing machines. The clack-clack of the ancient machines is loud and comforting. The women are wearing headscarves, but their faces are visible and their hands move fast. Almost all are widows, their husbands killed by the Taliban during the past five years.

They are working under an ACTED-funded 'work for food' program, receiving a kilo of wheat for every garment sewn. There is a long-term benefit, too, of teaching the women skills they can use when peace returns. The wall is festooned with dresses and children's clothes, as if this were a showroom. 'We'll make you something,' says Manesha's deputy, Aruzu, as she feels my locally made cotton shirt. 'This is a man's shirt – and not very good,' she says sniffily. 'We'll sew you one for free. Better than this.'

I take out my mini-disc. Having had the sensitivities of women here drummed into me so often, I wonder whether they will be reluctant to talk. It turns out to be the opposite, a deluge of opinion. The women interrupt each other to speak, barely waiting till I get my microphone to them before launching into their stories. They speak in Dari, and Manesha translates for me into Russian.

'My husband was killed by the Taliban, they came and destroyed our homes and killed our men. Now I am left with eight children. I must support them all.'

'The Taliban killed my husband. They beat him with cables for no reason, and he died in front of me. One month later I had my last child, my tenth child. Now life is very difficult for me. We want to return to live and work in our own homes, we do not like it here.'

'I came here when the Taliban conquered Taloqan. My husband was already dead, killed fighting the Taliban. Now we live in tents and we have no food. It is a difficult life. Can you help me?'

'If the Americans come here, we will have peace and a better life, and we will have schools and our children will learn, and it will be better for them.'

Then they all start pointing at one woman, and my Russian runs out for a moment while they are trying to explain her plight. Manesha says the word in Russian, but I don't know it. Then the woman pulls up her skirt to show me that she has lost a leg. 'This was caused during a Taliban bombing.'

She has a prosthetic, but it is still a shock and I find myself gulping.

I ask them about the burqa. This is a Northern Alliance village, why do they wear it? Some say tradition, some say security – in a war zone, anonymity is a help. Some don't like it and, in fact, in the refugee camps most women don't wear them simply because it is not practical to do so. It is difficult to put one on every time you leave a tent. This is one of the complaints about life in the camps, that men can see the faces of other men's wives.

Manesha wants to have her say about the burqa, too. 'It is hot, it is claustrophobic, and it is inconvenient. It is also dangerous, because you can't see out of it almost at all. I don't like it.'

Manesha's fourteen-year-old daughter, Sima, has been beside her throughout the interview. She has shining eyes and Manesha hugs her close, telling me proudly that she is a very good student. This year Sima officially becomes an adult and must wear the full veil. She has already had several offers of marriage from local families, but she is not yet resigned to the loss of her childhood freedom. Manesha wants her daughter to wait. She hopes that she, too, can have a university education. But that all depends on what happens next. Women can only be educated again if the Taliban are defeated.

I ask them about the markets – do they mind not being able to choose their own purchases? I joke that you can never trust men to go shopping. They agree vehemently. 'Yes, that's right, you can't. Men always bring back the wrong things.' It seems this is a universal truth.

Perhaps that explains why in defiance of the ban on women in the markets, you will see some, late on a Saturday afternoon as the bazaar is winding down, at the stalls selling materials. Food is one thing, but you definitely can't trust men to buy your clothes.

Manesha invites me to her home. She wants me to meet her husband, Nuraddin, and the rest of her brood of seven children. Manesha and Nuraddin are refugees, but they are not living in any of the camps here as both these enterprising university graduates have found jobs. They live in two mud-brick rooms, up narrow stairs, carved into the exterior wall of a house they share with three other families. The cooking fire downstairs is communal. In their rooms there is no furniture at all. They sit around the walls on mats by day, sleeping on the same mats at night.

But Manesha has brought her photographs with her to this new bare existence as a refugee. The fading albums contain evidence of another life. During Soviet times, Manesha studied economics in Moldova, near Poland. Her class photograph, in the stern Russian style, has small photos of every face separately, students at the bottom, the Professor and teachers at the top. '1983, ECONOMICS FACULTY' it says in Cyrillic script. There are also more casual photos of Manesha with her friends. They are wearing tight jeans and T-shirts, their hair is out, there's not a headscarf in sight.

'That is Tataiana,' says Manesha pointing to a blonde girl. 'I loved her. She was my best friend. I have lost contact with her since, since . . .' Manesha sighs, her ebullience crushed for a moment. 'I miss her.'

It seems the untold story of Afghanistan is that the best time here was during the Soviet era – for women certainly, and perhaps for men, too. There was education, travel, and more opportunities. Manesha lived in Moldova, Farahnaz in the Ukraine, the pharmacist I met in the market had studied in Czechoslovakia. They had experienced other peoples and cultures. Today most people only leave Afghanistan for a refugee camp on the country's borders.

We are having tea, served with sweets, as we look through the photographs. Manesha's children sit around us, all well behaved, including the youngest who is eighteen months old. Manesha says she does not want more children, but it's not entirely possible to predict as there is no contraception available.

Manesha's deputy at the sewing centre, Aruzu, drops by with her daughter. We sit in a circle on the floor and Aruzu sings bittersweet songs of love lost and betrayed. The girls join in. Then Manesha sings a Russian love song, investing all her longing for her former life into this sad Russian ballad. I record the haunting moment. Aruzu's eight-year-old daughter recites a poem about her life.

> *There is a house, but it is not my house.*
> *There are people, but they are not my people.*
> *There is weather, but it is not my country's weather.*
> *There are things, but they do not belong to me.*
> *I am a refugee.*

Entertainment is simpler here – stories and song, nothing more, yet none of the children complain they are bored and have nothing to do.

I ask Manesha about her marriage. After sixteen years she is very happy. Her family was liberal enough to allow her to marry the man of her choice, an Afghan student studying with her in Moldova.

'He was so handsome – I fell in love with him the moment I met him,' she says. 'And do you know, I feel the same way about him now that I did the first time I saw him all those years ago.' Manesha smiles at me, her eyes alight. 'I'm the happiest woman in Afghanistan.'

Darkness is closing in, there's no electricity, and in this context that cheesy phrase stops me in my tracks – she's 'the happiest girl in the whole USA', only she's living in a makeshift house, without light or heat or running water or sanitation.

'Would he take a second wife?' I ask.

'No,' says Manesha emphatically. 'I wouldn't let him. His parents pressured him to, but he resisted, so they gave up. He couldn't do it, he feels too much for me. It's love.' She is smiling as she repeats this in Russian, *Eta lubov, lubov.*

She breaks into her girlish laugh and I have tears in my eyes.

Saint Paul was right when he said 'There is Faith, Hope and Love, and the greatest of these is Love.'

Manesha confirms that the simple truths about women's lives are constant the world over. A good marriage is a good marriage, wherever you are. If you are married to someone who doesn't value you – or worse, beats you black and blue, as is sanctioned in Afghanistan – you are miserable and powerless. If you find a man who loves you and is kind to you, you're happy and powerful. Even here.

When Manesha introduces me to her husband, Nuraddin, I like him immediately. His eyes crease easily into lovely laughter lines, and he is a handsome, strong, reassuring man. I can see why she is happy. She is lucky, too, that her parents were willing to let her follow her heart. That is still extremely rare here.

Nuraddin walks me back to EBU in the dark. The compound is five minutes away, through a maze of mud walls, and although it is not late, it is pitch black here by 6 p.m. and I could never find the way on my own. After I've filed to Berlin, I am chatting to EBU manager Joris when we hear music floating out over the mud-brick walls. It is a rare sound so we follow it, and it leads us to an open door. We look in to see wild leaping and dancing, lit by shining lights that appear at first to be TV cameras, but turn out to be paraffin lamps, held high and flat, like torches, by some of the revellers.

Fifty men surround two singers and three drummers. They play wide, shallow drums, animal skins stretched tight across a wooden hemisphere. There is a space in the centre of the group where two men dance, whirling and banging sticks in time to the music as they leap. They provide the third component of the sound. The beat is fast and the tune hypnotic. This dark, wild festivity turns out to be a wedding party, though only men are celebrating, of course.

We walk into the light and I record the sound on my minidisc. The excitement in the air is magnified by the feelings directed to the only woman present, and with her face visible – me. Other female journalists here agree that generally for Afghan men we are not really women, we are more like Martians. But on some elemental level, they know we are women, and tonight that knowledge is floating out towards me on the waves of wild music.

Drinking all this in, Joris turns and says with the force of a prediction, 'Tonight, you will be married, too.'

'Right, *payechali* – time to leave,' I say in Russian. I switch off my mini-disc, and Joris and I beat a hasty retreat.

Chapter 6

I finally track down Farahnaz Nazir at the Médecins Sans Frontières office. She is happy to see me, and smiles warmly.

'Yes, yes, I will do an interview with you,' she says.

She explains that Northern Alliance officials did ask her to stop talking to journalists, but so many reporters want to interview her that she can't put them all off.

'I told the Northern Alliance that I would be talking. Why shouldn't I?' She clasps my hand.

We agree that I should come to see her in the mother and baby clinic at the refugee camp the following day.

It's hot and oppressive as I go down the hill to visit Farahnaz at the camp. Another dust storm is on its way. The heavy air blows gusts of grit and dust, and the sky is turning that strange yellow colour I recognise from before. I hope it won't be as severe as the last one. The MSF clinic is in a large tent at the bottom of the hill. Its sides are billowing out in the wind, like a sailing boat in a stormy sea, only we're in the desert.

This morning underweight children are being treated. Hot, unhappy babies are being weighed and deposited squealing in a sling attached to a hook, as if they were sides of lamb. Mothers sit on the floor feeding their thin babies high-protein biscuits, diluted with clean water. MSF supplies both free of charge. Flies crawl all over the babies and the bowls of food. Their weak cries are drowned out by the sound of the tent flapping.

Farahnaz is shimmering. She looks fresh, neat and beautiful in the overpowering heat. I tell her so.

'No. This is nothing. It climbed to fifty degrees here this summer.'

Other mothers whose babies no longer need treatment come by the clinic just to say hello, and to show Farahnaz their happy, healthy children.

'You know I am not doing my job for my salary, I am doing it for these children. They need help and it's necessary to take care,' says Farahnaz. 'I am also like a mother, the people at the camp call me mother, younger than me and older, and a mother must take care of her children. I take care of everyone.' Many baby girls in this camp are named after Farahnaz.

The thinnest baby I've ever seen is being carried in the arms of a woman dressed in black, with black diamond-shaped stencils on her cheeks. She is a nomad, a *kuchi*. Farahnaz says she is prepared to help everyone, it doesn't matter that this woman is not a refugee, she should also have the opportunity to feed her baby properly and to learn how to look after him so that he won't die simply from diarrhoea. The child looks like a skeleton, his eyes sunken, his cheekbones wide and protruding. When his mother unwraps his emaciated body, I can't bear to look.

Instead, I find myself watching a small boy called Juma. Friday. Baby Friday. He is small and sweet, and reminds me of my nephew at the same age. He is creamy-skinned, with beautiful dark eyes and curling lashes. Though he is almost a year old, he is the size of a three-month-old baby. His legs are spindly, long, but squashed up like a grasshopper's. If he held them out straight, he would actually be taller than a three-month-old, but he is not strong enough to stand. Juma's father died before he was born, and his mother remarried. She has fled to a refugee camp in Iran, leaving Juma with family here. But he is a burden to them and they do not look after him properly. He breaks my heart.

'I stand like a beggar woman, begging them to love him,' says Farahnaz.

Juma's chart shows that without love, food is not enough. He weighed less than four kilograms when he was admitted, and he began to improve on the high-protein biscuit diet. But then his weight dipped dangerously again, until he was thinner than when he was first being treated.

'His family do not always feed him, even though we give them the biscuits,' says Farahnaz.

I watch the sixteen-year-old girl feeding Juma. She is a cousin of his absent mother's. It is apparent that despite all Farahnaz's begging, she does not love him. She handles Juma roughly and he is listless in her arms. His eyes light up when he sees Farahnaz and he smiles – but only at her.

'I want to change his name to Azim, it means Great Achievement,' says Farahnaz. 'Maybe it will mean a change in his fortunes. "Friday" is a stupid name.'

I sit there concocting wild plans to adopt Juma and take him back to Moscow where at least I will care for him. It can't be worse than life in this sweltering fly-infested refugee camp where disease is rife and his life expectancy is low.

Would I really be prepared to adopt him? I surprise myself with the strength of my feelings. Perhaps it's because I so miss my nephew. I would take Juma if I could, just to give him a better chance at life, but the practical barriers are enormous. I discuss it with Farahnaz, and I realise the bureaucracy would defeat me. The bribes I would have to pay to three sets of corrupt officials – here, in Tajikistan, and in Russia – would bankrupt me, and there would be no guarantee of success.

My heart aches when Juma's teenage cousin wraps his cotton diaper around him, pulls him roughly onto her hip, and disappears back into the camp.

I wonder if he will still be alive when I come back next time.

When I fall asleep, his little face is the last thing I see.

Ahmed is working at the front of his metal workshop in one of the tumbledown shacks in the market. He is short and dark and looks much older than his thirty-two years. He has a gruff manner and is not wearing a turban. Ahmed can make you a chair from an old ammunition case or fashion you a drum for water, a wood-burning stove, or pitchers and buckets and other kitchen utensils, all from tin. All the journalists troop off to Ahmed for household necessities. His business is booming and as a result he can afford to take a new wife – his fourth.

Bill from Canadian broadcaster CBC wants to interview him about this and his fifteen children. I enjoy working with Bill so I go along, too. Ahmed stops work to answer Bill's questions, and a crowd quickly gathers, laughing at his answers to such personal questions.

'Yes, I earn more than twenty dollars a week – quite enough to support a new wife. I am a wealthy man,' says Ahmed leaning on his lathe. 'No, my three wives don't fight, in fact my first wife helped me choose the second one. And if they do disagree, well, I can sort them out. I am the man of the house after all.' There is ill-concealed menace in the jovial answer.

'Yes, fifteen children is a lot, it's true, but I think I know all their names. I am raising an anti-Taliban army all by myself.' He laughs. 'I will try to remember the names of any new children, too.'

He tells us he hasn't selected a new wife yet, but has already built her a room, which is almost complete, so all he has to do now is find the right one.

'You might think about my colleague,' Bill suggests, pointing at me, to a big laugh from the crowd. 'She's quite sweet once you get to know her.'

Ahmed's reply gets a bigger laugh, but our translator, Dr Aini, is suddenly shy, and won't tell us what Ahmed said. Later, he tells Bill that Ahmed said if he could have one 'like her' he would be married already.

'You see, he's a charmer – that's how he does it,' Bill says.

Of course, charm has nothing to do with how Ahmed does it. He does it because the society allows him to, if he can afford it, and it doesn't matter what the women think or feel about it. Islam allows a man to take up to four wives for specific reasons, such as if the first wife is sick or cannot conceive. But over time that has come to mean a man takes four wives if he can support them, no matter how good the health of his previous wives. Old men give away teenage girls from their brood of children, and with the marriage price they garner they marry other teenage girls themselves. In this way limited capital is exchanged from one hand to another, to shift girls from one house to another. All to the benefit of the men, first and foremost. Any benefit that may flow to the girls is coincidental.

The other bleak truth is that we journalists are funding a wave of marriages here. All the men who work for us – drivers, translators, cooks – are earning so much that they can afford new young wives. And they are invariably young – usually no more than fifteen years old, even if the men are fifty.

At the sewing centre, I ask Manesha if she thinks the later wives are ever happy. 'I think their lives are not good, they are over. Because if the man is a good man he loves his first wife and the children of his first wife the most, and not the later wives and children. There are some good men who also love their second and third wives, but this is rare. And the women fight, they try to avoid each other, there is always war in the house.' She sighs. 'This is the difficulty of life here with us, power resides with the man. The women have no say.'

Seventy years after a reforming Afghan monarch aimed to impose monogamy on Afghan men, for most the perception of family remains the harem. Men take new wives even in the refugee camps.

At my second visit to the sewing centre, the woman who helps Manesha run it reveals her greatest sorrow. We are having lunch when Aruzu tells me about her marriage. Her husband is a highly respected local surgeon and he has recently taken a second wife. Aruzu says it is the hardest thing that has happened to her. Harder than being a refugee and leaving her home in Taloqan for Khoja Bahauddin, which she freely describes as 'horrible'. It tears out her heart.

'I am tired of this, and am always saying to him, "Why did you do this? Why is she here? I don't want this." He did not want it either, it was arranged by his family, but he agreed to it and now my life has been spoilt.' Time has not reconciled Aruzu to the experience.

'If I had the means, I would leave my husband and take my children away from here, and it would be better for me and for them never to see this life again.'

Her friends Farahnaz and Manesha remind her to hold herself together for the sake of her children.

'We take care of Aruzu, and sometimes we force her to be quiet, for her children's sake,' says Farahnaz. 'Because if a second mother comes into the home and the first mother goes away, no one will take care of these children. Aruzu's children are so cute, they are wonderful children and they need to be loved.'

Aruzu has two children, a girl and a boy, and it is true they are remarkable. I particularly like her ten-year-old son, Kombis, who has adopted me. He is a great kid, helpful, clever and cheeky. Whenever I am in the markets he appears as if by magic to help me communicate with the stallholders, though he speaks no English. It is uncanny how he does it, and they all respect me more because I have a 'man' to intercede for me, even though that man is ten years old. 'Ah, she's with the doctor's son,' they say to each other.

So when Aruzu invites me to her home for dinner, I'm happy to accept for many reasons. I like her children, she is reputed to be a fantastic cook – 'the best cook in Khoja Bahauddin' – and I want to see the second wife. Aruzu takes me there after work at the sewing centre. The mud-brick house is large and they don't share it with any other families. We sit on mattresses on the floor, on a new silk rug that has just been smuggled out of Mazar-i-Sharif, the centre of Afghanistan's rug production. It has to be smuggled out because Mazar is currently in Taliban hands. The softness of the rug and the depth and beauty of its colours make the whole evening worthwhile, for this sensual experience alone. Like so many things in Afghanistan it's for sale, but the price is steep: US$3000. It's probably worth more than ten times that, but no one I know here has enough cash to buy it. Some of us can barely afford to pay our translators.

'Doctor', as Aruzu calls her husband, is a warm man in his forties who speaks some English. He studied in Kabul and has been a surgeon for twelve years. His mother lives with them, and she is there when I visit, as are Kombis and his eight-year-old sister, all sitting on mattresses around the wall. And there, like a spider in the web, is a beautiful girl, no more than twenty years old, who looks like their teenage daughter. Aruzu is a careworn woman in her late thirties. She wears a plain, drab dress and her hair is hidden under a scarf. The beautiful girl's hair is uncovered and she is wearing a stunning silk outfit with a patterned silver motif, repeated at her wrists and ankles (you notice ankles here where everyone sits on the floor). I'm surprised to see that she is wearing earrings and bangles, and is also the first woman I have seen in northern Afghanistan wearing make-up, carefully applied.

As if she really were the teenage daughter, instead of the new wife, the beautiful girl doesn't help prepare the dinner. Aruzu does that alone, working in the dark because we came home as the sun was setting, and of course there is no electricity. She won't allow me to help. On a waxed tablecloth placed on the sumptuous carpet, Aruzu serves a series of dishes, including a salad with bite, made with tomato, coriander, onions and chilli, and the local specialty called *mantu*, a kind of ravioli with tomato sauce, topped with goat's milk yoghurt. Both are simply delicious. She tells me that out of consideration for me she has not prepared the regional staple of rice cooked in goat's fat. She has watched me eating lunch at the sewing centre and could tell I didn't like it. This is a big sacrifice, since every meal in Afghanistan is served with rice.

There are more meat dishes, including a boiled sheep's head, which I am forced to decline. The family is a little disappointed, as it is traditional for the guest to partake of it before the other diners can eat. But I explain that I don't eat much meat, and they are soon all enjoying this local delicacy. For dessert there are local grapes, green and very sweet. This is without doubt the best meal I have had in Afghanistan. Aruzu beams with pleasure when I tell her this. All the family immediately beg me to stay the night or to promise to return for another meal.

But there is such tension around that dinner table – well, the tablecloth on the floor – that I feel uncomfortable. You get good at recognising repressed sexual feelings here. It is apparent that the beautiful girl obviously wants to touch her husband, but feels she cannot, so she flirts instead with his ten-year-old son. She holds the boy and hugs and pummels him. She is like his older sister, and yet not. Aruzu is patently hurt. And although our Doctor should be happy, reaping the rewards of a new young wife, he looks uncomfortable. No, he's definitely not a happy man.

When Aruzu is clearing up, which I am also not permitted to help with, I ask the Doctor why he's taken a second wife. He looks embarrassed and lies to me. In front of his non-

English speaking second wife he says, 'But I haven't. I have only one wife.'

If either woman had understood him, he'd have been lynched. I think I might have helped.

The next day I ask Farahnaz, who is a friend of Aruzu's, why the Doctor denied his second wife. She says it was because he was ashamed. He sent Aruzu and the children away to his father's house for safety's sake during a period of bombing. While they were there he took up with this young girl from a poor family who helped clean the house. When Aruzu returned it was already too late to prevent the marriage.

'He is not a peasant or an uneducated man who does not know any better. He knows it hurts her and he still did it. Because of that, he is hiding from you, from the Western journalist.'

Farahnaz says she does not think that she would stay with her husband if he took a second wife.

'It is very hurtful for the woman. I couldn't live with a second woman, when I know she is not better than me.' But Farahnaz explains it is harder here, because if you leave your husband you will usually lose your children.

'All people think she is a bad woman, she is not living with her husband, everyone is disappointed in this woman. Because of that women are staying with a man who takes second, third and fourth wives. And also here we worry about our children, because if the mother goes, they will not be safe, there is no one to take care of them. Maybe in the West, the government will take care of the baby, but here there is no chance for that.'

Having said all this, Farahnaz admits she would leave her marriage if her husband took a second wife. Her children are older. Her seventeen-year-old son works with her at Médecins Sans Frontières, she is a hard worker, and they would get by somehow. Then her face softens because she loves her husband and she doesn't think he would take another wife.

'We have a partnership. We make decisions together, we discuss everything together, and there is consultation. No one gives orders. We have studied or worked together since we first met at university more than twenty years ago. When I was a student he was in the year above me, and he took a year off and looked after our newborn baby so that I could study, and then we were together always after that. We even graduated together on the same day. And since then, for eighteen years we have lived and worked together, often in the same office!'

Farahnaz says that her husband helps her with everything – with the Women's Association and with the housework, and of course here he has to do all the shopping because of local rules forbidding women to go to the bazaar.

'I am successful because of my husband.' Farahnaz repeats a sentiment that successful women all around the world have told me, reversing the old saying that behind every great man there's a woman. Behind every great woman there's a man who's prepared to share the child care. But Farahnaz's relationship is about to be tested, due to an interview that she does. With me.

I am by no means the only journalist to interview Farahnaz Nazir. At this time when it feels like half the world's press has converged on Khoja Bahauddin, waiting for the US air strikes to begin, an interview with Farahnaz about women's issues is standard. Sometimes she's quite forthright, openly criticising the local administration for its treatment of women, although this is personally dangerous for her.

'We too much miss Ahmed Shah Massoud, he cared about the women. These men, these leaders, I do not know if they care about the women.'

With each interview she grows bolder, holding a press conference petitioning American President George W. Bush and UN Secretary-General Kofi Annan to take a stand about the plight of women in Afghanistan, including in areas controlled by the Northern Alliance.

These stories go out all over the world, but most are unseen and unheard by the local administration. The story I do with Farahnaz is much more low key, a general look at the position of women in northern Afghanistan, starting with the girls' school and including an interview with Farahnaz about the fate of her women's group. But it is broadcast on Voice of America's Persian service – and so is heard locally. The story includes reference to how local military commander Quazi Kobir refused to permit Farahnaz to hold baby hygiene classes for women. Although this is true, when Quazi Kobir hears it he doesn't like it. And in Khoja Bahauddin, his word is law. If Quazi Kobir doesn't like something, he can exact whatever revenge he likes.

He threatens to have Farahnaz killed.

She is of course terrified, and I am devastated that she should be in this position due to a broadcast of mine. I know this is a risk which activists take in a society without a rule of law, and Farahnaz knows this, too, because we've discussed it. In an interview for CBS TV, Farahnaz said she knew her outspoken stand could have terrible implications for her personally, but sometimes you just had to do what was right. Nevertheless, I am appalled that her life has been threatened, a threat she takes seriously.

Her husband is devastated, and so is Farahnaz. When we meet she is nervous, rattled, and unsure of herself. I half fear that she will blame me, but she hugs me close to let me know she understands it is not my fault. When we sit down at CBS to discuss what steps the family should take next, she falls apart. She is very different from the woman who was everyone's 'mother' at the refugee camp.

She tells me that Quazi Kobir sent his son-in-law to her home to tell her that he is so angry that he could easily kill her, but that he might become less angry if she did a second interview for an international broadcaster he listened to – the BBC Persian service or the VOA Persian service – retracting everything she had said about him.

The CBS journalists and I advise her not to do any more interviews with anyone at the moment, but just to lie low. Sometimes even murderous rages can blow over when the local leader is distracted by his next PR disaster.

'He will not forget,' Farahnaz says.

CBS comes to her aid, devoting time and resources to help rescue Farahnaz and her family, organising to take them on the next CBS convoy back to Tajikistan. 'Done it before once in Iraq,' veteran CBS producer Larry Doyle says gruffly. 'You hope you won't have to, and you hope it'll work if you do have to. Sometimes you bite the bear and sometimes the bear bites you.'

The plan is that once Farahnaz reaches Dushanbe she should apply for refugee status to a Western government. But Farahnaz is uneasy about leaving.

'Is this the time to leave Afghanistan? This is when Afghanistan needs me the most,' she says, sitting in the cramped CBS office in the house they share with rival network ABC. News reports are being compiled all around us.

'And if we go to Tajikistan, how long would we be stuck there?' continues Farahnaz. 'There is a big Afghan community there, you know. He could have me killed there, too. I don't think I would feel safe, and my husband does not want to go.'

It seems to me that while Quazi Kobir's reach might extend to Tajikistan, as Farahnaz fears, there is no doubt he has power here. I hold her hand and tell her, 'If you are frightened, you should go.'

Simple bureaucratic tasks become obstacles though. Farahnaz is surprised when we tell her each member of her family will need travel documents. 'But we only have one passport. It belongs to my husband.'

We explain that in the West, each of them will require a passport, and they should acquire them before they leave Afghanistan. This news seems to overwhelm her. 'Does Quazi Kobir issue passports?' she asks.

I don't know, but say I don't think so – surely that would be a function of the Foreign Ministry? I tell her that regardless of who issues passports she will need a photograph first.

'We have some in an album at home,' she says.

I explain to her that she will need proper passport photos, not family snaps cut out of an album. Having watched another man obtain a passport, I know there's a photographer in the market, and with the right photo even illegal documents can be paid for and obtained.

Farahnaz looks dismayed.

'But I'm a woman, I can't go to the market.'

She pauses, on the verge of tears and then says bitterly, with a flash of her former self, 'This is a stupid country.'

Farahnaz seems like a woman in shock, veering between fear and the desire to have things 'as they were before'. After she leaves, I discuss the situation with the CBS crew. They will continue with their massive effort to help her, including having their Dushanbe producer try to obtain passports for the family there – a complicated process since there is no postal service.

The forms have to be brought in by a person coming into Afghanistan overland from Dushanbe, filled in by Farahnaz here and then returned – with photos and cash – by another person travelling out to Dushanbe. We have begun this process, but Farahnaz has to be committed to following it through.

I hope that we can save Farahnaz and her family – I hope she will let us. I know that we will give it our best shot. But nothing is predictable in this fierce land, and it adds to my burden of guilt and worry.

Chapter 7

The next day we go to the front line to monitor the preparations for war. The drive to the front line takes almost two hours, even though it is little more than ten kilometres distance. A gravel path leading from Khoja Bahauddin out into the desert is soon pitted with craters, gouged into the earth by other vehicles. It's difficult driving if you're at the wheel, and little better if you're the passenger being bounced around. At some spots there are men dressed in rags, trying to fill holes and craters in the roads with gravel. A job that a bulldozer would do in a few hours takes these men – who have nothing more than shovels and hoes – weeks. I begin to wonder if we'll still be here when they finish this stretch.

A beggar woman is always waiting at the same spot in the road, running up and almost throwing herself in front of the cars. Most drivers stop to give her money, or to be more accurate, slow down to fling money at her. I wonder why she is always there, and if it is lucrative, why no one else muscles in on this spot. Her blue burqa is torn and filthy, and when she lifts it back to receive money from drivers at their windows, she has a vacant, damaged gaze. I fantasise that the drivers support her because they fear that otherwise she will put a curse on them. Maybe they just want to see a woman's face.

As we draw nearer to the front line, there are checkpoints manned by sixteen-year-olds whose Kalashnikovs are almost as big as they are. I am edgy with fear. In volatile situations, checkpoints are dangerous in themselves – in the South African townships, in the Middle East or here, there are no guarantees. Negotiating checkpoints is just that – a negotiation. This is the first time we are going to the front line here, and I am nervous. After talking to our translator, and looking at a permission that they plainly cannot read, the boys smile, drop their rope and let us through.

We drive up to Ai Khanoum hill. Its summit is honeycombed with trenches and bunkers. Russian T-55 tanks are covered with straw matting, their cannons pointing towards the mountains opposite where the Taliban are equally burrowed in.

There is not much action. Standing on top of the escarpment, which it seems is safe to do on this sleepy front line, you see an alluvial plain crisscrossed with streams. Between us and the enemy lie farms and villages, and the remains of the ancient Greek city of Ai Khanoum, which flourished here from 400 BC. British journalist Tim Judah tells me that Ai Khanoum was a fabulous, wealthy walled city, with a palace, temple, theatre, gymnasium and mansions. Archaeologists suggest it was sacked and burned at the end of the second century BC. 'It's once again in the middle of a war,' he explains.

The remains of Ai Khanoum were discovered in the 1960s and many of its treasures were displayed in the Kabul Museum. But the museum was vandalised, and its collections stolen and scattered. You can even buy Greek treasures from Ai Khanoum in the bazaar in Khoja Bahauddin. Authorities removed Ionic columns from Ai Khanoum, one step ahead of the looters, and put them into a restaurant in the town square to save them for the local area. We are told that the plain beneath us was bulldozed to facilitate looting, dredging up the buried treasures for locals to scavenge and sell.

A local aid worker says bitterly, 'During this two decades of war we have destroyed everything, we have even destroyed our own culture.'

When the front line is quiet like this, the soldiers 'turn it on' for the journalists, and we film them. Gotta get your 'bang

bang' for the bulletin. On this visit to Ai Khanoum hill a crew from Russian state television is also here. They ask the soldiers to fire their weapons so that they can film them. The soldiers oblige and the crew ask them to stop so that they can reposition the camera and film them from a second angle. I've never seen anything like it – a TV crew directing action while there is live fire! I can only think this must be how they do all their reporting with the Russian forces in Chechnya.

The front line is strung along a series of hilltops, and the commander explains to us how a battle would unfold. But it appears that nothing much is happening today – well, nothing that hasn't been orchestrated by other journalists – so we move on.

There are three front lines facing the enemy, one behind the other. The soldiers will only take the journalists they like or trust up to the first front line, closest to the Taliban, which they say is the most dangerous. They decide they like us. We drive through villages on the plain. Irrigated by the Kokcha River, this is the greenest area I have seen. There are actually fields and grasses, a break in the seemingly endless desert. A boy leading his emaciated cattle through the trees plays a tune on a handmade reed flute. The music is sweet and haunting.

Crops grow here, including thirsty crops such as wheat, rice and cotton, but many of the villagers have not been able to harvest any grain because of Taliban sniper fire. One village has a mill where water turns a huge smooth stone to grind wheat into flour. Because of the drought and the fighting, however, the mill has sat idle for years.

We drive on but the road ends at the Kokcha River and there is no bridge. The Northern Alliance says that our jeeps risk getting stuck in the river. If we don't have access to a Russian military truck, we will have to cross on horseback. Afghan boys with horses materialise, and so does a flourishing trade in front-line rides. Rides cost US$20 per person, but for half that amount you can cross the river by 'ferry', a raft made of two inflated tractor-tyre tubes, attached to a wooden frame. One correspondent says he's made the crossing on the carcass of a cow – but I don't believe this engaging traveller's tale.

In fact, very few brave the river on the makeshift rafts. Even now, reduced by the drought, the Kokcha is fast flowing and in parts as wide as a football field. Every year, dozens of people drown crossing here, especially those who are too poor to afford any type of transport. They try to cross on foot, and die because they can't swim.

We climb onto the horses, which have no stirrups or saddles, only a blanket on their backs. Afghan boys sit in front of us as we ford the river. A rush of adrenaline hits me, the kind that only danger can provide. *The current here is strong, will the horse make it across? Are those Taliban guns pointing at us?* The front line is so sleepy that I half suspect the soldiers are putting all of this on as adventure tourism for bored journalists. This first taste of fear is turning into something not dissimilar to fun.

The opposite bank is crowded with people waiting to cross back. The river, a green belt in the endless desert, teems with life. We ride up through an Afghan village to the front line at Puze Polihomri. Here, the Northern Alliance has cut deep, narrow trenches into the side of the mountain, opposite the Taliban positions at Qala Qata. At the top of the hill, just above the Northern Alliance forward positions, there is a cemetery.

The commander at Puze Polihomri is Major General Yusuf Muhammad, a fifty-year-old career soldier whose life encapsulates the contradictions and tragedies of Afghanistan. He was trained in Russia, rising through the ranks in the Communist army of Afghanistan, which fought against the Mujaheddin. However, since the defeat of the Soviets in 1989, he swapped sides to fight with the Mujaheddin in their factional wars. Now he is fighting with them against another sect of Islamic warriors, the Taliban.

The Uzbek general has no illusions about his chances of victory. He is one of the best-trained soldiers remaining in Afghanistan, and for him the war has been an endless series of retreats. In 1996 he fled from Kabul to Mazar-i-Sharif, when the Taliban took the capital. Then in 1998, when Mazar-i-Sharif also fell to the Taliban, he retreated to Taloqan. Last year Taloqan, too, fell.

Now, Muhammad is literally cornered in north-eastern Afghanistan. With his back to the Tajik border, he has the chance for one last offensive.

If he fails, there is nowhere in Afghanistan left to run to.

We are in the trench when it takes a few rounds of Taliban artillery fire. Throwing myself to the ground is instinctive. It's impossible to take any other action when you hear that sound. You have to spend weeks under fire to unlearn that innate response. The soldiers are more sanguine. They dodge and fire back. The front lines here are very close, no more than a few hundred metres apart. The two sides can hear and understand each other's cries of '*Dushman!*' – Enemy! After the artillery rounds, it is quiet again.

Two turbaned soldiers crouch in the trench, listening to walkie-talkies, monitoring Taliban radio traffic. This creates a strange intimacy with the enemy. I imagine two similar-looking men in the Taliban trenches across from us are doing the same thing. Civil war, a war of brothers, perverts the natural order. That's why the Northern Alliance soldiers focus on the 'foreign Taliban'. Hating them comes so much more naturally.

'I will kill the foreign Taliban, the Pakistanis and Arabs, but not the Afghan ones because they are my brothers,' says one soldier defiantly.

'Listen! They are talking in Arabic,' the soldiers with the walkie-talkies shout excitedly, providing further 'proof' the Taliban are mostly foreigners and not Afghans.

A shell lands not far from the trench. Some soldiers prepare tea, and grumble; but others are more worried – they fix their make-up.

Many Afghan men believe that mascara protects them from the evil eye and so, while the shells fly, soldiers apply mascara. Then they pass a tiny mirror from one grimy hand to another, to check they've done it properly.

Every image here is confusing. Women are masked, and men sit in trenches wearing make-up. I try to see what brand they are using, but so many hands have worn the logo away. I think it may have been Max Factor.

I can see the ad campaign now. *Max Factor – no Mujahed would be seen dead in anything else.*

The soldiers live behind the trenches in abandoned mud-brick villages. They live like the men of Alexander the Great who conquered the region around 2300 years ago; or the men of

Genghis Khan who sacked it more than 1500 years later. Life is basic. Here, too, there is no water or sanitation or electricity. The only modern objects in Afghanistan are weapons. This is part of the paradox of this place – people have made the leap into the twent-first century, but only for arms. Stinger missiles are symbols of Afghan modernism, yet they have to be delivered by mule.

Most of the soldiers in the camp are refugees from the Taliban, and when we visit their barracks they are making long rakes. The first troops to advance will be armed with these unlikely weapons. They will use them to clear any land mines lying in their path – not only fresh land mines laid by the Taliban, but those laid more than a decade ago by both sides during the Soviet wars.

Regional commander General Mehibullah concedes land mines pose a danger to his men – and to the civilians who live so close to the front lines here. But he defends the Northern Alliance practice of laying additional mines, saying they are required to protect his front lines. 'They are a necessary weapon in the war with the Taliban. But if our forces leave the area we will clear the mines, neutralising them by blowing them up,' he says.

He knows there are an estimated ten million land mines in Afghanistan, and in most of the country there has been neither the funding nor the opportunity to clear mines dating from the preceding two decades of conflict. 'We know where the mines are – we have the maps. But because of the intervening wars we have not been able to clear them.'

Many of the male correspondents go to the front line every day. They dress like soldiers and swagger instead of walking, carrying their cameras like weapons. They even speak in horrible clichés. 'I'm here for the war, baby,' a Greek reporter says to me, 'what are you here for?'

Since very little changes as we wait for American air strikes, I go to the front line once or twice a week, watching the slow preparations for war. Like the soldiers, my fear has morphed into boredom. At this stage we are only assessing the Northern Alliance's military readiness as there is no real fighting. So, instead of doing this every day, I decide to spend time with women, and at the refugee camps.

A disgruntled reporter from Moscow is losing patience, however. She says that nothing is real – not the front line and not the war. 'This is a Potemkin war,' she says. 'Next they'll be showing us cardboard cut-outs of soldiers on the hills.'

Everybody deals with the waiting differently.

This conflict is largely tribal, not religious. The Northern Alliance and the Taliban are both Muslims and both from the same sect: Sunnis. The Taliban soldiers also wear mascara in their trenches. But the Taliban are mainly Pashtuns from the south of Afghanistan, and the Northern Alliance is a coalition of Tajiks and Uzbeks from the north.

Very roughly the divide goes like this: the Pashtuns are Afghanistan's largest tribe, with a population of about six million, living mostly in the south, descended from the Persians who conquered the region more than 300 years ago. The Tajiks are the second largest tribe, with about four million people living in the north. The Hazaras live in the centre of the country. They are Shia Muslims – a different sect to the rest of the country. These four million people are the most Asiatic-looking Afghans, reputedly the descendants of Genghis Khan, whose Mongol hordes swept through Afghanistan 800 years ago. The mountains isolated the Hazaras and kept the strain pure – they still look like their Mongol ancestors. Two million Uzbeks live in the north-west of the country. The rest are a collection of smaller tribes, with even more exotic names. Imagh. Balouch. Turkmen. Qezelbash.

One of the reasons for Afghanistan's perpetual tribalism is its geography. Mountains cover three-quarters of the country. Each tribe is trapped in a valley by its geographical walls.

'This is the first post-modern conflict, because we are definitely at war but we don't know who the enemy is,' says English journalist Chris Stephen. Everybody likes this quip. One of his friends even inserts it into a story. The forces of world terrorism are hard to identify and pin down. Even solely in the context of Afghanistan, is the international coalition fighting Osama bin Laden or the Taliban?

At this time, the Taliban make that question easier to

answer by refusing to give up Osama bin Laden to be tried by Washington or the United Nations for his part in the September 11 attacks. In late September the 600 clerics of the Grand Islamic Council convene in Kabul to debate the issue – only the second time the council has gathered since the Taliban came to power in 1996.

Religious leaders from distant provinces leave their mosques and trek along mountain paths to the capital. Others cross from the refugee camps in Pakistan, home to around two million Afghans. Hundreds of poor, ill-educated clerics gather in Kabul to decide whether their country should go to war with the world's sole superpower.

In a world first, we are able to watch their deliberations. The Taliban usually forbid filming under their strict interpretation of Islam, but they allow cameras in to record part of this historic meeting. They reveal that at least some of the Taliban leadership understands the dire position its regime is in. But they fail to sway the conservatives. The Taliban refuse to give up Osama bin Laden, repeating that he is a guest in their country, though they compromise by asking him to leave voluntarily and expressing grief over the September 11 attacks. The Council also hedges its bets, declaring a Holy War against the United States if it attacks Afghanistan.

When this concession fails to mollify Washington, or to dampen down talk of war, the Taliban leadership attempts to avert US air strikes by announcing Osama bin Laden has gone into hiding and cannot be found. In a sign of their increasing desperation, they then claim Osama bin Laden is no longer in Afghanistan. As they celebrate the fifth anniversary of their rule on 25 September, the Taliban leaders are twisting and turning like fish on a line.

The Northern Alliance is quick to deny Osama bin Laden has left Afghanistan. Its Foreign Minister, Dr Abdullah, tells us he has received intelligence that Osama bin Laden remains in the south, in the Taliban-controlled section of the country. 'Osama bin Laden is in hiding in the Uruzgan province in the centre of Afghanistan, and his men have also been sighted in the city of Jalalabad, near the border with Pakistan. This indicates that bin Laden is likely to be constantly on the move,' says Dr Abdullah.

But 'Bin Laden is not in Afghanistan' stories run and run, long after the Taliban have fled. Pakistani President General Pervez Musharraf becomes the chief peddler of these speculations and gives us contradictory opinions on a weekly basis: Osama bin Laden is no longer in Afghanistan, he long ago departed; Osama bin Laden is in Afghanistan, but he has died. First he was killed, later his death is from kidney failure. Only his corpse is there. And if all that is wrong, Osama bin Laden is in Yemen or in Saudi Arabia, but nowhere near Pakistan.

American Secretary of Defense Donald Rumsfeld is more honest when he says, 'We do not know where he is.' But a journalist colleague perhaps sums it up best during an interview with a small Cincinnati radio station. They ask him, live on air, 'So, have you run into that bin Laden?' A true professional, he responds, 'No, he's a pretty elusive kind of guy . . .'

We are off to the front line again. I haven't been there for a week and I want to see if there are any developments. I go with two English journalists in a white Toyota Hilux. This is the first time I have been in a car that is not a Russian military jeep or pick-up. The boys agree the Toyota is more comfortable but not as effective in these dusty conditions. The Russian jeep's great strength is that it is so basic it can function anywhere and, perhaps more importantly, can be repaired anywhere. The driver says his Toyota was captured from a Taliban commander in an important battle a year ago. 'Now you are in Taliban car,' he chortles.

Osama bin Laden bought 5000 white Toyotas like this one for Taliban commanders. This was not simply generosity; he was functioning as de facto Defence Minister for the Taliban, financing the defence requirements of the nearly bankrupt 'failed state'.

So it is not just hospitality that precludes the Taliban from asking Osama bin Laden to leave Afghanistan. They have thrown in their lot with him, and they stand or fall with him. Bin Laden, one of fifty-seven children of a billionaire construction magnate, took refuge in Afghanistan in 1996, after Saudi Arabia froze his assets and forced him to leave the country.

Opposed to Saudi Arabia's co-operation with the United States, bin Laden strongly resisted the presence of US troops on Saudi soil during the Gulf War. More than 500,000 American troops were stationed there during the war, and some 20,000 soldiers remained afterwards. Bin Laden declared it was the duty of all Muslims to drive the US out of the Gulf States, and Saudi Arabia responded by stripping him of his citizenship and expelling him.

Bin Laden went first to Sudan and then to Afghanistan, where he had been off and on for fifteen years. He first arrived in Afghanistan to join the *jihad*, the Holy War against the Russians in 1980. An austere religious fanatic and business tycoon, bin Laden specialised in recruiting, financing and training the estimated 35,000 non-Afghan fighters who joined the Mujaheddin.

When he returned in 1996, bin Laden refurbished the camps he had helped build a decade earlier, during the Afghan war. He offered the facilities and access to thousands of his foreign fighters to the Taliban, who took power that September. Bin Laden's private army of Islamic warriors, which he trained and funded, became a key prop of the Taliban regime.

The Taliban owe bin Laden too much to push him out now. But driving along the dusty, bumpy track back to the front line, I wonder whether a master tactician – and traitor – like Joseph Stalin would have let such loyalty hamper him? If it came to a choice between saving an ally and saving himself, Stalin would always save himself. As an Australian friend observes later: 'On 10 September the Taliban were in control of Afghanistan. They've played a shocking hand.'

Driving in our Taliban Toyota, we pass the beggar woman. Our driver slows down to give her money before we reach the refugee camp on the flat by the river. A new military training camp has sprung up here so we stop and investigate. There are two lines of men training in the sand. A sergeant calls out orders to his men, sing-song commands that end with a rolling sound that he spits out from the back of his throat, like a Zulu war cry. His raggedy army marches out of step. Their uniforms are ill fitting and mismatched. Their weaponry is old.

We interview their commander, General Taj Mohammed. He relays the same message we consistently hear from Northern Alliance generals at different front-line camps: 'We are preparing for an offensive, but we need air support, and more weapons and equipment. I am awaiting instructions from the Defence Ministry, and my understanding is that the offensive will begin soon.'

We become spotters for Russian military equipment, telling each other when we see trucks carrying ammunition on the roads. Some Russian weaponry is being delivered over the mountains on horses and donkeys. This must be how Alexander the Great supplied his conquests here, too.

A Russian helicopter, a new part of the Northern Alliance air fleet, starts making low flights over Khoja Bahauddin.

'You see, its weapons bracket is empty – the pilot is obviously being trained,' says Andrei, a Russian journalist who has reported extensively from Chechnya, as we watch the helicopter swoop over us again and again. Thank God for the Russian contingent. Most of the arms used by both sides here are Russian, or in fact Soviet, and under the patient coaching of my Russian colleagues, I am learning to distinguish one piece of weaponry from another.

Andrei, a former dissident who spent two years in a Soviet labour camp, is the cleverest and most modest of the Russian journalists. I enjoy learning about arms – and Russian writers – from him. English is his third language, but he has a remarkable turn of phrase and great breadth of knowledge. He tells me about the descendants of Alexander the Great living here in the Pamir Mountains, the lick of Afghanistan that stretches out into China. 'They have profiles that could come from ancient Greek coins, they are blond, and they live here now, in Afghanistan. Instead of this silly war, let us go to the Pamirs and do a story there. Now that *would* be interesting.'

Chapter 8

Journalists 'adopt' different generals, forging relationships so they can learn about the progress of preparations for war and so that the generals will let them accompany their troops once the fighting starts. My favourite is General Attiqilah Bariolai, the Northern Alliance's Deputy Defence Minister. He is one of the new breed of Afghan military leaders. Young, charming and clever, the softly spoken general has done some training in the West. He is a snappy dresser, with mod suits in both local and Western styles. I have seen him wearing corduroy, but never a turban. When he invites journalists to dinner, there is a table, unusual enough here, set with crystal bowls.

General Bariolai reiterates the complaint we have heard in Dushanbe: the Northern Alliance wants America's respect as much as its weaponry. 'We want to be treated as equals. If Americans want to deal with us, they have to speak with us as a government with another government.'

He tells reporters the Northern Alliance, which has been fighting the Taliban for almost seven years, is the only force capable of defeating the Taliban on the ground. 'The bombing alone will never win this war. You have to follow up with ground forces and we are the ground force.'

Some journalists even go to live as guests of another general, Mamur Hassan. His compound is fifteen kilometres from Khoja Bahauddin, at Dashti Qala. It is a short distance, but significant here, where there are no proper roads. Depending on the weather, it can take more than two hours to reach Dashti Qala.

The Foreign Ministry is not pleased because it has no control over journalists living there. General Hassan collects an unusual group around him. There is the unforgettable Volker Handloik, a tall German with blond curly hair reaching past his shoulders, which he sometimes puts up in a bun. He wears blue glasses and a long quilted coat, a local *chapan,* but a multicoloured version no one else seems to have found. I never see anything like it in the market. He rides the General's horses, with his long blond hair flying behind him. Combat cameraman Andy Driver also lives here. He is a cockney, ex-SAS, and like so many of the real tough guys, a darling. Andy obtains the first footage of American Special Forces in the region, at a time when the Northern Alliance is denying they are present.

Northern Alliance officials order Andy Driver to move out of General Hassan's compound because his visa is not in order, but Andy hunkers down and General Hassan lets him stay on, prepared to defy the Alliance officials because he likes him. Andy is an Afghan man's kind of man. He's a good shot and, most importantly, a good rider. He and General Hassan sit poring over maps and discussing strategy till the early hours of the morning.

Mamur Hassan's compound is green and fertile and pleasantly relaxed, especially after the Foreign Ministry office. It's built around a garden and, while it has necessities like a radio room and an anti-aircraft battery, there are also orchards that geese wander through, and a large plane tree under which Mamur Hassan sits for interviews. With articles in international newspapers, and a long profile in the *New Yorker*, Hassan is becoming a celebrity warlord. He seems to me to be enjoying it.

General Hassan is charming, and we take tea. He has a round Uzbek face and wears an embroidered cap, which sets off his white whiskers and warm smile. I can't help thinking in other circumstances he would make a natural Santa Claus. But every time I interview him, he gives me a different assessment – of the war aims, of the timetable, of the number of his troops, of their readiness. Often he flatly contradicts what he said last time, only days before. It is hard to rely on his dates, figures or predictions. A three-year-old child who I presume is his grandson climbs up onto his lap, and Hassan seems more interested in playing with him than speaking to us. Afterwards I learn little Babur Shah is his son. He looks up from the boy and says he can call on more than 5000 soldiers. One thousand men live here with him in Dashti Qala. 'They are ready to fight for me whenever I order them to.'

It is very difficult to verify these numbers. I have not seen 1000 men here – though there could be 5000 men on call in the region for all I know. He says that the Northern Alliance feeds 600 of his soldiers, but that he makes up the shortfall out of his own pocket, providing everything else they need, such as clothing and medicine.

The Taliban say they have 20,000 to 30,000 men in this region. Northern Alliance intelligence supports this, but it is another unverifiable figure. However, it appears certain the Taliban forces do far outnumber those of the Northern Alliance. In the circumstances, how sure is Mamur Hassan of victory?

'We want to win more strongly. Victory is about will and our spirit is indomitable,' he says.

On another day, Hassan says that if the American air strikes are successful and Russia supplies the weapons it has promised, then it will be possible to defeat the Taliban – but it will take two months. This contradicts what he tells Jon Lee Anderson from the *New Yorker*. He complains to him that General Fahim has told him to collect all his soldiers and be at the ready, but he doesn't have sufficient resources. He only has food for 600 men and he has 1000 to feed. He argues that the conditions are not right for a sustained attack – in fact, in these conditions it's impossible.

In the first week of October we are frequently asking each other, will this offensive ever begin? What can we reliably report about it?

Thirty men from Dashti Qala set out to fight the Russians in 1979. Mamur Hassan says he is one of only two still alive.

They started out fighting locally, on their own, but once the US, Pakistan, and Saudi Arabia began covertly funding various Afghan factions, Hassan threw in his lot with the powerful Pashtun leader Gulbuddin Hekmatyar.

Hekmatyar is a notorious figure, reviled for his ferocious cruelty, particularly here among the Tajiks. In the 1970s, while at university, he and his supporters are alleged to have thrown acid in the faces of women who refused to wear the veil, and to have shot at the legs of women who wore no stockings. Though Hekmatyar later denied this, it has become part of Afghan political folklore.

Hekmatyar was also virulently anti-American, but in the 1980s when the US was supporting seven main factions in the Afghan war against the Soviets, Hekmatyar's received the largest amount of weapons and training. It was funnelled via Pakistan, and many said his greatest talent was that he knew how to schmooze the Pakistanis, positioning himself as their major ally inside Afghanistan.

Hekmatyar was Ahmed Shah Massoud's rival, and his Northern Alliance critics say that he killed more Mujaheddin than Russians, undermining the unity of the anti-Soviet forces. They argue that Hekmatyar spent the decade of the Soviet war safely in Pakistan stockpiling CIA-supplied weapons and money, while Massoud was fighting in the mountains with weapons stolen from dead Russian soldiers. Hekmatyar once boasted that he could keep fighting for twenty-five years without ever needing supplies.

In the 1990s Hekmatyar used his American-funded weaponry to lay waste to Kabul in one of the bloodiest sieges in modern warfare. Unwilling to share power with the other Mujaheddin factions, Hekmatyar pounded Kabul with hundreds of heavy rockets and mortars on a daily basis. He kept this up for three years, killing some 20,000 civilians, and wounding many more.

Unless he can make a dramatic comeback, this is what he will most likely be remembered for. He became Prime Minister in 1993 and then again in 1996 for a short period until the Taliban took over. Very much the forerunner of the Taliban, Hekmatyar envisaged an Islamic state where women would be banned from work and education, and a puritanical brand of extremist Islam would be enforced. 'If you liked Khomeini,' the Russians said as they were pulling out of Kabul in 1989, 'you'll love Hekmatyar.'

Hekmatyar's supporters included many of Osama bin Laden's foreign volunteers who later found their way into the Taliban. The creation of the Taliban weakened the cunning erratic Hekmatyar as Pakistan shifted its support to the new group of Pashtun warriors.

When the Taliban took over they condemned Hekmatyar to death and he fled to Iran. I am told by drivers, translators and aid workers that if he returned to Afghanistan, he would be torn limb from limb.

'At first I was a member of Hekmatyar's party, and I fought against the Soviets but also against other Afghans,' says Mamur Hassan. 'We killed a lot of people and destroyed many places, and I regret this. I tell my sons not to have anything to do with political parties.' So Mamur Hassan tells the *New Yorker*, when the Northern Alliance is cosying up to the United States. Who knows what he really thinks?

In classic Afghan fashion, in the mid-1980s Hassan switched sides, breaking with Hekmatyar and joining Massoud until the defeat of the Soviets in 1989. After the Russians left, Hassan rejected any further political involvement and returned to Dashti Qala. He works with the Northern Alliance but maintains his independence. His men, he says, owe their allegiance to him. Personally.

This is a plausible claim. Mamur Hassan is a clan leader in Dashti Qala, as was his father before him. This society is essentially feudal. Poor men owe their loyalty to the local leader who pays their way. They will follow him when he changes sides for whatever reasons he deems compelling, such as a change in the overall temperature of a war, or the offer of a large amount of cash. They will do this even mid-battle. If Mamur Hassan decides to switch sides and join the Taliban tomorrow, all his men will unquestioningly fight with him, for the Taliban, and against their present allies in the Northern Alliance. This is part of the mystery of Afghanistan.

While it is not an outcome I think likely, it is by no means impossible, and it is something I always bear in mind when coming to Hassan's leafy complex at Dashti Qala. The loyalties are old and complex, and pre-date Western involvement in this conflict. You never know when an Afghan warlord will turn or, as the British observed during their abortive campaigns here during the eighteenth and nineteenth centuries, you may be able to rent an Afghan, but you can never buy one.

If you follow the money, you see that plenty of people on both sides have tried to buy the Afghans over the past twenty-five years. During the decade of the Soviet war, it's estimated Russia spent more than US$40 billion fighting here, losing 15,000 of its own troops in a war that cost more than one million Afghan lives.

America also spent huge amounts here over the same period, in its largest covert action program since World War II, funnelling more than US$3.2 billion in guns and money to the Mujaheddin, and co-ordinating an equivalent amount from other countries, including Saudi Arabia.

It started in the summer of 1979, when Washington signed a secret directive to support the fledgling Mujaheddin movement, to the tune of US$30 million. That was six months before Soviet tanks rolled into Kabul.

This was the initiative of President Jimmy Carter's national security advisor, Zbigniew Brzezinski, whose aim – and he was quite open about this – was to destabilise the Soviet Union by fostering the spread of Islamic militancy in Central Asia. In 1980, Brzezinski was filmed standing on the Pakistani side of the Afghan border, wearing the wrong type of turban and rallying the Mujaheddin to 'wage a jihad!' against the Communists.

American journalist Bob Fitrakis wrote bitterly about this following September 11: 'The Mujaheddin took the message to heart. They're now waging a jihad against us.' Brzezinski played a critical role in shaping Washington's policy in Afghanistan, which was continued by successive Republican administrations. In 2001, as the US returns here to the last great battlefield of the Cold War, dragging the world's press behind it, this issue underpins our reporting.

We discuss whether September 11 is in any way 'payback' for America's policies in Central Asia, and specifically for the conduct of its foreign policy in Afghanistan in the 1980s. Is it simply bad luck or coincidence that Osama bin Laden based his al-Qaeda network here? Is America now 'reaping the whirlwind', or as some US officials put it bluntly – has America helped create its own Frankenstein's monster?

We learn the term 'blowback' – security service talk for supporting an unsavoury local leader because it suits your short-term ends, only to have him turn around and bite you later. Saddam Hussein is one striking example of blowback. Is Osama bin Laden another?

Three years ago, as the nature of the Taliban regime was becoming apparent, Zbigniew Brzeziński stood firm, denying to a French newspaper that he had any regrets. 'Regret what? That secret operation was an excellent idea. It had the effect of drawing the Russians into the Afghan trap and you want me to regret it?'

Asked specifically whether he regretted supporting the rise of Islamic fundamentalism and giving arms and advice to future terrorists, Brzezinski replied, 'What is most important to the history of the world? The Taliban or the collapse of the Soviet empire? Some stirred-up Moslems or the liberation of Central Europe and the end of the Cold War?'

Brzezinski still holds to this view today, maintaining he has no regrets, even post-September 11. He tells American journalist David Corn that the Carter administration funded the moderates, not the fundamentalists. His defence is robust, putting the blame squarely on the Soviet Union, which he says continued to support world terrorism during the 1980s while it was fighting in Afghanistan. He argues this was what set the stage for the Afghan civil war of the 1990s and the subsequent rise of the Taliban, not Pakistani machinations and the rockets and missiles the US supplied to the Mujaheddin.

Brzezinski does not seem to have heard of blowback, though he does concede one fault with US policy – the rapid exit of US forces once the Soviets had departed: 'That was immoral.'

But that immorality, of course, was down to later Republican administrations.

Once the last battle of the Cold War was won, there was nothing holding the West in Afghanistan – no oil, for example. Not enough natural gas to stick around for. In fact, the

West appeared confused and even repulsed by the bloodthirsty Mujaheddin it had armed.

It left, it seemed, without a backward glance.

On the ground, US desertion rankles. The distinction between the policies pursued by different administrations in Washington is lost on people here. Afghans want to know why the United States funded ten years of war here, and then, having supplied enough arms for the Mujaheddin to keep fighting for the following decade, too, just upped and left.

'Why has the world forgotten us?' is the most common question I am asked by ordinary people in the bazaars and refugee camps. I feel a stab of guilt.

In her clinic at the refugee camp, Farahnaz Nazir put it succinctly the first time I visited her there. She looked up from tending malnourished babies and said, 'The September 11 attacks were terrible, simply terrible. But the US is paying the price for its belief that Communism was more dangerous than Islamic fundamentalism. The US armed the fundamentalists and then when the Communists were defeated, the US just left the fundamentalists here to ferment. They washed their hands of us, and they left us to live with the fundamentalists. For years we have suffered under them, and now the US is suffering under them, too.'

For the Republican administration in Washington, 1985 was a turning point. President Reagan's government increased covert military aid to the Mujaheddin to US$250 million a year – double the amount spent in 1984. Under National Security Decision Directive 166, Washington secretly agreed to take US high-tech and military expertise to the Afghan battlefield. The possibility of trapping the Soviet Union in its own version of Vietnam was irresistible – and that's just what happened.

In 1985 the CIA started supplying the Mujaheddin with satellite reconnaissance data of Soviet targets, plans for military operations and intercepts of Soviet communications. But that was just the beginning. In 1986 the US provided the Mujaheddin with sophisticated Stinger anti-aircraft missiles. There is grainy NBC news footage of the brave anti-Communist forces receiving their weapons. It is hilarious –

anyone can be cast as an ally in the war against Communism, including turbaned Islamic militants on mules.

The US program was that the CIA would provide funds, weapons and supervision for the Mujaheddin, but direct contact would be left to Pakistan's intelligence service, the ISI. With the Stinger missiles, for example, it worked like this: In June 1986 Pakistani intelligence officers received training on the missiles in the United States, and then returned to Pakistan, taking with them a new US invention – an electronic simulator – to teach the fifth-century warriors how to use the state-of-the-art missiles.

By 1987, 65,000 tonnes of arms were being supplied, and CIA and Pentagon specialists were constantly travelling to the new ISI headquarters at Rawalpindi.

It's worth noting that over the decade of the Afghan war, the ISI grew from a small outfit of a few thousand operatives to an organisation of more than 150,000, with a US$2 billion budget. In many ways this war cemented Pakistan's role as America's ally in the sub-continent. In the Cold War context of the time, 'socialist' India was Russia's partner, and an alliance with Pakistan redressed that balance.

By 1988, the annual amount being pumped to the Mujaheddin reached a massive US$700 million. The US was even shipping Tennessee mules to Afghanistan to carry all the weapons over the mountains. A decade later, Afghanistan was still littered with rusted American shipping containers, some refashioned by scavenging locals to serve as doors, workshops, stores and even gaols.

Recruits, money and equipment were distributed to the Mujaheddin factions by an organisation based in Pakistan called Office of Services, *Maktab al Khidamat*, known by its acronym MAK. One of three people who ran MAK was Osama bin Laden.

In 1986, bin Laden brought heavy construction equipment from Saudi Arabia to Afghanistan. Using his degree in civil engineering, his business expertise and family funds, he built training camps, and roads to reach them. Some were dug deep into the mountains. These are the camps now dubbed 'terrorist universities' by Washington. They were built in collaboration with the ISI and the CIA.

Bin Laden established al-Qaeda (the Base) between 1987 and 1988 to run these camps and other business enterprises. It is a tightly run holding company, integrating the operations of his armed forces with other 'legitimate' businesses.

In 1989, bin Laden took overall charge of MAK.

This history was known throughout the 1990s, reported on in detail in American newspapers, but it appeared irrelevant in light of the collapse of Communism. Debate over many issues, including the wisdom of arming Islamic militants and the policy of spawning a huge increase in opium production, was swept under the carpet.

But following September 11, the kaleidoscope has shifted, refracting these events in a new and more damaging light. It now seems incredible that in 1986 CIA chief William Casey supported an ISI proposal to recruit young Muslims from around the world to join the Afghan jihad. American investigative journalist John Cooley has revealed that Muslims were recruited within the US for the Mujaheddin, and were trained at Camp Peary, a CIA training camp in Virginia.

Surely this is blowback with a capital B? It seems that as in Saddam Hussein's Iraq, America has helped train and arm its worst enemy.

The CIA is scrambling for cover, claiming that though it supported Afghan fighters, including international Muslim brigades, it did not have any direct dealings with Osama bin Laden. He was not one of 'ours', they argue. But the web is so tangled that it doesn't make much difference. Bin Laden was, if not 'ours', then on 'our' side. He was linked to ISI, and ISI was 'ours', taking CIA money and spending it for 'us' in Afghanistan.

The left-wing analysis is that bin Laden has simply continued to do the job he was doing in Afghanistan in the 1980s – funding, feeding and training mercenaries. First it was for the ISI and, behind the scenes, the CIA. Later it became for the Taliban.

After a decade of fighting, the Soviets withdrew from Afghanistan in February 1989. The country fell to the heavily armed Mujaheddin, who turned on each other, plunging Afghanistan into seven more years of bitter warfare. This conflict swallowed up the Western dollars that had flowed here, and claimed tens of thousands more civilian lives.

By 1994 the country was in chaos, close to disintegration. Small-time commanders controlled huge arsenals and large numbers of mercenaries. They took control of trade and smuggling routes. On the road between Quetta in Pakistan and Kandahar, a distance of only 130 kilometres, twenty different groups put up chains and demanded twenty separate tolls. It didn't matter that you'd just paid ten kilometres back – if you didn't pay here, too, you'd be shot. Looting, theft and rape were commonplace. Afghanistan was utterly lawless.

When religious students from the south of the country, calling themselves the Taliban, stepped in offering peace and order, a grateful war-weary nation accepted. The tiny doctrinaire group conquered more than half the country without firing a shot. Town after town acceded to their tough brand of Islam in order to obtain relief from the chaos and bloodshed around them. However, most people never saw their new leader, Mullah Mohammed Omar. This is perhaps the strangest feature of the takeover. In a scenario unimaginable almost anywhere else in the world, in either a dictatorship or a democracy, there were no appearances and no photo opportunities. Mullah Omar was a name only. People were utterly oppressed by an invisible autocrat, his edicts enforced by brutal religious police.

One of the few people to have actually seen Mullah Omar is the Pakistani journalist and author Ahmed Rashid. His book is the one all the journalists in Afghanistan are reading. Everyone has a copy of *Taliban* except me, since I came in such a hurry, without any Afghan reference books. I read my friends' copies, whenever one is free, dipping into Taliban history in Khoja Bahauddin until someone wants their book back. Rashid says there is an 'entire factory of myths' to explain how a group of ill-equipped religious students took on and subdued the rapacious Kandahar warlords. Sex, in fact sexual perversion, features in all of them.

The most frequently told story concerns events in Kandahar in 1994, when a warlord abducted two teenage girls, shaved their heads, and allowed his men to repeatedly gang rape them. The Taliban took action. Mullah Omar gathered some thirty

Talibs who had only sixteen rifles between them – not even one per man – in Afghanistan, a sign of their poverty and desperation. But they attacked the base, freed the girls and hanged the warlord from the barrel of a tank. Crucially, they captured a huge quantity of arms and ammunition.

Some months later two Kandahar commanders were involved in a dispute over a young boy they both wanted to sodomise. Once again the Taliban took on the sexually perverse evil-doers and won, punishing the paedophiles and freeing the boy. As their reputation for heroism spread, the public began to appeal to Taliban leader Mullah Mohammed Omar to sort out other local disputes. Rashid describes Mullah Omar emerging as a 'Robin Hood figure, helping the poor against the rapacious commanders. His prestige grew because he asked for no reward or credit from those he helped, only demanding that they follow him to create a just Islamic system.'

But once Afghanistan was under the control of the idealistic Taliban, the people found their yoke of repression and suffering had only tightened. And despite the vigilant presence of the Taliban's religious police, as well as public amputations and executions, the war did not end.

After all this, the country is now suffering its worst drought in seventy years, bringing with it the real threat of famine. I am here at this time as a guest of the Mujaheddin who helped bring Afghanistan to its knees. It feels as if all Four Horsemen of the Apocalypse are riding in, and it's difficult to know how people keep going. The truth is, the effort of endurance kills many, or shortens their lives.

Increasingly, I feel my job is irrelevant to the real needs of this country. What is the point in covering the long, slow lead-up to a conflict when people are starving? By early October, I am reporting more and more about the struggle to feed people.

A truck drives into the centre of a clearing marked out with a string fence in the desert near Khoja Bahauddin. It contains a precious cargo. Not weapons but food. French aid agency ACTED is distributing fifty tonnes of wheat, the first food aid here in three months.

Hundreds of people line up outside the string fence on this flat piece of stony desert near the Qumkishlak refugee camp.

The people are hungry, but there is no fighting. Guards with switches keep the children in line. Inside the clearing, men wait by the truck. Sacks of grain are loaded onto their shoulders. They carry them a short distance to a blue tarpaulin laid on the ground. The sacks are split, their contents falling in a white river on the dusty surface, making a satisfying, sibilant sound.

The refugees stand patiently, covering their noses because the dust is ferocious. Women are also in the queue, bright absences in their burqas.

When enough grain has been poured out, the aid workers signal to them to begin coming forward. One by one, they run up to a table inside the string fence. They smear an inky thumbprint on a file, to show they have collected their family's quota, and then go to the tarpaulin where they receive three kilos of wheatflour. It's poured into their clothing with a big plastic scoop. They make a well in the long pyjama tails of their suits to receive it. A woman in a blue burqa carries her flour in a red scarf. One small child, coming to collect the precious grain, suddenly freezes in panic. It is too heavy. She is terrified she will drop it. Her father comes forward to help her carry her load.

ACTED logistician Eric Le Guin tells me, 'This amount will support 2000 families for a month, and 150 tonnes more is on its way, along with oil and sugar, which are cooking staples here.'

The people receiving this food aid are some of the 10,000 refugees who arrived in this region just over a year ago, after the Taliban conquered the nearby town of Taloqan. As Afghanistan's crippling drought continued, they soon became utterly reliant on food aid. During this period there was also a decline in relations between the Taliban and the outside world, leading to delays and sporadic food delivery by international aid agencies, just when it was needed most. This left some of these refugees at the point of starvation. Many survived by eating boiled grass.

'Yes, we boiled grass, and we ate it, there was nothing else. The children were hungry, we were all hungry,' says Nasr, the head of a large family living in the Qumkishlak camp. He is standing on a hill above the camp. Leaning on a stick, with a grey beard and a grey turban, he looks like an Old Testament prophet. His face is weathered and lined. I am shocked when he says he is only fifty years old.

The children gather around him, including his grand-children, most of them with skin lesions and the bleached hair consistent with malnutrition. One small girl is startlingly beautiful, with perfect features and huge, glowing eyes. In the West she would become a supermodel. But when she smiles her face is also lined, like that of a woman in her thirties. She is nine years old. She follows me all day at the refugee camp, smiling often, tearing at my heartstrings with her luminous beauty and her dismal future.

'We have to live here, what else can we do?' Nasr asks. 'The Taliban persecuted us, beating us with sticks. They would have killed us, just because we were Tajiks. We ran away, taking nothing but the clothes we stood in.'

The translator I am working with at the camp is Dr Ashraf Aini. He fled Taloqan at the same time as Nasr and his family. I can see that he is edgy here. Dr Aini, who speaks flawless Russian and English, is an urbane, witty man in his early forties. He works at the local hospital at night, but earns ten times his monthly salary working as a translator for Canadian CBC during the day.

'I left everything behind, absolutely everything. I had only two hours, so I gathered up my wife and children and we fled,' he says.

The sun is setting. I can hardly see Dr Aini for the stinging dust and smoke from the fires in the camp. The refugees are winter-proofing their dwellings. What this amounts to is build-ing mud-brick walls around their tents, in the hope that they will then withstand sub-zero temperatures. We are surrounded by swarming crowds of curious people and children. The beau-tiful nine-year-old stays close as I ask Dr Aini why he decided on this precipitate flight.

'We heard about the conditions for people living in Taliban-controlled areas, the massive killings of people in the north, the burning of villages, and we fled in fear.' He adds vehe-mently, 'There must be no compromise with such people. The Taliban cannot be included in any broad-based government in the future.'

Not all his leaders agree. This controversial issue consumes much of our attention as alternatives to all-out war are canvassed. When journalists ask General Bariolai whether a compromise allowing the Taliban to participate in government could be reached, he says no compromise deal could ever include the Taliban leadership. Men like Mullah Omar, he says, can have no say in the future of the country. 'They are nothing but agents of Pakistan. They brought foreigners here to kill Afghans. They educated boys of thirteen or fifteen in Pakistan to destroy our history, our museums and our archives.'

But General Bariolai would be willing to co-operate with lower-ranked Taliban. If they defected now, he would be willing to see them participate in decisions on how the country should be run. General Mamur Hassan tells me that he agrees. 'After the fighting, when we succeed, compromise is possible. Yes, I can even foresee the possibility of co-operation with the Taliban. I could sit in government with a former Talib, yes.'

In the late 1990s Iranian director Mohsen Makhmalbaf was filming near the refugee camp at Zabol on the Iranian border. He was making his searing movie *Kandahar*, about a woman returning from the West to see the sister she had left behind in Afghanistan.

'I never forget those nights of filming *Kandahar*. While our team searched the deserts with flashlights, we would see dying refugees like herds of sheep left in the desert. When we took those that we thought were dying of cholera to hospitals in Zabol, we realised that they were dying of hunger. Since those days and nights of seeing so many people starving to death, I haven't been able to forgive myself for eating any meals.'

Makhmalbaf was there to choose extras for his film. The Iranian authorities explained there had been an influx of illegal refugees, and the camp could not afford to feed so many people, although they hadn't eaten for a week. When the film crew offered to provide meals, the Iranian authorities were very welcoming, aware they could not cope. Makhmalbaf fed some 400 people. Most were children who had fainted of hunger in their mothers' arms. 'For an hour we were crying and distributing bread and fruits. The authorities expressed grief and regret and said that it took a long time for budget approvals, and kept saying that the flow of hungry refugees was far greater than what they could manage. This is the story of a country that's been ravaged by its own nature, history, economy, politics and the unkindness of its neighbours.'

As people in the south anticipate American air strikes, more refugees are beginning to arrive in Khoja Bahauddin, clambering up the inhospitable mountains in a journey that can take days or even weeks on foot.

The ACTED aid agency is pre-positioning food and assistance so that it is able to respond quickly if the need arises, and this trickle of refugees turns into a flood. The agency is concerned that the onset of winter will make its job much more difficult. In northern Afghanistan most of the population lives in remote regions. In winter many villages cannot be reached by cars and trucks – instead camels and donkeys have to be loaded with supplies, to cross the mountain paths. In some areas, the aid agencies have to send messengers to ask people to walk for two or three days to a lower village to collect the donated food.

I file a report on the situation for every channel I broadcast to. As I'm waiting for my feed at EBU, or hunched over a satellite phone on the dusty balcony at Massoud's house, in my mind's eye I see the beautiful nine-year-old in the refugee camp. She was born after the defeat of Communism and has known nothing but war and suffering. What will her future hold?

Chapter 9

It's early October and Khoja Bahauddin continues to be hot, dusty and unrelenting. I find myself besieged by self-doubt, lacerating myself with the thought that other people are better journalists, and achieve more. Some redoubtable women even manage to do this job and to have children. In my current negative mood, I am certain that they have better contacts than I do, and file better stories, not to mention manage their finances better.

I find myself in tears on the bleached grass at the ACTED compound. I can't understand why I am so upset, until I realise I have lost all track of time here, in this timeless place, and on top of everything it is my birthday, which I thought was still two days away. This prompts more tears.

Sitting in the dust crying, I look up and realise that to make matters worse, I am in the direct line of sight of nine satellite phones, which is expressly forbidden because of the dangerous rays they emit. If I don't stop soon, even my tears will be radioactive.

I try to talk myself round. Covering this story is a feat of endurance. It's about getting through the low patches and keeping going. Then I call home. Sometimes you just need the reassurance of hearing familiar voices. My sister tells me my nephew's well, and they've been watching my reports.

I perk up. Her considered opinion? 'I liked your hair.' I should have known. Perhaps I shouldn't worry so much. It seems no one is paying attention to anything I file in any event.

I spend the rest of my birthday on a hot dusty plain, seven kilometres from the Taliban front line, watching the Northern Alliance put on a show of military might. Looking for a lift, I ask the Greek reporter if he is going out there and he replies, 'No. I'm here for the war, not a training exercise.'

I catch a ride with a colleague from APTN instead.

Four thousand troops parade in the sand at Bydengak. Their uniforms and boots are Iranian and new, but their weapons are Russian and old, including ten rocket launchers, two dozen armoured personnel carriers and eighteen tanks. Some of the tanks, Soviet T-55s, date from the 1960s, a few from the 1950s. The men are here to swear allegiance to their new military commander, General Mohammed Fahim.

Ahmed Shah Massoud's successor is squat and stocky, with a squashed prize-fighter's face. He has none of Massoud's elegance or charisma. Standing in an open Russian jeep and speaking through a megaphone, he tells his men the Northern Alliance welcomes proposed Western support in fighting the Taliban. But he stresses that the Northern Alliance will continue to fight against the Taliban whether or not it receives Western help.

All the vehicles and tanks are plastered with posters of Massoud, and General Fahim pays tribute to his predecessor, the Lion of the Panjshir.

'We have been fighting against terrorism for more than two decades. We sacrificed our greatest leader Ahmed Shah Massoud in this fight, and we will continue to fight the Taliban, even if we fight alone.'

The sentiments are stirring but the performance is wooden. Perhaps the comparison with Massoud highlights General Fahim's colourlessness. He may be very able, but the strongest impression here in the bleak desert of northern Afghanistan is that the Northern Alliance is still reeling from Massoud's loss.

After the exercise is over, I ask Commander Mohammed Daoud about the Northern Alliance's weapon supplies.

'We have been promised new weapons from Iran and

Russia, but we haven't received them here yet. Don't worry, we are also asking,' he replies.

Russia has made a commitment to supply the Northern Alliance with arms but it seems the weaponry has yet to be distributed to the troops.

I spot the Greek reporter out here and can't resist saying, 'Oh, you made it – even though it's only a military exercise, not a war.'

'Sometimes the war starts from a military exercise,' he swaggers. Hide of a rhinoceros.

I decide to give Washington until Monday 8 October, and if nothing happens I'm going to return to Moscow, to replenish my stocks of food, water, money and equipment. We calculate a week here is equivalent to a month anywhere else, and by Monday I will have been here for two weeks.

'Yes, you must stay till the weekend,' a CBS journalist says, 'our Washington reporter says that something will happen soon.'

An ABC journalist agrees. 'Our Washington correspondent is very well connected and he never leaves Washington unless the sky is falling in, and he's preparing to accompany the Secretary of State on a visit to this region. That means something's up.'

So on the basis of rumours and gossip I stay to see the start of the conflict in Afghanistan. American air strikes begin on Sunday 7 October, one day before I'm thinking of leaving. We are alerted not by Washington, but by Dr Abdullah, the Foreign Minister of the Northern Alliance. He announces at a press conference that air strikes are only a matter of hours away, and says Northern Alliance front-line units have been ordered to cease shelling, so they won't be mistaken for Taliban positions.

We tend to take Dr Abdullah's pronouncements with a pinch of salt because he has alerted us to 'imminent' US air strikes before. But usually when we press him, 'imminent' is a matter of days away. 'Hours' is more dramatic, and my news desk is interested. So is every other news desk. The European Broadcasting Union, EBU, can't process all its bookings. As their satellite phone goes into meltdown, there is excitement in the air, but still no facts. Journalists are queuing up for ten-minute slots of satellite time, booked back to back all night. I do an interview for Deutsche Welle, explaining the circumstances and saying that American air strikes are no more than speculation at this stage. As I say goodbye to Berlin, take out my earpiece and give up my spot in front of the camera to the next journalist, Bruno from EBU comes up to whisper that air strikes have begun. Thank God my report wasn't live and we have time to retape it.

The air strikes are terrifying for the people of Kabul who have no air-raid shelters to go to and have to sit out the attacks in their homes, clutching frightened children close to them. However, to us it's just a job. Journalists are often accused of being vultures and feeding on other people's misery. *If it bleeds, it leads*. You certainly can't let yourself experience every painful thing you see, or you couldn't survive. I meet an Irish reporter who says she just got in tonight, wasn't that lucky, and I understand her completely. She *was* lucky. And since she files for Irish broadcaster RTE, which I also do, she lets me use her satellite phone. So I'm lucky, too.

We work around the clock reporting on the air strikes, though Kabul is actually hundreds of kilometres from here. There are few Western journalists in Kabul. The closest teams are in the Panjshir Valley, some fifty kilometres north of the city, but I know of one correspondent who describes himself as being 'just north of Kabul', when he is in fact north of the Panjshir Valley, a good two or three days' journey from Kabul. For most of us, though, it seems 'Afghanistan' is a specific enough location at this stage. No matter where you are in the country, even if you are nowhere near the bombing, news organisations will take stories from you.

When you are not on the spot, only as close as you can get to the spot, your access to information is limited, making it extremely frustrating when Berlin or Washington or Sydney is crossing to you live for an 'update'. I am trying to glean what information I can, and it is a tense night.

I am filing for three news broadcasters on three different continents, which involves juggling time zones, bulletins, extra live inserts, and then extra bulletins as Deutsche Welle responds to the air strikes by extending to a rolling twenty-four-hour news service. To do this I have to borrow satellite phones, which are in heavy use. But the tension affects the men around me differently – I start receiving declarations of love.

I'm stunned. I've been doing live shots from this exact same spot for two weeks, attracting no one, and tonight of all nights, when I don't have time to listen to men emboldened by bombs into thinking about sex, they are everywhere. One makes his proposal in Russian, which makes me even more grumpy, since I have to concentrate to listen to Russian and I don't have time to concentrate on anything but the news.

The locals are equally affected. They stand wrapped in their woollen blankets at the edge of the pool of light cast by the camera, listening intently as I do pieces to camera in a language they don't understand. They've never gathered to watch before, and one hits his head with his hands, telling an EBU technician that he is 'sick with love'.

He's not sick with love, he's just sick with bombs.

I file around the clock for thirty-six hours, on the air strikes, where they are targeted, how many bombs are being dropped, how much damage is being caused, and speculating on the efficacy of such strikes in a country like Afghanistan, where there is no real infrastructure to damage. In bombing Belgrade, NATO could destroy electricity stations, plunge cities into darkness, and punish the government of Slobodan Milosevic. It is not clear whether the same is true here, where there is almost no electricity anywhere in the country.

The most difficult question to answer tonight, and over the next few weeks, is the extent of the civilian casualties resulting from the bombings. Those figures will only become clear when we can verify them independently after the Taliban leave Kabul. This lack of information doesn't stop the news programs asking us now though. My biggest nightmare is being asked questions live on air I don't know the answer to. 'So, Irris Makler in northern Afghanistan, what impact are the air strikes having in terms of the loss of civilian life?' Takes some fancy footwork to get out of that one.

I catch some sleep on the cold concrete floor at EBU in between live shots. EBU staff are putting in long hours, too, and a strange sleep-deprived hysteria grips us all. At 4 a.m. Maxim, a cameraman from Moscow, makes me 'special coffee for women' – it sounds better in Russian, and it tastes great. He laces coffee with brandy and sugar to wake me up and make me lively enough to talk to an international audience about a war I can't see and don't yet understand.

This is one of the biggest changes wrought by twenty-four-hour rolling news. It has transformed journalists from reporters into 'experts' – which we are not, by definition. Now instead of going out to discover what is happening, and report on it, we stand at a feed point and tell the audience what some-one else has told us.

The following day Bruno brings out his CD player. The strains of very slinky jazz greet people arriving at EBU's outdoor office to file. Reverting to the DJ he once was, he plays tracks for different journalists. 'And a special track for my favourite team – the guys from China, who are going home today,' Bruno says in a smooth voice. They are actually from Taiwan, but today who cares?

'Here it is – gentlemen, this one's for you, "The Green, Green Grass of Home".'

They look expectant. Their English is not fluent, so they don't really know what's coming, but when they hear the song they have tears in their eyes. They sing along, until Bruno reminds them why they're here.

'Your feed is in two minutes, when the song is finished,' he croons in his syrupy DJ voice.

They listen till the end and scamper off to do their live shot.

Suddenly I'm laughing. It's surreal, karaoke in the middle of a war, then rushing off to tell your home audience in a serious voice all about the latest developments 'live from northern Afghanistan'.

Chapter 10

He gave you manna to eat in the desert, something your fathers had never known, to humble and to test you so that in the end it might go well with you. (Deuteronomy 8:16)

It falls like manna from heaven over the desert of Afghanistan. Yellow, plastic manna, in a carpet over the stony ground.

Within a week of the air strikes, the US is dropping food from the sky for those starving in northern Afghanistan, and people are soon fighting over it.

Each package contains a ready-to-eat vegetarian meal, sufficient for a day's rations, of the type issued to American troops. Each is marked 'humanitarian aid – a gift from the people of the United States', but this is written only in English, which almost none of the recipients can read.

Hundreds of people from the nearby refugee camps run up to collect the donated food, carrying the yellow packets on their heads and wrapped in scarves or the material of their clothes.

But once they snatch their booty, many people are clearly confused. The food includes items unfamiliar to Afghans, such as peanut butter, strawberry jam and pop tarts, as well as layers and layers of packaging.

A child squeezes peanut butter out of its vacuum-sealed packaging into the dust, in front of American TV cameras. 'You can't film that,' says an American journalist. 'Why not?' asks his Russian cameraman. Some people feed the food aid to their donkeys. They have to be shown how to eat and prepare such unusual food. But the US government has not put any advisers on the ground to do this part of the job.

The instructions on the packets are quite complex – some confuse me, and English is my first language. Fortunately, exposure to the 'Meals Ready to Eat' the NBC crews have brought means I can explain to people what to do from personal experience. Once we show them how to eat the pre-packaged food, they politely declare it is quite tasty.

The food packages land over a wide area. In some places, people fight over them. In other places, further away from the refugee camps, men with jeeps and trucks appear and collect huge quantities of the packages, loading them into their vehicles, and guarding them with guns. They say they are planning to distribute this food aid. But there's no way of knowing whether that's true. An American TV crew follows one truck full of contraband packages and after half an hour of changing stories and directions, the drivers are shamed into giving the food out to the poor. 'I feel like I did my good deed for the day,' says the cameraman.

This experience encapsulates the problems with this method of delivering food aid, for when there is no news crew who happen to be in the right place at the right time, what then?

Local aid agencies are critical. They confirm that with humanitarian aid dropped in this way by plane, it's difficult to police the distribution and to ensure the food reaches the right people.

'It's not targeted, so it's wasteful, too much gets lost, some people get ten packages, some get none. This is a bad method of delivering aid, especially when resources are so scarce,' Eric Le Guen from ACTED explains at an interview in a refugee camp.

I tell him the story of the news crew and the trucks collecting the packages.

'Exactly. That's why we think it's a bad idea.'

He humbled you, causing you to hunger and then feeding you with manna, which neither you nor your fathers had known, to teach you that man does not live on bread alone but on every word that comes from the mouth of the Lord. (Deuteronomy 8:3)

This is a controversial project, even within the US. Criticism also comes from an unusual American source, an aid agency descended from the Knights of Malta, who were last in these parts during the Crusades, putting Muslims to the sword. Now the modern-day Knights – working under the trade name 'Knightsbridge' – are here to deliver food and tents to refugees in northern Afghanistan. Despite persistent rumours of links to the CIA, American Knight of Malta Ed Artis is scathing about the US food drop.

'Whoever came up with this concept had bad information. The colour of the packets, the method of delivery, the contents of the packets, that person should be fired. The people don't eat these things. The Russians when they were here dropped yellow cluster bombs on these people. They have been oppressed, they are starving, but they have a little dignity left. Don't throw food at them. They're not animals.'

In addition, says Artis, no humanitarian drops have been made in the Mazar-i-Sharif and Bamian regions, which are cut off from the rest of the world by a Taliban blockade – and where arguably the need is greater. He says the unavoidable conclusion is that the US has dropped the food aid here because this is where the journalists are.

Artis is a character. A decorated Vietnam veteran and retired combat medic, he calls himself 'Sir Edward' on his card – they are knights, remember? He is a red-faced Californian in his fifties, surviving mostly on sugar cubes. 'I'll lose forty pounds on this trip, just like the last,' he says with a twinkle, grabbing another cube from the NBC stash.

Then he adds more seriously, 'I was a warrior – but I came back from multiple tours of Vietnam and thought that I could wage peace as well.'

Much of the Knights' aid work is self-funded, and he boasts that not one cent of money received in donations goes on administration. 'I got a beat-up old car, my house is paid for, what else do people usually spend their money on?'

In a delicious American touch, he says part of the funding of his aid work comes from a book deal and the possibility of a Hollywood movie. One of the major studios has taken out an option on his life story. 'So that's two hundred thousand dollars in the kitty.'

Then he turns serious.

'This is not a business, it's an avocation that turned into a vocation. Walking around refugee camps you cannot but feel impelled to do something. Cast-offs in the rest of the world can save a life here. I'm just an agent for the child, for the widow, for the elderly, I'm just glad I can do it.'

On his modern-day crusade, for Ed Artis, almost anything goes.

'We go to the front line ahead of the NGOs [non-government organisations] at the threshold of the migration of refugees, providing care and comfort. We draw in some of the other NGOs who might not think it's safe. When we've been here for a while, they see that we're not dead, and they might bring in their larger operations.'

He says he's delivered food to front lines as the bombs drop in Albania and Chechnya. He brings clippings with him, to show us that he is who he says he is – interesting that he feels this necessary. The articles from small-time US papers recount that he smuggled tonnes of medicines into Cambodian refugee camps and defied Taliban fighter jets to fly medical help to the Hazara people in the interior of Afghanistan, when no other humanitarian organisation could go there. He also says he managed to persuade the Albanian mafia to guard medical supplies for Kosovo refugees through his connections with the New York underworld. 'But that's a long story . . .' He denies point blank he is gun running or that his exploits are a cover for intelligence gathering.

In Khoja Bahauddin, Ed Artis is sometimes in the company of 'Bob', a strange American in a dark jacket and dark glasses. 'Bob' is pleased that I file for Voice of America, and is always sympathetic to me about the amount of money the US government is 'ripping out' of the broadcasting service. His job is never explained, and we suspect him of being a Special Forces officer. His plans are shadowy, and he says he may be accompanying Ed when he goes to Choyab – a town four hours west

– to deliver aid to starving refugees. 'Bob' may not be serious about this, but Ed is.

'You don't know anyone who wants to donate half a million dollars for tents? I know where I could get them right away, if you did,' he says.

Ed Artis tells reporters that instead of dropping food on people, the humanitarian aid should be given to non-government organisations that can go and distribute it on a one-on-one basis.

'You have to give the aid to the NGOs that have the balls to go on the ground.'

We soon see the yellow US food packages on sale in the bazaar. Someone is making a profit out of US largesse. But at least the packaging doesn't go to waste. Kids use the yellow plastic bags to carry their school things. You see them from a distance, walking beside donkeys, with their small US-issue yellow plastic bags. They are the perfect size for children who don't have schoolbooks.

Two weeks later, the US broadcasts messages on radio in local languages, warning Afghans not to confuse the food aid it is dropping with the cluster bombs it is also dropping, as both come in yellow packages.

I find the War Against Terror is becoming more and more surreal.

I go out to gauge local reaction to the US bombing. In the Qumkishlak refugee camp, I find Nasr again, the patriarch who was eating boiled rice and looked ninety even though he was only fifty. His family has received a second donation of oil and sugar, and he welcomes the air strikes.

'It is good that America helps us,' says Nasr. 'For a long time America abandoned us. Afghanistan needs help.'

At my favourite moneychanger's, a small shack facing the main square in Khoja Bahauddin, the men sit cross-legged on rugs discussing the air strikes. The American dollar has lost half of its value against the Afghan currency, the afghani, in the space of a week, instantly making goods twice as expensive. The moneychangers say that the effective increase in the value of the afghani is a vote of confidence in the American military action, and indicates faith the economy will improve. If the war is going badly then the afghani will plummet again. But they are also making a tidy profit, as they gleefully admit.

'It's good. It's good for business. Of course we profit if the dollar falls,' says Shaqib, the chief moneychanger, looking up from his game of chess. He joins the drivers, translators and owners of generators as the new rich in Khoja Bahauddin. 'But it's also good for Afghanistan, if it means the Taliban are defeated. The Taliban are very bad and Afghanistan needs peace.'

But even those who welcome the air strikes are worried about their relatives in the south. In the square I meet Mahmudullah, a man in his forties who left Kabul three months ago with his teenage son, fearing the boy risked being conscripted into the Taliban army. Mahmudullah's three daughters and their families remained behind in Kabul. He does not know if they have suffered during the air strikes.

'It is difficult to contact them, they have no telephone.'

A man squats on his haunches on the floor of a dark shop across from the moneychanger's. Salahuddin is one of a group of men waiting to be called to the pedal-operated CB radio, plugged into a car battery, which allows them to contact Kabul. This is how they check on their families' safety. They use a method of communication originally devised by the military in a country without communications, now adapted again for civilian use. They call a similar shop in Kabul, give a name and address, and a runner there goes to alert the family to the call from the north. Then they come with him to the shop, and call again to speak to their relatives.

'Hello, hello, yes, please go to the following address and ask for Amonallah,' Salahuddin tells the operator.

This cumbersome method of communication can sometimes take the best part of a day. But here that seems not to matter.

'Yes, I spoke to my brother-in-law. My sister and the children are all well. My mother, too. We can't say too much because we know the Taliban are listening in, and we don't want them to punish the family. So we only discuss matters very generally, but they say everyone is well, Allah be praised.'

Salahuddin can also tell me that the Kabul telephone exchange has been hit during the air strikes, because he usually leaves a message asking his family to call him by phone at a number here, but they are no longer able to do that as all the phones in their region have gone down.

On Wednesday 10 October, the US bombs its first targets here in the north, in the nearby town of Taloqan. War is coming closer. By Friday people fleeing Taloqan begin to trickle into Khoja Bahauddin. I'm with two friends buying supplies in the town square – cartons of juice, cans of Pepsi, sultanas – when the stallholder says that his friend has just arrived from Taloqan.

Gul Ahmad stands in the back of the shack, behind dusty rows of goods. He is a twenty-eight-year-old merchant, as dusty as the produce. He describes how he watched the American bombs dropping on Taloqan. He was awake all night, and saw American bombers strike airfields and destroy the Taliban's military helicopters. He says the fire at the airfield burned until the following morning.

'It terrified me. I could see that war was coming,' he says.

Fearful of war and the impact it would have on his business, Gul Ahmad loaded his possessions onto forty donkeys. Every image here is biblical – even the numbers resonate from the Old Testament. He didn't load his goods onto twenty-three donkeys. It had to be forty. The next night, he and a group of ten others walked out with their possessions, to escape Taloqan. They hiked for twenty-four hours over the mountains to reach Khoja Bahauddin.

Gul Ahmad says some Taliban commanders have run away from Taloqan, taking their families with them. He saw them packing their belongings and families into their jeeps before they fled. This is more than Gul Ahmad did. He left his family behind to face the Taliban and the bombings. He says those fleeing Taloqan were mostly 'foreign' Taliban commanders, from Pakistan and Arab countries. Later, however, we hear it is the foreign Taliban who are the more determined fighters, staying on until after the local Afghans have given up or switched sides.

I want to ask Gul Ahmad more, including why he left his family behind while saving his goods, but he is reluctant to keep talking.

'No more,' he shakes his head and moves further back inside the shop.

We walk away, talking about this interview. If Gul Ahmad is right, the American bombing in the north of Afghanistan is weakening the Taliban.

It seems that the air strikes have not changed much militarily here. The Northern Alliance is waiting for the US to smash the Taliban before it begins its offensive, and it is still waiting on large-scale weapons delivery from Russia.

Officially, Military Commander General Fahim welcomes the US intervention against the Taliban, and the promised support for the Northern Alliance. But he is not revealing his tactics, on or off the record, including the timing and direction of any military push. It's understood that he wishes to secure the north of Afghanistan first, recapturing the town of Mazar-i-Sharif before heading south to attack the capital, Kabul.

This strategy of starting the ground war here in the north is understood to be less popular with Washington, which wants a quick victory, easy to explain to the American people. 'Everyone understands the concept of capturing the capital city. The name Mazar-i-Sharif doesn't mean anything to Mom and Pop sitting at home watching TV in the US,' an American journalist explains.

But what the Northern Alliance leaders are hoping for is that after a couple of military defeats, Taliban commanders will begin to defect, either because they want to be on the winning side or because they would be paid. It's a domino theory – the hope is that once one or two commanders defect, others will follow. In this scenario, the northern territories, where we are, will fall first, and the rest of the country will follow without major fighting.

That's why every account of a defection is seized upon by Northern Alliance leaders and gloatingly reported – and then so hotly denied by the Taliban.

The man the Northern Alliance is pinning its hopes on at Mazar-i-Sharif is Uzbek warlord Rashid Dostum. He is a larger than life figure, an ex-Communist who recreated himself as an Islamic warrior, while remaining a lover of wine, women and song. He famously said of the Taliban, 'We will not submit to a government where there's no whiskey and no music.' A giant of a man, he has a reputation for brutality, with allegations that his troops committed atrocities against civilians in Kabul in the early 1990s and then in the north near Mazar-i-Sharif towards the end of the decade. Dostum is once again outside Mazar-i-Sharif, his men in a pocket surrounded on three sides by Taliban troops who have taken and retaken the city twice since expelling Dostum in 1997.

On 13 October General Dostum tells British journalist Tim Judah by satellite phone that within the last twenty-four hours a Taliban commander called Kazi Abdul Hai has defected, bringing 4000 men with him. But within days, General Dostum is forced to admit Kazi Abdul Hai has switched back to the Taliban. He claims some of the Taliban leader's 4000 troops have remained with the Northern Alliance.

The problem with this story is that we can't verify any of it: whether Kazi Abdul Hai actually has 4000 men, whether he ever really defected, or whether once he defected back some of his men chose to stay with the Northern Alliance. There are Taliban forces between us in Khoja Bahauddin and General Dostum south of Mazar-i-Sharif. He can't get to us and, more importantly, we can't get to him.

The significance of these defections – so incomprehensible to a Western observer – is that they indicate which way the wind of victory will blow. At this point in mid-October it seems that the wind is still changeable, and that you couldn't chart a reliable course on it.

The French aid agency ACTED has opened its doors as a guesthouse, providing lovely rooms before it, too, is overrun by journalists, as happened at the Foreign Ministry. My Deutsche Welle colleague Christoph Wanner has a room there, and I am sitting outside writing when I hear his satellite phone ring. I run in to answer it, and am asked for a journalist I've never heard of.

I explain that he's not here, and that I don't know him. The caller says he is from *Neue Zürcher Zeitung* newspaper in Switzerland, and that he needs to find a freelance journalist. Do I know any?

I tell him that I am freelance, but that unfortunately I don't speak German. The man from the NZZ is not deterred.

'That doesn't matter – you can write the article in English, and we can translate it. But I need 800 words on the most recent events, in a hurry, and can you wind in some local reaction to the bombings, especially from the refugees?'

Before I know it I am agreeing, and the efficient Swiss newspaper is taking my bank account details so that they can pay me directly. So this is how I come to be shouting my copy down a poor satphone line to a German woman who can't really speak English.

'Bitte to repeat that last sentence.'

'It's the first sentence, and it reads as follows . . .'

I have to repeat each sentence twice to Frau Brunner, after which she says, 'Ja, now I am content, please go on.'

At this snail's pace, Frau Brunner records my copy, which is beginning to sound lame even to my own ears, until she objects, 'But vy have you called him a town crier?'

'It's his job – he is a town crier.'

'Oh – vot it is?'

'It's . . . it's a town crier. He walks through villages making announcements.'

'Oh.' She does not sound convinced.

'It's a word, in English, it's a word.'

We struggle on through three more sentences, until Frau Brunner exclaims, discouragingly from my point of view, 'But vy haf you written ze sentence like zat?'

Chris Stephen, listening in and laughing, says I should have replied, 'Because, madam, in English it scans!'

I am not so bold, and repeat the sentence for the third time.

'Ja, I think I understand vot you are trying to say,' Frau Brunner says doubtfully. 'I am content, please go on.'

I shudder to think what that piece looked like translated into German.

Later in the week, I file at EBU until 2 a.m. for 'The Today Show', a morning television program for Channel Nine Australia. They want to know about the effect of the continuous US air strikes in terms of morale on both the Taliban and the Northern Alliance. They are also interested in the military preparedness of Northern Alliance troops for a ground offensive and whether the Russian weapons that have been promised are getting through. I drive along the dark, bumpy road to the Foreign Ministry, exhausted. I have been putting in sixteen-hour days and working till 2 a.m. all week. I don't sleep very well because when I get home the NBC contingent work all night, filing to the United States during their day.

The thought of my sleeping bag has never been so inviting. I sleep much better since I switched the short, plasticky sleeping bag bought for me in Dushanbe, for a warm high-quality one made of modern fibres 'good to minus fifteen celsius', that belongs to the Northern Alliance. Two officials gave it to a gorgeous blonde reporter from Finland whom they found irresistible. She left without the sleeping bag and, after five days of looking at it lying crumpled on the floor of my room, I took it – well, swapped it – for my short second-rate one. I've squared this with my conscience as I've also bought two mattresses in the market, which I will leave here when I go. It's almost a fair exchange.

I'm thinking fondly of my new Northern Alliance sleeping bag when a teenager with a gun peers in the car window and waves us through the checkpoint on the road to the compound. We reach the Foreign Ministry, I say good night to the driver, and walk in to the dark compound, where one small light is shining. A guard, another teenager with a gun, comes up and starts to shout at me, pointing at his watch and making it clear that this is the Dari version of 'And what time do you call this, missy?'

I find myself shouting back, 'Don't you wag your finger at me as though I'm the sixteen-year-old and you're my father. Where do you think I've been anyway? Out having a good time at Khoja Bahauddin's famous nightspots? I've been working, I don't choose to come home at 2 a.m., it's my job . . .'

I trail off mid-sentence, realising that I am shouting, in English, at a teenager with a gun, in a culture where they use them, and where women's lives are worth nothing. I'm losing it. I don't shout at guys with guns, especially at two in the morning. It's time for a break.

I've been here three weeks, which is longer than most other journalists. The vast majority spend no more than two weeks here, before they are replaced by a new crew. Many don't last a week. It's hard to file to hourly deadlines from the fifth century. Maybe it's time to go home, and pick up some money and equipment before coming back.

It proves as hard to get out of Afghanistan as it was to get in . . . you can check out any time you like, but you can never leave.

There are no reliable flights to Tajikistan. People wait for days, scanning the skies for a mythical helicopter that doesn't turn up. Or, when one finally appears, so many journalists scramble to get onto it that it is overladen and is forced to crash land. That's what happens to five of the European journalists I flew into Afghanistan with from Dushanbe on Chopper Number 3, was it only three weeks ago? It feels like a lifetime. Waiting in the Panjshir Valley for a flight out of Afghanistan, they had been promised that they would definitely fly on the next chopper out. However, when one finally turns up, days later, they find that they are competing for seats with the Northern Alliance military who need to ferry men and a dead body back up north. The journalists say they and their gear must have priority. The soldiers say they and their body must have priority. Neither backs down.

The pilot says he can't take so many – but in the end he gives in and takes everyone. The overladen, poorly serviced chopper takes off above the mountains, carrying soldiers, journalists, gear and corpse, but then its emergency lights come on, and the pilot says they will not make it. He tries to perform an emergency landing right where they are at that moment – above a mountain in the middle of nowhere. The soldiers start chanting *Allah Hu Akbar* – God Is Great – preparing to meet their maker. My friends are sure they are going to die. The chopper hits the ground hard, but miraculously, no one is killed, or even seriously hurt.

They climb out of the wreckage, with no idea where they are. There is nothing in sight. The nearest village, Rustak, is seven kilometres down the mountain. Villagers scramble up the steep slope. They have never seen foreigners and are poor beyond describing. They form a line to help the journalists carry their heavy silver boxes of TV gear, and climb down the

mountain in a strange procession – the journalists, the barefoot villagers, the soldiers. Everybody is carrying something:
gear, backpacks and, of course, the corpse. The dead Northern
Alliance soldier is being borne down the mountain by his
comrades and a boy from Rustak.

When they reach the village, the grateful journalists then
hire a jeep and drive back to Khoja Bahauddin.

This salutary tale reinforces that the best way to get in and
out of here now is by road. The route requires driving to the
Tajik border, which is actually at the Pyang River, and then
crossing the river by barge. It's recommended you do this stage
of the journey at night, because Taliban snipers are sitting in
the mountain opposite, and have attacked a convoy here.

Once you've crossed safely, it's a six-hour drive back to
Dushanbe. Since there is nothing on the Tajik side of the river
except reeds, you have to co-ordinate a car to drive down from
Dushanbe to meet you there.

This requires a good deal of planning, not to mention bribing of border guards along the way, but luckily for me the BBC
has a correspondent coming in the next day. He is due to ring
in and if he does they may be able to hold his driver, and get
him to wait for me on the other side of the river.

I'm leaving more suddenly than I thought. As soon as
I adjust to the idea, I find that I am thrilled.

The BBC's safety officer picks me up, and I feel very grand
because we are in the Beeb's armoured car, which last did
service in Kosovo. We drive back along the familiar bumpy
road to the river, for the border is just down from the front
line that we know so well. It's dark when we reach the river
crossing. There is a small mud-brick building, where three
turbaned men sit on mats on the floor. This dark room, lit by
a lantern, is the Afghan border post. The small flame casts
long shadows on the wall and on their guns, as one of the men
notes on a piece of paper that I am departing Afghanistan.
'Passport number? Father's name?'

They make a notation in pen in my passport as well. They
have no stamp.

I greet the incoming BBC correspondent and settle down
to wait for the barge. I look over the dark stretch of water that
the Persians called the mighty Oxus when they ruled this

region hundreds of years ago. It is reduced in size by drought and time and decades of Soviet water diversion schemes, which are draining the river and the seas it feeds, the fallout of a disastrous experiment with growing cotton in the desert.

My favourite book on travel in Central Asia is written by Fitzroy MacLean. He was a British MP and one of the founders of the SAS, but is most famous for being the model for James Bond. MacLean was in Moscow in the 1930s as a diplomat, and wrote about his travels in Stalin's Russia, as well as his adventures and flirtations during World War II, in a wonderfully entertaining book called *Eastern Approaches*. It's urbane, flamboyant and moving, leaving you shaken *and* stirred.

Fitzroy MacLean crossed by river from Russia into Afghanistan, the same trip I am about to do. Despite the passage of seventy years and the demise of Communism, the experience has changed very little.

Now there is only one barge. In the 1930s when MacLean travelled, there were three paddle boats, but two were out of action and the third was undergoing a complete overhaul. Though it had a grand name – the *Seventeenth Party Congress* – MacLean notes acerbically that 'to judge by her antiquated appearance, she must have been built long before the Communist Party was ever thought of'. The *Seventeenth Party Congress* was also 'handicapped by the absence of an engine motor of any kind. Eventually it was decided to take the motor out of one of the first two and transfer it to the third. It turned out to be an ordinary unadapted tractor motor from the Stalin factory.'

Once the work was done, Fitzroy MacLean boarded the boat. 'The Red Flag was hoisted. The crew of seven counted and recounted in case any should try to escape. The tractor engine (an anxious moment) started up. And we set out on our somewhat unsteady course across the Oxus.'

When I first read *Eastern Approaches*, by my favourite dashing hero, I didn't imagine I would one day be standing at the same river, doing the same trip, only in an even more basic vessel.

The *Seventeenth Party Congress* was a boat with a frame and a roof. Our barge is just a pontoon, with no protection from the elements. Our barge is also powered by a tractor motor – surely it couldn't still be the same one, handed on

150

from vessel to vessel, down the years? I put this thought out of my mind as I throw my bags on. The barge hasn't got a crew of seven, but it does have a captain, a kindly man in a military uniform, who speaks Russian.

I stand and listen to the barge putt-putting through the calm, dark water. The sound hums through my feet. Taliban gunmen are in the mountains overlooking us, but I feel a great sense of peace and accomplishment. I am leaving Afghanistan.

I remember that I have some Afghan currency with me, which I meant to leave behind for a friend. On impulse, I offer it to the barge captain instead. It will be of absolutely no use anywhere else in the world. In fact, it can't even be used in southern Afghanistan, since it's 'up-money', only valid here in the north. But the captain refuses. 'It will be bad for Afghanistan. Then you will write that we take money and enrich ourselves,' he says sternly in Russian. I blush in the dark. Oh God, I've struck one of the only honest men in Afghanistan – and I wasn't even trying to bribe him.

I hear some desultory gunshots in the hills, but nothing disrupts our slow glide through the water. We bump into the bank. Tajikistan. I heave my bag over one shoulder, grab my laptop, bid farewell to the captain and walk off the barge.

I climb up the sandy riverbank and stand in the pitch darkness looking for a man I've never met who is going to take me to Dushanbe. No one appears, and I keep walking, suddenly nervous.

Then a figure rounds a bend in the path, takes all my gear in that insistent Russian 'You are a woman, you cannot carry a bag' way, and introduces himself.

'Hello. My name is Anton. You are Irris,' he says carefully in heavily accented English.

When I reply in Russian he is so relieved that he does not have to struggle in English I can almost hear him smile in the dark. He introduces me to Sasha, a Russian soldier, not that I can really see either of them. Anton says that if I am not in a hurry, after we clear the Tajik border post, rather than driving all the way to Dushanbe tonight, we should drive for two hours to a Russian army base where we can spend the night. 'We can then complete our journey more safely and comfortably in daylight tomorrow.'

151

This sounds like an excellent plan and we drive up along a sandy path to the border post, which is surrounded by barbed wire and watchtowers, as befits the furthest outpost of the former Soviet Union. It is manned by Russian soldiers, making it feel very much as if it still is the Soviet Union, although Tajikistan became independent ten years ago. The soldiers are a regiment from Vorkuta, the northernmost settlement in Russia, within the Arctic Circle. It is dark there for eight months of the year. What a contrast this hot, dry desert must be.

The border guard is sitting in a small room with velour curtains and a camp bed in the corner. He is wearing military pants and T-shirt, and the ubiquitous Russian slippers, *tapochki*. Anton is also from Vorkuta, which is why he is a perfect person to smooth us through customs here – and why the BBC chose him for the job. The BBC are so organised that the whole thing, bribes and all, works like clockwork, and we are in and out in a matter of minutes.

I smile in wonder as we clear the border post and drive along a paved road. Both seem like miracles.

Anton tells me about Vorkuta. It is a bleak name, full of blood and fear – like saying you come from the Nazi death camps of Auschwitz or Treblinka. Vorkuta was one of the most terrible outposts of the Gulag, the Soviet labour camps. It is in a position so far north in the Arctic that in fact it is not really habitable. No town could have been founded there without the use of slaves whose lives were expendable. From its inception in the 1930s, freezing inmates worked without proper food or clothing to build the camp, and slave labourers were sent there until the 1950s because Vorkuta sits above a huge seam of coal.

The camps and the mines consumed and extinguished hundreds of thousands of lives. The first of the death camps was set up in 1943, and within a year more than one-third of the thirty prisons were death camps. Their purpose was to kill their inmates, but the Communists didn't need crematoria, they just used the climate. When the temperature plunged to minus forty and blizzards howled, prisoners were kept in lightly boarded tents. The only flooring was sawdust

152

sprinkled onto permafrost. The prisoners hauled coal for twelve hours a day, and within three weeks they were broken.

Anton's grandfather was sent to Vorkuta after World War II for some misdemeanour invented by Communist bureaucrats, and froze to death. He says his mother is now used to the bleak, dark cold and couldn't live anywhere else. 'Now already in October it is minus thirty-five degrees and dark all the time.'

Anton invites me to Vorkuta, and says he will put me up if I want to do a story there after this war is over. The best way to reach Vorkuta is by train, a three-day journey, but more reliable than going by plane, especially in winter. You can wait at Siberian airports for days for planes that are cancelled and never come.

'It is an interesting place, you know, the cultural life is quite strong because all the people were dissidents and intellectuals,' he says.

As we drive into a Russian army barracks in Tajikistan, I wonder whether I could brave somewhere as cold and bleak as Vorkuta. To tell the truth, in my Australian way I'm more frightened of winter in the Arctic than of war in Afghanistan. Just the thought of Vorkuta makes these barracks seem inviting, though the toilets here are not much better than in Khoja Bahauddin. I unfurl my Northern Alliance sleeping bag onto a sofa, a vast improvement to the floor I'm used to sleeping on, and fall asleep exhausted.

In the morning, after breakfasting on packaged chocolate cakes that Anton has thoughtfully brought, we leave our soldier with his comrades and continue our drive to Dushanbe. I marvel at what a difference a border makes. Just fifty kilometres out of Afghanistan, in the poorest country in Central Asia, there are paved roads, cars and shops.

The drive is also one of the most beautiful I have ever done in my life. The gaunt brown mountains on this side of the Hindu Kush are stunning, and halfway along the drive, as we climb higher, they snake around a clear aquamarine lake, red-brown rocks marching down to meet the turquoise water. This beauty spot is man-made, flooded as part of a Soviet hydro-electricity project. It is breathtaking, as if the red rocks and rugged scenery of central Australia were set by a calm turquoise sea.

We stop at a *chaikhana*, a traditional teahouse, by the side of the road. It has three open-air 'rooms' with a roof but no walls and a raised platform where you sit cross-legged to eat. First, you wash your hands at a faucet in a pipe near the road, which has a small towel hanging nearby for you to dry your hands. After Afghanistan, this small gesture towards public service seems so civilised and so touching. The restaurant owner comes out smiling, with two fish from the nearby stream flip-flopping in his hands. I instinctively reach out to catch them. 'Yes, we will have those,' says Anton, and they are thrown onto a pan on a blackened grill, and cooked there by the side of the road. When the man reappears with two little live quails, we decline. There is too much food already – a salad of fresh vegetables, dense sour pomegranate juice and rounds of freshly baked chewy white naan bread.

Across the road from the *chaikhana* is a tiny, perfect mosque, with exquisite silver detail on its roof. It is the height of an ordinary house and the width of a very small room. I've never seen such a small doll's house of a mosque, and the café owner explains it's for prayers 'to go'. It's for travellers who want to stop to pray and quickly resume their journey. Hearing us ask questions, a diner at another table realises that we are visitors and comes to introduce himself and invite us to his home. The hospitality here is spontaneous and warm.

I delight in the food, savouring the fresh ingredients. The sun is shining. My hair is uncovered and I feel free, of dust, shit, and tension. Anton is reading a dog-eared book of Persian poetry. 'It's good to read these poems in the lands where they were written,' he explains earnestly.

We drive on to Dushanbe, and an unexpectedly joyful reunion with the *dezhurnaya* at the Hotel Tajikistan who had seemed so stern when I first visited.

'You are back safely, thank God, *dai bog*, we have been worried about you.'

Her close attention to my life started out as the coldly professional interest of the spy, but it is warming into something more personal and genuine.

'You have been in Afghanistan? What was it like? For the women, yes the poor women . . . and no water? And no sewerage? Vay, vay, vay. but I am so happy to see you safe, thank God, thank God.'

I am overwhelmed by her concern and the luxury of a bed and a working toilet. Did I ever think of this hotel as basic? It seems very grand now.

The Hotel Tajikistan has never had it so good. The joint is packed, and the revelling in the bars is feverish, almost demented. Journalists coming out are delirious with happiness to have escaped, and desperate for all they were deprived of in Afghanistan. The bars and the hookers do a roaring trade. Journalists going back to Khoja Bahauddin know exactly what they are facing, and party as if they are on the *Titanic*. The bars and the hookers do a roaring trade with them, too. I've never known an atmosphere like it.

There is also a new selection of service industries springing up, including 'airlines' run by companies that usually provide mercenaries and 'logistical support' to both sides in war zones – *coups our specialty*. They are run by ex-SAS soldiers, and have innocuous names like Executive Outcomes and Global Solutions. Some are in Tajikistan, branching out from their usual tinpot dictator clientele, to try to profit from the huge captive market of journalists wanting to get into Afghanistan. One is run by an Englishman who has come with his own helicopter, and is charging US$4000 per person for the thirty-minute flight to Khoja Bahauddin. He has plenty of takers, even at this inflated price, but as days pass without his helicopter moving, he's growing more and more desperate. He is one of those wonderful people who become funnier and funnier as the situation grows more and more dire. He tells bleak, hilarious stories about the frustration of dealing with Tajik bureaucracy.

'This is nothing – you want to know real misery. Real misery is being twenty-one years old, standing at attention in the freezing cold, with your huge fat sergeant in front of you, his mouth three inches from your nose, his spit hitting you as he bawls "It's only going to get worse. And if you want sympathy, son, you'll find it in the dictionary – between shit and syphilis." '

Despite his buoyant attitude, his helicopter never reaches Afghanistan.

I want to leave Dushanbe – and not on his chopper. I go to the airport and buy a Tajik Air ticket to Moscow for the following day. I pay only a small bribe of US$30 to a uniformed man for this 'express service'.

I'm going home.

Chapter 11

AFGHANISTAN, 25 OCTOBER 2001

In the blink of an eye, which is really about a week, I am back. Back at the Hotel Tajikistan, back at the Tajik border post – 'I remember you,' one of the border guards says in Russian, smiling as he stamps me through – and back at the Pyang River. I stand on the riverbank in the early afternoon, looking across the calm, grey water. Greeting the captain loading my gear onto the barge, I'm preparing to cross this physical border and a border within myself, to go back into Afghanistan, and back in time once more.

While it is literally true that if I stayed in Moscow there would be nothing to file on as no broadcaster is taking any other 'foreign' stories, that isn't why I'm here. I'm here because I want to cover the biggest breaking story in the world, the one at the top of every news bulletin. Nevertheless, I have to steel myself to re-experience the reality of Khoja Bahauddin. On a practical level, I think I've kitted myself out better, but it seems that I still haven't brought enough money or deodorant or tampons or face cream, because this time I end up staying for weeks and weeks.

I return to Afghanistan in late October, just as the US starts a massive air assault in the north, at the front line further down this river, bombing Taliban positions in the mountains above Qala Qata. It also turns out to be the worst week of the war for the US, and it is interesting to watch from here, where the war is actually being conducted, how Washington handles the crisis in other international and domestic arenas, far from the squalor of Afghanistan.

Pressure is growing to end the bombing campaign, now more than three weeks old, with questions being asked about its efficacy, since the huge and sustained use of US airpower seems to be yielding disappointingly little in terms of results on the ground. In Europe, particularly, this has attracted strong criticism, and the White House is nervous about attacks in the American media.

In addition there are high-profile blunders. For the second time in ten days, American warplanes hit a Red Cross warehouse in Kabul. Two 2000-pound guided weapons are dropped on the warehouse on the night of 25 October, and a B-52 bomber delivers three more 2000-pound smart bombs the next morning. In the earlier strike ten days ago, a building was flattened and a guard injured. This time desperately needed relief goods such as food, tents and blankets are destroyed. They were earmarked for the city's disabled. The Red Cross says that the warehouse – now in flames – had its emblem on the roof, clearly distinguishable from the air. It calls the attacks 'a violation of international humanitarian law'.

A third bomb misses the warehouse but hits a residential area of Kabul 250 metres to the south. Washington apologises. The Pentagon also admits it expected a speedier victory. In late October, Rear Admiral John Stuffelbeem acknowledges that the Taliban are proving to be tough warriors, and that he is a bit surprised at how doggedly they are holding on to power.

The bombing wakes me up.

It's my first morning back in Khoja Bahauddin, and I am once again sleeping on the floor, in a room with snoring strangers. At 6 a.m. a heavy rumble shakes the ground, like the beginning of an earthquake. It seems to be coming from far underneath me, and the windows in the house start to rattle. It's repeated – boom, boom, boom – thirty minutes later. I lie there trying to imagine what those huge bombs must feel like in the mountains at Qala Qata if they shake the earth here twelve kilometres away.

I reach for my short-wave radio. Within an hour the BBC is reporting massive bombing here. It was the right decision to return.

Today we must go to the front line. I team up with two other journalists for the jolting drive on the familiar path to the hill at Ai Khanoum. We pass through the checkpoint and drive up the hill, scanning the sky. It's a cloudy grey, and cool, as if rain threatens. We dismiss this possibility, as it hasn't rained in three years.

As we clamber over the top of the escarpment, a B-52 loops ponderously overhead, dropping bombs on the Taliban positions. They fall in a series, causing the mountain opposite to kick up its guts, in spectacular coloured clouds. It ends with one huge ear-splitting, ground-shaking blast.

The mountains look as if they are exploding, and from a distance, this destruction has a macabre beauty. But it is the sound which is overwhelming, cracking and rolling like thunder, and reverberating in the ground beneath our feet, all the way over on this mountain. This is sound you feel as well as hear.

Four Afghan men squat on the ridge watching the bombing, one wearing the shiny black patent-leather shoes which are the strangest part of the male winter wardrobe here. They are like slippers, and the men explain they are easy to clean mud off, not that there's much need for that now, with such a severe drought.

It's as if we are at a fireworks display. Plumes from the last bomb hang in the sky and then disperse. The next set of bombers loops lazily in. 'B Pinjao Du, B Pinjao Du,' the men point at the sky, shouting 'B-52' in Dari.

Ai Khanoum hill, where we are standing, falls within the margin of error for the US bombs, but with the carnival-like atmosphere I never feel seriously worried. A plump grey-haired man is sitting on a ridge behind me with a walkie-talkie clutched to his turban, listening to Taliban radio traffic. General Aziz says the Taliban are panicking, they are shouting that a man has died. 'They are calling for an ambulance. Most of the talking is in Arabic. They are saying that three positions have been destroyed and nine men have died.'

It does not seem like a very large return for such a huge investment of airpower. As we drive down the hill to go home and file, I remember the comment attributed to President Bush at the beginning of the war – what's the point of using a two million dollar missile to destroy a ten dollar tent?

And, what's more, the Northern Alliance isn't even grateful.

Deputy Defence Minister General Bariolai says that the US selected the targets for the bombings at Qala Qata without consulting them. He tells reporters that he is happy with one lot of 'extremely precise' bombing this week, which killed at least forty foreign Taliban fighters, but generally he is not satisfied with the intensity of the US air campaign.

'Even at Qala Qata, the ten bombs they dropped today are not enough,' Bariolai says, on a tour of his positions on Ai Khanoum hill. 'The mountain at Qala Qata is big and the Americans have hit two bunkers, but they have much more work to do. I understand that for American people, bombing some hill in Afghanistan might not seem as important as bombing Kandahar airport. But there is nothing left of Kandahar airport, while Taliban fighters have retreated to front lines like these. This is where you can really hurt the Taliban, and al-Qaeda.'

The Northern Alliance says it has information that key figures in the al-Qaeda network have retreated here to Qala Qata, including Juma Namangani, an Uzbek fundamentalist leader and one of Osama bin Laden's deputies.

General Bariolai's comments reflect the divergence of strategy between the Northern Alliance and the US over the focus of the ground war. The Northern Alliance wants to start any action here in the north, securing the power base from which they traditionally launch their attacks on Kabul. The US wants to destroy the Taliban strongholds in the south first.

General Bariolai is defensive when reporters ask about growing disappointment in the US over the lack of military action by Northern Alliance troops. He says the situation on the ground in northern Afghanistan is complex. 'We have several isolated enclaves, and supplying them with enough ammunition to start a major offensive is very difficult. But we will start the ground offensive before the winter sets in, and I hope by that time we will have more understanding with the Americans.'

The next day I am walking in the square when two men come up and ask me if I need a translator. This is quite a common experience here, as Afghans with even a smattering of English descend on Khoja Bahauddin from all over the country, lured by the possibility of earning US$100 a day working as translators for journalists. For the few Afghans lucky enough to be in work, that's more than a year's salary. In a week they can earn more money than they would see in five years.

Men with desperate eyes clutch crumpled pieces of paper saying they studied journalism in Kabul in the 1990s. They ask, 'Do you too much need help, gracious madam?' One journalist swears he was asked whether he needed a transformer.

But these two men are different. Older, edgier. They are brothers, both doctors, and they have just spent more than a week on the gruelling journey from Kabul, walking and catching lifts with any car that would stop, climbing up through the mountains to reach Khoja Bahauddin. They show me their hospital ID and ask me not to repeat their names as it could endanger them or the families they have left behind. Although they are opponents of the Taliban, they are Pashtun and they don't feel safe here in the north, in the Tajik heartland.

The brothers left Kabul the day after an American bombing raid killed four security staff at a mine-clearing agency funded by the UN. One of the men who died was a close friend of the younger doctor, Momar.

'I told him not to go to work that night, but he insisted that he had to, he was always so conscientious. When they found him his head had been severed, and his legs. There was nothing left but his trunk.'

Momar appears traumatised by his friend's death, but says this is not why he left Kabul. 'No, I left because I am afraid there will be punishments, reprisals against Pashtuns who stay.' He wants to leave Afghanistan and migrate to Europe, where he can work to support his extended family waiting back at home.

'Yes, the Taliban are evil, holding all Afghanistan to ransom for one Osama. Why is one man more important than all of us?'

But he can see no future for this country. After twenty-two years of war he is not confident this latest episode will stop the fighting or improve the situation generally. He wants to earn money and to lead a normal life.

Both men are likeable, responsible professionals. The older brother appears more jovial and less dejected, but he says Kabul is a frightened city. The American air strikes are terrifying. Every Friday the service at the mosque ends with the imam saying, 'Remember, we may not survive the week and we may not meet again.'

I walk with them across the square, but they do not want to do a formal interview.

'In fact, maybe it is better if you stop walking with us now – if it is known at the guesthouse that we have been talking to journalists, it could go badly for us.'

Perhaps they will have to rethink being translators then, I tell them sadly. I wish them luck for their long journey, filled with the prospect of so many impediments and so much heartache, as they attempt to go first to Dushanbe, then to Moscow and then to Europe, where – if they ever arrive safely – their qualifications will not be recognised and they will most likely be despised as cheating, lazy, dishonest asylum seekers.

We return to the front line, to see how the heavy US bombing affects the troops. We cross the Kokcha River on horseback, an easy ride today as the river is sluggish. As we ride into the first village we hear gunfire close by.

On the top of the Puze Polihomri hill, at the Northern Alliance forward position, there are about a dozen soldiers. They say they are too close to the American bombs, but otherwise morale is high. They tell us US soldiers were on this hill two days ago.

Canadian journalist Levon Sevunts spends many days on this front line. He is an Armenian who has emigrated to Canada, where he files for the *Montreal Gazette*. We met queuing for visas at the Tajik Foreign Ministry in Dushanbe, and I liked him instantly. I rate his work very highly, not least because he files in English, his *fourth* language, after Armenian, Russian, and French, but also because he was a soldier in the Soviet army, and brings a conscript's eye and understanding to his coverage. He is also clear-headed and brave, prepared to stay overnight in the Northern Alliance's forward trenches during the US bombings. This takes courage since the front lines here are only hundreds of metres apart.

His day with the soldiers starts at 4.30 a.m. The men get up in the dark to pray, and then have breakfast – several cups of tea with brown bread. After eating, it's time to fight. They do this, says Levon, 'while the sun is behind their backs and blinding the Taliban gunners. After a short firefight, everybody waits for the US air strikes. The Taliban hunker down and stop responding to sporadic machine-gun fire. After each bombing run, Taliban soldiers fire a couple of rounds from their heavy machine guns, to let the Alliance soldiers know they are still there. The soldiers spend the rest of the day waiting for the orders for the offensive, killing time and trying not to get killed . . . They play cards and *gorodki*, a game taught to them by a Russian TV crew, using machine gun casings as their targets instead of cylindrical sticks.'

War. Still ninety per cent boredom and ten per cent panic.

The only other entertainment for the soldiers is watching a firefight in the valley below. There are two houses with a field between them. One house is controlled by the Taliban, the other by the Northern Alliance. These positions are 300 metres apart. Levon Sevunts reports that 'Soldiers cheer every time the shots come from the Alliance side and curse when the Taliban house responds. The houses belonged to one family before the war, they say.' He adds dryly: 'There is not much talk about the future: why bother worrying about something that might not happen?'

At this time the US suffers another blow, with the capture and execution of Pashtun leader Abdul Haq. The portly, balding forty-three-year-old was one of the most famous Afghan commanders during the war against the Soviets, when he was injured many times and lost a leg in a famous gun battle. Part of his legend was that he was the Indestructible Abdul Haq. He survived – he always survived, until now.

He was a fierce opponent of the Taliban and an influential figure in the huge community of Afghan exiles. He'd lived in Dubai for the past decade, running a successful business.

Following the September 11 attacks, he volunteered to return to Afghanistan, to rally anti-Taliban opposition among the Pashtuns, and in many ways, for the CIA, Haq seemed an ideal candidate.

He was a Pashtun, like the bulk of the Taliban's supporters, and he was acting as emissary of exiled King Mohammed Zaher Shah. Despite his record as a hero of the war against the Russians, Haq was not tainted by the post-Soviet bloodbath inside Afghanistan since he did not take part in the Islamic civil war of the early 1990s. He had also paid a huge personal price for his opposition to the Taliban. In January 1999 his wife and eleven-year-old son were assassinated, and the Taliban were the chief suspects.

Most importantly, the US administration knew him of old. He had dealings with the CIA and the Pakistani intelligence service, the ISI, during the anti-Soviet jihad, and in the mid-1980s had met with Margaret Thatcher and Ronald Reagan, when the CIA had dubbed him 'Hollywood Haq'. The extent of CIA involvement in his mission is still unclear. There are some accounts that he went into Afghanistan with CIA blessing and assistance. It is known he made a request to Washington, via intermediaries influential in President Reagan's time, to delay US air strikes until he had a chance to return to Afghanistan. This was turned down. There are reports that Haq requested substantial help from the CIA, including the provision of arms, but that the CIA turned this down also. According to this version of events, all that the CIA offered Haq was the one item he had in abundance – satellite phones. Suspicious that the CIA wanted to track his movements, Haq turned them down.

Looking at the sad sequence of events, it seems that Haq's was one of the missions that the CIA knew about, but had not co-ordinated and planned well enough – particularly in case of the need for rescue.

On Tuesday 23 October, Haq crossed into Afghanistan from Peshawar in Pakistan with nineteen men. The group was only lightly armed.

Within thirty-six hours, having penetrated less than twenty kilometres into Afghanistan, they were ambushed in a mountain gorge. Abdul Haq was trapped by an enemy employing

Pavel Zelensky

Helicopters were the only way in and out when we first arrived in Afghanistan before the road was opened. But although the ageing, ill-maintained Russian military choppers were a dangerous option, locals and journalists waited for them anxiously.

Jonathan Mossek

The severe drought meant that there was not much fresh produce. This man has laid his walnuts out on a tarpaulin on the ground in the square at Khoja Bahauddin.

Above: 'It's like travelling with Madonna!' When I went to the markets, 100 men followed me from one stall to the next. One of my exasperated male colleagues snapped these five photos of the men who turned out to watch me buy apples.

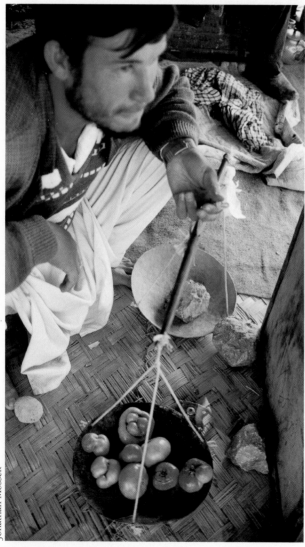

Jonathan Mossek

'One rock – or two?' The veggie man weighs out his tomatoes in rocks.

Left: Market day at Khoja Bahauddin. You could buy glorious fabrics – but women were forbidden to shop, by order of the local commander. Instead they had to rely on men to choose their clothes and fabrics for them.

Muslim girls in Afghanistan can show their faces until they are fourteen . . . After that they have to cover up and wear the burqa, a tent with a small mesh screen at eye level, allowing limited vision and breathing. Women's faces were never seen in Khoja Bahauddin – and they were often alone like this woman.

Jonathan Mossek

This woman is begging at the car window – a common experience as poverty escalated during the drought and two decades of war.

Pavel Zelensky

Another woman lies in the road, begging. She hopes people will throw money from passing cars.

Pavel Zelensky

Jonathan Mossek

Children in Afghanistan grow up quickly – they seem to have the faces of adults, and young children frequently have to look after babies.

This boy is selling sweets and matches. Other children supported their families by selling plastic bags to shoppers in the markets.

This boy lost a leg stepping on a mine.

Many illnesses that are treatable in the West, like trachoma, lead to children losing their eyes in Afghanistan.

Despite the harshness of their lives, these children in Taloqan appear happy. They have never had any toys other than a hoop to play with.

Jonathan Mossek

These two men are moneychangers – counting their cash before the dust storm hits and stops business for the day.

Above: The yellow air is the signal to these girls that they have to run back to the refugee camp, where their only refuge from the savage storm will be canvas tents.

Left: The Northern Alliance's charismatic military leader Ahmed Shah Massoud was assassinated by al-Qaeda in Khoja Bahauddin, two days before the September 11 attacks in New York.

Below: An Afghan prays on the roof of the house where Massoud was assassinated. I lived in this house for almost a month.

NBC cameraman Tom Streithorst behind Taliban front lines on the first day after Taloqan fell. Taliban soldiers had fled so recently their discarded tea leaves were still wet.

Me and Shah Mahmood, driver extraordinaire and the funniest man in northern Afghanistan.

NBC sound recordist Jonathan Mossek at one of the refugee camps ringing Khoja Bahauddin, which housed some 30,000 Tajik refugees from the Taliban.

Irris Makler

After we receive the first reports that Taloqan has fallen and the Taliban have retreated, refugees load their goods onto horses and camels, ford rivers and travel down mined roads to return home.

Horses, still one of the most common forms of transport, share the river with tanks.

Interviewing Northern Alliance soldiers after they have defeated the Taliban and liberated the nearby town of Taloqan.

Unexploded US bombs lying on a path in northern Afghanistan. This is a common feature in much of the country, where roads are also heavily mined.

Another common sight – tanks have become almost part of the scenic beauty of Afghanistan.

NBC reporter Jim Maceda and computer engineer Jim Bruton. Five minutes after this happy snap was taken near the summit of one of the highest mountain ranges in the world, our jeep lost its brakes and clutch, and overturned.

Waiting – so much a feature of life in Central Asia. We tell a local that in the West time is precious, like gold. 'Here time is like stone,' he replies.

Kabul – a city destroyed. This was not the result of US or Russian bombing. Afghans did this to themselves, during the Muslim civil wars from 1992 to 1996. People live in the ruins.

Jonathan Mossek

Pavel Zelensky

The NBC house in Kabul's upmarket diplomatic section came with a little something extra – an unexploded 500-pound US bomb in our kitchen.

Pavel Zelensky

Kabul's absurdly overdressed traffic police – when I was in Kabul they stood at empty crossings.

On the helicopter out – we finally made it – flying over the Hindu Kush to Tajikistan with the Russian emergency services.

the same tactics he had used in that very region when he had fought the Soviets ten years earlier.

Taliban soldiers blocked both ends of the Alikhel gorge. Though Haq and his men fought fiercely for twelve hours, they were no match for the well-armed Taliban troops. As the situation grew more desperate, Haq called his office in Peshawar by satellite phone, asking them to contact Washington. Haq's office sent word to an old CIA contact from the days when he was America's freedom-loving ally.

According to British journalist Jason Burke, the CIA's response was not encouraging. It said that it could track Haq's position from his satellite phone, but that it could not help as the terrain was too rough for it to land any rescue aircraft. The CIA received reports on the progress of the battle and an unmanned American plane attacked just after midnight.

It was too late. An hour earlier, Haq's aide had made his last call. Haq's office in Peshawar told Jason Burke that they heard sobbing and screaming and the crackle of automatic gunfire – and then the line went dead.

Taliban spokesman Mohammed Tayyab Agha said Haq was captured as he tried to flee from his hiding place on horseback. He was taken to the capital and interrogated. Then, in accordance with a fatwa issued by Mullah Omar and the Taliban's council of clerics in September, he was hanged as a traitor, a 'spy for the US and Britain'.

At 1 p.m. on Friday, less than seventy-two hours after entering Afghanistan, Abdul Haq was swinging from a makeshift gallows. Nine of the men who accompanied him were also dead.

Some Northern Alliance officials suggest to me that Haq's death is due to a failure of intelligence, that after a decade in exile in Dubai running a successful business, he had lost touch with the rough realities on the ground here. Others argue that such a speedy, desperate end could only be the result of betrayal, a sting operation organised by the agents of Pakistan's intelligence service, the favoured hand behind every conspiracy here.

The official US response is muted, expressing regret over Haq's death and the failure of his mission. Senior US government officials mention Haq only when asked, and then dispassionately. 'Clearly he was, among other Afghans, a person who opposed the Taliban,' says Defense Secretary Donald Rumsfeld. 'And it's certainly regrettable that he was killed.'

The administration moves to distance itself from this failed military action. In CIA briefings, old assessments are dredged up in which Haq was described as 'unruly and immature'. The CIA is also quoted as saying that he moved too quickly. It is left to right-wing columnists in the US to rail against the 'bungled CIA operation' and the betrayal of freedom-loving allies.

These events come at the end of a bad week for the US. One American journalist says to me pensively, 'Why do I feel that despite all our airpower, so far the Taliban is winning?'

The most active front in this war remains Mazar-i-Sharif, a major city of 250,000 people 250 kilometres to our west.

The city, famous for its white doves, is named for an important Muslim shrine, the grave of Ali, son-in-law of the Prophet Mohammed, and is especially holy to Shia Muslims. Historically it prided itself on being an enlightened cosmopolitan city, and for fifteen years it avoided the worst of the war. While Kabul was being destroyed, life went on as usual in Mazar-i-Sharif. Women were studying in Mazar when all the universities in Kabul had been shut down. A wide variety of people lived in Mazar, even before it welcomed refugees fleeing the Taliban, such as actors and singers from Kabul who could no longer perform there after the Taliban captured the capital.

All this changed in 1997, when the Taliban captured Mazar as well. Thousands died in some of the bloodiest massacres of the Afghan war. There was a spate of terrible revenge killings as the Taliban took the city, lost it and took it again.

Now fighting continues in Mazar, with reports that Northern Alliance troops led by General Rashid Dostum have captured villages on the road to the city. Then the Taliban claims its forces have recaptured them.

We can't verify these reports for ourselves because the front remains unreachable. Northern Alliance troops, which have massed to the south of the town, are in a pocket surrounded on three sides by Taliban forces. When the US wants to provide ammunition and supplies to these troops, they drop them in by helicopter. We would have to cross Taliban lines to reach Mazar from here.

Strategically, Mazar has two prizes for the Northern Alliance: a working airport and a road link to Uzbekistan, about sixty-five kilometres to the north, where US and British forces are being deployed. Once they hold this road, the US will be able to supply the Northern Alliance with much-needed military equipment.

As the air strikes continue, reports filter through that Taliban leaders in Mazar are becoming increasingly desperate and punishing citizens to cement their control over the city. They know Mazar is not their heartland. As a warning to its people, the Taliban hold a public hanging at Hazrat Ali, the famous blue-tiled shrine to the son-in-law of the Prophet. According to three eye-witnesses, in mid-October the Taliban brought five men to the shrine at around the time of evening prayers. Their hands were bound and the Taliban identified them as Northern Alliance military personnel, although it is not clear if they were Northern Alliance or simply unlucky civilians. Taliban officials ran a rope through an arch just west of the shrine, about seven or eight feet off the ground, and then tied the rope around the necks of the men. The officials pulled at the ropes, but this did not provide enough pressure to fully lift the men off the ground. Two of the witnesses say the officials then had to tie the ropes to vehicles on either side of the arch to complete the botched hanging at the holy site.

Nineteen-year-old Ahmed Umid watched the execution from nearby. 'It is difficult to watch five people being hanged in front of you in such a wild way,' he says. 'As the word spread, I can say that almost fifty per cent of people in Mazar did not have dinner that night because they were feeling so sad.'

Ed Artis, Knight of Malta and aid worker superman, is trying to get into Mazar to deliver humanitarian aid, and says he has Northern Alliance support. 'We're considering going out to Tashkent, getting some cold-weather gear and some better communications equipment, and going into Mazar – before it falls. The technique may not be 100 per cent kosher or legal, but our Northern Alliance advisers now trust us, they know we're not in the government business, we're not in the God business, and they'll get us in the safest way possible, whether on foot or by donkey.'

I point out that it is very dangerous to walk across Taliban territory for a week in order to deliver food aid, and there are not many other aid agencies that would do it. The UN pulled all its people out of Afghanistan as soon as the air strikes started.

'We're here to help the people and do whatever it takes. It's always been a rule of mine to hide in plain sight. I got no guarantees of living through the night, let alone surviving a trek through Taliban territory.'

I pursue this point. The Taliban had an ambivalent relationship with aid agencies even before the air strikes, engineering the expulsion of most of them from Kabul in 1999. If they catch an American aid worker crossing their territories now on foot, they would immediately execute him as a spy. And for Ed Artis it is even more dangerous, since we've heard rumours that the Taliban have put a bounty on his head.

He concedes all this, but says, 'If we don't go, if we let the Taliban threaten us, if we let Osama bin Laden threaten us, then they continue to win the war on terrorism. If they want to kill me they can do it here or in the US, we know now their reach is beyond the borders of Afghanistan. They can get me anywhere that I am. If I let them intimidate me into not doing what I believe then I am part of the problem not the solution.'

After that rousing speech, I'd join the CIA, too. I thank him and the agency for the interview. Though I can't help liking him, I'm not sure how much of his story to believe. How much aid could you carry on foot across enemy lines, just for starters? Sir Edward Artis is one of the strange collection of characters you meet in war zones, but if he does succeed in delivering food and tents behind the lines, or even here in Northern Alliance territory, he will be doing some tangible good. Sometimes I get the feeling that this is more than can be said for the rest of us.

Journalists are also working to get into the region near Mazar, angling for a seat on any Northern Alliance helicopter going in to supply Dostum's isolated pocket of fighters. So far, no one has been successful. A German producer promises he can get me a seat on the chopper when he goes in. He is well connected to the Northern Alliance and he has interviewed Dostum before, so maybe he could get a seat for himself and his cameraman. But I can't help thinking what a funny situation we are in when a man offers every female he speaks to a one-way ticket to the spot where the fighting is fiercest – and where there is no exit strategy.

I don't really think the offer will come through, and think of it more as a war-zone pick-up line. But if it did, I don't know whether I'd take it. It would be too dangerous to be surrounded on all sides by Taliban if things went wrong. As an experienced front-line cameraman says to me, 'You've always got to know two things: how you're getting in and how you're getting out. If you don't know those, you don't go.'

In the meantime we make do with speaking to General Dostum via satellite phone. He remains feisty. 'We need more support, especially more weapons, and then we will fight on the ground for the United States. We will succeed in defeating the Taliban.'

Dostum says he is progressing and makes one concession that we don't hear from the Northern Alliance here. He says American Special Forces soldiers are working with his men in a training capacity. The Northern Alliance denies they are on the ground in Khoja Bahauddin. But we know the Special Forces are here, and there is competition among the journalists to be the first to find and to film or interview them. The CIA arrived first, before the Special Forces – and two days after me, I am pleased to learn. Always good when the journos beat the spooks onto the ground. The first operative to make it also flew in in a Russian military chopper, but unlike us he went straight to the Panjshir Valley. One other difference is that he was carrying a large strapped metal suitcase containing US$3 million. Oh, and he probably had better communications gear with him than I did.

This agent tells American journalist Bob Woodward that he always laughs when he sees a movie where someone carries $1 million in a small attaché case, because it just wouldn't fit. Woodward calls this fifty-nine-year-old CIA man Gary. He has been with the Agency for thirty-two years, working under-cover in Tehran and Islamabad, and as station chief in Kabul in the 1980s. He was weeks from retirement on September 11, but a man with his experience who also spoke two local languages was too useful to let go.

Gary sticks around for one more Central Asian adventure, codename Operation Jawbreaker. His task is to persuade the Northern Alliance to work with the US, including receiving US forces. His method is simple: dole out the dosh. He's done it before, during the late 1990s, taking cash into Afghanistan in lots of US$200,000 for distribution to anti-Taliban fighters.

But this time he's armed with serious money. Gary's first meeting in the Panjshir is with Muhammed Arif Sawari, who heads the Northern Alliance's intelligence and security service. Gary places a bundle of cash on the table: US$500,000 in stacks of $100 bills. He tells Woodward he believed it would be 'more impressive than the usual $200,000, the best way to say: We're here, we're serious, here's money, we know you need it.'

Gary tells Arif they want the Northern Alliance to spend the money on food, weapons and intelligence operations. Washington wants a partner on the ground, and it is also planning to send in small units of its own Special Forces soldiers to help the local fighters. Arif tells Gary that the Northern Alliance welcomes him.

The next day, 27 September, Gary meets with General Mohammed Fahim, the Northern Alliance military commander, and Dr Abdullah, the Foreign Minister, in the Panjshir Valley. For two men, double the money. He puts $1 million on the table, explaining it's theirs to use as they see fit.

General Fahim welcomes the United States.

There are lots of ways to win a war.

The bombings at Qala Qata continue, and we continue to go to watch. After one colossal bombardment, we learn that the US is dropping bombs five times as large, known as Daisy Cutters, in the east of the country where Osama bin Laden is rumoured to be hiding. The Daisy Cutter – named because of the circular pattern of destruction it leaves – is the most powerful non-nuclear weapon in the US arsenal. While most conventional bombs weigh 500 to 2000 pounds, the Daisy Cutter is a 15,000-pound automobile-sized bomb, so large that it has to be dropped from a cargo plane and floated down by parachute. It is designed to explode a metre above the ground and to incinerate anything within 600 metres.

I try to imagine what the impact of those Daisy Cutter bombs must be as we drive back from the front line to Mamur Hassan's to see what information he has. The General is busy, but quickly says that according to his sources, nine positions out of 300 have been destroyed, and around sixty Taliban soldiers killed. Like General Bariolai, he is critical of the US bombing campaign, and says the Northern Alliance is waiting for greater results before it commences any military action on the ground. He also says he is still waiting for the weapons and equipment that have been promised by Russia.

Washington and the Islamic warriors remain uncomfortable bedfellows. Despite the cash handouts, the unholy alliance does not appear to be becoming any easier with time.

Chapter 12

Many locals remember me and seem happy that I have come back. An informal taxi service develops. I enjoy walking around Khoja Bahauddin, as it is the only exercise I get, but every so often cars will drive past me and screech to a halt. The driver will stick his head out the window and say 'EBU? BBC?' They are always enormously pleased when I accompany them on the five-minute drive to the European Broadcasting Union, repeating happily the only words we have in common, 'EBU' and 'BBC'. And because it smacks of normality, of a more easy exchange between men and women, I like it, too.

I find a new house to live in, the only two-storey building in Khoja Bahauddin, which really only means that it's a building with basement rooms as well. It's located around the corner from EBU, making it easier for me to get home after I file late at night. The time difference with Australia means I am always one of EBU's last bookings, doing a 1 a.m. live shot for the next day's breakfast TV for Channel 9. Then I can walk home through the inky Afghan night.

The new house has large rooms and possibly the worst toilet in Khoja Bahauddin – which is saying something. Its fundamental flaw is that it's been poorly dug. Like every outhouse here, it has no door, but the slit in the mud is positioned so that the wall does not hide you and you can be seen squatting by anyone walking by. It is also more filthy and rancid smelling than most, and frankly I hate it.

There is also a concrete bathroom which all the inhabitants of the house share – a floor with a drain and a tin drum with water in it. The water is delivered by a sweet grey donkey, which has white flanks and delicate feet. If you pay extra for firewood, the water may be heated on some mornings, and the bare rooms have carpet on the concrete floor. That's the extent of the facilities. It's BYO mattress, lamp, table or chair. And of course, if you want electricity it's BYO generator, too. And BYO candles. Sometimes the strangely sleepy Afghan teenager in charge of the house will boil water for you on a gas ring, but that's it. The Foreign Ministry is charging US$25 per night for a space on the floor here, in a room with four others, a fair whack for sleeping on concrete. Apparently they slug Japanese TV US$250 for the same spot, so I suppose we should count our blessings.

The house does, however, have two lovely Russian photographers who are friendly and helpful, and talk to me in that peculiar mix of Russian and English that is developing into my second language here. We have dinner together, comparing notes about how we spent our day, and they let me use their generator to charge my laptop at night. Some Spanish TV guys move in, and there is a strange collection of fly-by-nights downstairs, including Americans in khaki army gear, dark sunglasses, webbing, the whole box and dice, who call me 'ma'am' and file for the right-wing *Soldier of Fortune* magazine. Rob Schulteis, a fascinating journalist and author, files for both *Soldier of Fortune* and *Mother Jones*, a right-wing jab followed by a left-wing hook that leads me to believe he must be a good writer. He is also an Afghan 'veteran' who has been reporting here since the 1970s. He has written a book, *Night Letters*, about the civil war fought here during the 1990s.

We have vehement arguments about Abdul Haq. He was not naïve or 'soft' after years in Dubai, says Rob. 'These Taliban are a new breed of people, this is not the old Afghanistan, this type of behaviour would not have happened ten years ago.'

I wasn't here then, of course, but this seems to me like an overly romantic view. These warlords were a tough bunch of guys, even then. After all, Haq had been aligned with Hekmatyar, who laid siege to Kabul for three years, raining US-supplied rockets and missiles on the city. Haq's brother was a governor in Nangarhar province who funded his fighters through opium cultivation. There is not one of those Mujaheddin leaders, even the 'sainted' Ahmed Shah Massoud, without blood on his hands.

Rob argues that the Taliban are a quantum leap beyond the Mujaheddin in cruelty and extremism. They starved an entire people, the Hazaras, by blocking the roads to the region around Bamian and refusing to allow UN food convoys through – the first time food was used as a weapon in twenty years of conflict. The Taliban's oppression of women is on a scale never before seen even in the most backward rural sections of Afghanistan – and it is being imposed on all women, including those who led very different lives in the capital.

I am sitting and talking to the blue-eyed, slightly fey Rob Schulteis on the roof of our house. With the sun warm on our backs, we toss this argument back and forth. It is true that the Taliban have brought a new and much more restrictive version of Islam to a country that was traditionally immensely tolerant. Eighty per cent of Afghans belonged to the Sunni Hanifi sect, the most tolerant of the four schools of Islamic teaching. But the Mujaheddin were the start of the change.

Rob says he wants to write about the Taliban and sexual perversion. It is a murky subject for a clear day. The view from this slightly elevated spot is stunning. The mountains that are often obscured by dust or clouds are visible today, and they have a gaunt, bare beauty that suits an Australian eye. Autumn is clearly the best season in Khoja Bahauddin.

Rob pulls out a tin of *naswar*, a mixture of tobacco and spices, which Afghan men hold in their mouths between their lower lips and gums. As he takes some, he says that he was born an expatriate, but that he will probably convert to Islam after this trip. When I ask him why, he says, 'Because I want to belong.'

Following the failure of Abdul Haq's mission, US hopes are pinned on another English-speaking Pashtun politician opposed to the Taliban, Hamed Karzai. Subsequently he becomes known as the leader backed by the former king, the interim Afghan assembly and the West, to try to rebuild a central government, as well as the man whose stylishness turns him into the most surprising fashion icon of the new century. This is reflected in articles with titles such as 'The man who has single-handedly brought capes back into fashion' and 'Hamed Karzai is in da house, yo, yo'.

In early October he's simply another former Mujahed, a potential emissary for King Zaher Shah, entering southern Afghanistan with a group of armed men to try to rally Opposition forces.

In fact, the tall, well-dressed Karzai is Afghan royalty. At forty-three years old he is a youthful politician by Western standards, but in Afghanistan he has exceeded the average male life span. He heads a 500,000-strong Pashtun clan from the Kandahar region, the direct descendants of the first king of Afghanistan, Ahmad Shah Durrani.

Karzai's grandfather was a Speaker of the parliament, and his father was a deputy during the reign of King Zaher Shah. In July 1999 his father was assassinated while walking home from evening prayers at a mosque in Quetta in Pakistan. The murder is believed to have been carried out by the Taliban.

Although Karzai was Westernised and moderate, initially the Taliban trusted him because of his important tribal position. Before they seized power they sought him out and offered him the post of their United Nations ambassador, a position which he declined.

Karzai has said that he did not initially oppose the Taliban, believing them to be good, honest people, friends from the jihad against the Soviets. He only became suspicious when people he didn't recognise began to appear at meetings and to take over the Taliban movement. Karzai believes these men to have been Pakistani intelligence. After that he became an opponent of the Taliban and their 'foreign' influence in Afghan politics.

Following the September 11 attacks, Karzai formulated a plan, similar to Abdul Haq's, to infiltrate the south of the country in order to encourage Pashtun tribal leaders to fight the Taliban. He also planned to convene a *Loya Jirga*, the national gathering that traditionally chooses an Afghan leader, to elect a replacement for the Taliban.

The softly spoken Karzai appears to have been more diplomatically adroit than Abdul Haq. He gained the support of Afghanistan's former king, and crucially also that of Washington, obtaining a commitment from the US to arm any Afghans who split from the Taliban. He was also brave. His training was as a political scientist, and he'd never been a military leader or fighter, so entering the Taliban's heartland to foment opposition took guts.

Washington asked Karzai to wait until it gave him the green light. He received it on 8 October, twenty-four hours after the American air strikes began. With the approval of US Defense Secretary Donald Rumsfeld and CIA Director George Tenet, Hamed Karzai and a group of his men left for southern Afghanistan.

They entered Afghanistan from Karzai's home in the Pakistani border city of Quetta and travelled by donkey across the mountains on tracks too rough for a four-wheel-drive. In his desperately poor ancestral homelands in the Uruzgan province, Karzai trekked from village to village, rallying support for an attack against the Taliban.

But on Thursday 1 November, it was the Taliban who attacked him. During a traditional debate among tribal leaders in the village of Dehrawut, the alarm went up. Taliban fighters were entering the town.

There was a fierce gun battle, during which Karzai and his men received American air support. Karzai reaped the benefits of better co-ordination with the US than Abdul Haq had managed in his tragic campaign two weeks earlier. The Pentagon confirmed that US planes fired missiles at Karzai's opponents.

Karzai escaped but his whereabouts were unknown. He was believed to be working his way across the hills towards the safety of Northern Alliance territory, or back to Pakistan. He failed to appear at the first spot he had told his family he was heading for. For the second time in two weeks, CIA-backed opposition forces were in trouble.

The next day we contact Karzai's brother, Ahmed Walid Karzai, in Pakistan by satellite phone. He says that Hamed Karzai remains inside Afghanistan and is continuing to organise resistance against the Taliban. He says he has spoken to him, he is well, and all his men escaped from the fight with only one injured.

Ahmed Walid Karzai confirms that his brother has been talking with some Taliban commanders about them defecting. He says that Mujaheddin leaders are gathering at the family home in Pakistan, waiting for a signal from Hamed Karzai to cross the border and join him.

But in early November, the Taliban announce they have hanged three tribal elders in Kandahar for backing Karzai's rebellion. This is a direct warning to the West and their own nationals that their intelligence is still effective.

On 2 November the drought breaks. After a gap of three years, it begins to rain, a steady downpour that we initially greet with glee. I know that rain does not necessarily mean the end of a drought, that it's about the quantity of rain, and when and where it falls, but I am so busy wondering about the implications for the region that I don't think about the implications for us. They turn out to be horrendous. By the next morning, the dust everywhere has turned to mud.

Just when you think Khoja Bahauddin can't get any more miserable, it does.

The mud has become an oozing, sucking, filthy prison. Everything is bleak and grey and our lives become even more circumscribed. It reminds me of the mud-spattered accounts of soldiers' lives from World War I. I find myself grumbling that I haven't signed up for Flanders field, or the Battle of the Somme. All right, all right, minus the trenches and the gassings and the shootings, but still . . .

I go to visit my friends from the British tabloid press, and end up having to stay the night, sleeping on a mattress, with a blanket improvised from three jackets. I am trapped because the walk to my house, which usually takes seven minutes, has turned into a sea of mud. It's too risky to attempt it at night, for in certain spots the path is already so gooey you can sink. Also the trenches in the ground outside my house have filled with water, and the new deep pools are dangerous in the dark.

Even the journey across their yard to the toilet is fraught. The toilets, never my favourite part of life here, are slowly leaking and toppling inwards, as the mud walls sink back into the mud floor from which they were built. Squelching in, and then squatting above the wet clay, there is the dispiriting sound of rain dripping *inside* the small structure. I feel as if at any moment the whole edifice will ooze back into the ground, naturally when I'm here rather than any of the boys. I can see the funeral service now – ashes to ashes, dust to dust, mud to mud.

Walking back to the house involves avoiding the puddles, the worst patches of ankle-turning clay and the only occupant of the yard, the bedraggled satellite phone, which is slowly sinking into the ground as well. One of the photographers snaps this dreary scene, and captions the picture 'Sat phone with toilet and hay'. That's before the sodden pile of hay on the wall topples into the neighbour's yard. Then it's just 'Sat phone with toilet'.

Another British journalist tells me that one night she slips and slides into the outhouse only to find a donkey and three chickens have taken refuge there. She chases the donkey away, but decides to let the chickens stay. 'They had so politely put their heads under their wings, I felt they were saying, "We won't look", so I didn't have the heart to push them out into the rain.'

The other grim feature of the rain is it binds everything together. The two keynotes of life in Khoja Bahauddin – dust and shit – are now coalescing. As they amalgamate everywhere, nothing is ever clean. Everything stinks. Your hands after you do up your shoelaces are fetid.

During this time, while I'm camped out with the *Mirror* boys, I hear a story I never quite recover from, and one which makes me vow never to go to the toilet again. A female journalist is perched on the mud, squatting over the toilet hole, when she hears giggling. She looks out, and she can't see anyone. But some instinct makes her look down, to see that two boys have climbed *into* the toilet, so they can look up at her. Those boys were willing to stand in a privy on a pile of excrement and be shat on just so that they could stare up at a woman. I guess they recognised it doesn't make much difference where you stand in Khoja Bahauddin. It is all mud and shit, just different quantities of each.

After three days of remorseless, relentless, endless rain, just when I can't bear it any longer, the downpour stops.

I am thrilled at the end to our enforced inactivity. But we are warned that the heavy rain has repositioned the land mines that litter the area, making driving increasingly dangerous. Once-safe roads in this remote region may now be full of mines. And we won't know till we set one off.

When I first see Sarah from the *Daily Mail* I can't believe my eyes. It takes me only a moment to realise what is wrong. She's not wearing a headscarf. Her long, red hair is cascading to her waist, and she's wearing tight jeans, a white T-shirt and a leather jacket. In this environment, what she's wearing has the impact of watching a woman walk naked down a city street in the West. But Sarah says she has had enough. She did wear a scarf for a while, but it didn't stop anyone staring.

'So I've decided that I won't cover my hair any more, since it makes no difference.'

This is part of the paradox of Afghanistan – in the north, no one insists she covers her hair. If this were Saudi Arabia or Pakistan, or Taliban-controlled Afghanistan, she'd probably be lynched.

Later we go together to the front line to watch the bombing. It is the first clear day following the rain, and there is a strange feeling of reprieve as we wait for the US cluster bombs to fall. 'Which is worse – the dust or the mud?' we ask each other, as we step over the puddles and sniff the clean, rain-washed air. We eat Sarah's pistachio nuts while she sings 1960s songs and dances as we wait for the bombs to drop.

An Afghan man whom we don't know says she looks very happy.

'Yes, it's a beautiful day,' she replies.

'Are you happy that bombs are being dropped on my country?'

Sarah backtracks. 'I wasn't talking about politics, just about the weather.'

US jets have bombed the mountains here almost every day for the past week. At the forward positions on the front line at Puze Polihomri, Major General Yusuf Muhammad watches the bombing. He walks back to a safer spot, satisfied.

'They should have been doing this from day one.'

His troops controlled the Qala Qata hills opposite six months ago, but they were pushed back further and further, until they dug at the village cemetery, on the top of this mountain.

'The Taliban enjoyed numerical superiority, they had better equipment and facilities,' he says. 'But now the American bombing has levelled the playing field for us.'

Muhammad's men are Uzbeks, as are many of the Taliban soldiers in the hills opposite. But the men here have little sympathy for their compatriots.

'They allied themselves with the terrorists and now they are paying the price,' says one of the soldiers.

I visit my friends at other news organisations, to gather news, or at least the rumours that pass for news. All the broadcasters I file to want to know only one thing: will there be a ground war, and when and where will it start? Since none of us has any hard information, we discuss this question for hours, swapping rumours we have heard from generals at different front-line camps, till our original rumour returns, inflated but recognisable.

The other hot topic is the huge cost of this war – not for the combatants but for the media. The big news organisations are spending millions of dollars every week. BBC News has exceeded its entire annual budget, and is being bailed out by the Director General from week to week.

'Our money will run out on Friday – so go on, have some of our instant noodles,' they offer cheerfully.

All my NBC friends have left, but the house shared by the American networks ABC and CBS is now so well organised that they have a percolator and proper coffee, making morning visits a special pleasure. They are building 'winter quarters' so that staff will not have to continue sleeping in tents when it gets cold. Every time I visit, the work is further advanced. Ten rooms are being built on the edge of the compound, and I sit watching Afghan labourers on the ground throwing the bricks they have made up to workers on the roof. Their movements are quick, fluid and mesmerising. It makes me think that if things were different, they would be good cricketers, like the Pakistanis who are their neighbours.

One of the CBS techs tells me that the favourite part of his working day is buying petrol. 'You can't just buy petrol, you have to choose it. It's not pure here, they have various grades, and if you're not careful and you get the wrong one, it simply won't power the generators. You have to make sure it hasn't been adulterated too much. So I go from vat to vat, checking, smelling, testing – this one's too light, I don't like the smell of that one – as if it was wine.'

One morning when I have to go to the Foreign Ministry compound, I visit Massoud's house. A new NBC contingent is camped out there, the old crowd having been so keen to see the back of the place that they could barely spare ten minutes for a handover.

Veteran reporter Jim Maceda is here now. He is funny and friendly, and driven, as all successful correspondents have to be, and we discuss the latest developments in the conflict. He has set up an office in a dark corridor, right outside the room where Massoud was assassinated. On his dusty table he has a satellite phone, and a laptop with email and the wires. It is one of those miracles of modern communications that Jim can access information from all around the world in this remote spot. He is always happy to share what he knows.

'I used to live in this house with NBC,' I tell him, 'and your colleagues were very kind to me.'

I meet the rest of the crew and, for the second time, they are a great bunch of guys, welcoming and interesting.

Your first impressions of people are so crucial. I walk up onto the roof with its panoramic view of the river and the town beneath. There a cameraman who looks like Kevin Costner is filming the Russian military helicopters swooping past, and reading a history by Herodotus in between shots. This is an unusual guy. He's a New Yorker called Tom

Streithorst, and I sit talking to him while one of Massoud's bodyguards prays just beyond the tripod. Tom is funny and clever and there's something about this setting – with the Islamic warriors and the sunshine and the Taliban over the ridge – that imparts an extra edge to every exchange. The pheromones of war.

Tom summarises what he's learning from Herodotus: 'This place used to be the centre of the world. When Manhattan was inhabited by hunter-gatherers, an Afghan invented algebra. When London was an outpost on the edge of the world, this place was the centre of trade between Russia and China. Afghans invented the axle, and therefore the chariot, and conquered much of the known world. Look at them now.' We gaze down from the roof.

A child carrying firewood walks past us bent double, as much a beast of burden as the donkey that usually does this job. He passes camels, and men guiding donkeys bringing water up from the river. Tom is right, it is incredible to look at this society, and to wonder where our own self-confident civilisation will end up in a thousand years' time. Could it be such a steep decline?

The NBC crew invite me to join them for lunch, the perennial plastic packaged Meals Ready to Eat. Cheese tortellinis still rule. They have an American conversation, utterly different to the British conversations at the BBC house – the cadences, the subject matter, the energy, the humour. One of the pluses of being Australian is being able to understand the jokes in both languages.

The NBC guys are still concerned about anthrax, which was sent to their head office at the Rockefeller Center in New York. But it's not all serious. One of them is in mourning because BBC radio reported this morning that the 1960s are now officially forty years ago.

'That means I'm so old,' he wails.

I remind him of the old hippie saying, 'If you can remember the 60s, then you weren't really there.' He cheers up slightly.

'Stay as long as you can,' says Tom, 'it's good to have you here. We need some oestrogen in this sea of testosterone, it's a relief, you know.'

I tell them that I cooked dinner last time I was here, regaling them with the story of the wonderful Babette's Feast, with its 'tablecloth' and candlelight and wine.

They look down at the same grimy table, covered in dirty dishes and cups, with a packet of Rice Krispies and part of an opened Meal Ready to Eat, flies trailing over everything. They ask entreatingly, 'Could you do it again?'

I tell them that it was probably an unrepeatable experience, but I might be able to cook something more modest.

Jonathan, the sound recordist who works with Tom, says he will help. He's a dark-haired, funny New Yorker in his late twenties, who looks and sounds Hispanic, but turns out to be Jewish, the son of an Israeli father. This adds another layer to the experience of being in Afghanistan, but the possible dangers don't deter him.

'I was freelancing for NBC news in New York on September 11, so I've been on this story right from the start,' he says. 'We worked round the clock for the first three days, and from then I knew I had to come to Afghanistan.'

I cover my hair with a scarf and we go to the markets to buy vegetables. The approach of winter means that there is even less choice than before. The mounds of vegetables on the dusty sheets on the ground are smaller and mingier. Most of the tomatoes are green, and you have to pick out the few remaining orangey ones. The carrots are a pale yellow and look like turnips, or long radishes. There are still chillies, garlic, onions and potatoes, and a dried herb mixture that we decide to try, too. Flies swarm over everything. 'Don't use your hands!' Jonathan stops the stallholder just as he is about to scoop the herbs out. He squats on the dusty sheet, looking bemused as Jonathan finds him a plastic bag, a small attempt at hygiene.

Jonathan enjoys the whole process, from communicating without a common language, to vegetables being weighed out in rocks. He can't get over the crowds that accompany us everywhere. I am by now inured to being watched and followed, and only notice them because he does.

We walk back through the bazaar, and hear an ear-splitting, blood-freezing scream from inside one stall. Jonathan snaps a pic and I ask what terrible cruelty is going on inside that dusty shack. 'It's a circumcision. The boy is four years old.' A man beams at us happily. We move away from the hellish sound as fast as we can, but it reverberates in my ears for a long time. Later Jonathan buys a carved wooden pipe, which turns out to be a circumcision tool. I never figure out the mechanics of that pipe. When he puts it to his lips at the bazaar – *Like this?* – the locals laugh helplessly.

We walk back via the new house that NBC is refitting in the centre of town. They are moving out of Massoud's house and into a building that will one day be the Khoja Bahauddin town council. I suspect it will be liberating for them to be away from close day-to-day contact with the Foreign Ministry, but moving their base – home, office and feed point for more than ten people who file around the clock – is an enormous logistical undertaking, especially as they have to keep churning out reports at the same time.

Their satellite engineer, Hans, has taken charge of this project. He is one of the most competent people I've ever encountered, so he should be able to do it if anyone can. He's never been outside the United States before. The first overseas trip for this Chicago home boy has been to Afghanistan, and he hasn't missed a beat. He selects the building for the new base, decides that for the sake of security it will need a wall, and goes to the town hall to investigate the title to the property, so he can make sure the wall is built in the correct place. Then he tackles the really important stuff. He builds a toilet.

'I need a forty-foot drop,' he says to the local builders, with that fantastic American clarity of vision.

'Oh no, we don't do those. Our toilets are only six feet deep. We only dig six-foot holes.'

'Do you ever dig any holes that are forty-foot down?'

'We dig wells . . .'

'In that case bring me a well digger!'

Hans is about to build the best toilet in Khoja Bahauddin, with a wooden toilet seat, inside a small wooden outhouse, which has a door that you can lock. NBC puts an end to squatting in Khoja Bahauddin! All glory to the US of A.

It is a beautiful day and, while we wait for Hans, Jonathan and I climb up onto the roof. NBC will do their 'live shots' from here. It overlooks the slaughterhouse and the public toilets and the town square, and is overlooked in turn by the mountains beyond. Living in close proximity to a mountain range, you gauge its moods at different times of the day. This afternoon the air is clear, and the desert stretches out to the peaks. They bank up grandly above us, every crag and facet sharply defined. Their eternal grandeur inspires confidences.

Jonathan and I are soon telling each other about our lives and our dreams, including the films we've made and the films we want to make. Jonathan reminds me of my favourite cousin in Australia. Is it time to go home when you start seeing your family in every new person you meet in Afghanistan?

When an Afghan boy comes up onto the roof, I write our names in Russian in my book. Bashir. Irris. Jonathan. It's funny how everyone loves the Cyrillic alphabet.

Then Hans is ready: 'G to G' – 'good to go', he translates for me – and we carry our vegetables back to Massoud's house. We cook on the balcony where the two-ring hotplate is still sitting. When I last lived here, the boys stuck a CD to the wall at this spot, and used it as their shaving mirror. Now Hans has rigged up a pizza oven. Jonathan smears the dusty Afghan bread with olive oil and garlic and the dried herbs from the market, and we bake it in Hans' oven. We make a real tomato sauce for the pasta, debating whether to add wine or parmesan cheese.

'Wine??? Where does this wine come from? Can we waste wine on this sauce?'

'Sure we can,' says Jonathan, splashing it in. 'It came with the house.'

All of the crew who are here tonight – around ten guys – sit down to dinner. It's a very happy meal. Producer Karl Bostic, tall, busy and gracious, asks everybody to say a few words about why they are here, and what the experience means to them. I am dumbfounded. This is not an Australian way to go on. Do they do this every night?

They say warm, funny things, about what an unusual bunch of guys this is and how they couldn't think of anyone they'd rather be stuck here with. Tom can lecture us about Herodotus, and Jonathan will tell anyone who will listen

185

about his current musical obsession: the Goldberg Variations. They propose a toast to Club Khoja: 'It's better to be in hell with friends than in paradise with assholes.'

I know what they mean, and I search for something significant to say to a group of complete strangers. I thank them for taking me in, a second time – once may be accidental, but twice . . . I tell them the thing I have been musing on ever since I have been here, which is how much men have looked after me.

'Women often dump on men, but I think I see men at their best. Working in a team, helping each other. It's a privilege actually.'

They seem to like that. 'When we move out next week, will you come and live with us?'

It's late and I stay the night. One guy clears a spot in the room, another finds me a spare sleeping bag, and a third provides me with a toothbrush and soap. It's as if they want a girl to look after. It makes me realise that for all the bravado – 'Women: you can't live with them, and you can't kill them' – most men actually miss women when they're not around. Wasn't what I expected to learn in a war zone.

Facilities have improved, and everyone has stretcher beds. I'm perched on mine, laughing with Jonathan about how the standards have improved since I last lived here. 'When we pioneers first came . . .'

It's funny to be back in Massoud's house, back in my old bedroom again. Ahmed Shah Massoud spent one of the last nights of his life in this room talking with a friend, Masood Khalili. The two men sat on the floor, where our packs and stretchers are now. Khalili says that he and Massoud looked out over the river and talked about everything, from poetry to politics.

I look out over the same river and think about how close Massoud was to death, though he did not know it. He was with an old friend, I am with new ones. Then a battle was raging at the front line near Kabul. It was in the back of both men's minds all night, but Massoud did not speak of it, instead seeking refuge in poetry. He read from a beautifully bound book of the verses of a famous

Persian Sufi poet, and asked his friend to recite one poem over and over again.

It was about friends spending time together, talking, and enjoying a night like many to come, though this night 'will never be repeated'.

Afghanistan reminds me that we must all try to live our lives with that awareness, appreciating every experience, including those we think we will enjoy again . . . for this night 'will never be repeated'.

Chapter 13

For the NBC guys, the reference point is Afghan men. They never see any Afghan women, except as shapeless figures, their burqas flapping like tents. They certainly never see their faces. Tom Streithorst says, 'I've been here for a month, and I've never heard an Afghan woman's voice.'

They live with Massoud's bodyguards, who have adopted them, playing chess, using their equipment and eating their food. The unforgettable Tom Baer, a huge man with a voice and a sense of humour to match, would retrieve his Leatherman knife from a different soldier every night.

'Can I have your knife?'

'Yes, but you have to give it back, I need it,' Tom would say sternly.

He'd have to go to get it back each time. He'd find the man asleep with the knife enclosed in his fist, like a small child.

It's odd this male addiction to knives. The great American novelist John Steinbeck visited Russia in 1946. He was one of the last Westerners permitted to travel through the Soviet Union, as the goodwill created by fighting as allies during World War II rapidly disintegrated into the Cold War, and such contacts became impossible. Not knowing what to expect, Steinbeck armed himself . . . with a pocketknife. It had 'a blade to take care of nearly all physical situations in the world, and some spiritual ones. It was equipped with blades that were scissors, with blades that were files, awls, saws, can-openers, beer-openers, corkscrews, tools for removing stones from a horse's foot, a blade for eating and a blade for murder, a screwdriver and a chisel. You could mend a watch with it or repair the Panama Canal.' Steinbeck had this wonderful pocketknife nearly two months, and the only thing he ever used it for was to cut sausage. Deadpan, he assures us that it cut sausage very well.

Every bloke from every news organisation has come to Afghanistan with a pocketknife. They know every feature on each other's models, as well as the colours they come in and what each can do. 'His is much better than mine, it has two extra blades,' one sighs enviously, as they compare knives at the table. Actually, 'compare' is the wrong word. They name the brand and the model and then sigh – they don't need to look to know that the other guy's is better.

Just to prove it is a guy thing, the Afghan men soon also know the difference between each knife, something I never really retain no matter how often it is shown to me.

I find Massoud's bodyguards – with the exception of Samim, a clansman of Massoud's – positively creepy. They speak no English, so we have to rely on other cues. The way they look at women leaves little to the imagination. One of them has a very unsettling stare. I try not to be around him when I am alone at the NBC house.

But the NBC boys react differently. They enjoy their time together and all the paradoxes of living with Islamic warriors. When one of the Americans catches a moth, the soldiers grab him and lecture him sternly about letting it go because 'It is a living creature'. Human life seems to be more expendable.

Jonathan and Samim become close. 'We are brothers,' they announce, cementing their bond in the Afghan way – having their photo taken holding Samim's gun. Jonathan decides he can be open with Samim, and tell him that he is Jewish. As the cameraman who works with Jonathan, Tom is angry. 'You've got to stop. It's dangerous. You'll get yourself killed – but what's worse, you'll get me killed along with you.'

Tom's right. Jews – and especially Israelis – cannot travel

to many Muslim countries, and if they do manage to slip in, it is not safe for them to reveal their religious identity. Jonathan says he just wants the Afghans to know that Jews don't have horns and tails, but he is taking a risk.

American Jewish journalist Daniel Pearl is later kidnapped while interviewing Islamic fundamentalists in Pakistan, and after some weeks in captivity, he is butchered like a sheep because of his religion. He is forced to intone 'I am Jewish, and my mother is Jewish,' before his head is pulled back and his throat slit. His murder and his last words are filmed.

We are transfixed with horror as this story unfolds, but in the Islamic state of Afghanistan, no one takes any action against Jonathan.

The only thing the NBC boys can't handle too well is that Afghan men walk around hand-in-hand, and sometimes want to hold their hands, too. Or sit too close behind them on the same chair when they are at their computers. There is a lot of 'boy love' here, apparently another reaction to the repression of women. The Taliban, having come to power in part by taking a stand against rampant paedophilia, also punish men suspected of homosexuality severely. One punishment involves standing the offender behind a wall and backing a vehicle into it, so that it falls on top of him. If he dies he deserved to die, if he survives he is capable of being 'reformed'. It is God's choice. Like the simple test for witches in fourteenth-century Europe: women suspected of witchcraft were thrown into a river, weighed down with stones. If they drowned, as they all inevitably did, they weren't witches. Sorry about that.

Taliban Chief of Staff Mullah Mohammed Hassan explains the problem this way: 'Our religious scholars are not agreed on the right kind of punishment for homosexuality. Some say we should take these sinners to a high wall and throw them down, while others say we should dig a hole beside a wall, bury them, and then push the wall down on top of them.'

Feeding the starving people takes second place to such important doctrinal questions. However, this ferocious punishment doesn't seem to be a very effective deterrent. As far as we can see here, homosexuality flourishes. In the Taliban stronghold of Kandahar, it is so common they joke that crows fly above the city with one wing clamped to their bums, just in case.

Despite all this, cameraman Tom Streithorst says he's never met men like these, and that he's learnt a lot from them.

'They are like heroes in the *Iliad*. Brave, hospitable, resourceful, hardy, loyal, unselfish, they never complain, they are never ironic. They play chess like champions. They are oddly gentle, these killers, cupping their hands around a moth, helping it escape. Afghanistan was never conquered, never colonised. Unlike most third-world peoples, Afghans have no sense of inferiority to the West, actually hardly any sense of the West at all. They do not doubt themselves. They do not compare themselves to Donald Trump or Michael Jordan or Brad Pitt. They envy no one. They are not post-modern, not even modern at all.'

Tom's twenty-first-century American assessment complements a nineteenth-century British account by diplomat Mountstuart Elphinstone. Sent to the region in 1809, six years later he produced one of the most remarkable books about Afghanistan, *An Account of the Kingdom of Caubul*. He says of Afghan men: 'Their vices are revenge, envy, avarice, rapacity and obstinacy. On the other hand they are fond of liberty, faithful to their friends, kind to their dependants, brave, hardy, frugal, laborious and prudent, and they are less disposed than the nations in the neighbourhood to falsehood, intrigue and deceit.' He reports an old man saying 'We are content with discord, we are content with alarms, we are content with blood, we will never be content with a master.' Perhaps such insights are still true. Elphinstone's experiences in the region, he would later say, cured him of ambition.

Still, Tom Streithorst is disturbed by an exchange about men and women he has with a teenager working as a translator.

'In America, do men beat their wives?' nineteen-year-old Fayoz asks him. Tom replies that no, in the West, wife beating is regarded as something a man should not do. Fayoz is confused. 'So do the women beat the men?'

Tom laughs and Fayoz tells him the following story. Two years ago in Taloqan, where Fayoz lived until it was conquered by the Taliban, one of his neighbours had been betrothed to a young girl. The wedding was a month away, but the boy had not seen his future bride. Impatient, he took a chance. He walked to her house and knocked on the door. She invited him in and made tea. They sat on the floor to drink it.

Her brother came home and saw a boy sitting with his sister. Although he knew it was her future husband, the brother got his AK-47 and shot them both dead.

'The boy's father is outraged and demands justice,' Tom recounts. 'The village elders reject his plea. They conclude that killing is justified as the boy was sitting with a woman who was not his relative. Killing the sister is never questioned. A small fine is paid to the boy's family and that's that. This is why premarital sex is rare in rural Afghanistan. By law it is only the women who are stoned, but the men can be shot by indignant fathers or brothers.'

Tom adds cynically 'You can see why in Afghanistan bestiality is less dangerous than heterosexuality. The donkey's father won't be looking for revenge.'

Sex and death. When you can't get one, it seems you focus on the other. We talk a lot about death, and who is more determined to win this war. 'You guys have got the gear, but do you want to win as much?' Again, the attitudes of Islam are very different to those of the secular West. We are aware that our rewards are in this life, Muslims' in the next. Massoud's bodyguards are constantly discussing sacrifice and martyrdom, and even the boy NBC employs to clean up at Massoud's house, who looks to us no more than thirteen years old, talks about his death and what's waiting for him in the afterlife. Everyone knows the reward waiting for the martyred Islamic warrior is seventy-two virgins. And shade. In the heat of the Middle East, where Islam was born, a garden with shade was as important as seventy-two virgins.

The NBC boys sit around discussing this. I hear them as I am writing a script.

I thought it was twenty-one virgins?

Oh, I thought it was 100.

Only twenty-one, I don't know if it would be worth it.

Tom Streithorst has the last word. 'I've been thinking about this. I'd want seventy virgins and two experienced older women to show the virgins what to do.'

I sense that here it is fear of women that underlies the rigidly enforced separation of the sexes. The terrorist who headed the September 11 attacks, Mohammed Atta, specifically instructed that no woman, including his mother, should attend his memorial service. And where in the West, repression of women has been traditionally framed in terms of protecting women from the lust of men, in Islam that is turned on its head. The Prophet said that when God created lust, he gave nine parts of desire to the woman. To man he gave only one.

Men have to be protected from the threat of being consumed by women's untrammelled lust. That's why women have to be locked away. Most of the men around me are separated from their wives and families. Since Afghan women only have a place in the private sphere, the men never see any other women at all. They live here with each other, in a world virtually without women.

In a world without women, men go to war.

There are advances on the front line at Mazar-i-Sharif. General Rashid Dostum is once again within twenty kilometres of the town. He was in this position two weeks ago, but he could not secure his gains and had to pull back. He could not defend the villages he had captured and could not supply the men so far ahead of his rear positions. There was also some squabbling with a rival warlord over who would take the credit. Now by satellite phone, General Dostum claims he has regained the same ground with American aid. He says eighteen British and American Special Forces officers are working with his men as advisers, helping to direct air strikes and pinpoint targets.

General Dostum says he has received airdrops of weapons and ammunition.

'American helicopters have dropped fifty AK-47 rifles, with 100 boxes of AK-47 ammunition, twenty boxes of rocket-propelled grenades and fifty boxes of ammunition for PK machine guns.'

General Dostum says this is a start, but he still needs more.

'I have 10,000 soldiers to equip. This won't go far among 10,000 men.'

The Taliban deny Dostum's forces have advanced, and claim they are repelling his attacks. But they concede that one disputed province has fallen to the Northern Alliance, and they are reinforcing their troops at Mazar.

Taliban resistance is also being weakened by the millions of dollars in covert money the US is spreading around Afghanistan. Gary, the CIA agent, is soon requesting and receiving an additional $10 million in cash to hand out, and the CIA believes it has bought off thousands of Taliban members. The prices are $10,000 for a low-level commander with dozens of fighters, and $50,000 for a bigger commander with hundreds of fighters.

Bob Woodward reports that one commander who's offered $50,000 to defect wants some time to think it over. The Special Forces A-team direct a precision bomb right outside his headquarters. 'The next day, they called the commander back. How about $40,000? He accepted.'

On Thursday 8 November Mamur Hassan predicts Mazar will fall within days.

'One of the most infamous Taliban commanders was killed and three others were captured yesterday,' Hassan tells reporters at his compound at Dashti Qala. 'The ferocious and ruthless Taliban Commander Gargaray was killed as the result of the US bombing near Mazar-i-Sharif. He was one of the most feared and despised Taliban commanders. We were worried when we learned about his appointment to the Mazar-i-Sharif front. We called him "The Dog", but now he's taken care of.'

Mamur Hassan also pays tribute to General Dostum, who captured the three other Taliban leaders.

Rashid Dostum's story reveals a lot about Afghan politics because his ability to bounce back can be attributed partly to his willingness to switch sides. Once a Communist commander, he has been allied to, and has betrayed, every other leader and political movement including the Taliban.

In his defence, it could be said that he generally only betrayed his 'friends' before they betrayed him. He was twice forced to flee his capital, Mazar-i-Sharif, and in 1997 he was forced to bribe his own soldiers in order to escape, after his second-in-command defected to the Taliban.

In the Soviet years, Dostum was a union boss working on a gas field. Then, finding his vocation as a soldier, he became the leader of an Uzbek militia fighting on the Soviet side. By the mid-1980s, he commanded 20,000 men, and controlled the northern provinces. He went on to join the government of Communist President Najibullah, fighting against the Mujaheddin and receiving a medal for his services.

But towards the end of Najibullah's rule, he saw the writing on the wall. In early 1992 he switched sides to fight with the Mujaheddin. It was this 1992 defection that brought down the Communist government. He allied himself with Massoud, and together they took Kabul. But the leaders who had been part of the anti-Communist resistance excluded Dostum from the new government. In the following five years, he fought with them and against them, switching allegiances within the many Mujaheddin camps whenever it seemed pragmatic to do so.

In 1994 General Dostum retreated to his power base here in the north, an area with a population of around five million people. While much of the rest of the country was in ruins, and warring Mujaheddin factions – including Dostum's – had destroyed Kabul, Mazar-i-Sharif was thriving. Dostum had an army and a sizeable air force, and support from the Russian, Uzbek and Turkish governments. He became known as an efficient administrator, running a largely secular fiefdom with a health service and higher education, both available to women. But he was also a harsh ruler. Criminals were publicly executed and justice was often summary.

When author Ahmed Rashid visited Dostum in his headquarters in the Qala-i-Janghi fortress outside Mazar during this time, he noticed that there were smears of blood and pieces of flesh in a corner of the courtyard. At first he thought a goat had been killed, until the guards explained that no, this was human flesh. Dostum had ordered a soldier accused of stealing to be tied to the tracks of a tank, which was then driven around until he was mincemeat.

I guess at least you save on bullets that way.

Dostum's followers called him Pasha, a title used by some of the region's ancient kings, and he appeared to have ambitions to emerge as the new ruler of Afghanistan. No Uzbek has ruled here for 500 years, since the fourteenth-century Uzbek horseman Tamerlane conquered Afghanistan and started an empire that stretched from Baghdad to China.

But by 1997 comparisons with Tamerlane appeared to be no more than hubris, for in May the Taliban attacked Mazar, defeating Rashid Dostum and forcing him to flee. Dostum's defeat was partly due to betrayal from within his own ranks, and was followed by a series of double crossings, which led to some of the worst massacres of Afghanistan's civil war.

First, one of General Dostum's senior commanders, Abdul Malik Pehlawan, defected to the Taliban. Malik did a deal with the Taliban that gave them the city. At that point, Dostum was forced to flee to the border with Uzbekistan, leaving his vehicles and much of his money. But when Malik realised that what he understood to be a power-sharing arrangement was, in fact, a Taliban takeover, the deal fell apart. Pakistani diplomats and ISI officers flew in to the city to try to help the Taliban renegotiate. However, this failed when Malik switched sides again, and the Taliban's brutal fundamentalism provoked an uprising among the people of Mazar, the most liberal city in Afghanistan.

The Taliban were subjected to their most punishing defeat since they had begun their roll across Afghanistan in 1994. They lost approximately 3000 soldiers in ten weeks of fighting, with a further 3500 taken prisoner. These figures include 250 Pakistani soldiers killed and 750 captured. The Taliban withdrew from Mazar-i-Sharif in July 1997.

After taking refuge in Turkey, Dostum returned in early 1998. In order to discredit Malik, his disloyal deputy, Dostum revealed that Malik's men had massacred some 2000 Taliban soldiers. One of Malik's generals admitted that they had crammed around 1250 captured Taliban fighters into airless containers, leaving them to bake to death in the blistering sun. When the containers were opened the bodies were found to have turned black.

Paik Chong-Hyun, a UN special rapporteur who investigated the Taliban deaths, wrote in his report that many bodies were also tossed down deep wells, then hand grenades were thrown in, and the wells were bulldozed over.

In a desert land, who would poison a well?

Dostum was unable to unite the anti-Taliban opposition. In August 1998, the Taliban again bribed their way through the Northern Alliance front lines. Mazar-i-Sharif fell to the Taliban for a second time. When they came into town they extracted a bitter revenge for their losses the previous year, killing civilians indiscriminately. 'A Taliban commander said that Mullah Omar had given them permission to kill for two hours, but they killed for two days,' writes Ahmed Rashid.

The streets were piled high with corpses, which were not allowed to be buried for six days, in breach of instructions in the Koran. A Tajik man who escaped the massacre said dogs were eating human flesh, and the smell was intolerable.

Hazara prisoners were locked in containers, in direct revenge for the deaths of the Taliban soldiers the previous year, and 300 men suffocated to death in this way. All in all, estimates are that some 6000 people were massacred by the Taliban during this retaliatory killing frenzy.

General Dostum was forced to flee into exile a second time as the Taliban took over the territory he once ruled. He returned to Afghanistan only in June 2001, when he reached a compromise with Ahmed Shah Massoud, his former enemy, to join the Northern Alliance and fight the Taliban. Following Massoud's assassination, Dostum was not appointed to succeed him as military commander. However, Dostum's is now the most active front. It seems that when the war will start, it will start there, in the north, a fight for Mazar.

So cometh the hour, cometh the man, and this is the man who has come. This knight, with no shine left in his armour, holds the Northern Alliance's future in his hands. If Mazar-i-Sharif falls, it is widely assumed that the Northern Alliance will take control of the rest of the north, and then the capital Kabul.

On a personal note, it's our future, too, up here in the north where the fighting will be. In the back of our minds is the knowledge that if Dostum fails, the Taliban will most likely overrun Khoja Bahauddin, where we are living.

Our hopes are pinned on him, too. He's all we've got.

Chapter 14

NBC is moving its stores of food, water, furniture, generators, petrol, tools, first-aid kits, cameras, batteries, laptops, edit packs, telephones, videophones and satellite equipment out of Massoud's house, just as we hear the first confused reports that Mazar is falling.

Details are sketchy. It appears that a Northern Alliance commander fighting with Dostum, General Ustad Atta, has marched into Mazar from the south, capturing the power station and the city's strategically important airfields. His 2500-strong troops have met with no resistance. About 7500 of General Dostum's men attack from the south-west, capturing the military base at Ferkededadi. US military sources report that the Mazar-i-Sharif hospital is tending to hundreds of Taliban casualties. Taliban forces are reported to be fleeing south, towards Kandahar, and hundreds of Taliban soldiers are said to be defecting.

We obtain what corroboration we can. Foreign Ministry officials here say they are monitoring Taliban radio traffic and confirm that the Taliban forces are withdrawing from the city. General Mamur Hassan says that a large number of Taliban soldiers drowned while trying to escape by crossing a river to our west. The Northern Alliance attributes this victory to greater co-ordination between the American air force and its troops on the ground.

I call Voice of America to fire off a quick radio news report.

'Oh, hi Irris,' says a sleepy voice in Washington. 'Yes, we have your earlier piece about fighting at Mazar.'

'No – you can't use that. Mazar is falling,' I tell him.

'Mazar is falling?'

'*Yes*. Mazar is falling. I've written a piece.'

'You've written a piece?'

Sometimes dealing with the news desk can drive you crazy. Of course I've written a piece, it's the news, and it's breaking, but at this rate it'll never get on air because of our little comedy routine. I finally file for VOA.

I also do a live broadcast for Deutsche Welle and for Australia, and we move into NBC's new house after midnight on the night Mazar falls. It is the closest thing to paradise in Khoja Bahauddin.

I'm exhausted, but I don't sleep well, despite the luxury of a stretcher bed to lay my sleeping bag on. I am filled with adrenaline, plans and doubts, as the war we have all been waiting for has finally begun.

The next day, Saturday 10 November, Taliban radio confirms that its troops have left Mazar-i-Sharif, but says this is merely a strategic withdrawal. There are unconfirmed reports of further Northern Alliance gains north of Mazar, clearing a land corridor to Uzbekistan where US troops are stationed.

Mamur Hassan says he is planning to start his offensive at Qala Qata, breaking through the Taliban lines and launching an offensive to capture Taloqan and then Kunduz. He has had to postpone the attack, waiting for one more US bombing raid, which has been delayed by bad weather.

My friend the Canadian journalist Levon Sevunts goes to the front line. He reports that the Northern Alliance forces are getting ready for the big push. Trucks are unloading ammunition, and soldiers are busy digging tank positions at the top of the Puze Pulihomri hill. Taliban soldiers don't respond to the sporadic firing from the Northern Alliance trenches. Instead, they reply over the walkie-talkies, with taunts.

'That's it, you must have fired your last shell,' a Taliban soldier says to a machine gunner who has just fired six shots in the direction of the Taliban positions in the valley below.

'Get your stinking head out of the trenches and you'll see if this was the last shell,' the gunner responds.

Inoyatullah, a twenty-six-year-old fighter, tells Levon that they speak with the Taliban soldiers several times a day.

'It gets boring here, there is nothing to do,' Inoyatullah says. 'So we talk on the walkie-talkies. They tell us to come to their side and we tell them to come to our side. If they are nice to us, we speak nicely to them. We don't like to swear and curse, we are Muslims.'

Inoyatullah says that often after shooting at each other, they ask about each other's health and family.

'But that doesn't prevent us from fighting.'

At a triumphant press conference, Northern Alliance Foreign Minister Dr Abdullah announces that troops are mobilising here, with columns of tanks and armoured personnel carriers moving towards the front line where US air strikes have been concentrated over the past two weeks. He confirms what Mamur Hassan has said, naming the Alliance's former regional headquarters of Taloqan as a military priority, followed by the next major town south, Kunduz.

There are already garbled reports of human rights abuses by Northern Alliance soldiers in Mazar-i-Sharif, but Dr Abdullah flatly denies them. At the press conference, I sit next to Johanne Sutton, a French radio journalist. She is dark-haired and shy, and she sympathises with me when the Northern Alliance boys – my former friends! – won't let me crouch down where I need to in order to get the best audio.

'No, you can't sit there,' they say, moving me off the patch of concrete that used to be my outdoor 'office' when I first came to Afghanistan. This is a problem because I don't have a long enough cable with me to reach Dr Abdullah from the chair near Johanne's. Since I am the only one they have moved, allowing all the men to stay where they are, I gear up for a full-scale argument, when a kind American reporter lends me a cable. Another outbreak of hostilities avoided! As we wait for Dr Abdullah, I chat to Johanne about the difficulties of working here. I can't conceive that the next day she will be dead.

Johanne is one of seven journalists who accompany a Northern Alliance brigade when it crosses the front line here at Dashti Qala, following retreating Taliban troops. The group includes Australian Paul McGeough, the striking blond-haired German e-mag reporter Volker Handloik, and my friend Levon Sevunts.

Commander Amer Bashir leads the brigade they accompany. On the day after Mazar falls, Saturday 10 November, the battle for Qala Qata begins. Mamur Hassan starts the battle theatrically, as befits a celebrity warlord, declaring, 'I order the men to start fighting.' Bashir and Mamur Hassan lead bravely, wandering openly in the line of Taliban fire. Commander Bashir wins the ridge near Qala Qata on Saturday, but loses it later in the evening when the Taliban advance and retake it.

The next day, Sunday, Commander Bashir takes the ridge again after an afternoon of fierce fighting, claiming he's killed about 100 Taliban soldiers who 'fought to the death', for the loss of ten of his own men.

The seven journalists accompany the advancing troops less than an hour after the Taliban retreat on the Sunday night. Commander Bashir warns them against it, saying it could be dangerous. 'There are mines near the Taliban trenches and the Taliban might launch a counteroffensive.' But Levon Sevunts later tells me that the temptation of seeing the Taliban trenches and bunkers dug into the hill is too strong to resist.

They climb on top of Commander Bashir's armoured personnel carrier, with Levon praying the Taliban haven't laid any anti-tank mines. 'We passed a first line of trenches similar to the Alliance trenches we had just left. Approaching the second line, we passed by an Alliance platoon marching toward Taliban positions. The second line of trenches had been bombed more heavily than the first, and a huge crater blocked our way. There was no sign of bodies or abandoned equipment. The fighting had subsided considerably and only occasional red tracer bullets could be seen flying gracefully from one position to another.'

But 100 metres further up the hill it becomes clear that the Taliban have not quit the ridge. The armoured personnel carrier comes under attack from three directions. At least one large machine gun and five AK-47s are firing, illuminating the dark night. People start jumping off. Sitting on the edge of the armoured personnel carrier, Volker Handloik is one of the first to jump. Two other journalists – Johanne Sutton and Pierre Billaud – follow.

Levon finds himself thinking, Mines and unfamiliar territory – don't jump!

'One of the last things I saw before the driver of the APC made a sharp left turn and started descending a steep hill was Volker in his green Uzbek coat rolling on the ground like a stuntman. Those who had nothing to hold onto fell off. I was thrown in the air as the APC jolted violently and landed one metre away, flat on my back atop the vehicle, holding onto the cannon.'

After several sharp turns in different directions, the armoured personnel carrier reaches a hollow where it can hide. Northern Alliance fighters who have been thrown off start showing up one by one, 'appearing like shadows from the darkness'. Soon only five people are missing: Volker and his interpreter, and Pierre, Johanne and their interpreter. They wait, calling out their names. There is no sign of them. Commander Bashir tells Australian journalist Paul McGeough he is confident the three foreign journalists will be rescued – after all, the armoured personnel carrier has passed dozens of his men walking in the dark.

But Bashir's confidence is misplaced. A Northern Alliance search team finds Johanne Sutton dead in a Taliban trench. They are forced to attack the trench to retrieve her body. They say there might be another body, but they can't get to it because of renewed Taliban fire. They bring Johanne Sutton back to the camp. Levon sees soldiers in tank helmets standing on the APC and shaking their heads in disbelief: 'Vay, vay, vay.'

'Can you come up with us to the Ministry of Defence?' the commander asks him. Levon clambers aboard the armoured personnel carrier again. 'We need somebody to hold her so she doesn't fall over.'

'Johanne's body lay sprawled on the back of a Russian-made armoured personnel carrier, her dead eyes staring into the billions of stars in the Afghan sky. There was nothing else

I could do for her but tie a shred of cloth around her head to close her half-open mouth and hold her lifeless hand for one last bumpy ride on Afghan roads on the back of an APC,' Levon wrote in his account of the night.

By daybreak it becomes known that the two other journalists and the two interpreters are also dead. They have been shot, but it's unclear whether they have been killed in crossfire, or whether Taliban soldiers executed them.

Paul McGeough accompanies Commander Bashir to search for the bodies. They find them, looted of all valuables, and bring them back to Khoja Bahauddin. The army will move on, but for the journalists, Afghanistan has proved to be their final journey.

We hear about the deaths the next morning as we are making our new home habitable. The news casts a pall over all of us. It is somehow unthinkable that someone who was sitting next to me at a press conference such a short time ago can now be dead. Or that all Volker's outrageous stylishness can have simply been extinguished. As my NBC friend Jonathan and I do our washing in tin pails on the balcony, we discuss whether the journalists took an unnecessary risk, and whether they should have waited longer before accompanying the troops on such a volatile battlefront. Everyone comes up to throw in an opinion.

It was foolhardy. The same ridge had changed hands twice the previous day. This is war, if you're covering a war you have to be 'in there' and be with the men to see what is really going on. *Levon survived.* But Levon is an ex-soldier, and he is savvy and physically fit. Of course Levon would survive, if anyone would. *You shouldn't jump off an APC into a battlefield when you are unarmed.* Sometimes if you stay on the APC, then you become the target. *Why were they on top of the APC, and not inside it, that shows they were running a ridiculous risk.* It was night time – what could they hope to see in the dark? That shows it wasn't about journalism – they were just bored.

The discussion goes round and round as we wring and rinse our clothes. And in the end the only incontrovertible fact is that three of our colleagues are dead, and we are here, doing our washing on a balcony in the sun. Even the smallest practicalities of life suddenly seem very precious.

At this time I have a premonition of my own death.

It's a jarring experience because it happens in the very ordinary context of filing a story at the TV feed point run by the European Broadcasting Union, EBU. Filing here at night has a religious quality. The glow from the EBU compound is the only light in the sky, in the utter inky darkness of night in northern Afghanistan. It draws us like the star guiding the three wise men. I arrive at the familiar dark door in the wall, with the makeshift office at the far end of the yard radiating light. The generator is humming, the soundtrack to our lives in northern Afghanistan, and Bruno Beeckman is saying suavely into a satellite phone, 'EBU Afghanistan, how may we help?'

So far, so normal. As I walk into the light, preparing to discuss the latest news, people come up to me and put their arms around me. Some are crying.

I'm mystified.

'What's wrong?'

They explain that they'd heard I was dead, a terrible rumour which quickly assumed the status of fact. Coming the day after the journalists and their interpreters were killed at the front line, it's plausible, and for the small and close community of journalists in Khoja Bahauddin, it's frightening. Another journalist dead, another friend lost. An Afghan boy at the house where I had been living before I moved in with NBC was the source of the rumour. I said goodbye when I moved out, and I've no idea why he told people I was dead.

I assure everyone standing around me in a circle at EBU that I will go and check with him about that, and joke that reports of my death have been greatly exaggerated, but seeing how shaken my colleagues are gives me a chill.

I walk back to the NBC house holding onto my torch very tight. The darkness is overwhelming, and watching the tiny light the torch throws, I feel vulnerable. I try to fight off the fear that my death has just been foretold, but there is no reassurance from the black Afghan night.

Chapter 15

In the light of day at the NBC house, my premonition of death seems less frightening, and I convince myself that it doesn't have any significance. Luckily, I'm distracted by a rapidly moving story, and by helping to organise our new house.

We send our washing out to local families, but since the rain the service has been much more erratic. Tom has been waiting for his clothes to come back for over a week. It's also become much more expensive. The prices have been creeping up, until when a bag of washing in Khoja Bahauddin costs the same as it would in New York, we suspect something is up. Later we learn that the oldest translator working for NBC, nicknamed the Professor, was adding a huge whack to the prices of everything from washing to drivers' salaries.

'Yep, we'll have to fire the Professor,' Tom says sadly. The Professor is a former teacher. He is balding with a flowing grey beard, a gentle voice and manner. He is Tom's favourite. NBC has been paying him more than the local annual salary every day for months. You can never tell who is going to fleece you.

My favourite local is Shah Mahmood. He is a driver with the worst car in Khoja Bahauddin, and a volatile temper, but he is so entertaining that everyone loves to drive with him. He is short, wiry and mercurial, his body pulsing with energy.

He answers a question with his entire frame, and has an elastic face and innate comic gift. Shah Mahmood is always laughing and so is everyone around him, even though he speaks no English. He teaches us all to say *burro b'chai* – 'let's go'. If he were living in New York he'd have an Afghan comedy channel within six months.

When Shah Mahmood tries on a pair of American sunglasses, he is immediately transformed into a rapper – 'Snoop' Mahmood. I know that Shah Mahmood probably would fleece us, as he's a 'wide boy', a chancer. But like with the CIA and the warlords, he may be a con man but he's our con man, and I adore him. I knew him when I first came, before this lot of NBC guys hired him as a driver. He was kind to me before I moved in with the people who pay his wages.

NBC producer Karl Bostic and I are driving with Shah Mahmood when he suggests coming with me to Australia.

'You. Me. Go. Australia,' which he pronounces A*h*-stral-y*a*.

'But Shah Mahmood, I live in Moscow.'

He adapts quickly.

'You. Me. Go. Moscow.'

Karl chips in, 'Shah Mahmood, if you want to drive to Moscow, you're going to have to get those brakes fixed.'

We finish setting up home. The satellite engineers connect this remote spot to New York and London, and we move our bags from the corridors into our rooms. Our bedrooms are luxurious – there are stretcher beds, curtains on the window, and we are only three to a room. I share with the two sound recordists, Jonathan and Stan. It's a pleasure not to be sharing a bedroom with a constantly changing cast of characters. On our first morning, when I do a yoga stretch, Jonathan says, 'Irris, it looks as if you're praying. In fact, it looks as if you're praying to Stan.'

I pray to Stan every day for the next two weeks.

That evening, I tell the NBC guys how grateful I am that they have taken me in.

'It's gotta be because you're a chick,' says Tom the cameraman. 'You're on the inside, and Tim from *USA Today*, he's here, too, but he's outside, in his tent.'

'Yeah, but it's a very cool tent . . .'

'Best tent in Khoj,' Tom agrees.

The house works very well. Everyone confides in me, about their lives and their heartaches and their sexual adventures. Everything's open here, it's as if we are on an extended plane flight, and I don't think these are things they share with each other. But I look out for them and they look out for me; in this hostile environment, that makes a big difference. And they make me laugh.

Jonathan wants to teach the Afghans we work with to knock on the door before they come into our rooms. Before NBC fires him, the Professor is in charge of the household, so Jonathan tries with him first.

'Okay, so you knock, go on, knock, and then I say come in and you come in. Let's try it, Professor.'

The Professor listens, bemused. He knocks and walks straight in.

Jonathan says, 'No, you knock and you wait, and then I say "come in", and then you come in.'

The Professor tries, but once again he knocks and comes in without waiting, and can't understand why he still hasn't got it right. The Professor and Jonathan fall about laughing, which makes it fun, if futile.

An American friend of mine has a small illustrated book called *Toilets of the world*, with examples from various cultures, in different materials and styles. I feel that the toilet that Hans built in Khoja Bahauddin deserves an honourable mention. It instantly changes my quality of life, as does the addition of hot water in the bathroom, now that it's getting colder. The bathroom here is the Khoja Bahauddin standard: a concrete room with a drain and two tin containers, both probably made by Ahmed from the market, on the look-out for wife number four. One container has cold water, and the other has water that has been boiled over a hob. There is a small pitcher for mixing the two, and *voila*! – my first warm 'shower' in weeks.

Producer Karl Bostic's slogan is *chera ney?* – 'why not?' Or, as the boys soon adapt the Dari, *chera fucking ney?* This breezy optimism is responsible for the improvement in living standards, and we are inspired to broaden our culinary horizons, too. We introduce 'take-out' to Khoja Bahauddin, and are now having goat shashlik delivered from across the road. You just return the steel skewers after you're done.

We walk out our front door, cross the border where there will one day be a wall, and jump across a sedentary pool of rancid muddy water, which men use as a urinal. Then we go round the corner to the shashlik joint, which doubles as a doss house. Men wrapped in blankets sleep on raised platforms. It is dark and filthy, another reason for preferring take-out. They broil the shashlik on an iron grill out front, putting two small pieces of meat and one piece of fat on each long skewer. When we ask for 'shashlik, hold the fat', they are so perplexed they give us the fat to take home in a separate bag. Who could not want the fat, it's the best part?

We give in to the take-out shashlik because no one can bear the 'Meals Ready to Eat' any longer. It went one cheese tortellini too far. And my vegetarianism is long out the window, though it's strange that the first meat I eat in twenty years turns out to be goat – not what you'd expect to fall off the wagon for.

Then we become ambitious. We decide to look beyond goat.

'Let's make chicken,' says Jonathan.

First you have to buy a chicken. No, in fact, first you have to catch a chicken. Outside our front door, near the slaughterhouse, there are chickens for sale, scratching around in mud and human excrement, God help us. Just shut your eyes and pick one. Amer, a local who used to live in Moscow, comes up at this moment, just as Jonathan and I are having second thoughts. Dubiously eyeing the ground, I check with Amer whether these chickens are any good. '*Charoshy, charoshy*' – good, good – he assures me emphatically in Russian. So Jonathan nominates the chickens that look best, from a distance, against this filthy background, and agrees a price.

'Ten US dollars for the three. I think I paid too much,' he says.

Then the owner of the chickens appoints a small boy to

catch them. The chickens run away as fast as their little legs can carry them, which is surprisingly fast, actually. It is amazing how they go from insouciant scratching in the dirt to frenzied escaping before we have even come for them, displaying an instinctive comprehension that danger is at hand. What's most interesting is that not all the chickens run, only the ones we want to buy.

The boy runs after them, and they run in the other direction, hopping over bicycle parts, puddles of mud, and through the crowds that have gathered to watch the purchase but are now only complicating the transaction. Then they turn around and run in the other direction, straight through the patch of ground used as a public toilet. *Bam*, the small boy doesn't miss a beat, he runs straight after them. Then when the chicken tires and he catches it, the small panting boy has to do it all again. Twice. We walk back, with Shah Mahmood carrying the chickens by their feet and clucking approvingly over their weight and feel.

'*Morgh* good' – chicken good – he says, mixing Dari and English in his delight. I teach him the English word, and he repeats 'chick-en' laughing. And then you really know it's Afghanistan, because once we get the chooks home, the locals fight over who gets to kill them.

After our purchase, I go driving into town with Shah Mahmood. I want him to stop in the square on the way back home, but he is clearly not happy. He uses his new English vocab to say 'chick-en' and to mime wringing its neck. I sigh. We go straight home. How can I stand between Shah Mahmood and such pleasures?

The chickens are stringy, but the meal we cook, with lots of garlic and potatoes, is delicious. We eat it on our concrete verandah, looking out over the wall which is slowly rising on the boundary of the NBC property. We feel like proud landowners. We watch the locals who work all day, breaking rocks with iron bars until they are the right shape. It is primitive, and back-breakingly difficult, though the men are very industrious.

'But you know what's amazing, at lunchtime, not one of them is to be found. It's as if they were unionised,' says Jonathan. 'They take a break at eleven – and there is nothing you could threaten them with to make them work.'

The eleven o'clock 'smoko' crosses all cultures.

The city of Taloqan falls to the Northern Alliance on the day after the three journalists die. The next day, Monday 12 November, Levon returns to Dushanbe, accompanying the corpses of our dead colleagues. Before he leaves, he shows me the piece he has written about the experience. It is very moving, but I think he ran a big risk for a guy with a wife and kids back in Montreal, and I find myself angry because I like him so much.

'We wanted to see the Taliban trenches before the Northern Alliance had a chance to interfere with them,' he says, and he appears tired and shattered by his experience, as if a light has been extinguished behind his eyes. I decide I won't press him now.

After we say goodbye to Levon, we decide to go down the Taloqan road. We take flak jackets and drive down to the front line we've been watching for weeks. It's almost unbelievable to think we will be able to cross it, like entering a special room you were forbidden access to as a child. Standing at the river crossing, I suddenly understand Levon's urge to see the Taliban trenches.

It is safer this morning than last night, twelve hours that may make the difference between life and death. It is still dangerous, of course, but there is a small distance between us and the front-line troops. It seems the Taliban really have left the ridge now.

The sky is pale blue and the river gleams turquoise, but the water is almost obscured by the chaos on the bank. The ground has been torn up by tank tracks and there are people, vehicles and animals everywhere. There are soldiers and refugee families, trucks, jeeps, APCs, horses and camels, all preparing to cross the river, or already in the water. Small piles of goods – some sacks and a table – wait patiently for their owner, a donkey saddled nearby. Trucks full of soldiers are crossing back and forth, bringing news from the front. We all listen urgently.

Refugee families squash themselves onto the backs of horses and camels. One animal can carry a man, a woman and a child, and their few possessions. They ford the river, wet up to their saddles, holding their bags aloft. Next they will have to travel down mined roads. At this stage we have only heard that Taloqan has been liberated, it is not confirmed, and the journey remains extremely dangerous, but the families are prepared to take any risk to return home, to see the houses and families they left behind more than a year ago.

I am with five American journalists, most from NBC. None of us are wearing our flak jackets. They are so heavy and cumbersome no one wears them unless they absolutely have to. Some TV journalists put them on while they are being filmed and take them off again afterwards.

As we wait to cross the river in our open-topped truck, one of the locals approaches Tom Streithorst and says, 'Give me your camera.' Turban fronts up to baseball cap, and I can see from the tilt of Tom's cap that he's not amused. He is not going to hand over a Betacam worth more than US$30,000, but the man is armed and will take some handling. It always makes the guys edgy to refuse a man with a gun.

Fortunately, we get the call to cross the river before there is an international incident. It's finally our turn to go into the territory that the Taliban controlled until yesterday. We mask our nerves by discussing food. Tom says he misses mozzarella and basil salad. Another journalist says pumpkin pie. The first shock is how familiar everything looks – this road could be any of the roads we travel down around Khoja Bahauddin.

We drive up a narrow, rutted path, between the high mud-brick walls of a village, and we are tossed about in the back of our truck. Only one vehicle at a time can pass through here. Even then it risks getting stuck or overturning if one of dozens of small bridges – in reality just a few logs bound together – gives way.

Our driver is careless, grazing walls and trees, and almost killing one of the children who run in groups on the road and climb onto the walls to watch us. 'Duck!' NBC producer Kevin Sites shouts as we drive under the branches of a large tree. Three small faces peek out, above a door in a wall. They are beautiful girls, with green eyes shining out of dirty faces framed with red scarves. Two girls wearing purple scarves sit on top of the wall.

211

Although every inch forward is hard won, we often have to reverse because trucks carrying soldiers are coming in the opposite direction. The only road rules seem to be that vehicles with guns have priority. We wave at them and check where they have come from, and whether Taloqan is free, and if the road is clear of Taliban. At this rate it's going to take us a long time to get anywhere.

Suddenly I hear shouting, 'No, no, no!' and a loud crash, almost before I feel the impact. Our driver has reversed into another wall with such force that he smashes it. Tonnes of mud brick come crashing down on our truck. It hits me on the back of the head, and I fall under the weight of it.

If it had been concrete I would be dead, but mud brick is surprisingly light, as I now know. I hear shouting, 'No. No, stop, for Chrissakes stop, you've hit a wall, someone's hurt,' as the boys come to help me.

Before they reach me, I emerge from the rubble. Five men are looking at me as if they are watching a resurrection.

'It's okay, I'm okay,' I tell them, brushing myself down.

'Are you sure? Are you hurt? You're not hurt at all? You must be hurt,' says Tom. 'There's an awful lot of mud brick here, you know.'

He's right. The tray of the truck is full of debris.

Jonathan says, 'I put my arm out to save you, but it was too quick. I really thought you were dead.'

'Well, all I can say is it's a miracle. Nothing hurts. I'm not even scratched.'

I feel a mixture of shock and relief. No one seems concerned about the wall we've knocked down, so we keep driving, and reversing, and driving until we make it through the village onto a wider stretch of path. There is still mortar fire in the hills as we stop another truck full of soldiers. They are on their way south to Kunduz, where they say as many as 20,000 Taliban soldiers are now surrounded. We ask them about the fighting here. They say they took Taliban prisoners, mainly foreign fighters.

'They were foreigners – look, we took their cards, and the letters they were writing.' They show us cards and letters, in Arabic and the Pakistani language Urdu. They also show us a Dari–Arabic dictionary. Before we leave we ask them about the land mines here.

'Yes, the road is still very heavily mined. Your driver should leave the road where it is indicated.'

The local sign for land mines is three small rocks laid across a path. But these roads may not have even these rudimentary warnings yet.

The men on the truck speak to our translator in Dari, gesticulating as they talk. It's hard when the discourse about your safety is being conducted in a language you don't understand. I get our translator to ask our driver if he knows where the land mines are.

'No, he says he does not know this road at all,' the translator informs me.

'Well, get him to ask these soldiers – they know!' I find myself snapping.

There is more stopping and shouting and hand waving, until the driver says he now knows which is the safe stretch. If I hadn't asked, would he have driven blindly down a mined road? We plough off the path, into a field. Other vehicles have taken the detour ahead of us and flattened the grass. This is an even more unstable ride, but it feels safer. When we return to the gravel path, three kilometres further on, two men are walking towards us.

It is a soldier and his prisoner. The Northern Alliance soldier looks like Omar Sharif, and his Taliban prisoner, a delicate handsome Pakistani with hair down to his shoulders, looks like Jesus. The soldier is carrying a gun and has bound his prisoner around the chest with a rope, as if he had tethered a goat. This is as sophisticated as it gets here. We interview both men, and Omar Sharif unties his prisoner for the camera. Abdul Manan looks about seventeen years old, but says he is twenty-two. He clutches at his side, wincing in pain, increasing his resemblance to Jesus. His clothes are ragged, and he has grass in his matted hair. He says he was on holiday in Afghanistan when the Taliban shanghaied him into their army.

I hear this frequently from captured Taliban prisoners. 'I was sightseeing in Kabul' is clearly a line they have been taught to trot out in case of capture. Omar Sharif says Abdul Manan was hiding in another room when the Northern Alliance killed his friends. And now he is here. He is thin and

213

thirsty, and he winces again. Producer Kevin Sites offers him some water, and he is drinking from the NBC bottle just as a truck full of Northern Alliance soldiers comes into view behind him.

I wonder what their reaction will be. Tom, who is shooting the interview, says he pulled out to a wide shot, waiting for violence. 'I *wanted* Jesus beat up on camera in front of me. I was disappointed when he wasn't. I was even pissed off when Kevin gave him the water. Isn't it funny what this place does to you?'

The soldiers don't attack the prisoner, and Omar Sharif says he feels no guilt about shooting at him or at any of the Taliban soldiers he killed. 'I have been a refugee for two years. The Taliban took our wives, our land and our children.'

The interview over, the truck full of soldiers drives off towards the new front line. Omar Sharif re-ties his prisoner, clamping the rope around his chest and arms, and they walk together in the opposite direction, down a dusty lane. We watch them leave. Both are thin, filthy and poor, and neither is in uniform. Victor and vanquished are bound together in a way that seems to summarise this conflict.

When they are out of sight, we continue in the direction of Taloqan. US bombs, which were targeting the Taliban trenches, have left huge craters here by the side of the road. We also see land mines studded in the soil around them. The trenches are already crawling with locals who are looting them, stealing back what the Taliban originally stole from them. It is not much. One man is removing a blue door. Another is taking some sacking. The trenches are poor and dark. The Taliban soldiers departed so recently their discarded tea leaves are still wet. They were grilling mice to survive. The ferocity of the American bombing at close quarters must have been terrifying.

The sun is setting, and we decide to turn back. We did not intend to stay overnight. We stop by General Bariolai's head-quarters and he cheerfully describes the battle he has fought and what lies ahead. He says that the Northern Alliance has taken Herat in the west, and its troops are now twenty kilometres from the gates of Kabul. He also says the Northern Alliance will be ready to attack Kabul within the next few days. Having watched and waited here for so long, the speed of this offensive is bewildering.

We go back in the dark, and I file on all that we have seen today, trying to predict a timetable for the conflict. I write by hand in my battered exercise book, by the light of a paraffin lamp. Then I carry that lamp inside to use a satellite phone, which is sitting next to banks of TV equipment. It's a strange combination. NBC has set up a massive television operation, running all their state-of-the-art equipment from the generator, but there are still no lights.

I look up to see Maurice, the Kiwi cameraman, at the door. In case he needs the satphone, I tell him I won't be long.

'Yes, I'll just put the cat out, and I'll be coming to bed,' he replies cheekily.

We both laugh. I didn't realise how domestic I sounded.

Taking my paraffin lamp, I go back outside to write my next piece. We are receiving the first reports that Taliban leaders are loading up their cars and fleeing Kabul.

It's cold as I sit down at the table on the concrete balcony, the candle's shadow flickering across my pages. Tim from *USA Today* is out here, too. He can't sleep, even though he has the best tent in Khoja Bahauddin. My last live shot is for Deutsche Welle's 11 p.m. bulletin, which works out at 3 a.m. local time, and Jonathan and Tim sit up with me, talking into the cold night, huddled on the balcony under the gleaming sky. We go to bed just before dawn, while down south, Northern Alliance troops are entering Kabul. When we wake up the next day, Tuesday 13 November, Kabul has fallen.

I thought General Bariolai was being optimistic when he predicted yesterday that it would take a week. I can't believe that the Taliban have simply abandoned the capital they had vowed to defend to the bitter end. I discuss the speed of this collapse with our translator, Halim. He is forty-eight years old, with a wonderfully refined face, good English, and a roguish sense of humour. He has the most extraordinary laugh, like The Riddler in *Batman*. He lived in Germany for five years, selling used cars, and is always bringing us Greek antiquities to buy.

I enjoy hearing Halim's opinions, and he has an unusual take on the Taliban's speedy retreat across the country.

'Yes, it is a sign that the people were sick of them because they were so boring.'

215

Halim is actually learning a new word, 'boring', which he uses incorrectly in many sentences, but I like this angle on things. It wasn't just the Taliban's cruelty that made them so unpopular, it was also that they enforced dreariness, and made people's lives so drab.

This is not unlike the end of the Soviet Union. The Communists were atheists and the Taliban are religious fanatics – they were polar opposites in ideological terms, but both inflicted greyness on people.

I am busy filing all day on the flight of the Taliban's leadership from Kabul. They took care to clear out the country's coffers before they left and also seized eight Christian aid workers whom they had charged with proselytising Muslims, a crime punishable by death. It appears they regard the Westerners as a bargaining chip in any negotiations with Coalition forces.

I also file on the big news of the day: the Northern Alliance's victorious entry into Kabul. Joyful crowds swarmed onto the streets at dawn to cheer the troops on. There are the first reports of men shaving off their beards to celebrate the Taliban's departure, and of looting by soldiers as well. Every news desk wants an analysis of Washington's demand that the Northern Alliance troops should stay out of the capital. The Northern Alliance says it has to intervene to secure the capital and prevent a dangerous power vacuum from developing. Will the US succeed in imposing this unrealistic demand on the Alliance leadership? Are events moving too quickly for Washington to control?

Now Kabul is free, we can't keep on reporting on events there from up here in the north. It is three weeks since I returned to Afghanistan, and though I was thinking about leaving, I can't go home now. The logic of history is pushing us towards Kabul. When I go to the European Broadcasting Union to file, I hear about a convoy of journalists preparing to drive first to Taloqan, and then over the mountains to Kabul.

Should we join? I discuss this with NBC correspondent Jim Maceda. We pore over the map. The roads from the north aren't yet secure, or free of land mines. The main highway south is one of the few good roads in Afghanistan, and the journey should take little more than a day, but the Taliban still control stretches of this road. There are reports that some 20,000 Taliban soldiers, Afghans and desperate foreign fighters are surrounded further south, near the town of Kunduz. A siege is developing.

So that road's out.

Instead we will have to travel to Kabul across the Hindu Kush, the highest mountain range in this mountainous country. It's not reassuring to learn that Hindu Kush means 'Hindu slaughter'. Conditions are so rugged that this journey of less than 500 kilometres takes four days. It involves driving off road, in winter, in Russian military jeeps, along goat tracks strewn with land mines. The wrecks of vehicles destroyed by mines sit as grim warnings along the paths. There are also no guarantees that our vehicles will be able to cross the passes at the summit. The winter snows have begun and many of the paths are already impassable.

When a BBC crew did this trip three weeks ago, the pass was blocked and they had to transfer two tonnes of gear onto thirty-five donkeys, and ride across, through snow reaching up to their saddles. The price was an added complication. The Afghan horsemen used to charge ten dollars per animal in pre-air strike days. But they upped their prices mid-ride, demanding US$5000 from the BBC, and pulling out their guns to collect payment. That's a cautionary tale.

We look at the maps again. The best ones are printed in Russian, from the days of the Soviet war in the 1980s. We can't make out much, which doesn't stop us returning to them frowningly over and over. NBC decides it will join the convoy. Do I want to come with them? It is expensive and dangerous, with drivers now charging up to US$3000 per car – more than thirty years' salary – for the mountain journey.

I take a deep breath. I suppose I do, though I am very frightened of this drive, which I have been avoiding for six weeks. I didn't travel down to the Panjshir Valley because of the demands of this journey and other journalists' tales of near-death experiences, as well as the difficulty of making it back out. I don't want to go, but now that the war has been fought and 'won' in four days, I find myself agreeing to do the drive that terrifies me.

There are many farewells to make. My best friends Tom and Jonathan are staying behind. Jonathan will be going home to New York. Tom is staying on, but will remain in Khoj to pack up the gear. I hope he will come to Kabul next week, but there are no guarantees. I'm sad to say goodbye to both of them.

I file till very late, as the fall of Kabul is big news. The presenter of Ireland's most prestigious breakfast program ends our interview by saying, 'Look after yourself and God bless.' I can't think of any other national broadcaster who would be so solicitous during a live bulletin. Who could not love filing for the Irish?

I'm cold and tired by the time I come back to the room, but too tense and scared to sleep. Jonathan is up and I confess to him how frightened I am. There are no safety nets, and this journey breaks all the rules about knowing how you will get out. If we need to, if someone's sick, or we have an accident, or hit a land mine, I have no idea how we will ever get off that mountain.

Jonathan tries to reassure me, in whispers so as not to wake Stan, that everything will be all right, and that this crazy journey is the right thing to do. I suddenly remember how when I worked for ABC Australia, and we were filming at a remote spot somewhere on a mountain in Laos or PNG, the sound recordist used to say 'Right, this is the place – if your appendix bursts now, you're dead. No one can save you.'

Jonathan laughs, but says, 'You'll be good,' using that unintentionally comforting New York phrase, before adding, 'after all, you're the toughest sheila I know.'

I'm not so sure, and in the morning as I'm packing to leave, Jonathan changes his mind.

'I don't think you should go, I've got a bad feeling about this trip.'

'Jonathan! You're not allowed to say that. Even if you think it.'

'I know, I know, but I do think it . . .'

He tries to make up for it by plying me with useful gifts.

'Here, take this torch, you'll need it. And a knife. I can't believe that you don't have a knife.'

Knives again – but he's right. I do need both.

'Please, please be safe,' he says as I pack the pocketknife. I carry my bags outside for the last time, and promise to be as careful as I can, brushing aside that premonition of death two nights ago. I beg him to take care, too, and looking around the desolate vista of Khoja Bahauddin, I have a sudden moment of clarity. This is not the time to leave Afghanistan. We should both see this story through to the end.

'Jonathan, don't go to New York. Come to Kabul!'

Chapter 16

OVER THE HINDU KUSH, 14 NOVEMBER 2001

'You. Me. Go. Kabul.' I say to Shah Mahmood.

Shah Mahmood's small intense face lights up as he repeats 'Kabul' and slaps me on the back, laughing.

Seven of us are travelling on this journey over the Hindu Kush, excluding our drivers. Producer Kevin Sites, reporter Jim Maceda, engineer Jim Bruton, Maurice the Kiwi cameraman, Stan his sound recordist, and our translator Halim.

There are three vehicles, and I'm travelling with the two Jims, in Shah Mahmood's jeep. It's an old Russian military jeep, olive green, battered and dusty, like everything else in northern Afghanistan, with no brakes, clutch or suspension to speak of. It's the worst car in the convoy, but Shah Mahmood is driving it, so I don't mind. He is eccentric and quite wild, but perversely I feel safe with him. I realise that I've known him the whole time I've been in Afghanistan.

We pack our gear into the back of the jeep. Two doors open onto a small area behind the back seats, where we pile our luggage and provisions for the long journey. We take enough food, water, petrol and first aid kits for five days. The other vehicles have more petrol and all the generators, editing gear and videophones. 'Laptops on top,' we remind each other. As it turns out all this ensures is that whenever we have to brake suddenly our laptops go flying, injuring us and them.

We climb in. It's 14 November and Northern Alliance troops have entered Kabul, despite calls from Washington to hold back. Like everyone on the ground – journalists, Northern Alliance leaders, perhaps even some Taliban leaders – officials in Washington have been caught off guard by the speed of the Taliban collapse. The US fears the situation will spiral out of its control and that it will merely replace one set of Islamic militants with another. However, when we discuss this in the jeep we agree that it is impossible to ask victorious troops to stay outside a city in these circumstances. In the end, Washington does wring a concession out of the Northern Alliance: that they will go in and secure the city, to ensure that the Taliban really have left, and then they will withdraw, waiting for the new multi-party interim government to take control. They will do this to prevent a power vacuum from developing, which in Afghanistan is code for a takeover of sections of the city by armed bandits. Soon we'll be able to gauge for ourselves whether this is being put into effect.

We stop in at the Foreign Ministry to meet the other vehicles leaving in the convoy. The office and Massoud's house are both empty. It is the end of an era. All the ornate heavy furniture is being loaded onto a truck for relocation to Taloqan. Khoja Bahauddin is reverting to being the sleepy, irrelevant backwater it always was. This is the quickest shutdown I've ever seen.

I feel a moment's nostalgia, but it's a bright, cool morning and the beginning of a new adventure puts us in fine spirits as we jolt along the well-worn path to the river. 'I'm in the mood for the Shah ma dude,' carols Jim Maceda.

Shah Mahmood laughs, an infectious sound.

Contemplating the perilous drive ahead, I check with the boys, 'Why do we do this?'

'Because out here, we know we are alive,' says Jim Maceda.

'I can be myself here in a way I am not back home,' Jim Bruton offers reflectively, but certainly, in his distinctive Southern drawl. 'These extremes place demands on you that you never face in ordinary life. Rising to those challenges – that's what I'm here for.'

I tell them that an English journalist says he's here for the 'kicks and chicks and cash and chaos'. They both smile. Okay, so that's nailed them. But what am I doing here? Danger is invigorating and addictive but being the boys' own adventure girl doesn't seem like enough of an explanation at the moment. Frankly, I think we're crazy.

At Dashti Qala, the sky is a dazzling blue above the bare brown mountains, and the river that we know so well is once again full of traffic. In fact, today, Wednesday, three days after the Taliban have retreated from this front line, the river is crowded with people, animals and vehicles.

The riverflat is muddier than when we were here two days ago, but the most significant difference is in the state of the river itself. Where before it was sluggish and quiet, today it is fast moving and swollen. We stand on the flat, looking out, and see a dispiriting sight. A Russian jeep just like ours is stuck in the middle of the muddy water, submerged up to its roof. The owner is standing barefoot on top of it, his pants rolled up to his knees, shouting half-heartedly at someone on the shore. He has the defeated air of a man who knows rescue will take some time.

We discuss our situation and conclude that the only way we'll make it across is if we are towed, but what vehicle could do the job? On cue one chugs into view. It's an old Soviet T-54 tank, straight out of a Russian war movie, except for the turbaned Afghan fighters sitting on top of it.

For US$50 they agree to haul us across the river. Shah Mahmood attaches our jeep to the tank with a rope, and the soldiers wave at us from the tank top as it starts up with a muffled roar and jerks forward. Shah Mahmood steers intently, and the rope pulls and holds. Some water comes in under my door, but with much shouting in Dari and waving of hands, we are towed across the river between trucks, horses and camels. It's a thrilling start.

'At my age, this is better than sex,' Jim Maceda jokes.

Others in higher vehicles pay for horses to ride across in front of them, feeling out how deep the water is, so they know where it's safe to drive.

The exhilarating crossing is followed by hours of slow progress through the villages of the Q'urogh Mountains. We pass the wall our truck crashed into two days ago and I am surprised at what a huge chunk we tore out of it. When we are clear of the villages, we drive along unmarked tracks through the desert of northern Afghanistan. Our wheels kick up clouds of sand, and the drivers stop to fight over whether the Taliban laid land mines here before they fled. Shah Mahmood opens the door and stands with one foot on the car seat, the other on the door handle to give him height, looking out over the jeep's roof and surveying the desert. His calf muscle, like all of him, is twitching with tension.

'No, it is this way. We must go this way.' Shah Mahmood is certain.

The drivers get out of the cars to shout at each other. After close to an hour of vehement disagreement, we change direction, backtracking through the sand, and circling around in the opposite direction. Shah Mahmood is furious with his fellow drivers. 'This is the wrong way. This will take us hours more.'

They are furious with Shah Mahmood. 'He is crazy. He wants to take us across the land mines. This desert has changed since we were last here. It is not good enough to say "*inshallah* we won't be killed".'

We lurch through rocky outcrops, the jeep's gears crunching with a terrible grinding noise. It is hard going. Shah Mahmood's jeep basically has no suspension, and we jolt painfully over craters, taking our position from a river that has dried up during the drought. Eucalyptus and birch trees still grow there. There is a dusty waterwheel in the dry riverbed, ancient vines trailing over it like spider webs. We drive along tank tracks through the hills, passing trucks carrying soldiers also headed for Taloqan. The dust billows up until it covers the windscreen and the road and we can't see the path in front of us. 'Stop. Shah Mahmood, stop! Wait until the dust settles and you can see the road,' Jim Maceda says as he peers ahead from the front seat. We seem to have lost everyone else in the convoy.

'Are they behind us?' he asks.

Jim Bruton looks through the back window and replies, 'I don't know. I can't see a thing.'

When we rejoin the path that Shah Mahmood was heading for three hours earlier he is once again furious about the waste of time. He shouts in Dari, and Jim Maceda shouts back at him in English. Neither can understand the other, but everything is clear.

'Yes, Shah Mahmood, it took longer, but we couldn't take the risk. There could have been land mines there.'

Shah Mahmood responds furiously in Dari.

'I bet you he was right and we could have gone this way after all,' I say.

We'll never know. When we finally crawl into Taloqan that evening, there's dust in every crevice of our bodies.

The road into Taloqan is clogged with returning refugees and soldiers. Military trucks swerve around donkey carts and people on foot. Everyone, including Shah Mahmood, is blaring their horns.

The first thing that we notice about Taloqan is that its main street is paved, and that some houses are built of concrete rather than mud. The land here is not as badly affected by the drought as the desert area we have just left. Food stalls are stocked with fresh vegetables, of much better quality than any we saw further north. There are large, creamy-coloured cauliflowers, red apples and purplish pomegranates with shiny rinds. Bakery windows are full of bread, and sides of lamb hang from hooks.

After Khoja Bahauddin this is a big, busy city. We are wide-eyed.

One of the translators travelling in the convoy with us, Fayoz, is nineteen years old, and this is his home. He was living in Khoja Bahauddin with his father and is now returning to see his mother, sisters and brothers for the first time in almost eighteen months.

'This is the best day of me,' he says, beaming.

We go to the Foreign Ministry. Zubair is there, proud, no longer the diffident man I met reeling from the shock of Massoud's death almost two months ago. I congratulate him on the Northern Alliance's return to Taloqan.

He says that we cannot continue our journey tonight as the road is not yet safe, and suggests an address of a house we might be able to stay in. It turns out to be a single-storey building from which the Taliban only recently departed. Their slogans are still scrawled in huge curving black Arabic script on the walls, but otherwise they have left nothing. It is bleak and empty, with cement walls and floors, and the stink from the filth-encrusted bathroom pervades the whole building. Though the light is fading and everyone is tired, I hope we can do better than to live in Taliban dirt.

We go to look at a second house, which is in a compound with a number of empty buildings. The windows are broken, but it has better security, cosier rooms, and a garden area with a camp oven. Once, it would have been appealing, a compound which could house many families who would meet in the fertile garden. Even now, empty, the garden grey with dust, it retains some of that charm, and so we decide to stay. We buy a carpet for the floor. The owner of the house brings mattresses. And I put my sleeping bag beside Stan's, for old times' sake.

Outside, the streets of Taloqan are heaving and joyous.

'The Taliban are gone and now we can listen to music and shave our beards and go out at night. We couldn't go out at night during the Taliban times,' says twenty-four-year-old Freydon. He is clean shaven, revelling in the street with his friend Safiollah.

'The first thing we did after they left is we went to the barbers and we shaved off our beards. Then we turned on our tapes, then we threw away our turbans,' he says, counting off the signs of freedom on his fingers.

In the bazaar, barbers are doing a roaring trade. Men queue patiently to have their beards shaved. Inside, the mirrors are cracked, the walls are covered with ancient travel posters so faded it is difficult to divine which country they are advertising. The barbers wield their scissors energetically, and everyone, staff and customers, is smiling broadly. The snipping sound reminds me of the old Australian shearer's song . . . *click go the shears, boys*.

Outside there is music. We follow the sound through the bazaar, like the Pied Piper's children, to a *chaikhana*, a teahouse, where men gather for kebab and rice. The owner, Nafisullah, welcomes us. He is also smiling. There's an epidemic of smiling in Taloqan.

Nafisullah is playing a tape of Afghan pop star Farhad Darya, which he kept hidden from the Taliban's brutal religious police for more than a year.

'We love music and for two years here when the Taliban were in power we did not hear it. You know that without music people are dead,' he says.

Everything here appears festive. Carts are drawn by horses adorned with bobbles and bells. A particularly splendid black horse with multicoloured braids and red bobbles pulls a wooden cart carrying four passengers. Two men with guns across their knees face forwards, and two blue burqas face backwards. It jingles by.

We go back to base to file about the celebrations in Taloqan, and about the war still to be fought thirty-five kilometres down the road in Kunduz. The estimated 20,000 retreating Taliban fighters remain trapped there. Six thousand of them are understood to be 'foreign' fighters from Pakistan, Chechnya and many Arab countries, trained and paid by Osama bin Laden.

The Northern Alliance is planning to attack Kunduz, but Commander Mohammed Daoud holds a press conference in the garden outside the Foreign Ministry here to announce that he is postponing the offensive at the request of the local mayor. The mayor hopes to separate the Afghan fighters from the 'international terrorists' at Kunduz. Low-ranking Taliban will be given an opportunity to defect.

'But for high-ranking and foreign Taliban, there will be no deal. They will all be tried.'

General Daoud also says that two Pakistani jets have landed in Kunduz over the past forty-eight hours, and according to Northern Alliance information Pakistan is evacuating its military personnel from the besieged city.

At the press conference we ask him about disturbing rumours that the Taliban have not left Taloqan, and that there are militias in hiding here, preparing an attack from within the city. General Daoud concedes that it is possible, for one of his brigades was fired on and some of his men were killed when they entered a compound here yesterday. 'That is why my soldiers are mopping up house by house.'

He tells us that the eight Christian aid workers have been

freed by Northern Alliance troops and that Hamed Karzai is back in Kandahar.

The snake is shedding one skin and growing another.

General Daoud tells American journalist Jon Lee Anderson that the former Taliban commander in Taloqan is in 'a safe location'. Jon's translator discovers that the safe location is Daoud's home, and he talks the guards into letting them in.

The Taliban commander, Mullah Shabir Ahmed, agrees to meet them. A pale man in his mid-thirties, with a long reddish beard, Mullah Ahmed is being held in a building just inside the front gate. His room is small and he sits near its sole window, an AK-47 resting on the sill behind him. It gives a new dimension to 'house arrest', living as your enemy's guest and being allowed to keep your guns.

'I was studying at a *madrasa* in Pakistan,' says Mullah Ahmed, 'and when the Taliban began I joined and entered Afghanistan with them, filled with pure Islamic feeling. In the beginning, this feeling we had was splendid, but, more recently, we have begun having doubts about some of the commanders who are with the Taliban,' he says, alluding to the foreign fighters.

'Following the martyrdom of Ahmed Shah Massoud, we realised that outside hands, terrorists, were involved in the movement.' He's on solid ground with this line here in Taloqan, Massoud's old capital. 'So, for the good of the country, we decided to come over to the Northern Alliance.'

He and the two commanders under him, who are also now being held here at Daoud's house, remained behind in Taloqan and turned themselves over to General Daoud, along with several hundred fighters. The rest of the Taliban retreated to Kunduz. Mullah Ahmed says he stayed on to ensure the security of the town, and he personally called General Daoud to tell him the way into Taloqan was safe.

This was how Taloqan was reconquered by the Northern Alliance.

The Taliban leader has not revised his Muslim beliefs. 'I am still proud of the name Taliban.' The attacks on the World Trade Center and the Pentagon, he claims, were not the actions of the Taliban, but of terrorists. 'It's hurtful to hear the Taliban

227

name insulted, and to see it used by others who have their own purposes in mind.'

He says he supports the rules against rape, pederasty, fornication, gambling and drinking alcohol. And also the importance of beards. 'These are things commanded by the messenger of Islam.'

Mullah Ahmed says that he doesn't agree with all of the Taliban edicts, like the ban on music and kite flying, though it appears he was happy enough to enforce them, ordering the religious police to beat people who broke the rules. He says he opposed the Taliban's destruction of the giant Buddhas at Bamian.

'They posed no danger to Islam, and they were part of Afghanistan's history.'

It seems that despite what General Daoud indicated at the press conference, it is also part of Afghanistan's history that this man will not be punished for his support of the Taliban and his top-level role in the regional Taliban power structure, simply because he has defected.

Locals are not impressed. The owner of a Taloqan bookstore, Ghulam Sarwar Akbari, tells Jon Lee Anderson he is 'at a loss' about this merging of the two forces. 'Yesterday, Shabir Ahmed was a mullah wearing a black turban, and today he is living in Daoud Khan's house! And there are others who were wearing turbans and are now in *pakuls*, walking the streets.' Akbari is appalled. 'Every time a new government comes into power, the local strongmen change their disguises. They face up to no responsibility for the misfortune their wars cause to the civilians.'

I ask every person I interview about the side switching, since it is the most incomprehensible strand of the conflict for me. Some explain it in terms of poverty. Poor fighters join whoever is powerful. If the man who is paying you switches sides, you switch sides with him. It is feudal, like the structure in Europe in medieval times. Some explain it in terms of the absence of nationalism. In this region, people don't feel themselves Afghans, they are more closely defined by their tribes. You go where the tribal leader goes.

Many people blame foreigners for the plight of Afghanistan and the rash of side switching. They remind me that America helped the Mujaheddin in order to defeat the Soviets, but that after the Mujaheddin were victorious, America didn't stay to help them create a good government. If America had stayed, they argue, all this side switching would never have happened.

Others also blame the foreigners for cementing the rule of the gun, which allowed fighters to gain control of the country and push out or kill Afghanistan's educated elite. Now, people say, the few who remain are powerless to speak out, in the land where the Kalashnikov is king.

Everywhere, people look to these same foreigners whom they blame for their predicament to intervene and enforce a reasonable political solution. Like a mantra, every man I interview repeats that he is sick of war.

Walking in the bazaar I realise that this whole story can be understood through hats. Fashion explains everything. If a man wears a black turban and a long beard he is Taliban. If he wears a coloured scarf and *pakul*, the grey cap favoured by Ahmed Shah Massoud, he is with the Northern Alliance – or perhaps a foreign journalist (more and more of my colleagues seem to be wearing this kit whenever I see them).

A hat-seller in the bazaar in Taloqan says he almost sold out of *pakuls* earlier this week, in the days before the city fell. The Taliban once threatened to shoot anyone wearing the *pakul*, the symbol of Massoud. But now it's the Taliban's own soldiers who are queuing up at the hat stall to buy them. When a war is being won through defections, it's important to show distinctly where your new loyalties lie.

The Taliban had a ludicrously strict dress code. Men were compelled to wear the local pyjama suit (a good choice – I now have two pairs) and they had to wear it with a waistcoat, which had to be striped. The long blanket men wrap around themselves in winter was also compulsory, as were turbans. These had to be worn with a long, loose end hanging below the shoulder. Decrees were posted in public, signed by Mullah Mohammed Omar himself, saying that those who did not wear their turbans crooked would go to gaol. Beards had to be long enough to be clenched in a fist and protrude at the far end.

Although there is something almost comical about the dour, bleak Taliban as Style Nazis, the sanctions were serious. Any man who didn't obey would be locked in a container – a punishment with a terrible history of death in northern Afghanistan. No wonder everyone is rushing to buy Northern Alliance outfits.

We all sleep in one room, seven of us lining the walls, head to toe, Afghan style. A large lamp gives off some heat in the centre of the room and our translator, Halim, tells us about his wife. 'She is so old and so ugly – you can't believe it. Her teeth are so long. She is sixty years old and I am only forty-eight, that is twelve years older than me. It is time I took a younger wife.'

He has his eye on an educated younger woman, perhaps one who used to work at a university, a woman in her twenties. That would be ideal.

It's a strange bedtime story.

I dream of hideous hags with grey hair and long teeth, and am woken before dawn by lengthy calls to prayer. A new moon has been spotted in the sky above Mecca. The Muslim holy month of Ramadan has begun. I lie in my sleeping bag, listening to the muezzin and remember all the column inches devoted to whether there would be fighting here during Ramadan. Most of the country has fallen before Ramadan began.

In the morning we pack to leave Taloqan. The Professor appears bearing Stan's laundry and a piece of audio equipment he'd left behind in Khoja Bahauddin. Stan is touched. He feared he would never see it again. Even though we are about to sack the Professor for stealing from us, he is also kind and helpful – one of the paradoxes of relationships in this place. Perhaps you can't have a real relationship with people so much poorer than you. You almost have to expect them to steal from you.

There are continuing reports of marauding Taliban gangs. It's not safe to stay any longer. The siege in Kunduz is a fascinating developing story, but when I check with Deutsche Welle and Voice of America they want me to move on. 'Get to Kabul.'

The Foreign Ministry is organising a convoy to the capital, theoretically one where we'll stay in contact with the other vehicles and won't lose each other. But before we can join, we have to find a new driver. The rough road has caused Shah Mahmood's jeep to break down one time too many, and he has to stay in Taloqan for major repairs. We will have to continue without him. I'm heartbroken, but he promises that once he returns to Khoja Bahauddin, he will come to Kabul with the rest of the NBC crew.

The women's activist Farahnaz Nazir, whose interview with me earned her a death threat from Khoja Bahauddin's military commander, is also travelling to Kabul in this convoy. It is wonderful to see her and her family here. They are accompanying CBS, who can no longer take them to the safety of Tajikistan because they are not going there themselves. The fall of Kabul has changed everyone's plans.

Farahnaz is worried because among the Northern Alliance soldiers assigned to the convoy are some men loyal to Quazi Kobir, the commander who threatened her life. The men assigned to protect us are dangerous for her, and they make it plain they know where she is. She feels as if her guards are her gaolers. Even the house CBS rents in Taloqan turns out to be owned by Quazi Kobir. Farahnaz doesn't sleep a wink all night.

I remember my first interview with Farahnaz, when the only threats she had received were from disgruntled local men in Khoja Bahauddin, not its all-powerful military commander.

'Do you think that without freedom we are alive?' she said. 'Women are alive, but it's not life, we are a dead body that moves, with no permission to act. Women are only sitting at home. It is better to die than to live this life.'

Farahnaz and her family plan to apply for asylum in Canada, following a suggestion from a CBS correspondent who is Canadian. I don't think there's any point in Farahnaz applying to Australia. Its current policies on accepting asylum seekers are very tough, so I also encourage Farahnaz to apply to Canada. Any application in either country will be made more difficult, of course, because Farahnaz's oppressor comes from our allies against the Taliban, the Northern Alliance.

We find a new driver. Jamal is more quiet and modest than Shah Mahmood. While he is also an excellent driver and a skilled mechanic, his Russian jeep turns out to be in pretty bad shape, too. Battling across the rough tracks on these forbidding mountains destroys vehicles.

We line up for the convoy at a bridge at the western end of town. If you follow this road for fifty kilometres you will reach Kunduz. Although it is the best road and the most direct route, we can't take it because of the Taliban fighters trapped there.

Instead we travel through a plain dotted with small wheat farms. Snow-capped mountains surround us on all sides. About thirty kilometres away, the front line in the battle for Kunduz begins at a river near the village of Bangi. Taliban and Northern Alliance forces face each other, less than a kilometre apart. We turn off before Bangi, where children stand guard over patches of wheat, spread out to dry along the road. We avoid the wheat and the children, and regretfully leave the paved road behind. We start bouncing along the gravel paths once more and begin our ascent.

The nearness of the Taliban makes everybody nervous. Our convoy's armed guards include Samim, one of Massoud's bodyguards who lived with us in Khoja Bahauddin. We are genuinely happy to see each other. 'Is Jonathan here?' he asks about his Jewish 'blood brother'. Samim is returning to his village in the Panjshir Valley for the first time since the Northern Alliance victory.

We drive along these dusty foothills for most of the day. Strange, empty white cones dot the landscape, abandoned tents stopped up with stones. Here, people don't pack up their tents when they go home – they just leave them, in case they have to return. In Afghanistan, people have no confidence that they won't be refugees over and over again.

When we stop anywhere, crowds of men surround us. Had they started to get used to us in Khoja Bahauddin? It seems that the attention there had begun to abate slightly. Here it is unremitting, open-mouthed, slack-jawed staring once more.

At the village of Naharine we stop as our drivers are arguing once again.

'What is it?' I ask.

Halim explains that the drivers are uncertain what to do because the word is that the Salang Pass, which they'd hoped to take, is closed, and the road is mined.

'Why would they drive up a mined road to a closed pass?' I ask Halim. 'What else are they fighting about?'

'Where to go next.'

After some time they agree that if we take a longer detour via a lower pass, the Hawaq, we might make it across because it won't be blocked by snow. My heart sinks as it will take significantly longer, but at this point it doesn't seem we have many options.

'*Burro b'chai* – let's go,' I say sombrely.

Our jeep turns off the path and starts climbing up into the mountains an hour before sunset. Driving cross-country, up-hill, in a heavily mined area, is a bone-jolting and terrifying combination. We veer up a rocky stream to avoid land mines and are soon driving through this landscape in the pitch-black Afghan night. Even though there is water in the creeks, the dust has not abated; it streams towards us out of the dark, picked out by our headlights. The drive continues into the night, on narrow ridges, above high cliffs, with walls of rock above us and icy rivers far below.

We follow hairpin bends, frightening enough to traverse in our jeep which fits on the path, but there are huge trucks, too, reversing up and downhill because the paths are too narrow to allow them to turn. They have developed this strange zig-zag, taking one section forwards, then the next section backwards, from ramp to ramp, in order to negotiate this part of the drive. I watch this push-me pull-you progress in the darkness in disbelief. Sometimes two trucks meet back to back, one reversing uphill in the dark, the other reversing downhill. I have never seen anything like it anywhere else in the world.

We manage to make it across this mountain – without reversing – but then on the next peak, in the middle of a rocky outcrop, our jeep loses its drive shaft. Impatient cars from our convoy, caught behind us, begin tooting and cursing, as if we have stopped on a mountainside in the middle of nowhere, on a freezing night, out of choice.

Our driver, Jamal, takes his toolbox and lies under the jeep, while other cars edge past on the narrow path, spraying him with gravel. It is very dark, and Jim Bruton lights the under-carriage of the jeep with a torch. I keep moving to maintain body warmth. The stars offer consolation, spilled out across the sky in a gleaming carpet, so close and so dense I feel I could reach out and touch them. I fear it is going to be a long, cold night, but within half an hour Jamal has inserted a pin into the drive shaft, and it appears to be holding. We continue bumping along the rocky path.

In his book *Eastern Approaches*, Fitzroy MacLean records that he was travelling in the same region in the 1930s, when the gear stick on his truck also broke down. A spare part was missing, so they searched about for alternatives. In his James Bond way he found a metal collar stud that fitted, and 'well-pleased' with his resourcefulness he proceeded 'contentedly' on his way. While driving along a mountain path, 'negotiat-ing hair-pin bends in the dark at fifty miles per hour with a wall of rock rising on one side and a rushing torrent at the bottom of a precipice on the other, I wondered sleepily how the collar stud, which occupied so important a place in the steering gear, was standing up to the strain.' It's that 'sleepily' that lets you know he really is James Bond. After our drive shaft has been fixed, and the temporary pin inserted, none of us is quite so sleepy, even though we are all by now exhausted.

We are the last to arrive at the village of Andarrob. It's after midnight, but the good news is that we don't have to sleep in the car as there's a guesthouse here.

In Andarrob a guesthouse is a room with a raised platform on which 100 men sleep side by side. Well, 100 men and me. It is also the first chance for men who have been fasting all day to eat, so they are breaking out their food. After eating, the Afghan practice is to roll yourself in the blankets you wear, and just sleep in whatever nook you find.

But we don't have it too bad. An American journalist describes the guesthouse he stays in as the worst place he's ever been. 'Crack addicts in New York have it better than this, and I've filmed with crack addicts, I know,' he tells me. 'It's like some medieval inn, we climb up into our room through a ladder and it's the filthiest place I've ever been. Spiders wouldn't even go in there it's so filthy. I don't want to unroll my sleeping bag onto that dirt. And it is freezing. We have to sleep in all our clothes. But that isn't the worst thing. The worst thing is the smell. The air is dense with the stench of centuries of travellers. Or maybe they've buried someone in there. All I know is that I had to put my socks over my nose while I slept so that I could breathe.'

So, relatively speaking our Andarrob guesthouse is all right. I unroll my sleeping bag between the two Jims, feeling as exhausted as if I've been travelling since medieval times myself. I'm also losing my sense of humour. There's nowhere to wash and we've just calculated that the detour via the Hawaq Pass could add another two days to this trip. That's if snow has not blocked the pass. If snow has blocked the pass, it could take even longer.

I grumble as I get into my sleeping bag, berating myself for having come on this journey in the first place. Jim Bruton tells me to stop, there's nothing I can do about it, I certainly can't go back, but his pep-talk only makes me feel worse, because now I feel trapped as well. I fall asleep in a very dark mood only to be shaken awake four hours later. The drivers want to make an early start so that they have time to eat before their daily fast begins. Every soldier here comes to shake me awake – it's an irresistible lure, I can see that, a woman in the joint – but I'm never at my best in the mornings and after the seventh soldier has his hands on my feet, I'm forced to sit up and bark at them to leave me alone.

Once again, with no water in sight, we proceed on our way. The air is becoming thinner and clearer. At various spots you can still hear artillery fire in the hills. The tracks are sprinkled with matchstick hamlets and at each one the villagers come out to watch us pass. The crowds never include women. Perhaps they watch from behind the closed shutters of their shacks. The men stand in a row, solemn, dirty and curious. Though it's winter, many are barefoot. They are wearing heavier clothes than the people in Khoja Bahauddin, made of wool.

We are climbing so high that the snowy mountain peaks are no longer above us, but around us, in a white embrace. We leave the cliffs behind and we are out in the open, above them, with the sun gleaming on the snow all around us. There is a feeling of release, and here on the roof of the world, last night's tantrum appears ridiculous.

As we ascend there is less and less oxygen and our jeep needs repairs more and more often. We are stopping every half hour, so that our driver, Jamal, can carry out frenzied tinkering beneath the bonnet. Soon we are stationary for longer than we are moving, and all the other vehicles in the convoy are overtaking us. The jeep stalls in the middle of an icy creek as we are inching over its rocky bed. Jamal has to perch on the freezing slippery stones to do the repairs, with Jim Bruton holding him upright.

We finally continue on our way and at the next pit stop, Jamal takes a photo of the three of us. Five minutes later the jeep loses its brake and clutch simultaneously, sliding backwards on a mountain path near the snow-covered summit of the Hawaq Pass.

Only Jamal's quick response saves our lives. He turns the steering wheel, hard left, into the mountain rather than away from it, preventing the jeep from tumbling off the cliff and plunging into the river hundreds of metres below. But when the jeep backs up into the mountain it rolls over instead. The sickening lurch sideways feels as if it is happening in slow motion and I'm not frightened – not immediately, anyway – just incredulous.

Miraculously, no one is hurt. But when the jeep stabilises I'm lying on my side with all our gear and Jim Bruton on top of me, and I can smell the petrol that we need in order to continue our journey dripping over us. We climb out shakily through the window and hoick everything out. We are standing beside the overturned jeep with our bags piled around us when a car from our convoy drives by and a woman sticks her head out of the window. She sneers and says, 'We're not going to stop to help you, because you didn't help us earlier.'

I'm astounded – even if she did think this was a punishment we deserved, what would possess her to say it? We could easily have died ten minutes ago. In another ten minutes, it could be her. I'm also confused; I have no idea what she means, because I remember that we did stop to help her earlier today. Extremes bring out the best and the worst in people – they test you and not everyone passes the test. By contrast, an Italian journalist, seeing our predicament, stops his truck a kilometre along the path and walks back down to offer help. 'If it turns out that your jeep can't drive any further, don't worry. We have room in our truck for you and your bags.'

We accept this kind offer, and when we start walking up to his truck, I realise that any exercise at this altitude is surprisingly difficult, and that simply walking towards us was an act of remarkable generosity.

With the aid of one of the other NBC vehicles, we right the jeep, though the driver of the second vehicle complains bitterly throughout the operation that this is not what he was hired to do, he was hired to drive directly to Kabul and not to delay by stopping to help rescue other vehicles. Halim translates all these complaints to me until I finally ask him to tell the driver to shut up, that as long as he's being paid, for Godsake, could he stop whingeing. I am the only person here not being paid on a daily basis and I am not whingeing, I say, self-righteously, forgetting about my tantrum last night.

Jamal patches up our jeep so that it can drive, although its door is broken and has to be tied shut with a piece of wire. We will need to siphon petrol from the generator we are carrying to enable it to continue.

I am not sure that I want to continue the journey in this unreliable jeep, now minus a door we can close. Just as I am thinking that I might opt for the Italian journalist's truck, it backs down the path towards us and becomes bogged in the mud and snow. I can't believe it. This afternoon is starting to feel cursed.

Our resurrected jeep now tries to extricate the truck. The huge wheels turn, and the engine whirrs, but it soon becomes a hopeless whine as the truck digs itself deeper and deeper into its prison of icy mud. Men shout orders at each other in a variety of languages. They try again and again. Nothing. If anything, the situation is worse. The men become angrier and the wheels spin themselves deeper into the hole. Before they come to blows, we decide that we need a bigger vehicle with snow chains.

In the end, with only about two hours of daylight remaining, we have to leave the truck, which only stopped in order to save us, on a mountain in the middle of nowhere. The friendly, decent Italian journalist, whom I only ever know as Ivo from *La Stampa*, never once looks at me accusingly or hints that this predicament is in any way our fault. I will never forget his kindness, and I promise him that we will go to find a truck before the light fades, or that we will return for him.

Turning to look at them over my shoulder, I feel a wrench as we drive away. Our jeep limps over the Hawaq Pass. It is snowing, in stinging flurries, but it is passable, as our drivers had promised. I feel queasy as I look over the side, reliving the jeep's roll. 'Get over it, Irris,' says Jim Bruton. It's the right advice.

We see a truck with snow chains and flag it down, explaining where our trapped colleagues are and sending it to help. Relieved, we drive on. Barely an hour later, we see a jeep broken down by the side of the road. It belongs to the woman who jeered at us. We stop to help. We don't need to say anything.

Once over the Hawaq Pass, we drive down into the Panjshir Valley, a 200-kilometre-long canyon that stretches almost all the way to Kabul. It is overwhelmingly beautiful, hairpin bends above a crystal river, jagged rock faces seeming to tumble all the way down to the water. It has a wild grandeur and a self-contained ruggedness. Soviet-era tanks still litter the route. The road is narrowed by mudslides, making driving here dangerous, even if you are not in a vehicle prone to losing its brake and clutch.

'Not so close to the edge, don't drive so close to the edge,' Jim Maceda pleads with Jamal fruitlessly.

It is immediately apparent why this was the place where the Soviet army foundered. These unrelenting cliffs favour guerrilla fighters. Even with the use of modern weapons, wars in these mountains find no conclusion. Standing here it seems that Ahmed Shah Massoud owed his victory to the Panjshir Valley.

In the dog-eared article by Mohsen Makhmalbaf that I'm still carrying with me, the Iranian film-maker argues that if Afghanistan were not mountainous, it's conceivable that the Soviets could have conquered it. Geography is destiny.

Perhaps, as Makhmalbaf suggests, the true fighters of Afghanistan are not its hungry people but the high mountains that don't surrender.

Panjshir means five lions, and locals say that the sixth lion was Ahmed Shah Massoud, *Shir-e-Panjshir*. He was born here and he is buried here. His tomb is in a shallow cave burrowed into a hillside at Jangalak on the 'Chief of the Martyr's Hill'. The sun is setting as we drive past the Jangalak memorial. Massoud has a spectacular view from his resting place.

We drive on in the dark until we reach Bazarak, the village where Massoud was born and where his widow and six children still live.

Here we find another guesthouse, for our fourth night on the road. This one is built above a brook, but it is too cold and dark to wash now. At the guesthouse, I bump into an American colleague, a tough war correspondent, the veteran of many front lines who says that if there's no other road out of Kabul, he'll simply stay there, and take out Afghan citizenship. Nothing would induce him to do this drive again. His joke comforts me, making my constant fear seem reasonable.

Stan sets up the satellite phone, as he does every night, to call back to base. He was late last night since we arrived in Andarrob after midnight, and Tom in Khoja Bahauddin told him they were ten minutes away from calling the US Air Force to report us missing. Tonight it is not so late, although it is already dark when I chat to Jonathan on the satphone, sitting on a tiny bridge above a small brook, squashed between two jeeps. I tell him about our jeep rolling.

'I thought I told you to be careful,' he chides me.

'Next time you have a bad feeling about something, I'm going to listen,' I say ruefully.

Jonathan says he's not going home, he's coming to Kabul. This news makes me both happy and worried – a constant combination in Afghanistan.

'Please tell me that you guys are not driving all that gear along these goat tracks.'

'I think that's the plan.'

'Don't do it! It's a death trap,' I warn him. 'You should take the main road through Kunduz and risk the Taliban for five miles, it can't be worse than this trip.'

Jonathan clearly thinks I'm mad. To humour me, he tells me about the strange time they've been having in Khoja Bahauddin, where they are the only journalists left.

'We were sitting on the roof of the house at sunset, a bit out of it, when we saw an American Chinook helicopter, you know the one with two rotors. But we weren't in work mode, so it took us a moment or two of watching it to wake up to what it was, and to realise that we should film it. Then it was like Vietnam. We ran down to where it was landing, blades whirring against this amazing pink sunset, and out hop these American Special Forces officers. They were happy to be interviewed, so we beamed them in to the breakfast show, live.'

When it works, there's nothing like television.

We sleep in one room, once again arranged along the walls like furniture. I brush my teeth in the icy crystal water, the cleanest I've ever tasted. Then I remember a Russian producer in Dushanbe begging me, 'Whatever you do, don't drink the water in the Panjshir, it looks clean, but it isn't.' Oh well.

The Panjshir Valley is the Northern Alliance's heartland. The Taliban never conquered the Panjshir, partly due to its geography, and partly also due to tribal loyalties. The hardy, volatile mountain people in the Panjshir are mostly Tajiks, not Pashtuns like the Taliban. They are overjoyed at the Taliban's retreat from Kabul, crowding around to talk and to cheer whenever we stop our cars.

At its southern end, the Panjshir Valley opens into the Shomali plains, at the bottom of which, three hours south, lies Kabul. This fertile area was once dotted with farms, but in order to create a buffer zone and remove any chance of cover for Northern Alliance soldiers preparing to attack Kabul, the Taliban burnt the farms and the fields here in 1997 and 1998. Thousands of families were left homeless. The plains are desolate, dotted with blasted vehicles, ruined tanks, and collapsed houses, their broken walls covered with bullet holes and starbursts from shellfire.

Our translator, Halim, is saddened. He has not been to Kabul for more than a decade. 'I remember it was all vineyards here,' he says. 'This area was once so beautiful.'

There is nothing left now. As we drive on, Halim is overwhelmed. He struggles to find the right word.

'It is so boring.'

I feel I have to explain, 'No, Halim, that is not a good way to use the word boring.'

The road is still obscured, but in a gap between the clouds of dust, the city of Kabul is suddenly spread out beneath us. 'Kabul!' we say to each other excitedly, before it disappears behind another cloud. We see it, and we feel it getting nearer, too. Our bodies are no longer braced for impact, and we aren't hitting our heads on the roof of the jeep. We are driving along a paved road, and the relief is delicious.

This is the road the Northern Alliance forces took five days ago as they fought their way into the capital. It is strewn with burnt-out Russian tanks and armoured personnel carriers. In the weeks leading up to the Taliban's retreat from Kabul, American jets pounded the front-line positions here heavily, leaving the road torn up and impassable. Looking at the bomb craters, Maurice, who drove into Kuwait city in 1992, says US bombing is more precisely targeted now. The weaponry has improved in the intervening ten years. We swerve around the huge craters, taking care not to stray too far off course because the surrounding area has not yet been cleared of mines. But after days grinding along a mountainside, it's a relief to be on a real road. And it means we are nearing our destination.

We are driving into a divided, uncertain city, but a city nonetheless. I have mixed feelings: tremendous relief because that terrible route is behind us, and anticipation because so much new lies ahead.

Jim Maceda was last in Kabul in 1980, and he is looking forward to returning. But in my mind I run through all that I know about Kabul, and it's mostly terrifying. While outside the window, devastated villages zoom by, images from news reports flick through my head like snapshots.

They go back to the time the Northern Alliance conquered Kabul in the early 1990s, and the Mujaheddin of Ahmed Shah

Massoud emptied libraries at Kabul University, burning books on a pyre. I also remember pictures of a soldier executing a government office worker as Northern Alliance troops entered Kabul in 1992. Someone documented his death, photograph by photograph, with nightmarish precision, from the moment the soldier forced the worker to leave his office at gunpoint, until the end when the soldier dragged the corpse away, using the same cloth with which he had tied the worker's wrists only minutes before, smearing blood behind him.

Kabul is a city without heroes. The images from Taliban times are even more terrible. I remember pictures of a man being grabbed by the Taliban's religious police, who were forcibly cutting his hair. They said it prevented his forehead touching the ground when he prayed, letting the Devil stand between him and God. His face was a mask of terror because he did not know what they would do to him next.

The stories of the women are especially painful, such as the pregnant woman who walked to a clinic because she needed treatment. On the way she felt giddy and raised her burqa to take some deep breaths. A Talib beat her repeatedly for show-ing her face. She lay in the street bleeding, but no man dared to help her because he would also be beaten. She struggled alone to the clinic and lost her baby.

The public amputations and executions produced the most disturbing images – filmed by brave men and women who smuggled the pictures out of Kabul in order to show the world the true nature of the Taliban regime. I have seen a photo-graph I will never forget of a man with three left hands. It was a Taliban soldier parading through Kabul, holding two left hands. He dangled them from his index finger by a piece of material tied around their index fingers. The hands seemed to be clasping one another. They were the hands of thieves. Amputations, like beheadings, were carried out in football stadiums.

There is footage from the first public execution of a woman found guilty of murdering her husband, watched by thousands in the Kabul football stadium. Although several minutes before the execution the husband's family announced that they forgave the woman, which under Islamic law meant that she no longer had to be executed, Taliban officials said it was too late. The execution had been announced over the radio. The condemned woman was brought into the centre of the football stadium, and knelt, wearing a burqa, even now, even in death, anonymous. How were we to know this was the right woman? A Taliban soldier took aim with his Kalashnikov, but suddenly the woman stood and tried to flee. She was forced back down and shot three times in the back of the head. The execution was watched by her seven children, all crying loudly for their mother.

I try to re-focus on the scenery outside the window, but these images distract me. I am ambivalent about entering Kabul, fearful of what I will find.

Chapter 17

I'm distracted from grave political issues by something more immediate. Almost the first thing we find in Kabul is the bomb in our kitchen. You can't relax here for one second!

This is my third brush with death in a week, coming after our car rolled, and the wall collapsed onto me near the Taliban front line. Although I've emerged each time without a scratch, I don't know how much more I can take. I am becoming too familiar with the jolt of shock as it happens, followed by the adrenaline rush, *I'm alive, I'm alive*, and then the stab of fear once you calm down and realise what a close call it was.

I'd been so sure that I had to see this story through, and persuaded Jonathan in Khoja Bahauddin to also come to Kabul, but now I find myself wanting to leave.

I can't avoid feeling that three brushes with death is a significant number. Does danger come in threes? Will the next one get me? Or am I safe now because I've had three near misses? That's the problem with tea leaves, you can read them any way you want.

I try not to dwell on the fact that all three experiences happened in the week after that eerie premonition in Khoja Bahauddin, when everyone was told I was dead. Am I a marked woman, already a walking ghost?

I don't think of myself as superstitious, but in a war zone, when your colleagues are dying, the truth is everyone is superstitious. No atheists in foxholes, and no one here who doesn't believe that the lucky rabbit's paw, carried in their left pocket, never the right, was what saved them from being killed yesterday.

You take to examining every event for meaning, seeing providence in the fall of a stone. 'That wouldn't have happened to me,' you reassure yourself on hearing a journalist has been killed, 'I'd have done it differently.' You weigh risks, and assess them relative to other risks in this dangerous place. Going to the front line eighteen hours after the Taliban withdraw is okay – but only three hours afterwards is foolhardy. Driving down the main highway south is dangerous – crossing the Hindu Kush in a broken-down old Russian military jeep is reasonable.

But the lesson of Afghanistan is that it's never safe to exhale, to think, 'I'm all right here', even standing in your kitchen. You have to stay alert, keyed up, until you leave. Even going for a drive or a walk is dangerous, since death is waiting for you down every path. The UN estimates that as much as seventy per cent of Afghanistan is covered in land mines. If you set one off, and are lucky enough to survive, your injuries will be terrible, as the high number of maimed victims of mines here can attest. There are US bombs, stray bullets, and all the usual dangers of being in a war zone, exacerbated by the fact that in Afghanistan everyone has a gun. At least one.

So you take all this in, and navigate around it, sometimes with lucky charms, sometimes with alcohol, sometimes with love affairs. Anything to keep your luck afloat. Because in the end, no matter how careful you are, I believe it is luck. That's how I keep going.

Now I'm worried that my luck has run out. When we find the bomb in our kitchen, I discuss this with the UN mine man, Ross Chamberlain. In his kind, laid-back Australian way, he helps convince me that an unexploded bomb is only a middle-order danger, not a serious one. After all, there were unexploded bombs in London for years after World War II. And this bomb wasn't directed specifically at me, so it doesn't count as a real 'third time unlucky'.

To cheer me up, Ross tells me that there is a UN bar in

Kabul where alcohol has been available throughout Taliban times. The UN brings the booze in solely for its staff and other aid workers. No journalists are allowed, but there are ways of getting around that, too. Ross will be happy to help, only not straight away because at a little party two nights ago the UN boys, returning to Kabul for the first time since September 11, drank their bar dry.

I find myself smiling. Suddenly there seems to be a way to live between the rules here. Maybe I don't have to leave Afghanistan straight away after all. I decide I'll sleep on it. If I ever find a place to sleep.

Accommodation is at a premium in Kabul. The Taliban weren't big on tourism, so there are almost no habitable hotels, and now media from all over the world are arriving. My NBC friends are looking for a new house, and in the meantime they are bunking up with other NBC colleagues at the Intercontinental Hotel.

The word 'Intercontinental' conjures up images of luxury rooms, fluffy bathrobes and sumptuous service. But of course, the Intercontinental in Kabul is different. It's fallen on hard times since its heyday in the 1960s, when it was part of the famous hotel chain. The large, squat building on top of a ridge in the centre of the city has a spectacular view, and a ballroom, but that's about all that's left of its former grandeur. Despite faded signs promising a 'Beauty Parlour' and 'Night Club', they are long gone, and most rooms have no phones, no heating, no water and no sanitation. In the lobby you have to dodge the buckets that collect water from leaking pipes. Management says the pipes burst when a high-ranking Taliban official emptied his gun into the ceiling. Exactly why is never explained. Maybe it was frustration over the slow service in the restaurant.

But despite all this the Intercon is the best hotel in Kabul. It is the place to be – if you can find a room.

In the five days since the collapse of the Taliban, broadcasters from all over the world have set up here. Fortunately, the hotel has a large, easily accessible flat roof. It is like a TV factory, with rows of satellite dishes beaming at the stars, and rows of cameras pointing at rows of correspondents, talking away to their national audiences, with the vista of the city behind them. The hotel has electricity, but if everyone plugged in they would short circuit the building, so each broadcaster has its own generators, and tents to protect all this expensive equipment from the elements. These are also lined up in rows on the roof, as if a circus has blown in to town, which in a way it has.

The Intercon is the most practical place to be if you want to file at night, because Kabul has a rigidly enforced 10 p.m. curfew. Broadcasting to Europe, the United States and Australia, I can't avoid filing at night, so for many reasons this hotel looks like the best bet.

But the man at the front desk is adamant. There are no rooms at the Intercon. He would like to help, but he shows me a waiting list of hundreds of journalists. Knowing it's futile, I scrawl my name on the bottom and sit despondently in the lobby, wondering what to do next. I am psyching myself up to check out the rest of Kabul's dodgy hotels when Adriana, a journalist I'd known slightly in the north, comes up to say hello. She arrived yesterday, and it turns out she has the most sought after commodity in the capital – a spare bed in her room here.

'It's only for one night. After that we will see what we can do,' she says in her musical Mexican accent. The room has no toilet, no water, no ceiling and no heating – but it does have a bed, and the offer of a place to stay drops into my lap when I am desperate. This kindness from someone I hardly know reminds me that covering this conflict has not been all about fear. It has also been about good fortune, overcoming problems with the help of strangers, and forging friendships. My luck, I decide, will hold.

Chapter 18

Oh, the beautiful city of Kabul wears a rugged mountain skirt,
And the rose is jealous of its lash-like thorns.
The dust of Kabul's blowing soil smarts lightly in my eyes,
But I love her, for knowledge and love both come from
    her dust.

I sing bright praises to her colourful tulips,
The beauty of her trees makes me blush.
How sparkling the water flows from Pul-i-Mastaan!
May Allah protect such beauty from the evil eye of man!

I am reading this love song to Kabul by the seventeenth-century poet Saib-e-Tabrizi as we drive around the city and see the overwhelming scale of destruction war has wrought. Despite the poet's plea, Kabul has not been protected from the evil eye of man.

I have never seen devastation on such a scale so long after a war. The city lies in ruins, with entire sections obliterated. In some areas, it is like an archaeological dig. We drive for miles and see nothing but ruins. Row after row, block after block, street after street of damaged shells of buildings. Buildings whose roofs have caved in. Buildings where only one wall is left standing, and it's been pierced by tank shells. Buildings where concrete joists and iron girders list out to the sides, with half a storey still hanging by a steel thread as if it will fall at any moment. But it's been like this for five years or more – some parts of the city were destroyed almost ten years ago. Rusty cars lie upside down, riddled with bullet holes. There's the wreck of an old Soviet ambulance. In five years, no one has bothered to remove anything but the tyres.

People move in and around the rubble as if it were a normal city, but it looks as if they've returned to Pompeii or the fort of Masada, and simply resumed living there. In places market stalls nestle among the ruins. Sometimes a wall, the only part of a building that remains standing, has a billboard on it. This is the only concession to the present, to repair. In the evenings, smoke wafts above the collapsed buildings. People are building fires so they can stay warm or perhaps cook before they sleep beneath the lee of the broken walls.

I cannot think of any other city that compares, unless I reach back into history. This rivals the pictures of Berlin or Dresden after World War II, or Hiroshima and Nagasaki after the atomic bomb was dropped. Today, the Chechen capital Grozny also lies in ruins, but that war is more recent. Here the ruins already have the patina of age, as if they were relics that Afghans have cherished, instead of being something they are too poor and despairing to repair.

A whole generation, including some of the teenagers translating for us, have known nothing but war. Sabi is a nineteen-year-old from the Panjshir Valley and we drive through the ruins of Kabul listening to his favourite tape. He is a great fan of *Titanic*. 'Did you like it? It is my favourite. The story is too sad.' He plays his pirated cassette of the score, with its glitches and sudden stops, over and over again. It provides a surreal soundtrack to the devastation. I want to tell Sabi that what is 'too sad' is outside the window, but for him, this is just Kabul.

Does he feel he is living on a doomed vessel? The UN's Special Representative for Afghanistan, Lakhdar Brahimi, graphically described the country as a 'failed state which looks like an infected wound. You don't even know where to start cleaning it.' Driving here, I have an inkling of what he means.

The destruction occurred in layers, caused not by the American bombardment which just ended, nor by the decade-long war with the Soviets, but mostly by the bitter civil war of the 1990s. Afghans did this to themselves. Like a forensic pathologist, our translator tracks the destruction, explaining which Muslim warlord caused what damage. American journalist Jon Lee Anderson, whom I meet at different points covering this conflict, says of the experience, 'We are examining the city the way one assesses the age of a dead tree by counting the rings in its stump.'

Whenever we get out of the car, locals come up. They are quick to blame the Mujaheddin warlord Gulbuddin Hekmatyar for the destruction. 'Gulbuddin! Gulbuddin!' they say, pointing at the ruins with the Afghan habit of referring to people by their first names that is so disconcerting in the context of warlords and war criminals. It feels far too personal.

We get back in the car, and Sabi has *Titanic* at full volume as we drive further into the rubble. He gives me his wide, sunny smile as we go to the front lines of each of the Mujaheddin factions.

In 1989, Ahmed Shah Massoud attacked the city with rockets, attempting to seize it from Communist President Najibullah. General Dostum fought with Najibullah until 1992, when he switched sides and joined Massoud. Together they took Kabul. Hekmatyar then started his campaign, pounding the city with his stash of US-made rockets for three years. As a result, Kabul had no electricity and no running water, and the lives of the civilians who survived the attacks were absolutely desperate.

More factional fighting followed, but the intricacies of attack and betrayal, betrayal and counterattack, soon become mind numbing. We drive and drive and the ruins fan out in front of us.

I re-read the seventeenth-century poem as an antidote to present day reality. I love the line 'knowledge and love both come from her dust', though I don't sense either in the dust here now, just bitterness and resignation and the need to make do, to survive in the face of all odds. It is apparent in the angle of a woman's back, bent under her burqa, as if she is carrying a burden; in the defeated way a man trudges, hauling fire-wood to the corner where he now sleeps.

At the Intercon, the postcards on sale acknowledge the city's devastation. They show tourist sites – the ornate Darulaman Palace, the long, low, beautiful Id Gah mosque, founded in the 1890s – as they were in their heyday, accompanied by inserts of the same sites, as they are today in ruins.

They're the saddest postcards I've ever seen.

On my second day, I go back to the NBC house with the bomb in the kitchen to see the other sites in the cross-section of neat, tree-lined streets that were bombed on 12 November.

This wealthy suburb of Wazir Akhbar Khan was once the capital's diplomatic sector. Expensive homes are hidden behind high fences. There are almost no cars, though ancient yellow taxis drive by frequently. You don't have to wait long for a cab in Wazir Akhbar Khan. Architecture here seems to have stopped in the 1970s, when Kabul was still on the 'hippy trail' for Western tourists. The King was deposed in 1973, and the Soviets invaded in 1979, so perhaps that fixes the dates for the last construction boom.

This section of Kabul is like a low-rent 1970s Canberra or Brasilia, representing the last time when Afghanistan seemed to have some kind of future. One house has a downstairs bar, with a wall-sized mural of belly dancers. Four curvy Persian women are picked out in red and white on a black background, in cartoon style. They are doing an erotic dance, wearing bras and harem pants, with acres of flesh showing above and below their belly buttons. It's a shock, and a reminder that there was once sex here before the Taliban.

When the Taliban commanders fled Wazir Akhbar Khan a week ago, they cleared their homes of personal possessions, but left the basements stashed with weapons. There are rooms packed from floor to ceiling with all types of guns, and wooden crates full of ammunition, with Russian writing stamped on the side, some broken open with rounds spilling out. This was all the Taliban had, and this is how they enforced five years of repressive rule throughout Afghanistan. They built no roads and no infrastructure – they had no source of political power apart from these guns, yet they fled and left them.

Locals tell me, 'Many Arabs lived here.' 'Arabs' is what Afghans call the foreign soldiers who fought with the Taliban, most recruited and funded by Osama bin Laden. Two streets away from the NBC house, an American missile hit a parked car, leaving a mangled wreck.

In the next street, another bomb hit a house opposite the home of a Taliban commander. It's a mass of rubble, as our house would have been had our bomb exploded. Standing on mounds of mud brick, locals from the surrounding streets say the house was a bakery, and no Taliban lived here. People living in the house behind were injured in the explosion. These residents are suspicious and unhappy. 'Does America want to take over Afghanistan?' one man with a white turban asks me, troubled. I tell him I don't think so.

Another man, wearing an embroidered blue cap, asks the reverse question. 'Will America stay long enough to help us fix our problems?' He gestures at the rubble, 'America has abandoned us before.'

I don't know the answer to this one.

'Let's go to the zoo!'

The offer comes at breakfast at the Intercon. Breakfast is the most sociable meal of the day in a city with a curfew and where most of us work at night. The service is so slow that we spend a long time over the sweet toast and weak coffee, with the wintry Afghan sun spilling over our tables, and some of my best leads for stories come from here.

I've bumped into Chris Stephen, a friend from Moscow who files for a number of English and Scottish newspapers. He was in the Panjshir Valley when Kabul fell, and accompanied the Northern Alliance troops into the city. He says he does a zoo in every war zone.

'You always get a great story. I did a piece at the Sarajevo zoo, and that's the one story that everyone remembers. They didn't have much food left, and they had to decide who to feed – whether they were going to sacrifice the small animals to keep feeding the big bear.'

So we go to the zoo. It sits on the former front line, at the cross-section of two Mujaheddin factions' territories. A lonely lion roars. The animals here are grisly survivors. Not all of them made it, of course: the elephant enclosure took a direct hit during the civil war, and other unfortunate creatures were turned into meals for hungry fighters. There are only seventeen animals left.

Some of the enclosures are in ruins, but compared to the surrounding streets, it's not too bad. The zoo is in a pleasant, dusty park, and walking here is enjoyable. Attendance has doubled since the Taliban fled.

'It is a sign that people are less tired and sad than they were during Taliban times. They are happier, so they come out to see the city. Also in the Taliban times it was not really possible for women and children to come out to the zoo, only men,' says zookeeper Sher Agha, known by his nickname, Omar.

Two hundred people now come here every day to see the seventeen malnourished animals, including an Afghan mountain cat and a small black bear so neglected and miserable that it hurts to look at him. His name is Khers and his snout is raw, swollen and bleeding. Zoo officials say Taliban visitors would tease Khers by holding out food, then smack him on the nose with sticks when he reached for it, though his injuries look more severe than that to me.

The zoo has one lion, which is ancient, injured and almost completely blind, but the king of the jungle remains king with the public. During the time of Communist President Najibullah, the zoo boasted seven lions. Marjan is the only one left. He is fawn with a dark mane now peppered with grey, and he is so decrepit that he allows cameramen into his cage without attacking them. 'It's beautiful!' exclaims NBC translator Halim. 'We could pat him.'

Marjan – named after an Afghan precious stone – is forty-eight years old, much older than the life expectancy of most lions in the wild, especially if, like Marjan, they have only one eye and half their face has been blown away. He was imported from a German zoo in the 1970s, and lived an ordinary zoo life, which in Kabul meant dodging bullets and rockets, until in 1995 a soldier entered his cage to celebrate a victory in the Mujaheddin factional wars. The zoo was so close to the front line, it just seemed the thing to do, like dropping into your local for a celebratory drink. Marjan reportedly left the soldier alone until he started baiting a lioness. Unfortunately for the soldier, she turned out to be Marjan's mate. Marjan ate him.

The soldier's brother returned the next day looking for revenge. He lobbed a grenade into Marjan's cage. 'When Marjan pounced on it thinking it was food, he lost one eye and ninety-five per cent of his sight in the other,' says the zookeeper.

The resilient lion pulled through – as the zoo then had to do. Although the zoo had survived the rocket attacks of the civil war, the emergence of the Taliban regime in 1996 posed a more serious threat. The Taliban leadership wanted to shut it down because it was 'unIslamic', banning animals along with all other forms of entertainment. Zookeeper Omar went to the faculty of Islamic studies at the University of Kabul to ask them to defend the zoo. The academics put their lives on the line for the animals.

'They wrote down everything in the Koran that referred to animals and the Prophet Mohammed,' says Omar. 'I collected them all and presented them to the Ministry of Justice.'

The zoo owes its survival to Omar. Now his struggle is to keep the animals fed. There's very little food and the zoo's staff of eleven hasn't been paid for months. There's no money left to prepare the animals' cages for winter.

Omar says the Northern Alliance is providing some food and medicine for the zoo, but it's not enough. He goes to the markets to beg for food, and generous butchers give him their off-cuts. 'But then when I go back two days later, they say "But we gave you food – what did you do with it?" and I have to explain that Marjan is a lion and he eats a lot.'

Despite the difficulties, Omar sees better times ahead. The Northern Alliance has promised it will increase funding for the zoo, and Omar is happy to take this on trust and borrow money to buy food and other necessities. He is living up to the sign outside the zoo: 'God created animals. People must be good to them.'

I know there is interest from foreign zoos in providing assistance, so I ask Omar about that.

'Yes, a German zoo has promised us to take our bear and cure his nose and bring us two bears in his place.' Omar looks pleased.

Chris asks if he would give away Marjan the lion if it meant a better life for him. 'No, no, this is his home, and the people of Kabul need their lion.'

'How about a swap?'

'Maybe I would consider a swap . . . but the foreign zoo would have to bring the new lion here first before I would let Marjan go. I would call the new lion Opal. It is also a precious stone.'

All the world's press descends on the zoo. Omar has a twinkling smile, a deep, warm storyteller's voice, and an inspiring tale of suffering and survival, which includes that guaranteed ratings winner: furry animals. The Kabul zoo is a magnet to the British tabloids, who are obsessed with animal stories.

The first story about Marjan leads to 'zoo wars', as my friend Barbara from Britain's *Mail on Sunday* puts it. Her paper has long served on this furry front line. It once sent a reporter to Libya to rescue a rabbit, abandoned by British diplomats fleeing the embassy during a crisis. The *Mail on Sunday* adopts Marjan, providing more than US$5000 to feed him for a year. A rival London newspaper sends its correspondent in Kabul to the zoo to check whether the *Mail on Sunday* has paid up, and whether Marjan is reclining contentedly after the lion equivalent of a three-course meal and after-dinner mints. (No scoop there. To the disappointment of its rival, the *Mail* turns out to be feeding Marjan royally.)

London news desks assign reporters in a war zone to such ridiculous jobs because of the memory of a ten-year-old tabloid rivalry over a Spanish donkey called Blackie. In the early 1990s, tender British hearts ached over reports that 'Blackie' (real name Nero) risked being crushed to death during a fair near Madrid. A British animal rights campaigner went to Spain to save the donkey, hotly pursued by reporters from *The Sun* and *Daily Star*. Not wasting any time, *The Sun* reporter bought Blackie, to take her in triumph back to the UK. He left her in a local farmer's field, while he went for lunch – another time-honoured tabloid tradition – and came back to find that his *Daily Star* rival had stolen the donkey from under his nose, paying for her a second time and spiriting her back to Dover.

So *The Sun* reporter purchased a second donkey, claiming that she too was Blackie, and took her to London as well, just a squidge less triumphantly. A third journalist, from the London *Times*, trooped out to Spain to establish how two rival papers were both claiming to have rescued the one donkey.

Very amusing – but that was mainland Europe and this is Afghanistan during a war. It is dangerous to work here and there's an endless array of other stories to be done. Soon, however, there is even infighting within the *Mail* newspaper itself – internal battles over whether the Daily or the Sunday paper should adopt Marjan. Things look bad, with the Sunday preparing to protect its lion from the Daily, until sanity prevails back in London. After top-level negotiations, it's decided that the *Sunday Mail* can keep Marjan, and the *Daily Mail* can adopt the zoo's wretched bear, with his bleeding nose.

Barbara has her photo taken with Marjan and Omar, holding a framed sponsorship form that says 'Adopted by *Mail on Sunday* readers'.

'Can you believe that this is what I am doing in Kabul?' she wails.

At least Marjan is being fed, and when he dies in his sleep two months later – possibly from a surfeit of regular meals, but maybe just from old age – his demise is noted in the British parliament. Six MPs sign an early day motion mourning his loss and stating that the poor mutilated creature came to symbolise the suffering of Afghanistan. They call on the new government in Afghanistan to honour Marjan's memory by banning cock-fighting and dog-fighting, which are emerging following the overthrow of the Taliban.

It seems Barbara's work wasn't all in vain, though I can't help wondering if the death of an Afghan human would prompt an early day motion in the British parliament.

It's showtime in Kabul.

For the first time since the Taliban fled, cinemas are being reopened. The Taliban banned every conceivable form of entertainment – not that there was that much available, limited as it was by war and poverty. But movies, TV, videos, music, painting, photography, even kite flying and chess were banned. Singing and dancing were also banned, including at weddings, where for centuries they had been the highlight of celebrations, and this was how hundreds of musicians and dancers made a living. The Taliban's Military Chief of Staff, Mullah Mohammed Hassan, explained what he envisaged people should do for entertainment. 'They can go to parks and see the flowers and from this they can learn about Islam.'

No bread, no circuses in life during Taliban times. Actually, that's not strictly true – there was one form of acceptable public entertainment. You could go to the football stadium to watch someone being put to death, or having a hand or a foot amputated. This was such a breathtakingly bleak vision of life. The Taliban actually did not believe in any type of culture. How extraordinary that they should have triumphed at the end of the twentieth century, when Western society was dominated by entertainment.

So the return of movies has great significance, and the Bakhtar cinema in the town centre is full. Crowds of excitable armed men in turbans spill round the corner, waiting for the next session. Movies will run during the day, though not at night because of the curfew.

The Bakhtar is showing *The Ascension,* a film about the Mujaheddin victory over the Soviets in the 1980s. But although films, especially Bollywood love films, were extremely popular here, there are no women in sight. This triumphant return to the cinema is for men only.

The cinema's manager explains that this is simply because of the chaos at the front gate, with all sessions packed out.

'Women used to sit in the balcony with their husbands and children, and will be welcome again as soon as things calm down.'

You have to buy your tickets and then you have to hand in your weapons, much as we would check in our coats in the West. Wooden tables are set out, with weapons sorted according to type. Kalashnikovs lie on top in long rows, then pistols. Knives are on the bottom.

The men file in. The screen is an old canvas cloth painted white, the chairs are uncomfortable and the air smells musty. But all 750 seats are full, with 250 more customers crammed into the aisles. They are here for a wild afternoon reliving their earlier victories.

'I've seen this film before, but that's not important,' says one seventeen-year-old. 'I just wanted to see the first film that was playing after all these years.'

'This is a good day – it's too good,' says a twenty-five-year-old Pashtun, waiting in a queue for the next sold-out screening. 'We are all happy, because once again there are movies and music.'

'I was beaten by the Taliban religious police because they caught me with a video,' says a twenty-two-year-old. 'They beat me so hard, they fractured my skull.' He removes his cap to show me a scar on his head. I am concerned, but his friends are all smiling. 'And now we can go to the movies again!' he finishes triumphantly. All his friends laugh uproariously.

The mood in the cinema is exultant, until the ancient projector breaks down twenty minutes into the film. Howls of frustration fill the hall. Fortunately it's soon fixed, and the crowd's good humour is restored. After some wild cheering everyone settles back down to enjoying the defeat of the Soviets.

This movie is one of the few made by the Mujaheddin after the Russian retreat. Essentially propaganda, it depicts heroic Afghans fighting in the desert to defeat a brutal invader. In many ways it echoes the one Hollywood hero flick set in Afghanistan – *Rambo III*. It has the same storybook quality and bad guys versus good guys set-ups, except that unlike the Stallone blockbuster, it was actually filmed here. Going on the response tonight, the audiences here love this stuff as much as Western audiences love *Rambo* – as much as I suspect this audience would love *Rambo*, too, if they got the chance to see it.

In the 1970s, Pakistanis would go to Kabul to shop and to watch movies from India and elsewhere. A Pakistani professor now living in the US recalls, 'For us it meant an escape from the dreary life in Pakistan's parched plains. The Afghans traditionally loved commerce, a passion that has now sadly been overtaken by war-making instincts. Kabul had a sprinkling of Sikh traders and shopkeepers, which indicated to outsiders like us that free trade would ultimately catapult the Afghans to a Hong Kong-like environment.'

Even when war shattered these dreams, there remained fourteen cinemas that showed Indian movies, and studios that made films imitating the popular Indian product. All these vanished during Taliban times. As Iranian film-maker Mohsen Makhmalbaf points out, in a world where thousands of films are made every year, nothing was produced in Afghanistan.

Since the Taliban fled last week, the manager of the Bakhtar cinema has been cleaning away five years of accumulated dust and grime to prepare for this reopening. He has also been trying to get his hands on films the Taliban had locked away in the Ministry of Information. I wonder why they didn't destroy them, since they destroyed art works in museums? Perhaps the Taliban held some secret showings – just of their favourites, the least corrupting action films, of course.

The Taliban banned films, like they banned so much other entertainment, on the grounds the activities were unIslamic, frivolous distractions that took away from the serious pursuit of religion. Films and music 'created a strain in the mind and hampered the study of Islam', according to Taliban Minister for Education Mullah Abdul Hanifi.

On the same grounds, the Taliban regarded all portrayals of the human form as inappropriate. Some newspapers, for example, had pictures, but only of buildings or landscapes – never of people. However, the Taliban bent their own rules for the security services, requiring pictures in passports and other identity documents.

Later, while covering this conflict, a friend goes to the Taliban stronghold of Kandahar where, despite all the prohibitions, photographers' studios continued working during Taliban times. And they weren't just doing passport shots. He finds photos of men in groups of twos and threes, their arms snaked around each other, staring at the camera. They are wearing eye make-up. Their expressions are 'come hither' in an Afghan male-separatist kind of way. The photos are black and white, but they have been treated, and printed edged with colour. It is eerie, like looking at Taliban porn.

Even with God's uncompromising holy warriors, it seems some rules were selectively enforced.

'Films are not prohibited by Islam,' says the cinema owner at the Bakhtar. 'The Taliban banned movies for their own political objectives.' He is laying in a stock of Indian action films. He has already pulled out ten old movie posters and plastered

259

them on the walls. Afghanistan was India's third biggest market after the US and the UK, and the Bollywood industry is thrilled at the departure of the Taliban. Within days, Indian industry mags are filled with articles discussing the new political reality and its projected impact on the bottom line.

'People love the action films,' says the cinema owner. He is interrupted by a roar from the crowd. 'You see! Love stories too, yes, maybe later.'

I tell him that from my experience with young Afghan men, *Titanic* could be a money-spinner.

Journalists attend all events that are evidence of the resumption of normal life: first movie, first football match, first TV broadcast, first women to return to university. We see that people who have no money for food are buying movie tickets. Sales of satellite TVs are soaring. Cosmetics and high-heeled shoes are flying off shelves, along with DVDs and videos imported from Pakistan.

Halim was right. The Taliban *were* boring. People are rebelling.

Further reports are emerging that atrocities may have been committed by Northern Alliance troops in Mazar-i-Sharif, after they liberated the city on 9 November. Local Taliban soldiers fleeing from Mazar abandoned a contingent of around 1000 Pakistani fighters. It's alleged that Northern Alliance troops trapped the Pakistanis in the Sultan Razia girls' school on the outskirts of the city and shot hundreds of them.

'We gave them warnings to surrender,' says a spokesman for a militia, the Hizb-i-Wahdat, fighting with the Northern Alliance. 'They asked us to send representatives over several times, but unfortunately they shot them. Finally we gave the order to attack them. Some 200 of the Pakistanis have been killed.'

Reporters on the spot assess that more than 500 have been killed, but it remains unclear whether these Pakistani volunteers, many of whom had only just arrived in Afghanistan, were killed in battle or executed after surrendering. It is known that they continued to resist for at least forty-eight hours after Mazar fell.

There are graphic photographs of the dead lying in the girls' school. The bodies lie in pools of blood, their limbs thrown out at unnatural angles amid piles of rubble. Most have no shoes. Their clothes are more brightly coloured than Afghan men's clothes, and the blues and reds compete with the pools of blood to add a garish horror to the scenes.

But when the Red Cross enters the city, it says it is unable to shed any light on the matter. Head of operations for Central Asia Olivier Durr says, 'We cannot say whether these people had been brutally executed or whether it was the result of fighting.'

He confirms the Red Cross has found between 400 and 600 bodies, but says he is unable to comment on reports of massacres in Mazar-i-Sharif. 'Even before our expatriate staff entered the city, our Afghan colleagues started to collect and bury quite a number of bodies,' Durr says. He reports that about 180 have already been buried.

When we discuss this story at breakfast at the Intercon the next morning, English journalist Chris Stephen tells me that during his first week here, after coming in from the Panjshir Valley with the Northern Alliance troops, he heard there were still pockets of Taliban resistance to the north of Kabul. He went there to see whether it was true that some of the fiercest foreign fighters were holed up, terrorising the local population. What he found were three dead bodies. The locals gathered around, and he asked them if they knew who'd done it. They confessed immediately and proudly.

'You know how in Bosnia if you found any bodies, and you asked who did it, the locals would look at the ground, shuffle their feet, and say, "No, it wasn't us." Well, here they say, "Yeah man, we killed them! They were Arabs!"'

Chris confirms that the dead soldiers were part of the brigade of foreign fighters brought to Afghanistan by Osama bin Laden. They were abandoned by the Taliban in their hasty retreat from Kabul, and became trapped north of the city by the rapid Northern Alliance advance. When the soldiers snuck out at night, and tried to go south to Kandahar to rejoin the Taliban, they attacked the neighbouring population on their way. The locals weren't having any of that and if they caught them, they killed them.

Standing around the three dead soldiers, local men started to pelt the bodies with stones so that Chris would be in no doubt what they felt about the foreign fighters who took over Afghanistan.

A stone ricocheted off one of the bodies, hitting Chris in the chest. The Afghans were immediately contrite and concerned. 'Sorry. Sorry. Are you all right? We didn't mean to hurt you. Are you sure you're all right?'

The Indira Gandhi Children's Hospital is in the centre of Kabul. It is a tall 1970s-era building, and it is remarkably free of the scars of war, until you get inside. Doctors have not been paid for four months, as the Taliban diverted health-care funds to the war effort. The Director of the hospital, paediatric surgeon Dr Mustafa Zimrai, says this has led to an increase in the number of children dying, as poorer patients cannot afford to buy medicines.

'Yes, we have seen an increase of ten to fifteen per cent in the number of children dying over the past months. Yes, that's very high. We hope now that the NGOs [non-government organisations] are returning, they will help provide us with medication, food and instruments. The government money has not yet returned, no.'

I walk up the stairs and three women sweep by, gossiping and laughing. Their heads are covered with scarves but they are not wearing burqas. It is a surprise to see women's faces. The light in the corridors is extraordinary – soft, opaque, like a painting by the sixteenth-century Flemish artist Breughel. Framed against a wall, as if she had stepped out of one of those paintings, is a mother holding a crying child. Zainab's hair is swathed in an orange scarf, she has broad cheekbones and was clearly once a very beautiful woman. Care has aged her. Her child Shakrilljah, the size of an eighteen-month-old Western toddler, is painfully thin. I am shocked when she says this skeletal boy is five years old. He has a bandage on his sunken cheek, where a naso-gastric tube has been inserted. His cry is repetitive and listless. Though Shakrilljah is very sick, he lacks the energy to do more than moan.

Zainab carries him back upstairs to the ward where malnourished children are treated. She has been referred here by a local clinic because her son's condition is deteriorating. Zainab is a single mother. Her husband stepped on a land mine soon after Shakrilljah was born and since then she has struggled to support her son on her own. The Taliban forbade women from working, so she was forced to rely on her extended family. But the drought made it difficult for her family to support her.

'Often we cannot find food, and we don't have money for rent, or for the bus to come to hospital.'

Like thirty-five per cent of young children in Kabul, Shakrilljah is suffering from malnutrition and that childhood killer, diarrhoea. Eighty-five thousand Afghan children under five die from diarrhoea-related illnesses every year.

Dr Asaf has been treating Shakrilljah. 'He has had persistent diarrhoea for three months, due to severe malnutrition.' He consults the boy's notes. 'He was in the hospital for five months once before, and then for a few days last month.'

Dr Asaf is a kind and helpful man in his thirties, wearing Western clothes. He speaks in English when he offers the following bleak assessment: 'I rate his likelihood of succumbing and dying at sixty per cent.'

I check with Dr Asaf whether this tiny boy could really be five years old. 'Yes, yes, older. He is almost five and a half.'

Dr Asaf questions Zainab, acting as our translator. 'The patient's mother says she was bringing Shakrilljah to this hospital when the air strikes began. The bombs were very strong, and all the windows in their house were smashed, and it was very cold and dangerous. So they went north to Najrob in the Panjshir Valley, but the clinic there has referred the patient back here. And now it is safe to come, but she had trouble to find the money.'

The story is punctuated by a cacophony of weak cries from all over the room, where another six children are being treated. All are dangerously underweight and some have had their mouths painted purple in order to treat one of the side-effects of malnutrition, a Vitamin B deficiency that leads to swelling of the mouth and tongue.

This hospital took in children injured during the US air strikes, and Dr Asaf volunteers to take us to that ward, too. I feel a pang as we leave Shakrilljah and his mother. It requires great generosity of spirit to let journalists into your life and to reveal yourself, and it is difficult simply to walk away from that, especially with a child you suspect may not survive.

Dr Asaf leads the way up the stairs. He was in Kabul during the air strikes, which he says were terrifying. 'Every person fears he will be hit and that he is at the last moment of his life. I was repeating words from the Koran, which a Muslim must do before he dies.'

'Did you really think you would die?' I ask him.

'Yes, I was very scared. I had sent my immediate family away, but I had my nephews with me and they were very frightened. They were crying and I held them to me, and to encourage them I told them that the planes would deliver apples and sweets for them, not bombs.'

He pauses outside the door of the ward.

'The people of Kabul and Afghanistan are very unfortunate. All we want now is for the world to be serious about Afghanistan.'

We go into the ward where the three most severely injured children remain, out of forty who were treated here. All were injured in misdirected air strikes. Two are lying patiently in full-body plaster casts – held together with sticks. It is a simple, very uncomfortable form of traction. They look like chickens on a spit. The third is a ten-year-old boy, Mohammed Salem, whose mother and four younger siblings are playing near his bed. Before they tell me what happened, they pull back the blanket to show me his injuries. One leg ends below the knee in a white stump, the other is in plaster up to the groin. I gulp, not knowing how to react. Dr Asaf says the boy will require further operations on his good leg, which has been yanked out of its socket and needs resetting.

'Perhaps he will go to Germany for this operation,' says Dr Asaf, 'we have not got the facilities to do it here.'

Mohammed Salem was asleep in his bed during a bombardment on the night of 12 October, the first of five attempts by American bombers to hit a Taliban house near the Bini-Hisar region of Kabul. Instead, the bomb hit the building next door to Mohammed Salem's home and a wall fell on him, crushing his leg. His brother, sleeping in the same room, received minor injuries. He has been in hospital ever since – for more than a month – but despite a succession of operations aimed at saving his leg, gangrene set in and amputation was required.

'I feel very bad,' says Mohammed Salem, 'because now I will not be able to run and play with the other boys.'

His mother, Lailahmah, is understandably distressed, but exhibits an extraordinary generosity when I ask her about the United States. 'I am very sad because my son is now handicapped. But on the other hand, I am a very little bit happy, because we are now free and the pressure of the Taliban is lifted from us.'

I ask Dr Asaf if he shares Lailahmah's feelings. Has the US bombing at least had a good result, in forcing the departure of the Taliban?

'I hope so, but we don't know. If the situation improves it is good, but if it doesn't then it isn't good. It depends on the results of these adventures. Until now it is not clear.'

The people of Kabul remain wary. It is not just that many are Pashtuns, from the same tribe as the Taliban. This is the city where tribal loyalties are weakest. But the history here has been that every time they thought it couldn't get any worse it did. I remember the terrible images of starvation, public amputations and beheadings, the burning of books. People here are braced for impact.

We're driving along one of the main roads south out of Kabul. In every pothole there lies a sleeping dog. The road is mined, of course, and we have to drive carefully, avoiding both mines and dogs. Where does the expression 'let sleeping dogs lie' come from, I wonder, as we swerve around another mangy bundle of fur lying on its side. Winter here is beautiful – jewel-bright days highlight a dusting of snow on the mountains that fringe the city. The sky is clear, the air is crisp, and if it weren't for the war-scarred buildings, it would feel peaceful. We drive past the royal palace, a grand ruin, perched on a hill.

I have joined my roommate, Adriana, and her friend, Spanish journalist Gustavo, on this trip. Three other Spanish journalists have come, too, so we are a big group, travelling in three cars to the abandoned al-Qaeda training camp at Rishkor.

This was al-Qaeda's regional base camp, where thousands of mercenaries were trained, and it is no more than half an hour's drive from the capital. As we get closer the road surrounding the camp is littered with destroyed vehicles, tanks without turrets, overturned armoured personnel carriers, and lorries on their sides, dripping petrol. It's like a World War I battle scene. Some ten ruined tanks have ended up in front of a war memorial, an ugly plinth of the type that you see all over the former Soviet Union. Further down the valley there is a ruin – a 'real' ruin for once, a seventeenth-century Persian walled town with a beautiful tower covered in blue tiles. The mountains overlook the scene inscrutably.

The vehicles were destroyed when the camp was bombed during the US air strikes early in November 2001.

'They had an army, this was an army, wasn't it?' says Gustavo, as we stand looking at the devastation. The scale of the scene before us is surprising. This is what al-Qaeda was amassing in the years the West turned its gaze from Afghanistan.

We drive for a further ten minutes, up to the gates of the camp itself. The sprawling camp covers a vast area of 100 square kilometres. We leave our cars, and a Northern Alliance soldier meets us at the gate. As we walk down a long path shaded by two rows of trees, I notice small garden patches – for vegetables? – fenced off with missile cases.

The Northern Alliance has posted a soldier here. Abdul Rahman fought against the al-Qaeda forces in this camp on 15 November. He says that despite the bombings there were still many Arabs and Pakistanis left.

'It took our Northern Alliance forces two to three days to clear them out. Some fought for only two hours but others resisted for more than two days before they fled. It was a fierce battle.'

We walk past some partially destroyed buildings into a clearing filled with rubble. It is a jumble of destroyed build-ings and wrecked vehicles, as if a fractious child had broken all his toys with one sweep of his hand. It covers a vast area, and I can't estimate how many buildings and jeeps were here, because I can't even see how far it stretches from this edge. We clamber over the rubble, and I pick up a tank manual in Russian, and a military training manual in Arabic.

Abdul Rahman shows us the instructions and the pictures of bombs in the training manual. There is a section on defen-sive tactics explaining how to set up heavy machine guns, and information about small arms, grenades, and ambushes. We look into the few mud-brick rooms at the edge of this area that were not destroyed in the bombardment.

One room appears to have been an office. Outside, there is a sign in Arabic listing the duties of a good Muslim, including 'All soldiers should obey the imam' and 'Muslims should not fight with one another'. We walk in, and everything crunches underfoot. 'Be careful, there could be mines here,' Adriana's translator warns me. I poke my head in to the next room which is small and dark and full of dusty papers, textbooks and newspapers, all in disarray on the floor. 'Office?'

'Office, office,' the Afghans confirm. I move carefully in case there are land mines, trying not to take any unnecessary steps as I pick up documents and books that look interesting to add to my stash. There is an invitation from the Cuban embassy, which Adriana and Gustavo are very interested in. There is another blank invitation from the Pakistani embassy, and a third, blank invitation from the British embassy. Were they trying to forge these? There are also dusty exercise books – lessons: maths, science, bombs. The translator leafs through one. 'This man is almost illiterate, the Arabic is very bad,' he says disdainfully.

The next room has a huge amount of weaponry and ammunition. There are rounds of ammunition in boxes, for a variety of weapons. We walk through cautiously. 'Is that a mine? Be careful,' I say to the translator as he steps near some flat circular metal object.

He and the Northern Alliance fighter laugh. 'No, it is ammunition – for machine guns.'

I am relieved.

'That's a Stinger missile – still in its box.' I gawp.

'Stinger, Stinger,' Abdul Rahman confirms.

'But – it's still here in its box,' I repeat stupidly.

When I tell Abdul Rahman that I am amazed at the scale of this place, he reminds me that Rishkor was al-Qaeda's main training camp. Did everyone in the region know what this was?

'Yes, everyone knew this was an al-Qaeda centre, because no one was allowed to pass too close and we saw Arabs and their families driving in. People were frightened,' says Abdul Rahman.

Why?

'Everyone was afraid of al-Qaeda, so every passer-by kept his head down and didn't dare look up when he was walking nearby. Al-Qaeda kept up the pressure on the people of the surrounding area, to keep them scared.'

Abdul Rahman says that during interrogation, a captured al-Qaeda prisoner told them that Abdul Haq was hanged here at Rishkor. I remember reading one report suggesting this was the location for the rebel Pashtun leader's execution.

'Where was he executed? Can you show us?'

We drive back to the area where the tanks lie broken, past the dormitory blocks, and walk up the hill. I expect a gibbet, but should have known better since even the last Communist President, Najibullah, was strung up in the street. When the Taliban took Kabul in 1996, they hanged Najibullah and his brother from a concrete traffic control post. There was no trial. Najibullah was beaten, castrated, and dragged behind a jeep before being killed. Taliban leader Mullah Mohammad Rabbani said the fifty-year-old former President deserved his fate. 'He killed so many Islamic people and was against Islam, and his crimes were so obvious that it had to happen. He was a Communist.'

This brutal execution was the first political act by the Taliban in Kabul, and it symbolised all that was to come.

Here at the al-Qaeda camp, it was even more basic. 'Criminals' met their end on a tree. The noose is still swinging over a branch. The rope is white above the noose, brown–red beneath it, stained with the blood of the men who died here. It is a chilling sight and as I am describing it into my microphone, there is a volley of artillery fire close by.

We are all a little jumpy and ask our translator to find out from the Northern Alliance fighter what is going on.

'Nothing,' he says, 'nothing.'

'What "nothing" is that?' Gustavo and I ask him.

Our translator questions Abdul Rahman again, and comes back with the gnomic Afghan reply, 'He says he doesn't know what it was, or why they are firing.'

This is such a volatile place still. And I have to admit it is only standing here, amid its ruins, that I have a sense of the vast scale of the al-Qaeda network.

We drive home via an adjoining valley where there are dozens of ammunition depots, in bunkers made of reinforced concrete. They contain thousands of mortars and heavy artillery of every size, as well as rockets and countless bullets. They were virtually untouched by the US bombing. The Northern Alliance has taken over the stockpile.

In Afghanistan, only a desperate group would abandon such a valuable resource.

It's amazing what you can find in Wazir Akbar Khan, the smart suburb where the NBC house with the bomb was located. When Kabul fell, journalists discovered all sorts of documents abandoned by fleeing Taliban and al-Qaeda leaders, including a flight simulator computer program and a list of flight schools in the US, as well as documents concerning chemical, biological and nuclear warfare. The flight simulator program is understood to be identical to one discovered in the luggage of Mohammed Atta, the leader of the September 11 hijackers.

In the same upmarket street where the NBC house was located, it's likely there was a chemical weapons plant. It is next door to the Save the Children charity, and Chris Stephen and English reporter Tim Judah are the first journalists to discover it. This is a big story – the first evidence from here that al-Qaeda and the Taliban were working towards producing chemical weapons.

Most of the chemicals were removed when the Taliban fled Kabul. The Save the Children workers say strangers came to tell them to stay home that day, warning them that it could be dangerous. They heeded the advice.

The guards let us into the building. It is dusty and dark, and still smells slightly of chemicals – or is that the power of suggestion? The organisation that worked here was called Ummah Tameer-E-Nau, or 'Reconstruction of the Muslim Nation'. It was founded by Pakistani nuclear scientist and inventor Dr Sultan Bashiruddin Mahmood, an Islamic scholar who had worked at the Pakistani Atomic Energy Commission for thirty-five years. He held many senior positions, and was also one of the designers of the Khushab nuclear plant in Punjab. He took early retirement in 1998 to protest moves by the Pakistani government to sign the Comprehensive Test Ban Treaty, which he strongly opposed.

After retiring, he founded this organisation to run development projects in Afghanistan. Most of its membership consisted of nuclear scientists and military officers, and it was affiliated to the Al Rashid Trust, an organisation the US banned for its links with al-Qaeda.

Ummah Tameer-E-Nau was one of the few organisations permitted by the Taliban to carry out relief work in Afghanistan, and the Taliban gave Bashiruddin permission to sign business agreements on their behalf. This strengthened suspicion that Bashiruddin's 'non-government organisation' was actually looking for nuclear hardware for the Taliban.

Chris shows me maps and documents that he found here in the building, including diagrams of hot-air balloons which suggest the organisation was investigating dispersing chemical weapons over a city from the air. There are many documents about anthrax written in English, including US Center for Disease Control anthrax-immunisation leaflets. There is a letter addressed to Abu Khabbab, Osama bin Laden's top chemical and biological weapons commander. There is anti-American and anti-Israeli propaganda. There is also an inflatable model of an American plane, like a child's bath toy – strange and strangely chilling in this context.

Bashiruddin managed Ummah Tameer-E-Nau in partnership with another Pakistani nuclear scientist, Abdul Majid, who had worked for him at the Atomic Energy Commission. Dr Mahmood and Dr Majid were arrested in late October on suspicion of developing a nuclear device for the Taliban and Osama bin Laden. The arrests by the Pakistani authorities followed tip-offs from the FBI, linking the scientists to Jihadi networks.

The two scientists admit they made several trips to Afghanistan, and met Osama bin Laden, but say they were simply doing charity work. Both deny transferring any nuclear-related information to Afghanistan and say they only ran education programs and helped poor Afghan farmers. Dr Mahmood claims he talked with bin Laden about plans for the rehabilitation of Afghanistan.

Both men were subsequently released without charge.

In late December, after we leave Afghanistan, the UN Security Council orders a global freeze on the assets of Ummah Tameer-E-Nau, declaring it to be a terrorist group. The assets of the two former nuclear scientists are also frozen.

There are later reports of the discovery of documents relating to the building of nuclear weapons, but there is no indication that al-Qaeda's nuclear work has gone beyond theory. Creating a nuclear weapon requires a set of further steps not mentioned in the al-Qaeda manuals. And I imagine they have to have better facilities and infrastructure than anything available in Afghanistan – like a reliable electricity source, just for starters.

But all in all, even though I don't think there are nuclear weapons plants in Kabul, I'm glad I'm living at the Intercon, and not here in Wazir Akbar Khan, where the houses are large and comfortable, but there are also chemical weapons plants and unexploded bombs, and huge weapons stashes in your basement.

Chapter 19

On my second visit to the Kabul Women's Hospital, I go with a man.

Chris Stephen's news desk wants him to interview a female doctor and he thinks the interview will be easier with a woman present. I agree to accompany him, mainly because I'd like to see the hospital's director again. Rahima Zafar Stanekzai is a remarkable woman. She worked as a doctor throughout Taliban times and in 1998 was appointed by the Taliban to run the Rabia Balkh Hospital, when she was still only twenty-nine. Her staff is almost entirely female and the facility receives no foreign funding.

We drive into town, past the legless beggars who perch in the middle of the road in their terrifying, suicidal bid to earn a living. Once in the centre, where carpets are on sale, flapping against the fences of one of Kabul's main streets, we stop near the markets and walk through the stalls selling bananas, biscuits, nuts and roasted pumpkin and sunflower seeds, and into the crowded driveway leading up to the hospital. Our translator has a word to the man on the gate and we are permitted to push through a canvas curtain to enter the hospital grounds.

To our left, women are queuing for treatment outside a small building, sitting on benches out of the sun. Fifty women of all ages have their burqas back over their heads so that they can see, and are chatting to each other. It's an ordinary hospital scene, but Chris says he has to stop himself from staring. In two months here, it is the first time he has seen an Afghan woman's face.

Chris is spellbound, and also feels he is doing something forbidden, which in local terms, of course, he is. We walk past the queues to the three-storey building at the front of the hospital complex. A small, energetic woman in white, her hair under a white scarf, bustles towards us. Dr Rahima, as she is called here, does not wear a burqa inside the hospital grounds. The proud mother of two daughters, she gave birth to her second baby four months ago and is still slightly plump.

On this second meeting, Dr Rahima is warm and welcoming. She has a capable face, which can appear stern until she smiles, and she has a sharp sense of humour.

'It is good that Osama bin Laden made his base here. Now the world knows there is a place called Afghanistan.'

There are other journalists here and we follow her on her rounds. The hospital is scrupulously clean, but its facilities are simple and it smells of urine. Although the stone floors gleam, the sheets on the bed are torn. Patients have to bring their own food and buy their own medicines. Dr Rahima shows us the poorly stocked laboratories, the operating theatres, and the wards where women are recovering from surgery.

She explains that the Taliban clamped down on the availability of women's health care. By September 1997, only twenty-five per cent of the medical and surgical hospital beds dedicated to adults were available for women. By May 1998 that figure declined to twenty per cent. Besides shutting female patients out of the hospitals, the Taliban also banned female staff, including physicians, nurses, pharmacists and technicians, from working in any of Kabul's twenty-two hospitals. That policy was reversed in 1998, when some women were allowed to return to their jobs in segregated hospitals. The doctors here say the Taliban decided to reverse their ban on women receiving medical treatment when their own wives and daughters began to fall ill. It was at this time that Dr Rahima was appointed director of the hospital.

She denies she is a Taliban doctor. A renowned internal

medicine specialist, she says she did not seek the appointment as director, but accepted it in order to help other women.

'It's not my decision, it's government decision. I never prefer to work as director. I am a doctor. I can work everywhere. My job is to treat patients.'

When we ask her why she became a doctor she responds, 'I like it. I like to help other people, and it was my father's great ambition for me, although he died when I was fourteen years old, before he saw me fulfil it.'

As we go into the next ward, she stops the male reporters, translators and cameramen from following.

'No, no, you can't come in here.'

She motions me forward and, uncertain where I am going, I walk into a delivery room just in time to watch a baby being born. I could have caught him.

I am unbearably moved by the sight of this new life, a baby born into freedom in Kabul, two weeks after the retreat of the Taliban. This chance encounter seems to embody so much hope. His mother is lying on a trolley with a pillow behind her back, which is unceremoniously yanked out from behind her the second the umbilical cord is cut. She slumps back flat. No one pays any more attention to her.

I record the baby's first cries as a midwife wipes him down and swaddles him. He is lucky to have made it this far – there is a high incidence of miscarriages and stillbirths here.

'Yes, very high,' says Dr Rahima. 'We have fifteen to twenty deliveries a day, and four patients today have dead foetuses. One was five months, and one seven months.'

Kabul hospitals report a doubling of the number of miscarriages over the past three years. As well, Afghanistan has one of the highest rates of infant and child mortality in the world – 16.3 per cent, compared to 7 per cent in other developing countries. A staggering 1700 mothers out of 100,000 die giving birth.

In 1998, the medical charity Physicians for Human Rights interviewed women living in Afghanistan and women who had fled to refugee camps in Pakistan, in order to assess the health impact of life under the Taliban. The majority reported a decline in their physical and mental health. Eighty per cent said their mental health had declined – hardly surprising given that these women had lost one or more members of their family in the war. More than two-thirds reported that they or a member of their family had been detained and abused by Taliban militia, and that their social activities were extremely restricted. There was a stream of Taliban edicts concerning women, new ones coming out all the time, further restricting their lives month by month. Initially make-up and high heels were banned, then shoes that made a noise while women walked. Then women were confined to their homes.

These edicts were enforced by the Religious Police, the emphatically named police for the 'Protection of Virtue and Prevention of Vice'. They were bands of religious zealots who walked around armed with whips, long sticks and Kalashnikovs, and went on rampages, forcing women off the streets of Kabul, even those covered from head to foot and wearing the correct 'quiet' shoes. A further set of edicts required households to blacken their windows so that women would not be visible from the street. Women were to spend all their time indoors, where not even sunlight could penetrate.

Many of the symptoms the women reported to researchers met the diagnostic criteria for Post-Traumatic Stress Disorder, and ninety-seven per cent demonstrated evidence of major depression.

Against this background, Dr Rahima's job as a physician was demanding as well as politically complex. Everyday dealings with the bureaucracy were challenging, for she could never meet with her bosses directly – she had to send a lower-ranking man instead.

'Oh, no, no. During Taliban times I never go to the Ministry for Public Health,' she laughs at our misunderstanding. 'My husband, yes, a man could go, but there was no permission for me to go. It was not good. It was a problem, but there was no remedy, so we should accept it.'

In her view, the worst thing about the Taliban was the lack of education. 'It means we will never escape from this culture of economic decline.'

Dr Rahima combines running the hospital with motherhood. I am amazed, as juggling work with two small children is difficult enough in the West, where there is some acceptance of the role of the working mother. Dr Rahima's husband is an administrator at the hospital. Chris asks how she finds being the boss of her husband.

'Yes, here I am the boss of my husband, but not at home,' she laughs.

Who is the boss at home?

'No – there is no boss at home. We are equals, we consult each other on every matter, there is no problem.'

This hospital is entirely locally funded, and doctors in Afghanistan are poorly paid. A doctor at the Women's Hospital received US$30 per month – until April 2001 when the Taliban unilaterally cut that sum in half, in order to save money. Then in July 2001, the Taliban ceased paying salaries altogether, diverting funds to the military instead. Dr Rahima says the number of deaths rose, as patients could not afford to buy medicines and there was no possibility of provision from the hospital. But all the staff has kept working, even the cleaners.

'That is the culture of our people,' says Dr Rahima, 'we never work for money. I am a doctor. I should help my poor people. Otherwise what is my job? Even in my private clinic that is our rule. We treat the patients, no matter if they are poor and cannot pay.'

When we ask about the burqa, she is dismissive. 'People here don't hate it, it is part of our culture and it is related to the situation in our country. In good times, when conditions are good, it is not necessary. In bad times, when conditions are bad, it is necessary. The burqa did not make the war, you know. If we thought that removing the burqa would bring peace, we would remove it straight away.'

Our interview is interrupted by a nurse who consults Dr Rahima about an emergency patient. Dr Rahima excuses herself and tells the nurse what to do until she can get there herself. All her working life has been spent dealing with the impact of war. She nominates the two most difficult periods in Kabul as the recent American air strikes, and the civil war during the early 1990s. Dr Rahima was then working in a general hospital, treating the victims of the Mujaheddin attacks.

'It was very sadfull for me. Every day I examined injured people. We had no electricity for three years – for three consecutive years. NGOs helped the hospital and we had electricity during operations and at night. But we also had problems with water and with sanitation. Yes, sometimes we had no water and no sewerage as well.'

Dr Rahima is aware that some of the Mujaheddin leaders who were responsible for the attacks on Kabul in the early 1990s are now part of Afghanistan's new interim government. She says she hopes that they will not repeat the past – or that the international community will not allow them to – so that Afghanistan can have a chance for the peace its people crave after twenty-three years of war.

But when asked to assess the chances for peace, Dr Rahima is cautious.

'We have only a fifty–fifty chance. It depends on the UN and especially America. This is the third time that the UN will make a decision regarding our country without removing the weapons from here. You know, Afghanistan is like a laboratory: every country has offloaded its arms, old and new, for them to be tried out here. Afghanistan does not produce guns, they are brought in here – by the Mujaheddin, by the Taliban, by Osama. It is now up to the UN and America to collect these weapons.'

She pauses reflectively. 'But you know, I have never seen peace. I was such a small child that I don't really remember it. If the UN decision fails, the people are waiting for the storm after the calm.'

We tell her that in English the expression works in reverse. We have calm before the storm. 'Many things here are in reverse,' she smiles.

She says she does not give in to despair and that being able to treat her suffering countrymen has given her a sense of purpose. Perhaps her most telling response comes when I ask her if she would ever consider leaving Afghanistan, having stayed throughout all these dark, hard years.

'I don't want to go overseas to earn more money. But the education of my children is my top priority. It depends what is available here for them in the future, that is what will determine what I do.'

Dr Rahima hugs me as we depart. Once again I am amazed by the women I have met here, and their courage, humour, strength and determination, despite all that they have had to endure.

The Taliban leadership imposed the strictest interpretation of Islam ever seen anywhere in the world, saying they were recreating the Prophet Mohammed's era, the sixth century.

'We want to live a life like the Prophet lived 1400 years ago and jihad is our right,' an aide to Mullah Omar, Mullah Wakil, explained. 'We want to recreate the time of the Prophet and we are only carrying out what the Afghan people wanted for the past fourteen years.'

But in fact, the Taliban were recreating their own narrow lives in poor, backward rural villages in Afghanistan. Mullah Omar was from such a small village in the south that he had never been to Kabul – 700 kilometres away – and wasn't interested in going, even when the Taliban triumphantly captured the city in 1996.

The Taliban's policies on women were also a reflection of their own narrow lives rather than the prescriptions of Islam, even in the Prophet's time. Many of the Taliban recruits were war orphans brought up in refugee camps, tutored in the *madrasas*, the religious schools in Pakistan. They had simply never known the company of women. They had been brought up in a totally male society where the exclusion of women became a symbol of manhood and commitment to the jihad. They felt threatened by the half of the human race they had never known, and were more comfortable locking them away.

The Taliban leaders asserted that if they gave women greater freedom they would lose face with their rank and file, and sexual experience would weaken the men as fighters. Their lives had to be devoted to jihad to the exclusion of all else. Ahmed Rashid argues that, ironically, this religious brotherhood, with its hermetically sealed way of life, was 'a direct throwback' to the Christian Crusaders who fought Islam during the twelfth century – an all-male military order motivated by religion to fight and to kill.

Soon their oppression of women became the definition of the Taliban's Islamic radicalism. They justified it by saying it was what the people wanted, though it always had to be imposed at gunpoint. The religious police would smash TV sets with clubs, close girls' schools, whip women wearing make-up beneath – *beneath*! – their burqas, and stand on street corners measuring men's beards, arresting them if they were not long enough. Many here say that the Taliban's religious extremism brought people to a level of misery unparalleled in Afghan history.

After more than a decade of war, poverty and corruption, this was what the *madrasas* vomited up from the margins of Afghan society.

'My name means gold,' says Zarmina, a lively twenty-one-year-old woman. 'And my sister is Nuriya – that means light.'

We are sitting on the floor in her family's flat in a Soviet building on the outskirts of Kabul. Chris Stephen and I are here to interview her older sister Fahima – 'her name means knowledge!' – who is a doctor. But Zarmina is quick and clever and cheeky, and she has taken over the morning.

She has a twin bother, Mohammed, who is studying medicine. 'When the Taliban ran away I shaved off my beard, but now it is cold and I am a little bit sorry. According to your opinion, is it well?' he asks, offering us his chin from all sides.

Zarmina also wanted to study medicine, but the Taliban came to power just as she finished her high school studies in 1996, and she was unable to go to university.

'I was very sad because for so many years I sat together in the class with my brother, and I was in the first place and Mohammed was in the second. Afterwards, when I have to leave school, I help him, so that he will do well, and I study myself maths and English at home.'

She's done a thorough job of teaching herself. Her English is of a high standard and she translates for all the family in the room. Once, when she interrupts her twin brother, he looks up at the ceiling in frustration, and Chris says he sympathises with him. He knows exactly how he feels as he also has a cleverer sister who used to drive him crazy.

Since the departure of the Taliban there has been a rumour that medical schools may now open to women in the new term. Zarmina would like to resume her studies and the life that was interrupted by the Taliban's ban on the education of

women. Like her older sister Fahima, she says she wants to
help people.

'And in Afghanistan, being a doctor is a prestige job.'

Chris tells her that in England doctors are also rich.

'Then I want to come to London!' she laughs impishly.

I suggest she should come and work as my translator. A
female translator would send shock waves through this place.
She is very enthusiastic, but says she has to consult her father.
We agree that she will come to the Intercontinental Hotel the
following day at 9.30 a.m. I am surprised when she doesn't
turn up. Later, after I make enquiries through various drivers
and translators, I learn that she did come with her sister
Nuriya, but the guards at the gate turned them away. Two
unaccompanied females can't just walk into a hotel. And naturally no one checked with me.

The first small steps are so hard. Zarmina lives far away
and by the time I make contact with her again, the momen-
tum is lost. Her father has persuaded her that working for me
would be too much for her to take on.

I am still living at the Intercontinental Hotel, my first accidental meeting with Adriana having turned us into permanent
and happy roommates. Our room is freezing and I am once
again sleeping under my Northern Alliance sleeping bag,
though on a bed this time. Each of the hotel's six floors has
an Afghan version of the *dezhurnaya,* only the floor lady here
is a man, of course.

He's in charge of important things like providing water and
unlocking doors, essential for rooms with only one key and
multiple occupants. Every morning he brings a steel pail full
of water, so that we can wash. Sometimes when we are lucky
he will bring two pails, one filled with warm water. One day
I look into his room and see him heating water in small pots
on a two-bar radiator. After that, I don't expect warm water
every day.

The view from our room is stunning, looking out over the
city to the tawny mountains surrounding Kabul. Adriana is
fun, hardworking, and determined. She is tiny, with red curls,
an irresistible smile and a beguiling Mexican accent. When
her cameraman refuses to work any longer in the difficult

conditions here, she remains, filming sequences herself with a borrowed Digi-cam, and training her translator to shoot her pieces to camera. She does three people's work, and finds good stories through a combination of determination and that other journalistic necessity – luck. When Adriana goes places, things happen in front of her camera.

The heavy hitters are also here; CNN's Christiane Amanpour is broadcasting with her signature calm and fluency from the roof of the Intercontinental. Soon CBS anchor Dan Rather will be here. John Simpson, head of the BBC's World Affairs Unit, has been here from the start. He has been reporting from Afghanistan for more than twenty years, and until recently was a hero of mine, for his signature pieces are big, bold and thoughtful, always delivered with a flourish. But I am shocked that coming into Kabul with the Northern Alliance troops, he broadcasts that 'the BBC has liberated Kabul'. He does it in both his radio and TV stories – so it's not accidental. His declaration on radio is followed by an interview with the British Home Secretary, David Blunkett, who says, 'I'm still reeling from the news that the BBC and John Simpson have taken Kabul.'

In the ensuing uproar in the UK, Simpson says he regrets the statement, explaining that he became over-excited in the heat of the moment. He tells BBC TV interviewer David Frost, 'What I should have said, of course, was that we brought the news to people in Kabul that they had been liberated. I kind of shortened it down from the first word to the last word of the sentence.'

Acknowledging that four or five of his BBC colleagues had been walking alongside him at the time of the 'liberation', he says: 'What can you do? I regret it. But I don't regret being there a long way in advance.'

The next day the headlines scream *Simpson sorry for liberating Kabul*.

Since she was one of the first journalists into Kabul, my friend Barbara Jones has the best room in the Intercon, with a double bed, a working toilet and running water – cold, of course. Other rooms on the first floor have some of these advantages, but none is as impressive as Barbara's, which has everything, plus a heater, cheese and biscuits, and sometimes even gin. Barbara has collected an eclectic group around her, and I particularly enjoy spending time with Ajay Shukla, a former Indian army tank commander, now defence correspondent for India's Star TV. 'That guy has the biggest audience here. He must broadcast to 500 million people,' an American reporter tells me, awestruck.

In addition to the best conversation in the Intercon, Ajay's major asset is having a cameraman who cooks. Narindra makes mouth-watering curries in the Intercon kitchen, while the cooks and waiters look on grumblingly, and brings them upstairs to Barbara's room.

This is a blessing, since the food at the Intercon is usually tasteless and always expensive, tending to dry, overcooked chicken flanked by small portions of grey cauliflower. Perhaps this is what Westerners wanted to eat in 1979. Luckily for me I am at the confluence of two groups whose cameramen whip up fabulous meals at the end of a long working day. Alberto, a Spanish cameraman who sometimes shoots for Adriana, is one of the 'waifs' for whom we provide floor space in our room. He cooks delicious Spanish feasts, with tortillas and chicken enchiladas, and paella. In Kabul! At the Intercon, renowned for inedible food, I eat superbly.

Life here is easier than in Khoja Bahauddin, even though very little at the Intercon actually functions. But it is such an improvement on what came before that we're thrilled. The hard work is that the thin air at this altitude makes it difficult to run up the eight floors to the roof, where the feed points are. Just reaching the fourth floor where NBC has its offices is memorable. I sometimes find myself leaning against the doorjamb, with my breathing constricted, unable to keep climbing. Just as well I don't have any ambitions regarding Everest.

The hotel is at the top of a hill, and our cars usually drive up through two checkpoints to the front doors, but suddenly one day, with no explanation, we are prevented from doing this any more. We have to stop at the first checkpoint and walk up the last 300 metres.

As we are grumbling about lugging our gear up the hill in this thin air, someone explains the new policy was initiated after a car tried to enter the hotel with a trunk full of explosives. We grumble a bit less after hearing that.

The following week I'm driving up with Sabi, the sweet, funny teenager, obsessed with the *Titanic* soundtrack. He's a Panjshiri from Massoud's village, with a radiant smile and an almost female prettiness. He's unhappy about not being allowed to drive to the top of the hill. He gets out of the car and, without warning, grabs one of the guards by the throat.

The driver and I rush to pull him off. The guard has a gun, and I don't want Sabi murdered in front of me.

People here are so volatile.

The second NBC crew is inching its way from Khoja Bahauddin, bringing more than ten tonnes of TV equipment across the Hindu Kush to Kabul. My friend Jonathan has put off his return to the States and is doing the journey with about ten NBC guys, including his cameraman Tom, producer Karl Bostic and the saintly satellite engineer Hans.

Personally, this is not a journey I think they should undertake in a huge Russian truck, reversing up and down those narrow mountain paths. If I were NBC management I'd have them wait until the siege of Kunduz is lifted and the highway becomes clear, when they can do the trip in a day and a half in relative safety. But it's not up to me, so the boys are on the trucks, and I'm worried about them.

At this time we hear desperate rumours that four of our colleagues have been killed on the road driving in from Pakistan. After twenty-four hours, the deaths of four journalists are confirmed – Reuters cameraman Harry Burton, and his Afghan colleague Azizullah Haidari, Spaniard Julio Fuentes and Italian Maria Grazia Il Cutuli. They were taken out of their cars and shot by the side of the road. The Intercon heaves with pain and grief.

There is a sense of community here, and even people who did not know the journalists personally mourn their loss. There is also a stab of cold fear: *Next time, it could be me.* Alcohol is procured and consumed, but it takes some time to dull the reality of our colleagues meeting such a brutal end on an Afghan roadside.

Even worse, after they're killed their bodies lie where

they've fallen for three days because no one dares to go thirty kilometres outside Kabul to collect them. It's a measure of the lawlessness of a country when even the ruling troops won't go to pick up corpses.

I talk to Maria Grazia Il Cutuli's colleague Andrea, from Italian newspaper *Corriere della Sera*. Once Maria's body finally is picked up off the side of the road by Northern Alliance troops, he has to go and identify her. This place makes many demands on you that are not strictly part of the job description.

I find myself thinking again about luck, and fate.

I did not know Australian cameraman Harry Burton personally, but everyone who did says he was a top bloke, funny, brave and caring, as well as being a great professional. Harry did everything right – he drove in during the day, not at night, in a convoy along a road that had been regarded as relatively safe. But he died, and another Australian journalist, who broke the rules by driving in at night, unescorted, along the same road, is here to tell the tale. In fact, Harry begged this Australian journalist to join his convoy, to do it properly, not to take stupid risks. But it was Harry who died, and it's his friend who is alive, telling me this story in Kabul.

At its daily briefings, the UN says it's no longer safe for us to drive in and out along the road where the ambush took place. This is a significant restriction as it is the main road in and out of Pakistan, and there is no other means of transport at the moment. When the UN says it will put on flights for us, you can almost hear the sigh of relief in the packed room. Then we learn that the UN will charge US$2500 for the one-hour flight to Pakistan. Up front, in cash. This same flight cost US$500 a year ago. People who don't have that kind of money or don't have a big news organisation that will put it up for them feel trapped.

Road convoys out to Pakistan slowly resume, despite the danger. The noticeboard downstairs at the Intercon makes painful reading as Reuters writes a letter reminding people that they have lost two beloved colleagues and begging other journalists not to take such risks. There is a reply signed 'The Crazy Press', explaining that journalists have to get in and out to cover such stories, even if they don't have the huge sums the UN is demanding for the flights.

Two Israeli journalists who are 'in hiding' in the Islamic state of Afghanistan, working under false names, decide that they will solve the problem by leaving together on the local bus to Jalalabad. I admire their ingenuity and daring, and they make it out safely. But later in the month two bandits board that same Jalalabad bus. They turn out to be former Taliban, and force all men without beards off the bus, and cut off their noses and ears, leaving them bleeding in a ditch by the side of the road.

It never stops.

But what shakes me, and almost sends me home, is the murder of Swedish cameraman Ulf Stromberg in Taloqan. He is shot during a robbery when bandits enter his room at night. His death deprives me of my 'I'd have done it differently' figleaf. We stayed in a house in the same area in Taloqan, also in a locked compound, without armed guards. It could have been us.

Ulf Stromberg was a father of three children, devoted to his work. His Swedish colleagues leave a letter downstairs at the Intercon, describing him as a great cameraman and a wonderful human being, always prepared to go the extra mile for the story and for his friends. 'We cannot describe our loss, or how much we will miss him.' I cry as I'm reading it, and seeing how upset I am, a friend says, 'No, you don't have to go home. Think of it as a drive-by shooting – it could happen anywhere. Here, LA, London.'

In Afghanistan, that's comfort.

The other side of this is that danger is an aphrodisiac. Surviving dangerous situations with someone you find attractive enhances every feeling. Relief at surviving is immediately swamped by desire for the person you survived with. When your colleagues are dying around you, it makes life – and love – more precious.

It's something the male correspondents have known for a while. But they don't talk about it because many of them are married, with a wife worrying and waiting at home. Some men speak to their wives twice a day on satellite phones from trenches in the middle of battlefields. Others simply have a good time, with whoever is around: journalists, aid workers, refugees or prostitutes. Some men, of course, do both.

There are women who know about this front-line buzz, too. The guys describe them as 'war groupies'. Women who do ten days in Afghanistan following fashion week in New York, and bring hairdryers and bust-firming creams to places where the bombs are dropping and there's no electricity. Well, not the type that you can plug a hairdryer into.

And in Kabul there's another factor that heightens sexual tension. This is still very much the Taliban's city, where sex was forbidden and women were stoned to death for adultery. Simply the idea of sex here, in this city, is so illicit as to be irresistible.

So it's dangerous, it's forbidden, it's alluring – but unfortunately it's also impossible because there is no privacy anywhere. People are once again crammed three or four to a room, once again in sleeping bags. For example, Adriana and I are the two permanent occupants of our room, but there is a floating population of needy journalist refugees we take in.

In order to arrange accommodation for friends and colleagues coming in to Kabul, Adriana becomes like a property developer at the Intercon – acquiring rooms as they become free, with no reference to the front desk. 'We'll put the Spanish guys in room 301, and we'll move to room 243, which has a ceiling. Afterwards, when my new cameraman comes, he will move in and they will move out. I am looking for a room for them.'

Every extra space is immediately snapped up by newcomers in need of somewhere to stay, so there's little chance of engineering a night alone with anyone you might fancy. Everyone tries though. You hear snatches of conversation as you pass people, dodging drips in the lobby, or emerging from the daily UN press briefing.

'I've done a deal where we get room 131, which has a working toilet, when that journalist goes. I'll be alone there.'

It's amazing that anyone has time for reporting. And then one miraculous day, it happens. We organise three rooms and four sets of journalists, so that the right combinations can be on their own.

One English reporter says she is going for the 'I did it Kabul' T-shirt and bumper sticker. And a redoubtable Eastern European journalist even has two lovers on the go concurrently, a mind-boggling feat of organisation and stamina, given the hours that she works as well as everything else.

The second NBC crew calls in to say they have completed half of their journey down the mountains. It is taking them even longer than it took us because of the large amount of gear they are hauling, and they are finding it hard going. They've celebrated Thanksgiving on this journey, and are spending the night outside in the open, on the snowline near the summit of the Hindu Kush, because one of their trucks has burst a tyre. They are patching the tyre past midnight in the freezing dark, and tomorrow they will see whether snow has blocked the Hawaq Pass, and if they can cross down into the Panjshir Valley, or whether they have to unload all their gear onto donkeys.

One of the engineers describes this trip as the craziest thing he has been asked to do in twenty years at NBC news. I am very worried about them during their dangerous snail's pace ascent, but in only a day or two more, *inshallah*, they will reach Kabul.

Chapter 20

B ini Hasr is a typical Afghan village thirty minutes west of Kabul. The paved road has petered out, there are mud-brick houses, and chickens, goats and children scatter in front of us on the gravel path. The mountains look down benignly from their great height. This is 'Anywhere, Afghanistan', and this inaccessible ordinariness was just what al-Qaeda was looking for.

They wanted an unremarkable house in an unremarkable village, for a small camp and safe house. When they found it, the Taliban 'persuaded' the owner to give it up. Now it's empty and in ruins. Osama bin Laden was allegedly staying here in late October, and the building was destroyed by an American cruise missile just hours after he left.

We walk into the yard. I am with Adriana and Chris Stephen. A massive blast has destroyed the main building, tearing off its roof and scattering debris and timber everywhere. The owner describes how in September the Taliban came to him and ordered him to give up this house. Initially, he refused.

'They ignored this and they beat me with cables for two weeks.' He shows us fading bruises on his arms.

He fought them, obtaining an eviction notice, which he shows us. It has the thumbprints of his illiterate neighbours, as required by law. But it made no difference, and in the end, when he couldn't endure the beatings any longer, he gave up his house to the Taliban. He says that twelve men came here.

'Six were Arabs and six Afghans. I knew one of them, Mullah Mahmud. They built a large gate in the wall to make easy access for their vehicles.' The owner shows us the new wooden gate in the mud-brick wall surrounding his compound. It is large enough to take jeeps and an armoured personnel carrier. 'They said they wanted it because it was a decent size and had such a high wall, and then they built a gate,' he grumbles.

I am surprised to see that they also built what looks like a sauna, a small, carefully constructed wood-panelled room. For al-Qaeda's Swedish brigade perhaps? It stands apart from the main building, near the standard-issue Afghan outhouse, and it doesn't look as if they had a chance to use it.

Officially, this became a regional office for a charity called WAAFA, which delivered aid to the poor in Afghanistan, and was also possibly used by al-Qaeda as a cover organisation.

'We helped them at the start,' says the owner. He wanted to keep an eye on his property. 'They were distributing rice and oil, along with the Taliban, but then they pushed us out. A guard who worked here, Amin, saw bin Laden here. He says they came in the night, with extra bodyguards.'

Amin is not here now, but Chris Stephen spoke to him on an earlier visit. The guard was a twenty-three-year-old who had come to Bini Hasr in late September, one of fifteen Talibs sent to work at the compound in order to release the Arab soldiers based here for military duty.

Amin told Chris that bin Laden arrived on 26 October, almost three weeks after the start of the bombing campaign – and the night before the attack that destroyed this camp. However, there was so much secrecy that the men were not even told it was bin Laden until after he left. All they were told was that they had to secure the entire village.

'He arrived at night, it was after eight, and he came in a big convoy of jeeps with 120 bodyguards,' Amin said. 'When he came into our camp he was completely surrounded by a wall of very tall men. They were so close together you could not see him at all – they were arranged so they could fire in three different directions.'

Amin said that he heard bin Laden talking to the camp commander, telling him that he would leave at eight o'clock the next morning to go to Kabul. Amin's understanding was that bin Laden planned to spend two days at the compound, using it as a base for visits to Kabul. But instead he left early the next morning, within hours of his arrival.

'He just got up at five, said his prayers, then left.'

Amin told Chris that just before 8 a.m. everyone in the camp was ordered to leave because a cruise-missile strike was coming.

Minutes later, two missiles hit, smashing the house in the centre of the camp compound. This chain of events sparked an immediate investigation by the al-Qaeda camp authorities who suspected there must be a spy in the camp. However, said Amin, they never found one.

The owner of the house corroborates part of the story. 'We heard that bin Laden left before the bombing that destroyed my house. Seven Taliban died in the bombing, they buried them in the cemetery here. One lost an arm. Then they loaded up the car and drove to Kandahar.'

Most of the property is now destroyed, and the compound is full of rubble. There are documents and stickers from WAAFA. Crunching through the debris, we pick them up and other documents, including more exercise books and letters written in Arabic. Last time he was here, Chris found ripped-up plane tickets, which he has pieced back together. They show that some of the operatives had flown into Iran in late October and made their way here after that.

I am standing in the rubble, looking at a WAAFA sticker – if it is true that this aid agency is a cover for a terrorist organisation, it seems to me to be horribly cynical. Aid work is difficult, demanding, poorly paid, at times heroic. It is the opposite of terrorism, and it can only make aid delivery more difficult if it is being used as a front by terrorist organisations. I trawl through the rubble wondering if the story can be true and if bin Laden really was here and avoided being killed in an air strike by a matter of hours. It is one person's account and very difficult to corroborate.

I find a bottle of medicine for ulcers in the rubble. So terrorists take Zantac, too? You don't think of a terrorist with indigestion. Although I suppose it is a pretty stressful job.

I'm thinking through all the implausibilities in the story – doesn't the property owner's version partly contradict the guard's version, because if they had a warning to get out, why did seven Taliban soldiers die in the missile strike? – when my eye alights on an empty birdcage. You don't think of a terrorist with a birdcage, either. *Bin Laden's birdcage.* I kneel to touch it. *But the bird has flown.* Something about the dusty rickety cane cage takes my fancy. I bring it back to the hotel along with the WAAFA and al-Qaeda documents.

Over time I become quite attached to my unusual al-Qaeda loot. It sits dustily in my room at the Intercon, a symbol of all the things I don't understand about this conflict – soldiers who swap sides, a society where women are confined, and terrorists who have ulcers and birdcages.

Over the next few days, Adriana and I go through the documents, wondering, as with the stuff we lifted from the Rishkor training camp, where the security services are. Why are journalists able to collect all these documents? Journalists will take information wherever they find it, but why are the CIA and MI5 letting us do this? Why haven't they been in and cleared these places out? This appears to be another Intelligence failure, following the American security services' failure to act on warnings about increased terrorist activity prior to September 11.

At the al-Qaeda headquarters at Khost, a series of terrorist training camps 150 kilometres south-east of Kabul, there is another interesting stash of al-Qaeda papers.

Once again they are found by a journalist. In late November British reporter Jason Burke becomes the first Westerner known to have visited Khost in five years.

After the Taliban captured the dusty east Afghan city in 1996, they virtually ceded it to Osama bin Laden and it became the base for the 'international brigade' operating in Afghanistan. Almost all of the thousands of Islamic militants trained in Afghanistan since bin Laden returned in 1996 have been through Khost.

The main training camp there is called Khaldan. It's where the men who carried out the 1998 bombings of the US embassies in East Africa were trained and selected. The FBI believes that at least two of the September 11 hijackers, possibly including the group's leader, Mohammed Atta, also trained there.

The al-Qaeda operatives cleared the main camp when they departed, but in the corner of a room where a bank of computers once stood, they left a small stack of documents. Jason Burke picks them up. They reveal that militants were being instructed in every aspect of terrorism. They include photocopied pages in English, apparently from manuals circulated by far-right extremists in the United States. 'This book may seem controversial and dangerous, but such information may someday be the lifeblood of freedom fighters,' explains one manual.

Another forty-one-page document, entitled *Assorted Nasties,* is a 'how to' guide to chemical weapons, detailing how to make biological and chemical weapons from household items. The chemical weapons range from mustard gas to sarin, and the manual also details a variety of different delivery mechanisms.

In the cellar of a house set aside for foreign recruits, Jason Burke sees barrels of chemicals. The entrance to the cellar is surrounded by dead birds, which seems to imply that operatives were using this building as a laboratory and experimenting with the manufacture of chemical weapons.

Burke discovers other manuals covering explosives manufacture, including car bombs and the favourite bomb designs of Middle East terrorists, as well as personal letters. The letters are fascinating. Several mention bin Laden by name. One, written to Khaldan instructor Abu Said by Yemeni trainer Abu Ziad, refers to orders received from bin Laden. 'I have sat and spoken to Sheikh Osama . . . and he has made arrangements for me to travel to Eritrea. I am going to stay there for a month and a half, then I am going to travel, and then I am praying to God that I will be martyred.'

The letters reveal that the recruits are eager to progress to assassinations and more advanced operations. One is from an Iraqi Kurd sent to Eritrea to train other militants. It says, 'Thank you Abu Said, for showing us how small people with faith can defeat the big people with equipment and power, who have no faith.' It is the Suicide Bomber's Hymn.

At the same time, in late November 2001, one of my Moscow colleagues, Alan Cullison from the *Wall Street Journal*, buys two computers at a Kabul computer store for US$1100. The laptop and the PC he buys have been looted from an al-Qaeda compound which was destroyed in a bombing raid in early November before Kabul fell. Alan went to the Kabul computer shop in the first place because his laptop had been smashed on the drive through the Hindu Kush. Usual story – his jeep lost its brakes and crashed into a truck. This actually saved his life, though it destroyed his gear.

'I was looking for one, and was much more interested in this laptop and the hard drive when I heard it was used by al-Qaeda.'

He tells me that he was also aware that because he arrived in Kabul a week after it fell, all the best al-Qaeda documents had already been snapped up by the journalists who had come in from the Panjshir with the victorious Northern Alliance troops. Two forms of necessity therefore drive him to find a great scoop.

It appears the hard drive he buys belonged to Mohammed Atef, a leading al-Qaeda commander killed in the raid. It contains material linking al-Qaeda to the September 11 attacks and to the murder of Ahmed Shah Massoud, as well as revealing efforts by al-Qaeda to obtain chemical weapons.

Alan's bosses at the *Wall Street Journal* back in New York instruct Alan to hand over the computers to American government authorities, for authentication and in case they contain any information that could prevent further terrorist attacks. I find this puzzling – why let Alan pay for the computers if you are simply going to hand them over?

Before the US government officials show up, Alan and fellow *Wall Street Journal* reporter Andrew Higgins copy as many of the files as they can. This turns out to be everything from the hard drive, but nothing from the laptop since they can't get past its password. They hand both computers over to the government officials in Kabul.

The government authenticates the computers. The *Wall*

Street Journal has access to some 1750 files – text, audio and video – detailing everything from housekeeping and internal squabbles to active missions.

There is also an outline of an al-Qaeda project to develop chemical and biological weapons, codenamed al-Zabadi, Arabic for curdled milk. Top al-Qaeda commander Ayman al-Zawahri, who survived the bombings that killed the owner of the hard drive, appears to be the author of one memo. 'The destructive power of these weapons is no less than that of nuclear weapons,' he writes, adding, 'we only became aware of them when the enemy drew our attention to them by repeatedly expressing concern that they can be produced simply.'

A video file made after September 11 uses television footage of people fleeing the World Trade Center, combined with a soundtrack of mocking chants and prayers in Arabic. Another video file contains a twenty-three-minute clip of Osama bin Laden denouncing the United States and enthusing over the September 11 attacks.

It just goes to show that even a car accident can lead you to a fantastic story. You can never tell where the news is lying in wait for you.

A convoy of huge dusty trucks lumbers into the Intercon one night in late November. I am standing on the balcony looking out from the NBC's fourth-floor offices, and we excitedly agree that this could be the second NBC crew, arriving from the treacherous drive across the Hindu Kush. Of course the lift is not working, so I take the stairs. Three dusty men are walking in as I reach the lobby. I am very relieved to see that it is my friends, tired and filthy, but safe.

'I've been so worried about you,' I say throwing my arms around Jonathan, whose black hair is grey with dust. He smells of dirt and danger, and I look up to see a camera rolling. Tom has been filming their entire trip. I receive dusty hugs from Hans and Tom just as NBC's chief producer comes down to greet them. 'Welcome to Hell.'

Delirious with tiredness and the joy of survival, they describe the terrible drive and their near misses. Jonathan says he found himself praying for the first time in years.

'The worst moment was when the truck was reversing up a mountain road at night. It was a ninety-degree hill, it was pitch dark, and I could hear rocks slipping beneath our wheels, falling off the mountain and down that endless, pitiless cliff into the dark water below.' Jonathan shudders.

'And we drove right into a minefield – our driver made a mistake, and we had to reverse out when he realised, along the exact same track, real slow,' Hans says.

Jonathan adds, 'We told our drivers that we wanted to reach a town we nominated – but what that meant was that they drove all night, without eating, and we'd arrive as the sun was rising so that they couldn't eat all day again, because it was Ramadan, and they were all stoned, so I really didn't trust their judgement or their reflexes.'

'Ah, it was nothing . . .' says Tom.

There are many reunions in Kabul. NBC has brought my favourite driver Shah Mahmood down from Khoja Bahauddin. Here in the big city he is even more 'Snoop Mahmood', with the sunglasses he borrows from the American boys, and his shiny new van, bought with the money he's earned working for NBC.

Jonathan says Shah Mahmood wasn't meant to come. 'We'd said goodbye to him, he was taking one of the engineers back to the border crossing with all the gear. But Shah Mahmood just dumped the engineer there at the Pyang River. He didn't stay to help him load two tonnes of gear onto the barge or negotiate for him in Dari, he just headed straight for us. So we are standing at the bank of the Kokcha ten kilometres away and we see a figure crossing the river on horseback, he's riding towards us through the water and he has an NBC dust mask over his face. After a while, we realise, it's Shah Mahmood. He says, *You. Me. Go. Kabul.* We had to take him.'

I am very happy to see NBC producer Babak Behnam. I last saw him two months ago, in that field outside the airport in Dushanbe, while I waited for Chopper Number 3. Babak was on the list for the 'fixed-wing' plane to the city of Faizabad. He fills me in on what he did next: driving across the Hindu Kush down into the Panjshir Valley, where he stayed –

without a break – until the fall of Kabul. He accompanied the Northern Alliance troops into Kabul, and has set up an NBC empire at the Intercon.

Babak has a wonderful older man, Mr Haidari, working for him. We all call him Joe, which is what he was called when he worked in the US in the 1950s, studying to be an air traffic controller. He returned to Afghanistan and worked in his profession until 1980, but when the jihad against the Communists began, the airport and its facilities were destroyed. The following two decades of war limited air travel in and out of the country. Planes landed and took off without using air traffic controllers. Joe was out of a job.

Joe is sweet, courteous, and dignified, with a grey beard and glasses, and a ready smile. He always wears an embroidered cap, not a turban, and speaks delightfully formal old-fashioned English – Philadelphia, circa 1955, right down to the speech patterns and the accent, which he has retained. It's like listening to someone from Philly, not a Kabuli. They should put him in a language lab, to record American English 'frozen' in the 1950s.

Joe works as Babak's fixer and 'local knowledge'. Strictly, Babak doesn't need a translator since he speaks Farsi, which means he can communicate in Dari. But while getting things done is first and foremost about language, it is also about influence and pulling strings and knowing a place. Joe provides all that, and still manages to go home for a sleep in the afternoon.

When Kabul TV station resumes transmissions for two hours a day, we pile into a car to have a look. I go with Babak and NBC reporter Jim Maceda. Joe sits with us in the back seat. He speaks to Babak in Dari, then turns to us, clearly concerned.

'I don't know what to do,' he says. 'Mr Babak exhorts me not to stand upon ceremony with him.'

We savour this wonderful phrase, and Jim Maceda responds, 'Well, if he exhorts you – then you mustn't stand on ceremony. Just tell him he's an asshole.'

Joe would never do that, trading insults is not his style. When he tells me about his life it reinforces the difficulties people at all stratas of society have faced here. Joe is middle class and educated, and once held a professional job, but he has lost contact with his son, who fled Afghanistan for Europe.

'We last heard from him seven years ago, and his mother is very worried,' Joe says gravely. 'Can you think of any way I could track him down? He was last in Germany, I believe.'

Seven years. It is so pitiful to have lost a child and not to know whether he is dead or in prison or simply unable to contact you because of the parlous state of everything, including communications, in your country.

'His mother is very worried,' Joe repeats, clearing his throat, sadly.

I want to write a story entitled 'We are the new Taliban', as we are living in their homes, driving their cars and eating in their restaurants.

The Herat restaurant is doing a roaring trade, packed every lunchtime during Ramadan, journos only, of course. This was the Taliban's favourite eatery, and was obviously a lucrative spot – more beggar women patrol outside here than anywhere else in Kabul. The restaurant is a large room with fifty aqua steel tables and benches. There's a narrow steel sink along one wall, with many taps, like a kindergarten bathroom, where you wash your hands. The mirror above the sink has a prayer stencilled on it in Arabic. The only decoration is faded tourist posters of Afghanistan. In a backroom there is a poster of the Buddha statues at Bamian. I don't know how the posters survived the Taliban when the statues didn't.

A man stands on the street outside the front of the restaurant, whipping up the Herat's specialty: shashlik, kebab and kofta, meatballs with cardamom, over hot coals. There's lamb and, of course, the ubiquitous goat. My favourite. In Afghanistan, Goat is the new Lamb. The Herat also makes great chips, and a tasty salad, but it's lucky I learned to eat meat in Khoja Bahauddin. This is food for your meat and potatoes kind of terrorist.

We try other restaurants, but – like the Taliban – we always come back to the Herat. Later there are conspiracy theories that an al-Qaeda movement that tries to infiltrate the Northern Alliance is codenamed Herat. Named for the Afghan city – or for this restaurant?

Barbara from the *Mail on Sunday* will soon be leaving the Intercon for a house previously owned by bin Laden's third wife. A British journalist is turning it into a media compound, having cleared out all Mrs bin Laden's videos and al-Qaeda documents first. She left in a hurry on 12 November with all the rest of the Taliban leadership. It's revealing that even bin Laden's wife was not better prepared, and didn't know the Taliban collapse was imminent. While Barbara writes a piece about the documents and tapes found in her new home, I decide to do something more frothy. I plan to go to a hairdresser and incorporate that into my 'We are the new Taliban' piece. I'm hoping to go the whole hog and have a Taliban facial – that would make a good headline! – but it turns out this word is simply not in the Afghan vocabulary.

Finding a beautician/hairdresser is not easy. These women's services were 'underground' during Taliban times, prohibited as frivolous and punishable by beatings from the Taliban religious police. We make enquiries and finally hear about a beauty parlour in a suburb called Micro-Rayon. When I hop in the car I don't realise that we have to drive for more than an hour across Kabul to find a hairdresser.

There is no shop front, so we ask at the address we have been given. In classic Afghan fashion, our initial discussions are with a six-year-old boy. This is judged more appropriate than an adult woman speaking to us. The small boy directs us to a house at the back of his street, from which a shy seventeen-year-old girl emerges. Yes, she has a secret salon, but she has never coloured anyone's hair or done any facials. She opens a drawer to show me her make-up collection. A few lipsticks, some mascara and rouge. She put this on women. Is that what I mean?

I decide that I need something more for a story, after all even soldiers wear make-up here, so we drive for another hour and a half back across Kabul. We stop at a second house, in an area that looks rural. A woman comes out to speak to us and, with chickens scratching at our feet, she tells me that her beauty parlour only does make-up. No hair and no facials. Even in an Afghan context, this doesn't really look like the spot for a ritzy salon.

Disappointed, we are almost back at the Intercon, when

the taxi driver enters into the spirit of the search, and says that he knows of a possible beauty parlour right here.

We stop outside a nondescript house, climb through a door in the wall and walk up a path and around a corner.

A man opens the front door and, after the translator explains what we want, he unleashes his family of six beautiful women, like Afghan goddesses. They are tall and dark-haired, with bright faces and welcoming smiles. They are thrilled to be interviewed as they operated a secret beauty parlour throughout Taliban times. We sit in a room empty except for a dressing table and a chair. This is clearly where business is conducted. They too have not heard of facials, and I never really succeed in explaining the concept. 'Face cream?' they ask, puzzled. But they did do make-up and, of course, hair.

The middle sister, Massouda, is the hairdresser. She has a long face, clever almond-shaped eyes and is startlingly lovely. There are no clients here at the moment for me to interview, but I am so taken with Massouda that I decide to let her colour my hair, just to see what the experience will be like and for the chance to talk to women in this most ordinary, non-political context. She looks at my hair. Yes, she can match the colour. If I come back tomorrow she will have some dye. Where will she find it? In the markets, she knows where. I agree to return tomorrow at 3 p.m. and her fourteen-year-old brother who speaks some English will be my translator. She gives me a radiant smile as we depart.

When I return the following day, the five girls crowd around as Massouda shows me the hair colour she has purchased. During the night I was wondering if this impulsive idea was such a good one – how far do you have to go for a story after all? At home I am very particular about which hairdresser I choose, but Kabul changes the rules for everything. Here it seems to be enough that the colour is made by L'Oreal, although the instructions are in German, which neither Massouda nor I can speak.

How bad can it be?

Massouda sits me in the chair in front of the mirror. Her sisters and mother sit on a bench nearby while she colours my hair with this home colour kit. I could have done it myself really, and so could the other women who come here. But

I suspect that there is something about the conversation and the time out of your day, and the pleasure of having someone else attend to you that is as irresistible here as it is in the West. Even if the Taliban will punish you if they find out.

The electricity dies suddenly, a frequent occurrence in Kabul. It's quite dark inside, but Massouda is careful and professional. We are soon all discussing our personal lives, with everything translated by the fourteen-year-old brother, the only boy in this bevy of girls.

Massouda is twenty-four and she is not married. I say that seems very old to remain single in a place where girls are married at fifteen. How did she manage it?

'I simply told my father that I didn't want to.'

We all laugh. In fact, of the five girls aged between seventeen and thirty, only the oldest is married. There is much giggling when I tell them that their father must be desperate by now.

'And you – why are you not married?' they ask me.

I tell Massouda that I simply didn't want to either; only in my society I have a bit more freedom to act on my decisions.

'But you are so beautiful, you should be married,' Massouda says. Her brother translates earnestly.

'No, no, *you* are so beautiful – *you* should be married,' I reply, to peals of laughter from all the sisters.

Two of Massouda's sisters were at university, but the arrival of the Taliban meant the end of their studies. One was studying medicine and she now seems sad, as if life has passed her by.

'You could go back to university, the faculty of medicine is being reopened to women,' I suggest.

'No, I can't, my studying days are behind me. I don't have enough memory to keep learning.'

Even though it is Ramadan, they bring me tea and sweets and oranges. It is only by strenuously protesting that I stop them from cooking me a meal while they are fasting. I ask Massouda how she started doing this work, and she tells me that initially she did it for her friends and then it became a business. 'Then other women came to see me, secretly, as this was forbidden by the Taliban. It was dangerous for women if the religious police found out.'

I tell her that in the West this is incomprehensible, and she looks down, serious for the first time since I have met her. 'Yes, here too.'

When the Taliban took Kabul in 1996, they shut down beauty, hair and make-up parlours, and women's bath houses – the only place where hot water was available. So many small cruelties. Tailors were ordered not to measure women for clothes. They learnt to keep their customers' measurements in their heads. You couldn't get fatter or – more likely here – thinner. And tailors couldn't measure new customers – a woman couldn't bring along her fifteen-year-old daughter for new clothes for the first time. Even fashion magazines were destroyed.

The Taliban prohibited the painted faces and hair that are so much a part of female culture throughout the Islamic world. These were deemed to be 'unIslamic', and bands of armed zealots patrolled the streets to punish any women they caught breaking these rules.

Sometimes women would meet in secret and put on make-up for themselves, for each other, and then wash it off before they went home, so that they would not be beaten by the religious police. In this warm room, with these lovely, happy women, that image makes me want to weep.

Massouda pauses. 'You know, I wanted to be a journalist like you.'

I offer her my career advice. 'You should try to learn some English, like your brother – and maybe some computer skills. If you get a chance to do a computer course at an aid agency you should grab it. That is the future.'

They are as fascinated with me and my life as I am with them. There is lots of laughter, and I enjoy this very warm, very female exchange.

'Will you come to have dinner with us? What present can we get for you?' they ask me.

I tell them that I don't want any presents, but I would like to come and have dinner. As we plan the most convenient time for them, taking into account the daily Ramadan fast, it occurs to me that the NBC guys might like to meet this family of amazing women.

'Could I bring a male friend with me to dinner – or would it be more difficult for you?' I ask.

They confer in Dari, and Massouda explains anxiously that of course I can bring any guest I wish, but if I bring a male friend then they will not be able to eat with me, their father is quite strict about such things.

I tell them that I don't want them cooking all evening and not able to eat, what would be the point of that, and they are pleased. What a shame though, both for the NBC guys and for them, that they can never meet.

When I wash the colour out of my hair, it is in a small concrete bathroom, with a sink and a mirror, and water brought in by bucket. But the electricity has come back on, so we can all examine the new colour approvingly. Massouda and L'Oreal have done a beautiful job. She beams and says that we must take a photograph together. I explain that my camera broke when we drove over the Hindu Kush, but she surprises me, replying that she has one.

When Massouda comes back with the camera she is wearing a gleaming gold Afghan traditional dress. I tell her she looks very beautiful, actually she looks like an Afghan queen, and she says that if I like it so much perhaps this is what they should give me as a present.

I insist they shouldn't and am even more amazed when Massouda does not want to take payment for her work. 'You are my guest and my friend,' she says. I am determined to pay, after all she had to buy the hair dye in the market. She reluctantly agrees, though she will not charge me, she will simply take whatever sum I nominate. Afghanistan is extraordinary – you are either being robbed blind or encounter this humbling generosity.

It is getting dark as I leave, and Massouda's dress gleams gold in the twilight. I walk up the hill to the Intercon and see two beggar women. The hands that they stick out from under the burqas have varnished nails.

In Kabul you see women on the street wearing burqas having their nails polished by small boys. It seems this is cheaper than buying a bottle of nail polish to use at home. Just because you're a beggar doesn't mean you don't care about the only part of you a man can see. Perhaps they also think it helps in their work if their hands are adorned.

Iranian film-maker Mohsen Makhmalbaf saw this through-

302

out the country when he was here during Taliban times. 'I told myself that this is a good sign that women under burqas still like living and, despite their poverty, care about their beauty to that extent. Later on, however, I reached the conclusion that it is not fair to isolate and imprison a woman in an environment or a certain costume and be content that she still puts on make-up.'

On Saturday 24 November the two-week siege of Kunduz ends. An estimated 5000 Afghan fighters surrender and are allowed to return home, but a different fate awaits the foreign mercenaries fighting for the Taliban. Top US officials, including Defense Secretary Donald Rumsfeld, publicly oppose any deal that would allow safe passage of foreign Taliban troops to Pakistan in exchange for their surrender.

Taliban commander Mullah Faizal goes from Kunduz to Mazar-i-Sharif to negotiate the surrender with General Dostum. He promises to hand over the 600 foreign fighters under his command from the Taliban's international brigade. In return he is promised safe passage back to Kandahar. The foreign volunteers duly travel for five hours across the desert, pitching up on the outskirts of Mazar-i-Sharif in the dark early hours of Saturday. They sleep, and wake to find themselves confronted by Dostum's men. The foreign fighters are furious, and there are some suggestions that they had been tricked into going to Mazar on the understanding they would attack it.

It appears that Mullah Faizal instructs them to give up their weapons, but fails to tell them they will be taken into custody. After three to four hours of negotiation the foreign fighters finally agree to surrender. They are disarmed by Dostum's troops, herded fifty at a time onto flatbed trucks and driven to Qala-i-Janghi, Dostum's vast nineteenth-century fortress headquarters on the outskirts of Mazar.

Journalists covering events in Mazar are also staying at Qala-i-Janghi – Fort of War – a huge old tree-filled compound, like a small town. When things begin to go badly wrong, this is how it all ends up on TV, beamed around the world.

It appears the men on two of the five trucks were not searched for concealed weapons. This allows a Chechen prisoner to detonate a hidden grenade at the fortress late on

Saturday afternoon, blowing himself up and killing two other prisoners and General Dostum's police chief, Nadir Ali. A second prisoner, detonating another hidden grenade, kills a senior Hazara commander. Despite these two attacks, the Northern Alliance guards are not reinforced.

Sunday 25 November is a big news day. 'The marines are now on a piece of Afghanistan,' the US announces, having landed 1500 troops in the Taliban stronghold of Kandahar. The marines are ferried in by helicopter to a base just outside Kandahar, on a hunting lodge owned by a Saudi prince. Their first task is to secure the base and to set up landing lights so that fixed-wing aircraft with more troops and equipment can land.

This is an incredibly bold move, taking it right up to the Taliban. It appears Washington doesn't trust the predominantly Tajik Northern Alliance in the Pashtun south, especially for the job of hunting down Osama bin Laden.

As we are busy reporting and analysing this new phase of the war, there are the first reports of a riot in Mazar. It erupts when the foreign fighters are brought in for interrogation at the Qala-i-Janghi fort.

The prisoners fear they are about to be shot, apparently because they are being tied up. Some 250 prisoners are bound by their guards, before the rest rebel. The second problem is the presence of two TV crews. The prisoners believe that the two crews, from Reuters and Germany's ARD, are soldiers, there to film their execution.

The riot starts among prisoners being interrogated by two CIA operatives. One is known to be thirty-two-year-old Johnny Spann, one of the agents active in Afghanistan since the war's beginning. The other is known by his codename, Dave. The two CIA agents are in an open area outside the cells. A group of prisoners is brought to meet them. The agents want to know where the prisoners are from and whether they have any links to al-Qaeda. The prisoners crowd around them. 'Why are you here?' Spann asks.

'To kill you,' comes the reply as one lunges at him.

Spann draws his pistol and shoots the man dead. The second agent shoots another Taliban soldier, then grabs an AK-47 from an Alliance guard and opens fire. According to eyewitness accounts given to one of the German TV team, the Taliban fighters wrestle Spann to the ground, kicking and beating him. Spann kills two more with his pistol before he disappears under the crush.

The Taliban soldiers then overpower the Alliance guards, killing them with their own weapons. The second agent, Dave, kills three more men, and then sprints to the main building along the north wall, where two Red Cross workers are meeting with the prison governor.

'He burst in and told us to get out of there,' says Simon Brooks, a Red Cross staff member. 'He was really shaken up. He said there were twenty dead Northern Alliance guys, and the Taliban were taking control of the fort.'

Dave stays behind to try to rescue Spann, while the two Red Cross workers climb up to the fort's parapet, hoist themselves over the wall and slide twenty metres down the other side. The TV crews run to find Dave, and are pinned down in the ensuing firefight. Dave uses a satellite phone belonging to a German TV journalist to call the US embassy in Uzbekistan and ask for reinforcements to storm the prison. This phone call is filmed by the German crew, and when it is seen in Germany, it causes a storm of protest. The journalist is accused of 'crossing the line' from observer of the war to participant, a notion that I find ludicrous, for when your life is at risk you will do whatever you can to save it – including call in the marines.

In the prison block, the Taliban free their comrades. They overcome the guards at the fort's weapons store, and clear out Dostum's arsenal of Kalashnikovs, grenades, mines, rocket launchers, mortars and ammunition. Now they are armed – and cornered. Bitter fighting with the Northern Alliance troops inside the fortress begins.

Two Northern Alliance tanks start firing into the Taliban area. The first international reinforcements arrive: around fifteen American and British Special Forces officers, based at the airport just outside the fort. They begin an assault.

An American officer in a Harley-Davidson cap and mirrored sunglasses raises Dave on the radio. *Time* magazine's Alex Perry is with him. 'Shit . . . shit . . . okay . . . Shit . . . okay. Hold on, buddy, we're coming to get you,' the officer tells Dave. After explaining the crisis to his commander, he points to the sky and says, 'Tell those guys to stop scratching their balls and fly.'

That night, American bombers pound the fort. A siege begins. After seven air strikes the British SAS commander re-establishes contact with Dave, still penned in with the TV crews. They are filming everything that happens. Dave has established that Johnny Spann is dead – the first American to die in combat in Afghanistan. Later during the night, Dave and the journalists escape over the north wall, bullets whizzing past them as they climb down. Their footage goes all around the world.

The American and British teams stay in position over night. Northern Alliance soldiers work with the Americans to pinpoint missiles into the fort. Fighting is constant. Throughout the three-day siege at least thirty bombing attacks are carried out by US warplanes and helicopter gunships.

On Monday morning, an American bomb goes astray, hitting a Northern Alliance position on the castle's outer wall. At least six soldiers are killed. Several American officers are also badly injured.

The air strikes continue all day. By nightfall, it seems that the number of surviving prisoners has fallen to around 100. An American soldier checks his night-vision goggles, and tells *Time* magazine, 'You don't want to leave here tonight, there's going to be quite a show.' The soldier uses a reporter's satellite phone to call his wife and tell her he might be on the TV news. 'Tape it all day, will you? Okay. Love you, babe.'

Explosions sound through the night. The blasts blow open doors fifteen kilometres away. A Taliban fighter who escapes is caught by local residents and hanged from a tree.

Early on Tuesday 27 November, the Northern Alliance estimates there are only about fifty survivors from the original 500 or so in the fort, and that they have no water or ammunition left. Their only food is horsemeat from Dostum's cavalry.

Trucks carrying 200 Northern Alliance troops arrive at the fortress, as US warplanes circle above. American and British Special Forces troops position themselves along the parapets, and around 100 Northern Alliance soldiers scale the south-west tower, firing on the Taliban below.

According to one report, Northern Alliance soldiers go room to room, killing anyone left alive, including the wounded, and firing bullets and rockets into corpses. The fighting ends Tuesday afternoon but the mopping up goes on for days. The dismembered corpses of hundreds of prisoners are strewn among rubble and dead horses, with buildings burning in the background. This battle in the War Against Terror – a new type of war – ends with these age-old images, and with the blood of men and horses mingling in the dust.

Reporters enter the fort from Wednesday. They are shocked by these images, but find the local soldiers unrepentant.

'We don't think the Pakistanis should have come here. We would be delighted if America dropped its bombs on Pakistan next,' a policeman tells a British reporter. 'If we had allowed the Taliban to surrender they would simply have started fighting again. We had no alternative but to kill them.'

The policeman is asked whether those who had their hands tied behind their backs were shot before they had been able to take cover.

'Many of them were concealing grenades. They could explode them and kill us. We are sorry that they were killed, because they were Muslims. But you also have to remember that they were terrorists.'

The Northern Alliance assesses that it has lost forty men in the battle, including three top commanders. Another 200 have been wounded.

'I'm very upset that my commanders have been killed,' says General Dostum. 'They all had children and families. We tried to treat the Taliban humanely. We gave them a chance to wash and to pray. But they attacked us. We could have tied their hands and legs but we didn't.'

Rashid Dostum was away, supervising the surrender at Kunduz, but he denies his forces ill-treated the foreign POWs. He is already under investigation for the battle earlier this month when Mazar-i-Sharif fell, where it's alleged that Pakistani fighters were massacred. Reports are also surfacing of his troops mistreating captured Taliban soldiers in Kunduz after the siege ended, closing them in containers without air and water for transport to prison in Sheberghan. It's alleged that hundreds may have died. General Dostum denies all the allegations.

At the ruined fort, Northern Alliance soldiers start looting. They take guns and ammunition and search the pockets of the dead for money. But it is the Taliban's new-looking sneakers that prove the biggest draw. Within minutes, the Northern Alliance fighters are throwing away their shoes and yanking the sneakers off the Taliban dead.

They have to be careful – many bodies are booby-trapped, including that of CIA agent Johnny Spann.

As late as Thursday, those removing bodies are still being shot at by Taliban fighters who have survived in the basements beneath the fort. First burning petrol is poured down into the basement to try to smoke out the survivors, then on Saturday it is flooded with freezing water. The stench of rotting human flesh at the entrance to the basement makes it almost impossible to breathe, and no more than five or six Taliban are thought to be alive inside. But eighty-six prisoners emerge, filthy, hungry, their faces black with smoke. They are given clothing and food – bananas, apples and pomegranates – and loaded onto trucks for removal to Sheberghan prison.

One of the prisoners says he's an American. The twenty-year-old, who has been wounded in the leg, does not give his name but says he is a convert to Islam from Washington. He spent time at a *madrasa* in Pakistan, and then came to Afghanistan to help the Taliban build a perfect Islamic government.

He turns out to be John Walker Lindh. He is dubbed the American Taliban, and charged with treason for his role in this conflict.

The US quickly finds itself on the defensive for its role in the Mazar fort siege. Kenton Keith, chief US spokesman, says at his daily press briefing in Islamabad, 'We are sorry that so many people did die in Mazar-i-Sharif.' He insists the bombing was 'not a massacre, not a reprisal . . . What happened in Mazar-i-Sharif was a pitched battle'.

However, this response fails to satisfy human rights groups who believe the US may have breached international law by bombing the Taliban forces, many of whom were tied up and unable to move. Keith says that when the Taliban soldiers stole weapons inside the fort, their status changed from prisoners back into combatants. Human rights lawyers say any response to an armed revolt by prisoners of war should be proportionate.

Amnesty International calls for a full investigation, a request endorsed by UNHCR. These calls are ignored, but then earlier UN inquiries into massacres in the same place didn't make a blind bit of difference. In 1997 some 2000 Taliban prisoners were murdered in Mazar, including the 1250 men left to bake to death in containers. In 1998 when the Taliban retook Mazar, they retaliated by massacring some 6000 people, including civilians. There were investigations by various human rights organisations, and at least we have a better idea of what happened, but these investigations never prevent the next massacre.

That's why I have little faith in the efficacy of UN inquiries, and I fear I've also been brutalised by this place into thinking it's kill or be killed. From my vantage point here, it seems that if you don't massacre the troops in the fortress, they will massacre you. Given the bloody history of the past five years in Mazar-i-Sharif, is any other outcome likely?

After all these brutal events, I feel I need some inspiration. I find it – unexpectedly – doing a story on land mines.

The Italian aid agency hospital is like no other in Kabul. It's in a compound in the centre of town, visible from far away because of the huge 'no guns' mural painted on its wall – a gun with a line through it like a no-smoking sign. Inside is a series of low buildings painted white. Clean, spacious, well-stocked wards surround gardens with roses and a children's playground. It is neat and peaceful – and utterly unexpected. It's a world-class facility, providing free food, medicine and treatment for all emergency patients, from war injuries to car crashes.

When all the major international aid agencies were leaving Afghanistan on 12 September, one was negotiating to return – Emergency, the Italian medical aid agency which treats victims of war. Over the past seven years Emergency has founded hospitals in Cambodia, Sierra Leone and northern

Iraq, but nowhere was it more difficult to set up a hospital than in Afghanistan under the Taliban.

Surgeon Gino Strada established Emergency in 1994, along with three colleagues. He is Director of the aid agency, and a working surgeon, and I catch him between operating lists. Strada is an outspoken man in his fifties, with a wild shock of silver-grey hair. He is feisty and funny and reminds me of a bird of prey. Walking out of theatre in his green surgical uniform, he looks for a cigarette. I tell him I am stunned by his hospital, I've seen nothing like it anywhere in Afghanistan.

'It shouldn't be a surprise. It should be like this all the time,' he says in his musically accented English. 'If you come to the third world, or so called third world, you cannot come here and provide third-world services. Then you better stay home. If I consider this hospital is not good enough for my daughter or my sister, then this hospital is not good enough for the Afghans, who have the same rights as my daughter or my sister.'

The chain-smoking Gino Strada is a breath of fresh air.

'I think this type of hospital is a different sign that you throw into this shuttered society. It's a place where you can slowly start to rebuild human relationships. It is quite strange, but the overall atmosphere in this hospital is quite joyful, which shows that every time you treat people with kindness and dignity, every kind of dialogue is possible, there are no more enemies. We have civilians here side by side with Mujaheddin and Taliban – and if we learn how to communicate and how to look each other in the eye, in the end there will be no need for Kalashnikovs, or B-52s.'

He gives me a piercing stare. Since setting up Emergency, Gino Strada has become a cult figure in Italy. 'Prime Minister Silvio Berlusconi attacked me in the Senate after I debated him on the television,' he chortles. It is like watching an eagle laugh.

Gino Strada is a hero for our times, direct, passionate and world-weary. He has spent five out of the past ten years in Afghanistan, risking his life in a war zone, in order to save the lives of victims of war. I am finding three months here gruelling. Five years would be unimaginably demanding, even with the spectacular Italian pasta feasts which he and colleague Dr Marco Garatti are renowned for cooking.

Strada had previously worked for the Red Cross until it wound back its provision of this type of surgery. 'We felt there was a big black hole for war victims, that there was no specialised agency geared towards treating them.'

Initially in 1994 a dinner with 150 friends in a restaurant in Milan funded a team and equipment to go to Rwanda. The genocide was at its height. They arrived in the shattered capital Kigali and reopened the surgery and maternity wards.

'During the day it was okay, there was a hole in the roof, and that let in enough light to allow us to operate. But at night Rwandan boys had to hold up torches, powered by car batteries. There was no water, no electricity, no nothing,' says Dr Gino, as he prefers to be called, in the Afghan fashion.

'We saw Rwanda at its worst. But the plus side was that we got fantastic coverage, and US$300,000 came in, and the organisation was really born. Today we have eighty-five groups in Italian cities and 50,000 regular subscribers. It's a big cultural movement.' Dr Gino looks satisfied. 'We've treated 210,000 people worldwide.'

Here in Kabul this November, despite the heavy US air strikes, most of the patients being treated at the Emergency hospital are mine victims – and most are children. 'We had fifteen mine injuries here and twenty to twenty-five in our hospital in the Panjshir, so that's more than one a day,' says Dr Gino.

I follow him into the ICU ward. Intensive care here has none of the sophisticated machinery of such wards in the West. Instead, monitoring is delivered via round-the-clock nursing. Dr Gino says studies have found the health outcomes in this simpler form of ICU are much the same, for a fraction of the cost, making it ideally suited to conditions in the developing world. The nurses in the ward are all Afghans. Three children and one adult are patients in the ward. The adult was injured in a car crash. All three children stepped on land mines. Dr Gino checks on the patients, and sends me on my own to the children's ward across the way.

There are ten patients – all land-mine victims, too. Most are too sick to talk. The nurse takes me from bed to bed.

'This boy is nine years old. He is from Kabul – he has a fractured left leg and right hand. This boy in the next bed

311

is eight years old. He was admitted on the same day.' He consults the chart. 'They played together. He has a fractured pelvis and has lost his right foot.'

The litany of injury continues. The children look small and vulnerable in their beds, their truncated limbs wrapped in bandages, and I find myself unable to meet the eyes of the mothers sitting by their sides.

Hamed is the oldest child in the ward. Even though he is fifteen he couldn't resist picking up a brightly coloured object on the ground near his home and trying to open it. It blew up in his hands. He lost fingers on both hands, his arm is fractured and he has wounds in his leg.

'I stood and fell and stood and fell three times,' he says, 'and then they brought me to this hospital. I try not to think about my lost fingers – there's no point thinking about things you have lost.'

But that's not an option for Gino Strada. When I return the next day he has failed to save another child who stepped on a land mine when playing near his home. The nine-year-old boy was one of the patients I had seen in the ICU ward. He died despite a lengthy operation. I catch Dr Gino outside afterwards, smoking, looking defeated and angry at the same time.

'How do I feel? I feel like I always do when a child dies, and for what, for nothing.' He exhales smoke. 'Dr Marco and I have operated on thousands of land-mine victims, thousands, and I can hardly remember three or four combatants.' He gives a derisory snort. 'All the rest are civilians.'

'It's not a weapon, it's a form of terrorism against the civilian population. People are maimed or killed today by land mines which were laid months or even years ago. The problem with land mines is that they don't discriminate, they don't have a target, they are just thrown like this –' he mimes the action '– in the fields, knowing that nine out of ten of the people who will be affected will be civilians, and probably a child, stepping on them.'

Land mines have taken a terrible toll here. Since 1979, 400,000 people have been killed, and another 400,000 injured. If no more are added from today, it is estimated that it will take fifty years to clear the country of mines. Crossing into Afghanistan from Iran, a sign warns visitors about strange-looking items: 'Every twenty-four hours seven people step on mines in Afghanistan. Be careful not to be one of them today and tomorrow.' A Canadian charity that came to defuse mines found the tragedy simply too vast, lost hope and went home.

Gino Strada looks out over the rose bushes to the small memorial to a kindergarten that was on this site. It was destroyed in a rocket attack in1994 during the civil war. Now there is a doll's house, some broken playground equipment and some other shattered relics of the childcare centre, and a small sign telling you what you are looking at and how many children died here.

'You can do what you like with peace agreements,' Dr Gino says bleakly, 'but if you have ten million land mines on the ground, they will kill or maim hundreds of thousands of people, regardless of whether the country is at war or at peace.'

I follow him under a covered walkway. There is a crack in the path. 'This is new. It's a result of the air strikes. Of course, we didn't expect such mammoth bombing when we designed this,' Dr Gino says dryly.

We go to the laundry, peeking through a curtain of green sails, hospital bedding hanging out to dry. Fifteen widows are working here, washing and ironing. They crowd around to show me that they are washing sheets and surgeon's gowns by hand. 'Machine nay', they explain, but despite the difficult work these jobs are highly sought after. Emergency hospitals give priority of employment for non-medical positions to the handicapped, poor widows and mine victims.

'There are six million refugees, one million maimed and even more dead over the past twenty years. I am not aware of one family that has not been touched by the war,' says Gino Strada.

Jonathan stands on the balcony outside my room at dusk, during a break in our filing schedules. The mountains are turning from brown to pink in the sunset, and the streetlights are just coming on. 'These are the city's skyscrapers,' he says, with his New York perspective. We look at the houses scattered all the way up the nearest mountain face, a few teetering above the rest. How do the people get up there, where there are no roads? And how did they build them?

Perhaps it is a festival as there are small bonfires all the way up the mountain and in the surrounding streets. People are burning pine cones. The fires and smoke add to the other-worldly atmosphere. 'We're in Kabul,' we say in disbelief, after all this time.

Jonathan has spent the day at the Ghazi sports stadium. Its refurbishment was paid for by the United Nations when the Taliban lifted their ban on football in 1997. But no aid agency workers were invited to the inauguration. No football match was scheduled. Instead it was used for public executions. Now it is once again to be used for sport.

Jonathan says there is still blood on the concrete wall at the entrance to the stadium. 'The blood has handprints in it, as if someone was being dragged along, and tried to hold onto the wall.'

Most of the executions were by shooting and there are shells on the grass. He says he looked under the stadium, too, where there are rooms. Their windows had been smashed, and he could peer in through the broken shards. He saw interrogation rooms, with chairs and hospital beds with ropes tied to them. 'I couldn't get the image out of my mind, of women tied to those beds and accused of being whores, and being beaten till they confessed. And do you know the most chilling thing? Outside, the Olympic rings are still there, still intact, from when the UN built it.'

To cheer him up, I show him bin Laden's birdcage. He laughs. 'That's a great idea. And when you get sick of it, you can make some money selling it on E-Bay.'

E-Bay is too much of a visitation from a different world for me to comprehend here.

The anthrax documents Chris Stephen found at the chemical weapons plant have the same effect on Jonathan. He is spooked as he sits on my bed reading them.

'Have you read these? This is terrible. Do you think they are the source of the anthrax attacks in the States?'

I'm lying on the floor, writing a news report by hand in my battered blue exercise book. I often do this since my laptop has never really recovered from the dust of Khoja Bahauddin. For quick radio news reports, I don't bother to plug in. Adriana is editing a TV news story with Alberto, on our only table. I look up at the crowded, messy room and think how much this demanding environment is sweetened by friendships with people who care about you. Newfound friends. Adriana. Barbara. Jonathan. I don't know if I could have survived so long without this sense of connection. Freelance, but not alone.

Maybe being here on my own forces me to reach out to people in a different way than I ever had to when I worked within a large organisation, with my own cameraman and producer.

We climb the stairs to the roof to file. One journalist has set up an outdoor office with a table, a chair and a light bulb shielded by an upside down red bucket. It gives his cold eyrie a slightly seedy, romantic air. Rick's café on a freezing concrete roof.

After I've fed my report, I climb between the satellite dishes and TV cameras to the NBC spot. Jonathan, Tom and I look out over the city, with the lights of Kabul shimmering below in the cold black night, and a carpet of stars above. We are comparing the gleaming night sky here, in the lower reaches of the Hindu Kush, with the stars above Khoja Bahauddin. It's what passes for entertainment when you're waiting for a 2 a.m. live shot.

Life is simpler here. I haven't seen a magazine or a movie in two months – if you don't count the Mujaheddin victory flick when it was showing for the first time, which I don't. There's no TV, no videos, no gym. There's Coke from Iran but no ice. No worries about 'administrivia' either – have I paid my mobile phone bill, do I need to move house, has the car insurance lapsed?

But soon it may be time to go back to the real world, with its sophistication and its problems, and to say goodbye to Kabul, and its gleaming sky, carpeted with stars.

Chapter 21

We work until the last moment before we leave.

Russia is returning to Afghanistan, a little over a decade after its army was chased out by the Mujaheddin in the Soviet Union's most crushing military defeat. This is a moment in history I never thought I would see. Perhaps it is no more stunning than some of the other volte-faces that September 11 has wrought, but standing here in Kabul it seems literally incredible.

I go to the former Soviet embassy compound in the centre of Kabul. It is a vast complex with a series of more than ten tower blocks, as well as other communal buildings, all utterly wrecked. It sits on a former front line, not far from the zoo. Though almost every building is destroyed, it is teeming with people. The families dispossessed from the Shomali plains have been squatting here for three years, ever since the Taliban set their farms and villages alight, burning them to the ground. An estimated 20,000 people live here in unspeakable conditions. The ruined tower blocks are filthy, overcrowded and desperate. It goes without saying that the compound has no electricity, but it also has no water or sanitation. International aid agencies deliver water. We see the truck drive in, and people lining up with plastic containers to collect their water rations.

The only areas that haven't been destroyed are two empty patches of concrete ground, which were once a large basketball court and an amphitheatre for outdoor films. For rigidly protected Russian embassy staff, this was probably the extent of entertainment in Kabul. Ah, the glories of Soviet diplomatic life.

It seems that Moscow wants to reclaim this compound, though God knows why – it would probably be better to nuke it and start again than attempt any repair job. But yesterday Russian officials came and held a meeting in the former school building to tell people to leave.

'But we have no place to go. The Taliban burnt our houses,' says a twenty-five-year-old father of four. 'Last year when one of our neighbours died we returned to our village at Karabach in the Shomali plains. We wanted to bury him near his home, but there is nothing there, every building has been destroyed, there is not even water, we had to bring water from Kabul for our stay.'

Sixty-five-year-old Wallamschi has grey hair, broken teeth and a filthy turban. He is one of the men crowding around me, and his story of dispossession is typical. At 3 a.m. one autumn day three years ago, Taliban rockets started raining down on Karabach. Within hours the village's 2000 people left, abandoning crops ripe for harvest. Most walked to the nearest village. They walked through the night.

'The women were crying, the children were cold and hungry. We'll never forget that night.'

The following day the Taliban bombed that village, too, forcing the refugees to flee again until they slowly made their way south to Kabul.

'Now the Russians just say to us "Please leave here" and we say we are not ready, we have nowhere to go,' Wallamschi says.

'Did they offer you somewhere else?'

'No – and we remember them from twelve years ago. They did nothing for us then. They are non-Muslims, and we don't accept them coming back to Afghanistan.'

Wallamschi wants to go back to the Shomali plains to rebuild his home in his village. When I ask him and the others their reaction to the Russian edict, they say they are surprised,

'But what can we do?' The idea that they are citizens with rights who cannot just be uprooted by the returning Russians, in the same way they were originally uprooted by the Taliban, has not penetrated here.

I am pleased when I learn that one of their leaders has gone to see the Minister for Immigration in the new interim administration. Perhaps the rules will change. Perhaps we are witnessing the embryonic beginnings of civic awareness and a negotiation process that will allow the people to return to their villages when help is available to rebuild them, and the Russians to repossess their compound without further dispossessing thousands of disadvantaged people.

At the end of November, leading al-Qaeda figure Ahmed Abdul Rahman is captured. He is a son of the blind Egyptian cleric said to have inspired the first World Trade Center bombing in 1993, and a mentor to Osama bin Laden. Washington says its bombs have killed six out of the top thirty-five al-Qaeda leaders – almost twenty per cent of the leadership.

But Osama bin Laden remains at large. When the CIA sent in its first agent, Gary, six weeks ago, he had two assignments: to talk the Northern Alliance into supporting the United States, and to capture and kill bin Laden. According to American journalist Bob Woodward, the head of the CIA counter-terrorism centre told Gary he wanted bin Laden's head in a box, so that he could take it and show it to the President.

'Well, that couldn't be any clearer,' was Gary's reply.

The failure to capture Osama bin Laden hangs over America's military operation. Now, in late November, there are reports that he has been sighted in the mountains near Tora Bora.

'Yeah, he was seen saying where the fuck's my birdcage?' says Jonathan.

We check on the map to see where Tora Bora is. It sounds like something out of the musical *South Pacific*, but we locate it in the east of Afghanistan. Tora Bora is in the White Mountains above Jalalabad, in the Nangarhar province, where Abdul Haq was ambushed. I'm trying to decide if I should go there or go home.

When it becomes apparent that the Taliban will soon

surrender Kandahar, Jonathan says I should go there instead. Tom and I look at him in disbelief. 'You? *You* telling me I should go to Kandahar? You didn't want me to go over the Hindu Kush. What's come over you?'

'Yeah man, what's come over you?' Tom looks interested.

'I think she'd never forgive herself if she didn't go.'

We investigate the possibilities of reaching Kandahar. At this stage, the road from Kabul is considered too dangerous. It's safer and easier to get in from Pakistan. The town of Quetta just on the Pakistani side of the border is actually closer to Kandahar than we are, which means less distance travelling inside Afghanistan. And then a rookie journalist who goes in from Quetta is captured, kyboshing these plans. The first reports (later dispelled) suggest that he has been sodomised by his Taliban captors. We look at each other, frozen in horror, make some half-hearted black jokes, and decide to put off our trip to Kandahar for the moment.

Ever since we woke up to the bomb in our kitchen on our first morning here, I've been interested in the work of the UN Mine Action Program, one of the first international agencies to return to Kabul following the collapse of the Taliban.

Deputy Director Ross Chamberlain is in charge of its most urgent task: locating and defusing the bombs that did not explode during the US air strikes. He has surveyed about ten sites so far.

It seems I'm not the only one interested in this story. The UN has had so many requests for interviews that Ross takes about forty journalists in a group to the three safest sites.

We stop in front of a house in the city centre that has been reduced to rubble. Outside soldiers have piled up all the hardware that was found in the wreckage, including anti-tank weaponry and machine guns. Although this is a civilian suburb, Washington claims these weapons are proof it was a legitimate target – a Taliban commander's home with an enormous quantity of arms. The next-door house wasn't hit but was abandoned on 12 November by fleeing Taliban commanders. It has an arsenal in the basement, a room five metres by seven metres stocked floor to ceiling with weapons – Kalashnikovs, rocket-propelled grenade launchers, missiles. Boxes and boxes of grenades and ammunition. A Northern Alliance soldier stands guard over the booty.

'One of the major reasons we brought you here is to show you this target. If you look behind you there is a hospital, so they had to be spot on to hit this because if they got it wrong there was going to be a big problem,' says Ross Chamberlain. 'So we brought you here just to see that they did this one right.'

The 500-pound bomb accurately hit a building only hundreds of metres from Kabul Children's Hospital. I think of the children I saw there, including malnourished five-year-old Shakrilljah, the size of a Western toddler, and Mohammed Salem who lost a leg in the bombing and will never again run with the other boys, and don't even want to calculate the 'what ifs'.

The bombs have a computer guidance system on the front directing them to their targets. But Ross Chamberlain says that in the city of Kabul many of the bombs went astray.

'There are more bad sites here in Kabul than good sites,' he says. 'Outside of Kabul they probably hit what they meant to, but there are a few errant bombs in Kabul.'

He estimates that thirty civilians lost their lives. 'It's thirty too many, but it's not a great number.'

One of the bombs fell far from its intended target of a military post on a hill in Kabul's north. Instead it hit a home down the hill in Kabul's equivalent of tenements, housing the city's poor. There is now nothing but rubble where a home once stood. Eight people died here.

A woman stands in the rubble wailing. Forty-three-year-old Arifa lost her husband and seven-year-old son that night, along with six members of her extended family: her husband's second wife and their five daughters.

'What should I think about America now?' says Arifa. 'My husband hoped that following the air strikes we would lead a peaceful life. Now he is dead and there is no one to support me or my remaining children.'

She stands with tears coursing down her cheeks, and then, as if she has suddenly become aware of us, she pulls her veil over her face and sobs uncontrollably.

Though the site appears to be completely destroyed, the Mine Action Program is checking in the rubble for any unexploded bombs, to ensure there will be no further casualties when people start rebuilding. If Ross Chamberlain locates any more bombs, he has to quickly co-ordinate their safe removal.

Four bombs have to be defused as a matter of urgency, two at the airport, and two within the city. One bomb has buried itself under the runway at Bagram air base and until it's defused, the airport cannot be reopened. Peter Le Soeuer is a consultant working with the Mine Agency. He says it is a particularly complex and difficult job.

'It's deep, and it's twisted, and it could take about two weeks to do. We hope that we can locate it and destroy it so that they can repair that section of the runway and get the airport operational as soon as possible.'

One of the urgent jobs is in a residential district of Kabul. At a press conference Ross explains it was one of three dropped in a line targeting Taliban commanders' homes. But the computer guidance units in the bombs appear to have failed, and all three went astray. One bomb destroyed a vehicle, another levelled a shop across the road from a Taliban commander's house and a third landed in the kitchen of a house owned by an Afghan businessman, where it failed to explode. As he's talking I realise he means 'our' bomb, in the NBC house, and it makes me a little queasy to realise it is one of Ross Chamberlain's most urgent tasks. It has proved more difficult to remove than was expected, which is why it hasn't been defused until now.

The owner of the house is less perturbed. The UN sealed off the premises after NBC left, but the owner has been letting TV crews in to film the bomb . . . for a US$100 fee. He tells everyone we knew all about the bomb when we rented the house, whatever we might pretend now. They pay their hundred bucks, get their shots and get out as quick as they can.

It's funny to stand in that street again, outside the house with the bomb in its kitchen, being interviewed by my colleagues, responding to the standard journalistic question 'How did you feel?' The boy selling balloons is at the other end of the street. I haven't seen him since our first day here.

His balloons gleam pastel in the wintry sun, like lollipops. I watch him, feeling carefree, as Ross Chamberlain explains the difficulties involved in defusing our bomb.

'The bad news about this bomb is it turned itself over in the air and it's gone through the roof tail first, so the tail, where the fuse is, is in the ground and we have the head, the pointy end of the bomb, sticking out of the ground. So what we are going to have to do is get the bomb out of the ground and get the fuse out,' he says. 'There are going to be a lot of people down here with a lot of sandbags, protecting everything around here, and then we go inside and cut the bomb out from the ground.'

He gives a slightly manic bomb defuser's laugh, and I suddenly realise that Ross has always reminded me of a laid-back Australian Jack Nicholson.

Soon the process is completed. This is one story we've seen all the way through. Everyone is kept well away when the bomb is cut out of the kitchen floor. But once this delicate manoeuvre is completed the bomb is deemed too dangerous to remove to a safe detonation spot, and it's detonated right here. The explosion is massive, shaking the entire street. I'm sure the boom can be heard on the other side of Kabul. The size of the explosion even surprises the professionals.

When this task is finished, the UN agency can go back to its main job, clearing Afghanistan of the ten million land mines which contaminate this country.

I go back to the Emergency hospital to finish my story on land mines. When I listen to Dr Gino Strada, I am amazed at how hard you have to work to give away money. From 1999 Dr Gino has been here setting up two hospitals, one in the Panjshir, and this one in Kabul. This facility was completed in November 2000, and then sat idle for five months while the Taliban refused to grant permission for it to open. The US$750,000 hospital, with US$1 million allocated and available for running costs, couldn't treat patients while Gino was negotiating with the Taliban over his right to run it independently. Gino was a tough negotiator – and found himself paying the price.

'They wanted to run the hospital, to appoint the staff.

None of this was acceptable. It took two to three months' negotiations before it opened in April, only for it to be shut down in May after armed aggression by the religious police of the Taliban. They climbed the walls armed with Kalashnikovs, and came in beating staff, national and international, arresting staff.'

His colleague, the softly spoken surgeon Dr Marco Garatti was here on the night. 'It was very frightening. They were beating staff for about an hour, I think. We couldn't get them out, they left when they decided to leave. We didn't know what was happening or why. I still don't understand it. We were the only NGO [non-government organisation] providing free medical care and free food for patients,' Dr Marco looks at me wryly. 'And the only kind of NGO without any mullah on top of us, which was probably not acceptable.'

After this setback, Dr Gino shut the hospital and transferred the international staff out of Afghanistan. He says this was a necessary protest against the Taliban's attack.

'You cannot have humanitarian agencies treated this way. But we commenced negotiations for reopening the hospital almost at once. I think I had met every minister in the Taliban government ten times and the negotiations were still ongoing on September 11.'

Following the attacks in the US, Dr Gino contacted the Taliban and said he was willing to reopen the hospital immediately. 'I felt there was a humanitarian disaster on the horizon. It was not difficult to predict.'

The Taliban agreed.

Dr Gino was in the Pakistani capital Islamabad, and at that time – on 12 September – the United Nations and the Red Cross were flying their staff out of Afghanistan. He asked for a seat on one of the empty planes flying in to evacuate them. He says that both the UN and the Red Cross refused, for 'security reasons', and because it 'would look contradictory'.

Instead Dr Gino had to undertake that dangerous five-day journey over the Hindu Kush, by jeep and on horseback to get back into Afghanistan. He crossed in from Pakistan via the Khyber Pass, and reached the Northern Alliance front lines in the Panjshir Valley. There he spent weeks negotiating with the Taliban to organise a front-line crossing into Kabul. This was further complicated by the start of US air strikes at the very same spot, around the Bagram air base, where he and his staff needed to cross.

'So, having negotiated a supposed ceasefire so that we could cross from the Panjshir down into Kabul, with staff from our Kabul hospital risking their lives to come up to Bagram to meet us, there was fighting and US bombing at the exact time when we were crossing.' He sits back. 'Still we made it.'

Dr Gino and his staff reached Kabul on 8 November. Within two days the hospital reopened, when the air strikes were at their fiercest, a time which he admits was very frightening.

'Bloody hell –' How he sings this English expression in his Italian accent '– it was terrifying! But our worry wasn't the very heavy rocketing and shelling, our worry was the real threat of being taken hostage by fanatics. On 12 November it was obvious something big was happening. Armed people were coming here, some Taliban and some Arabs, and someone stole one of our cars. I had given instructions to leave all the cars ready, with their keys in the ignition and filled with petrol, because it's better to lose ten vehicles than one person.'

That day the Taliban fled Kabul. After reciting this extraordinary tale, Gino Strada is scathing about the decision of the major aid agencies to leave Afghanistan.

'I think it remains a shame for many humanitarian aid agencies, the UN the first, what they've done in this country. Because it will be difficult for them to claim a humanitarian role when they left here between the 12 and 13 of September. It was obviously a political decision taken at a high level in New York, which doesn't surprise me, and just proves once again that these agencies have nothing, absolutely nothing, to do with humanitarian work . . . It doesn't mean that individuals are not committed or professional, a few are, but the institution as such is not designed for humanitarian reasons, otherwise, if there is one day when the NGOs should have come back to Afghanistan it was September 12th.'

Dr Gino explains his decision for Emergency to stay. 'It gives a sign to your national staff that when a situation is dangerous, you don't leave them alone, pretending from the roof of the Marriott Hotel in Islamabad that all the programs are going on regularly despite the absence of international staff, which is a fairy tale no one believes.' He looks at me sternly. 'You are telling your staff that if there is shit going on, let's share it.'

It is a refreshing experience to interview Gino Strada. So much journalism is about reporting on deal making, and compromise, and interviewing smooth, often venal 'organisation' men and women. Gino Strada is utterly different. He is so uncompromising and so unselfconsciously heroic, that it is a paradigm shift to be here in his abrasive, amusing company, in the most impressive medical facility in Afghanistan.

More amazing than his principled personal courage is the stand that he has taken on funding. Emergency turned down US$4 million from the Italian government as soon as Italy joined the International Coalition Against Terror, committing money and men to the fight in Afghanistan.

'That money is the money of politics and of war so we cannot accept it. We cannot accept money to look after Afghans injured by bombs dropped by the same people who are donating the money. So we would not accept one dollar from the US or British governments. We have a lot of Afghan friends, and we are here to help the Afghans not to bomb them, not to kill them. I would feel shamed to get one dollar from the pockets of those who are sending soldiers here.'

Flabbergasted I ask him how he will make up this huge shortfall. He says that he has already received US$1 million from ordinary Italian citizens, who donated the money as soon as they heard about Emergency's decision to refuse the government funding. He is convinced that he will find the rest.

In the meantime, the Emergency hospital continues to treat all patients – including Taliban prisoners. I meet two of them, brought from Kabul's main prison where they were not receiving treatment. Dr Gino went on a prison visit and asked for them to be brought here. 'They are young men with wounds, and they have to be treated, no matter who they are.'

The prisoners lie in bed in a ward with two guards, and I am amazed as always by their ordinariness. No one can speak to them as they speak no Dari. One is a Pakistani, the other an Arab.

'I had many meetings with the Taliban military commanders, and they are normal people, very normal. But they don't have stealth bombers, so they use terror weapons, and bacteriological and nuclear weapons if they can get their hands on them.'

If peace will come to Afghanistan, the Emergency hospital will stay, to treat land-mine victims. But Dr Gino will be off – in search of another war zone in which to work.

In early December, Northern Alliance President Burhanuddin Rabbani tells a press conference that Taliban who 'are not criminals' can take part in a future Afghan administration. 'Taliban authorities and officials can participate in the interim government as individuals, not as the Taliban party, if they are selected through the *Loya Jirga*,' he says.

In the ballroom at the Intercon, a Taliban minister sweeps in wearing a stylish cream and gold outfit, adjusts his matching turban, and defects to the Northern Alliance in front of our cameras. He is Deputy Interior Minister, the man responsible for the secret police, and can bring the Northern Alliance practical information that might be useful. But we are not sure what to make of this piece of theatre. The Northern Alliance thinks it's important – it has staged the defection for the world's press – yet it's not clear what it means in terms of the collapse of the Taliban leadership.

Perhaps the most significant feature of this defection is the failure to punish the Taliban leader.

There's a party at the NBC house. I'm due to file a feature for Irish radio, but they say they'll take it tomorrow. 'Och, Irris, go to the party, we won't have room for it tonight anyhow. If you file it tomorrow, we can do an interview with you afterwards as well.' They are so understanding and so delightfully Irish. If there's fun to be had, why would I consider filing?

So I go to the party with a clear conscience. The NBC house, like all the others in Wazir Akbar Khan, has the feel of 1960s suburbia. The main room downstairs is low and dark, separated from the dining room by a divider. It has a dingy orange sofa, and someone has made banana smoothies and a birthday cake. I feel I'm taking part in a teen sitcom, pre-*Friends*, more like a re-run of *Leave it to Beaver*. There is a changeover and a new lot of NBC crews are coming through, and there are also some newly arrived aid workers. There are introductions – *Irris, do you know Sally?* – as though we were in New York. But Kabul reasserts itself, because at 9.30 p.m. we have to leave just as the party is getting into full swing, and race to the Intercon, to make it back before the curfew.

The city is dark and empty. Shah Mahmood drives quickly through the checkpoints. No one stops us tonight. One night last week he was not so lucky. He got the journalists to the Intercon in time for 10 p.m., but as he was speeding back to the NBC house, he was stopped. Because he was out after curfew without a permit, he had to spend the night in a Kabul gaol. Apparently there's a password that will avoid a night behind bars, but he didn't know it, so it was off to prison for him. Fortunately while he was there, the other prisoners told him the password, so he says it was a night well spent. We pester Shah Mahmood to tell *us* the password. But he won't.

Tonight we make it back to the hotel by 9.45, and best of all, Shah Mahmood drives all the way up the hill. We don't have to get out and walk. It seems there's another password which you learn on payment of a five-dollar 'fee' to the guards at the Intercon gate. It's as bad as remembering all your different pin numbers.

Our time in Kabul is coming to an end. It's already December, and I've been covering this conflict from the start, and need a rest. A long rest, actually. In our last hours, we go shopping.

Unbelievably, the shopping is fantastic. The main shopping area is the wonderfully named Chicken Street. You can buy food, including luxury items like chocolate, dates, cheese, crackers, tuna, and olive oil. Here, too, there is hand cream, and those strange piles of fat that are the staples of female beauty.

There are also the famous Afghan rugs, sheepskin coats, leather bags, silver jewellery, silk scarves, engraved brass water jugs and teapots, glowing with the mystery of the Orient. The 1970s was the last time Western tourists were in Afghanistan in any numbers. Mazar-i-Sharif was a hippy hangout, then. 'The DJs were fantastic,' Bruno from EBU tells me – and I suppose being known for the best hash in the world had nothing to do with it?

Near the intersection of Chicken and Flower streets there is a tiny second-hand bookshop, crammed full of books in English, German and Russian. The English selection is small and highly idiosyncratic, stopping abruptly in the mid-1970s. There is nothing post 1976. No one came here after that.

So the storeowners are thrilled to see us – Westerners with cash in our pockets. I go with the NBC boys, who turn out to be much better shoppers than me. I tell them it's genetic, and their being American trumps my being female.

We all buy rugs at a shop that Jonathan has scouted out. There is a wonderful array of carpets in wool and silk, and kilim rugs so delicate and finely woven that they can only be hung on the wall. The colours are beguiling, rich reds, and cool creams, blended together in intricate patterns. The owner, Naim, welcomes us, and we climb steep stairs to sit in a small alcove while rugs are thrown down in front of us. I love the theatre of this – extolling the virtues of every rug, turning each over to scratch its back to make sure it's woven by hand and not by machine. I fall in love with more carpets than I need or can carry. This is one of the few times when it's just as well that I have so little cash left.

When I explain to Naim that, in a land without credit, I don't have enough money with me for all the purchases I would like to make, he generously offers to allow me to take the rugs, and pay the next time I come back.

'I couldn't do that.'

'But you will be back soon!' he exclaims.

I tell him there are no guarantees. It's money or nothing.

Jonathan is a tough bargainer, which I am not. He talks me out of a kilim and into a beautiful cream silk rug and a more practical red woollen one. We buy silk scarves and *pakuls*, the Tajik berets. *Do you think they have fleas?*

Tom is also a canny shopper who has great taste. Along with kilim rugs, he has bought some very snappy leather bags, and I follow him to the leather shop. We carry our carpets tied up in sheets, like bundles the stork brings. Next door, at Agmal's, I buy Afghan jewellery – ornate engraved silver earrings with lapis lazuli, which look antique, and a sleek silver choker, with strands of lapis in it, which looks modern. It contains so much silver that back in the real world it will set off the alarm every time I go through an airport security check, making sure I never forget Afghanistan.

In a dark, crowded store in Chicken Street, among a jumble of silver ornaments, I find an engraved tea pot that looks like Aladdin's lamp. It glows magically among ewers, water jugs, bowls, candle sticks, hanging lamps and embossed mirrors which sit in higgledy-piggledy piles beneath silver picture frames, nargilehs, daggers, and ivory-handled duelling pistols.

The light barely struggles in through the window. Motes of dust dance in a beam of slanted sunlight. Standing in this captivating treasure trove, scented with cardamon, candles and dusty silver, I actually find myself believing that if you rubbed the teapot, all your wishes would come true.

I give it to Jonathan as a memento of Kabul.

'Does this mean we will get out safely?' he asks.

Once again it is proving difficult to leave Afghanistan. Maurice and Stan from NBC have been trying for a week. We've had four farewells for them, but after driving for five hours up to the Panjshir Valley, and waiting all day, they return more and more dejected each time because the helicopters don't fly. After the fourth day NBC puts its producer in Dushanbe onto it and, even though she is working full time, so far she has not been successful in getting them out.

A large NBC contingent forms to leave with Stan and Maurice, Tom and Jonathan included. I decide that as no one is bribing full time to get me out of Afghanistan, I will join them if there's room. Jonathan says he'll stay with me if I don't get on the plane.

I say a sad farewell to the Intercon, and especially to Adriana and Barbara. We pack our possessions, but even with all my new shopping I still have fewer bags than the guys. I gather up my Afghan rugs and bin Laden's birdcage for the drive to the military air base at Bagram, where we hear that a fixed-wing aircraft is coming in.

Kabul's Soviet buildings peter out behind us. This final drive is probably the most beautiful we do in Afghanistan. The paved road cuts through a bare desert valley ringed by grand, forbidding mountains. To Jonathan it looks like Colorado. The road is almost empty, apart from the occasional bus crammed with refugees, some sitting on the roof with the luggage, returning to Kabul. This is still relatively rare because the millions of refugees in Iran and Pakistan don't yet trust the prospects for peace. It feels as if the road is ours, the land is ours.

There is a checkpoint, a building of mud stones, with a ragged flag on top. I never make out what flag it is, but it's colourful and a soldier is lying near it, sunbaking. The scene has a psychedelic feel and the soldier looks more like an American GI in Vietnam, or a Soviet soldier here in Afghanistan, than a local Islamic warrior. One of his comrades in arms tries to hit us for a bribe, but only half-heartedly. We drive on to find the road littered with the twisted carcasses of Soviet tanks. They are such a regular feature of the landscape they are almost part of the scenic beauty of Afghanistan. We reach a river, its bridge blown out during the bombing. It sits cut in two, a tank without a turret resting near it. We drive through the water, circling both.

The road ends at the utterly destroyed air base. As one of the few legitimate military targets in this country without infrastructure, Bagram was bombed heavily during the American air strikes. Many of the wooden shacks and mud-brick houses along the avenue leading to the base have been flattened. A house at the gates of the base took a direct hit, and has been cut in half, so everything inside it is visible, like looking into a doll's house. Colourful paintings lean at right angles on the wall. Was it a kindergarten? Could there be a childcare centre so close to a military base? Maybe, if the Russians built it, since in Soviet times every large work place had a kindergarten attached.

Once we arrive, we wait outside for hours, in the finest Central Asian tradition. There is a battered plane on a stick above the gates, a 1970s Soviet symbol that survived the bombing, but not much else is intact. Men wrapped in blankets stand around, though it is not clear what planes they are waiting to catch. Maurice looks at a sailing magazine, dreaming of his boat and hoping that today he will finally leave. I talk to the security chief at the base. He is a Tajik who fought by Massoud's side for twenty-four years. He is a tough, feisty tae kwon do expert, but his eyes fill with tears when he describes Massoud's death, and he looks down at the ground, suddenly lost. He says that in the old days, if he'd found a Russian or American here at Bagram, he'd have killed them – he passes his finger across his throat – *srazu*, straight away. *Srazu*, he repeats in Russian, for emphasis, frowning. But now that Massoud has gone, he sighs heavily again, these foreigners are traipsing all over Bagram and he does not know what to do.

He speaks to me in excellent Russian – much better than mine – that he learnt without formal lessons from the Russian prisoners of war he captured. He polished it up after the Soviets left, at international tae kwon do competitions, talking to the Russian competitors. Truth is always stranger than fiction.

I have been translating for Tom and Jonathan, however when our Tajik friend tells me that I am attractive but that Jonathan is *extremely* attractive, 'like a woman', code in these parts for liking it both ways, I decide not to translate that bit. Who knows what they get up to at those tae kwon do meets? I'm saved by the fact that there is suddenly movement, and we are allowed inside the airbase. We feel we are getting closer to Dushanbe, but in fact there is only more waiting.

We sit in rubble, planning our holidays. Tom says that the problem with being in Afghanistan is that you save all this money, and then you reward yourself with long, expensive holidays because you've been in Afghanistan. We are sitting in front of a bombed-out building, with no roof. It has a mural drawn in black charcoal on one of its two remaining walls. It is a military scene – are there any other kind here? – depicting a tank, and men shooting each other. One man is being shot although he has his hands up. You can see the bullets coming out of the rifle towards him. The figures look at once child-like and apocalyptic.

At around three o'clock we hear that our plane is not flying today, but a Russian military helicopter that arrived delivering aid will take some journalists back out. We go onto the tarmac, where Russian Special Forces soldiers in blue overalls are waiting by a huge chopper. There are also Afghan customs officials, Afghan soldiers, and US Special Forces soldiers milling about. It's hard to know who to negotiate with. Some journalists are already loading their stuff onto the Russian chopper. The blades are starting up and the Afghan customs official says that we have too much stuff to make it onto the chopper in time. To me this is a sign that he wants a back-hander, but Tom says we couldn't bribe Afghan officials in front of American soldiers. Maybe that's how you have to play it, but it does mean we don't get to fly.

I don't mind so much, because there is plenty to file on since Kandahar, the Taliban's last remaining power base, is falling. But Stan and Maurice are devastated. The drive back, even more beautiful as the sun is setting, is not a happy one for them. The light is clear and the mountains glow pink. Jonathan can't stop taking photos.

It is a slightly more tense group that repeats the trip out the next morning. I leave bin Laden's birdcage behind, and one of the translators runs up to the car with it. 'Don't forget this.' Once we are inside Bagram again, everyone is more cheerful following a call from Dushanbe. NBC's wonderfully efficient producer, Judy, says our plane is on the tarmac, with thirty journalists who are flying into Kabul already on board. We have lunch in the sun, in front of our apocalyptic mural. Rummaging in my bag, I discover a forgotten tin of caviar that someone had asked me to bring in to Afghanistan. We eat Russian caviar on American crackers in the warm winter sun at a military air base in Afghanistan, where the roads are so heavily mined that Tom says it's too dangerous to take a leak by the side of the road. Perfect.

American soldiers drive by on vehicles that look like military beach buggies and stop to say hello. Some are air force and some are Special Forces, and all have that naïveté that seems to characterise American soldiers abroad.

We chat with them, but the afternoon wears on and there is no sign of our plane. At four o'clock Judy rings to tell us the tragi-comic news that the plane's wheel fell off as it was taxiing and there will be no flight tonight. The boys are very dejected. Jonathan is cool and so is Hans, but Tom is starting to lose his sense of humour, and Stan and Maurice are increasingly desperate. Tomorrow will be their tenth day trying to leave Afghanistan. The drive back is even more beautiful than yesterday. At sunset the mountains flame pink, looking like huge slabs of rose quartz, before fading to amethyst and then brown.

At night, I file on the disappearance of Taliban leader Mullah Mohammed Omar following the surrender of Kandahar, and the search for Osama bin Laden in the mountains above Jalalabad.

'Thanks for that, will you be there tomorrow if we need anything?' the Voice of America news desk asks.

'I don't know – I wasn't meant to be here today,' I reply.

In Dushanbe, Judy switches to plan B – hiring a Russian emergency services helicopter that is flying in to Kabul with aid, for its return flight to Tajikistan. On our third day at Bagram, we see a huge double-rotored Russian chopper flying in and our hearts skip a collective beat. Then Judy emerges, a tiny figure, from the helicopter's huge belly, and we're thrilled.

A customs officer appears on the tarmac – 'Any rugs?' – and after paying the requisite bribes, we load our gear into a chopper so vast it's the size of a jet. Most of the interior is taken up by two huge fuel tanks which look like bombs, and we perch around them as the chopper lifts into the air.

Hans pulls six tiny bottles of Scotch out of his pocket. He was given them by a steward on his flight out of Chicago, and has kept them for more than two months in a 'dry' country, waiting for the flight home. It's a remarkable combination of forethought and discipline, and very stylish. He shares them around. What a guy.

The Russian aircrew offers us coffee, and I pour in my Scotch, drinking sweet, strong Irish coffee as I watch the mountains of the Hindu Kush rising to meet us. We barely skim them, the helicopter chugging between the peaks. The mountains are white, covered in deep falls of snow, beautiful and austere, like the cold folds of a robe on a marble statue, and I remember that they were bare and brown when I first flew in almost three months ago, sitting in Massoud's armchair.

We look down, trying to pick out the track we drove over when we crossed these mountains overland. From up here it is even more terrifying to think that we did that drive. The chopper is so noisy that we have to write each other notes on the only paper we can find – huge denominations of worthless Afghan currency. This flight is impossibly romantic and exhilarating, but it is also dangerous – that characteristically Afghan combination. The next helicopter out will crash with the loss of all on board.

I finish scribbling a message on a grimy blue 10,000-afghani note, and look up at the NBC boys, perched around the windows of this old Soviet aircraft. We've been through so much together I feel bonded to them. I understand war vets now – even if we never see each other again, it doesn't matter, I will always hold them in my heart. Though at this moment I remain focused on survival – the lesson of Afghanistan is that you can't exhale, and we haven't landed safely yet – I'm aware that this has been an extraordinary experience. I flew in with the Northern Alliance, and I'm flying out with the Russians, following the defeat of the Taliban. They say that journalism is the first draft of history. I was here before the ink dried.

As the helicopter travels slowly between the mountain peaks, images of Afghanistan imprint themselves over these snowy scenes. In my mind's eye I see laughing warriors sitting barefoot, and the radiant smiles of young men enraptured by the soundtrack of *Titanic*. I see soldiers in trenches fixing their mascara. I remember an ancient capital city in ruins, and casual violence and bloodshed – a Taliban prisoner tethered like a goat, and children with truncated limbs in hospital beds, the victims of land mines. I think of a nine-year-old girl so beautiful she made me catch my breath, living in the dust and surviving on boiled nettles. I remember the wonderful women I have met: a brilliant doctor, a hairdresser in a gold wedding dress, and I wish they and their daughters will have better lives, full of dignity and opportunities, the lives they deserve, not the cramped, forlorn existences, hidden away, that have been forced on them.

I pray that Farahnaz Nazir will be safe and that her family will receive asylum in the West, and that she won't be hunted down and killed for trying to make small improvements to the lives of destitute women.

But Afghanistan herself remains unrelenting and extreme to the very last. Will she have leaders capable of pulling the population out of this terrible situation, or will they continue to show the contempt for ordinary people that has reduced this mountain kingdom to the status of a failed state?

Nothing is predictable in this poverty-stricken slaughter-house, with a bloodthirsty past, a troubled present and a precarious future. Flying away from Afghanistan, I can only put my faith in hope for a better future. What did the poet sing? May Allah protect such beauty from the evil eye of man.

Postscript

Women's activist Farahnaz Nazir succeeded in leaving Afghanistan with her family in January 2002. Their first stop was a refugee camp in Iran. While they were there, Laura Bush, the wife of the US President, gave the International Women's Day address at the United Nations on 8 March 2002. She quoted Farahnaz on the need for change in Afghanistan, saying: 'As Farahnaz Nazir, founder of the Afghanistan Women's Association said, "Society is like a bird. It has two wings. And a bird cannot fly if one wing is broken."'

The journalists from CBS-TV and I wrote letters supporting Farahnaz's claim for asylum, but her application was made more difficult because the warlord who threatened her life was from our allies in the Northern Alliance rather than the Taliban. Nevertheless, after Farahnaz and her family spent three difficult months in Iran, I received the wonderful news that Canada would give them asylum. They moved to Ontario, where her children have started school and are adapting to Canadian life. Farahnaz and her husband are looking for work, while she continues to struggle for women's rights. Now that she is living in a peaceful country once more, Farahnaz says she sometimes blames herself for the dangers she inflicted on her family, but they're never angry with her – 'They love me and I am lucky.'

On her first Thanksgiving in Canada, Farahnaz wrote to tell me that she prayed for me and everybody 'who helped us to be safe here in Canada'. I was in tears. It seems part of the miracle of reporting from Afghanistan that a Muslim woman should pray for me while celebrating a Christian festival and building a new life. Farahnaz's rescue and the hope that she and her children will now be able to spread their own wings is my greatest joy from the past year.

Sources

PROLOGUE

I have read a number of accounts written in different eras by visitors to Kabul, including recent accounts by my colleagues. Jon Lee Anderson's article 'City of Dreams: A peace of sorts comes to Kabul' in the *New Yorker* magazine (24 December 2001), was particularly helpful.

I had long discussions with NBC sound recordist Jonathan Mossek about what we saw in the city, and I am grateful to him for sharing his visually precise memories.

British travel writer Robert Byron travelled in Afghanistan in the 1930s, and wrote a book called *The Road to Oxiana*. He took a stunning collection of photographs, which are now held in the Conway Collection of the Courtauld Institute of Art, Somerset House, London, and are available on their website:
http://www.courtauld.ac.uk/sub_index/herat_mazar/herat.html.

CHAPTER ONE

The murder of Paul Tatum occurred while the ABC TV bureau was in the Slavyanskaya Hotel. My producer, Slava Zelenin, and my predecessor, ABC TV correspondent Eric Campbell, were there on the day of the murder when Tatum's body was found. On arrival, they were greeted by the cleaners saying, 'Don't go upstairs, there are men with Kalashnikovs everywhere.' These events have been covered extensively in the Russian press, including the *Moscow Times*, *Moscow News* and *eXile* newspapers. On 7 November 1996 American senator Don Nickles called for a State Department investigation into the murder of the Oklahoma businessman. In August 2000, *eXile* reprinted an article from Russian newspaper *Stringer* called 'Death Wish 1996: Paul Tatum's last letter to the Russian prosecutor' by Aleksei Fomin, which covers this in depth. There is also coverage on websites, including:
http://gangstersinc.tripod.com/PaulTatum.html
http://www.megastories.com/russia/economy/dead.htm.

I consulted various websites for facts about Tajikistan. If you
want to read more about Dushanbe, useful sites include:
http://www.angelfire.com/rnb/bashiri/Dushanbe/Dushanbe.html
http://www.ceroi.net/reports/dushanbe/eng/city.htm
http://www.somoni.com/

CHAPTER TWO

I conducted interviews with UNHCR in Tajikistan about the Pyang
River refugee crisis. Prior to arriving I had read an excellent article
by my colleague Robin Dixon from the *LA Times*, who had been
there in the summer of 2001 when the crisis was at its height. Since
returning from Afghanistan I have read articles from aid agencies
working with the Pyang River refugees, including the United Nations
website, the Human Rights Watch website, and a religious aid organisation called the Adventist Development and Relief Agency. I have
also read reports from Radio Free Europe such as 'Tajikistan: No end
in sight to Afghan refugees' misery' by Bruce Pannier (Prague, 12
January 2001), and 'In Dust and Despair They Await Aid' by English
journalist Alice Thomson (31 October 2001, reprinted in *The Age*).

The article 'Limbs of No Body: World's indifference to the Afghan
tragedy' by Mohsen Makhmalbaf, which appeared in *The Iranian*
magazine (20 June 2001) is possibly the single most interesting,
insightful and moving piece I have read on Afghanistan. The quote
about the refugees at the Tajikistan border is on page 2 of the article,
and the quote about the Buddhas at Bamian on page 19. It is also available on the Iranian director's website: http://www.makhmalbaf.com.

I know some Tajik history from my own trips along the Silk
Road, but a useful website, which I cited for Chapter 1, is
http://www.angelfire.com/rnb/bashiri/Dushanbe/Dushanbe.
html. Ryszard Kapuscinski's *Imperium* was also a very useful source
material for this section, particularly on Tajikistan in the 1960s.

Northern Alliance allegations about the Taliban and Osama bin
Laden being behind Massoud's assassination were put to me first
by embassy staff in briefings in Dushanbe. Saleh Mohammed
Registani, at that time the embassy's military attaché in Moscow,
was very helpful on this. Later there was a wealth of US intelligence
to support the contention, as well as information from the hard drive
of an al-Qaeda computer that the Moscow correspondents of the
Wall Street Journal purchased in Kabul.

CHAPTER THREE

I have relied on a number of sources for the account of Ahmed
Shah Massoud's assassination, including interviews I did in

Dushanbe and Khoja Bahauddin with Northern Alliance figures. Among them were Massoud's former Chief of Security and Nasrine Gross, an Afghan–American woman who was living in the Foreign Ministry compound at the time of Massoud's assassination. I have also read widely on the subject, including: a reactive piece by Jon Lee Anderson called 'A Lion's Death' in the *New Yorker* (21 October 2001); an investigation by the *LA Times* called 'Slowly Stalking an Afghan "Lion"' by Craig Pyes and William C. Rempel (June 2002); and an unpublished account by NBC cameraman Tom Streithorst, which he has called 'In Afghanistan', and which he has been kind enough to let me read.

As for a more general history, Massoud is the world's most photographed Islamic warrior, and there are websites devoted to pictures of him. He was media friendly, and so his life and views are well documented. I have read newspaper articles over the years, including those by Anthony Lloyd in *The Times* and Robert Fisk in the *Independent*, and Marcus Warren's account of Massoud's funeral entitled 'I Hope Terrorism's End Will Start Here' in the UK *Daily Telegraph* (18 September 2001). ABC TV's 'Foreign Correspondent' program broadcast stories about Massoud, including one by Mark Davis in 1999, which was especially useful. For general information the BBC Online political history of Afghanistan was informative, as was the official Northern Alliance website Afghan-info.com.

I'm indebted to Jon Lee Anderson for the detailed description of Khoja Bahauddin in his article 'The Warlord' (*New Yorker*, 22 October 2001), which jogged my memory.

Accurate statistics about Afghanistan are difficult to establish, given the difficulty of collecting information in this chaotic war-ravaged country. I have relied on those quoted by Mohsen Makhmalbaf, and also those quoted by Ahmed Rashid in his seminal book *Taliban: Islam, Oil and the New Great Game in Central Asia*, particularly for statistics on the population of Afghanistan and its refugees.

The quote from Taliban Planning Minister Qari Din Mohammed was in an article entitled 'Taliban Reject Warnings of Aid Pull-out' (Agence France-Presse, 16 July 1998).

CHAPTER FOUR

There is an enormous amount of material on the Mujaheddin trafficking in opium throughout the 1980s. Drug trafficking funded the purchase of arms from the CIA, and this explosion of drug trafficking in armies backed by the US government was a pattern that was apparent in Central America and South East Asia as well as Afghanistan. Much of the research has been done by Alfred McCoy and is in an article he wrote entitled 'Drug Fallout', which appeared in *Progressive Magazine* in 1997. It was also the subject of a documentary series called 'Dealing with the Demon' in 1996 by ABC TV.

The figures on heroin exported from Afghanistan were quoted by Ustina Markus, Senior Analyst for the Brussels-based International Crisis Group. The report is available on ICG's website www.crisisweb.org and is entitled 'Central Asia: Drugs and conflict' (Report 25, 26 November 2001).

The quote from Mark Galeotti linking the Northern Alliance to drug smuggling is from 'Drugs Fund War' (*World Today*, Volume 57 Issue 12, December 2001, published by The Royal Institute of International Affairs). The *World Today* website is www.theworld-today.org. Dr Mark Galeotti is Director of the Organised Russian & Eurasian Crime Research Unit at Keele University, England.

The aid worker who said that the Taliban and the Northern Alliance continued drug trafficking across the front lines was quoted by Jon Lee Anderson on page 8 of 'In the Court of the Pretender: Who has the right to rule Afghanistan?' (*New Yorker* magazine, 5 November 2001, © Jon Lee Anderson 2001, reprinted with the permission of The Wylie Agency Inc.).

CHAPTER FIVE

Farahnaz Nazir's International Women's Day charter began with a demand that schools for girls and boys should reopen immediately. It also included a call for women to be respected and accorded basic human rights, with society creating conditions favourable to the development of women's minds, education, health, discipline, culture, spirit and economic wellbeing in accordance with national and international norms. It went on to demand that women be invited to participate fully in both government and in society.

The statistics on female health are from Ahmed Rashid's book *Taliban: Islam, Oil and the New Great Game in Central Asia*, and also from a Physicians for Human Rights report, published in the *Journal of the American Medical Association* entitled 'Women's Health and Human Rights in Afghanistan' (Vol. 280, 5 August 1998).

As to the contention that the best times in Afghanistan were during the Soviet era, in addition to my own interviews with educated women in Afghanistan, in 1987 the General Secretary of the Afghan Red Crescent Society told the *New York Times* that 'Women are the strongest supporters of the revolution. For the first time, our women have been given equal rights at the level of education, work, salaries and other areas.' She was a member of the Communist Party, but even Western diplomats conceded that rights for women were one of the few achievements of the 1978 revolution, although many women moved into higher jobs because so many men were away fighting the guerrillas. For more on this read 'Afghans Mix Sovietisation and Free Market' by Steven R. Weisman (*New York Times*, 15 May 1987). See also the Revolutionary Association of the Women of Afghanistan website: www.rawa.org.

CHAPTER SIX

The article 'Limbs of No Body' by Mohsen Makhmalbaf was useful when writing this chapter. Makhmalbaf is very interesting on the position of women in Afghanistan, and the history of polygamy and the perspective of family as harem.

CHAPTER SEVEN

The history of Ai Khanoum can be read in more detail in Tim Judah's article for the *New York Review of Books* entitled 'With the Northern Alliance' (15 November 2001).

The front line at Puze Polihomri was visited several times by *Montreal Gazette* reporter Levon Sevunts over a period of weeks, including living in the trenches with the soldiers. It was Levon who first told me to look out for soldiers wearing mascara. I have read all of his excellent reports for this period, and am indebted to him for making them available to me. He is a brave journalist and a generous colleague. For this section, I read his long interview with General Yusuf Muhammad entitled 'Bombs Focused on Hills: Northern Alliance expected to launch offensive on Mazar-i-Sharif soon' (*Montreal Gazette*, 5 November 2001).

The tribal history of Afghanistan, which is so critical to understanding its modern day politics, is explained at length by both Mohsen Makhmalbaf in 'Limbs of No Body' and Ahmed Rashid in *Taliban*.

Tim Judah quoted Chris Stephen's quip in 'With the Northern Alliance' (*New York Review of Books*, 15 November 2001, © NYRB 2001, reprinted with permission).

I have read wire reports from the Associated Press and Reuters on the Taliban's Grand Council to consider the US demand to hand over Osama bin Laden. I would like to pay tribute to the work of Kathy Gannon from the Associated Press, one of the few Western journalists to have lived in Kabul during the air strikes. She has reported from there over a period of more than fifteen years. The refutation of Taliban claims that Osama bin Laden had left Afghanistan was made by Northern Alliance Foreign Minister Dr Abdullah at a press conference in Khoja Bahauddin, September 2001.

For the history of Osama bin Laden covered here and later in the book I have referred to Ahmed Rashid's *Taliban: Islam, Oil and the New Great Game in Central Asia* and John Cooley's *Unholy Wars – Afghanistan, America and International Terrorism.*

CHAPTER EIGHT
General Bariolai made comments about relations with the US to a number of journalists, including Levon Sevunts who refers to it in his article 'Alliance Looking for US Respect' (*Montreal Gazette*, 1 November 2001).

The celebrity profile of Mamur Hassan by Jon Lee Anderson appeared in the *New Yorker* on 22 October 2001, aptly titled 'The Warlord' (© Jon Lee Anderson 2001, reprinted with the permission of The Wylie Agency Inc.). Quotes from Hassan throughout this chapter are from his interviews with me, or with Jon Lee Anderson.

Since the defeat of the Taliban, Pashtun warlord Gulbuddin Hekmatyar has returned to Afghanistan, so all this history is once again painfully relevant. I have read what has been written about this controversial figure in *Unholy Wars* by John Cooley and on two websites: RAWA (www.rawa.org) and http://www.comebackalive. com/df/dplaces/afghanis/index.htm. The latter has an entertainingly written work by brave gonzo journalist Robert Young Pelton. I have also consulted a series of investigative articles from the late 1980s, including: 'Will the Afghan Regime Remain or Fall?' by Rone Tempest (*Los Angeles Times*, 31 May 1988); 'Westernised Women Dread Return to a Veiled Existence' by Christina Lamb (*Financial Times*, 23 June 1989); 'Exiled and Excluded' by Lucy Mathen (*Guardian*, 30 August 1988); 'Kabul Women Shun Veils, See Rebel Threat to Status' by David B. Ottaway (*Washington Post*, 4 May 1988); and 'The Heroes With Tarnished Haloes' by George Arney (*Guardian*, 5 January 1988).

The allegation that Hekmatyar and his followers threw acid in women's faces is now part of Afghan political folklore, having been played up by the Russians before they withdrew in 1989. However, it also has a basis in fact. In 1988 Shafika Razminda, vice-chairwoman of the All-Afghanistan Women's Council, who was at university with Hekmatyar told the *Guardian* newspaper, 'In 1971, when women came out in public with no veil, Gulbaddin's supporters sprayed acid in their faces. When women wore stockings, they shot at their legs. Women more than [any] other hate this man' (George Arney, 'The Heroes with Tarnished Haloes', *Guardian*, 5 January 1988). See also 'Afghans mix Sovietisation and Free Market' by Steven R. Weisman (*New York Times*, 15 May 1987).

I have also read *Mad, Bad and Dangerous to Know* by Scott Burchill, lecturer in international relations at Deakin University, Melbourne. I would like to thank Scott for his assistance with this section of the book. All the history about Hekmatyar – the CIA's favourite warlord – was known during the 1980s. In March 1990, the US House Republican Research Committee of the Task Force on Terrorism and Unconventional Warfare, severely criticised the CIA and Pakistan's Inter-Services-Intelligence for their gross negligence in covering up the misconduct of Hekmatyar's Hezb-e-Islami faction during the Afghan civil war. The report also canvassed whether the ISI had propped up Hekmatyar as an ideal Muslim choice, while knowing that he was actually working for the Soviet KGB. Now, there is the ultimate conspiracy theory!

There are also allegations about Hekmatyar's involvement in drug trafficking. In May 1990, as the CIA operation in Afghanistan was winding down, the *Washington Post* published a front-page exposé charging that Hekmatyar was a major heroin manufacturer. The Post argued that US officials had refused to investigate charges of heroin dealing by its Afghan allies 'because US narcotics policy in Afghanistan has been subordinated to the war against Soviet influence there'.

In 1996, the former CIA director of the Afghan operation, Charles Cogan, admitted the CIA had indeed sacrificed the drug war to fight the Cold War. 'Our main mission was to do as much damage as possible to the Soviets. We didn't really have the resources or the time to devote to an investigation of the drug trade,' he told ABC TV. 'I don't think that we need to apologise for this. Every situation has its fallout . . . There was fallout in terms of drugs, yes. But the main objective was accomplished. The Soviets left Afghanistan.' (Interviews for 'Dealing with the Demon', ABC TV, 1996.)

'You can rent an Afghan, but you can never buy one' – Britain's relations with the Afghans in the nineteenth century, and their war for influence with Russia, are enthrallingly covered in *The Great Game – On Secret Service in High Asia* by Peter Hopkirk. His wife Kathleen Hopkirk has also written a wonderful book on the history of the region entitled *A Central Asian Companion*.

On the money trail, there is an enormous amount to read, both on the web and in print. I have read 'Operation Blowback' by Bob Fitrakis (*Columbus Alive* e-mag, October 2001). I have also read the famous 1998 interview with Zbigniew Brzezinski by William Blum from French newspaper *Le Nouvel Observateur* (the interview has been translated and reissued by the author via email). William Blum is the author of the books *Killing Hope: US military and CIA interventions since World War II* and *Rogue State: A guide to the world's only superpower*. The follow-up interview with Brzezinski, post-September 11, was by David Corn in 'Anthrax, Mujaheddin and the CIA' in AlterNet (19 October 2001). David Corn is the Washington editor of *The Nation* and a regular columnist for AlterNet.org.

I have also found a 1992 investigation of the CIA's role by the *Washington Post* invaluable (see 'Anatomy of a Victory: CIA's covert

Afghan war' by Steve Coll, 19 July 1992). Another interesting and useful resource is the 1992 book *The Bear Trap: Afghanistan's Untold Story* by former Pakistani ISI General Mohammed Yousaf, which includes a detailed account of his role and that of the CIA in Afghanistan.

Ahmed Rashid covers the CIA's role, and in particular William Casey's stand, in *Taliban: The Story of the Afghan Warlords* (p. 129). The training of international Muslim volunteers by the CIA was first revealed by John Cooley on American television. See also page 71 of John Cooley's *Unholy Wars*. I have also consulted two articles by Norm Dixon in *Green Left Weekly*: 'Taliban: Made by the USA' (10 October 2001) and 'How the CIA Created Osama bin Laden' (October 2001). There is a fascinating article from Jason Burke in the UK *Observer* newspaper called 'Frankenstein the CIA Created: Mujahadeen trained and funded by the US are among its deadliest foes' (17 January 1999).

The rise of the Taliban is most carefully documented by Ahmed Rashid in *Taliban: Islam, Oil and the New Great Game in Central Asia*, and the quote about Mullah Omar being like Robin Hood comes from page 25.

I covered the drought and the plight of the refugees in Khoja Bahauddin, and the quote from the ACTED aid agency comes from my interviews. I interviewed Dr Aini and General Hassan about the possibility of the Taliban participating in any national government. General Bariolai's opinion comes from his interview with Tim Judah, quoted in the *New York Review of Books*, 15 November 2001 (© NYRB 2001, reprinted with permission).

Mohsen Makhmalbaf's terrible experience with starving Afghan refugees in camps inside Iran is described on pages 11–12 of his article 'Limbs of No Body' (*see Bibliography*). British journalist Christina Lamb also visited refugee camps on the Afghan side of the Iranian border. In an article entitled 'They call this "the slaughterhouse"' (*Financial Times*, 9 December 2001) she describes these forgotten camps, where 800,000 people were starving, as the most terrible she had ever seen anywhere in the world.

CHAPTER TEN

The drops of US food aid were controversial at the time. The response of Eric Le Guin from ACTED is from my interview with him in October 2001 in Khoja Bahauddin. I interviewed Edward Artis, as did others including Jim Maceda from NBC and Levon Sevunts from the *Montreal Gazette*. Neil Barrett made a longer film for National Geographic Television, spending a week with Ed as he delivered aid to refugees at Choyab, four hours west of Khoja

Bahauddin. I have also read the publicity about the modern day Knights of Malta whom Artis brought with him to Afghanistan.

On the strategy of the war I have referred to a long article by Tim Judah for the *New York Review of Books* entitled 'With the Northern Alliance' (15 November 2001). On the controversial figure of Rashid Dostum, I have read 'The Treacherous General' by Patrick Cockburn (*Independent*, 1 December 2001), which is where the quote about not submitting to a government where there is no whiskey and no music comes from.

On the vexed question of verifying information about defecting Afghan generals, journalist Tim Judah spoke to Rashid Dostum about Kazi Abdul Hai's side switching, but stresses that none of Dostum's claims could be confirmed as General Dostum was in a region inaccessible to journalists. See 'War in the Dark' by Tim Judah (*New York Review of Books*, 29 November 2001).

The tale of the chopper crash landing was told to me by two of the survivors.

For me, one of the greatest thrills from this entire journey was realising that I was standing at the same spot and having the same experience as Fitzroy MacLean in the 1930s. I'd highly recommend his book *Eastern Approaches*.

For background about the gulag at Vorkuta I read Colin Thubron's travel book *In Siberia* and Ryszard Kapuscinski's *Imperium*. I received additional information about the labour camps at Vorkuta from Anton, who took me to Dushanbe. He worked for the BBC and was very well informed about the history of the gulag due to his own bitter family experience.

CHAPTER ELEVEN

The effect of negative reporting about the war on Washington powerbrokers was covered in *Bush At War* by Bob Woodward. I read the preview serialised in the *Washington Post* called 'A Struggle for the President's Heart and Mind' (17 November 2002). He reports that by the end of October, Condoleezza Rice and others in President Bush's inner circle were on edge as the administration was being 'murdered' in the media. Even leading conservatives, Bush's usual allies, were blasting the war effort.

The general justification for the bombing campaign, including fears of al-Qaeda chemical and nuclear weapons capability, was covered in an article by Matt Kelley entitled 'U.S. Hits Suspected Weapons Plant' (Associated Press, 12 November 2001).

The Red Cross warehouse was bombed twice, first on 16 October 2001 and then again on 25/26 October. 'Bombing the Red Cross' by William M. Arkin (*Washington Post*, 4 November 2001) is an excellent summary of all the issues and concerns being raised in the US at the time.

Like everyone else I heard Rear Admiral John Stuffelbeem's comments on World Service Radio on 25 October 2001. It was also reported by Agence France-Presse, in a report by Jim Mannion entitled 'Pentagon official "surprised" at Taliban's cling to power' (25 October 2001).

The exact text of George Bush's famous quote in the week after the September 11 attacks is: 'When I take action, I'm not going to fire a two million dollar missile at a ten dollar empty tent and hit a camel in the butt. It's going to be decisive.' This was quoted on CNN, 16 September 2001.

The account of soldiers spending their day in the trenches comes from Levon Sevunts' article 'Life in the Trenches' (*Montreal Gazette*, 8 November 2001).

I have read a variety of material about Abdul Haq, including an interview he gave to Anatol Lieven in Peshawar some two weeks before his death ('Voices from the Region', Carnegie Endowment for Peace, Washington, 11 October 2001). Haq had also   done an interview for the BBC shortly before his death, which I have seen. Jason Burke wrote an excellent piece from Peshawar after Haq's death ('Desperate Call From the Valley of Death: "Help us . . ." ', *Observer*, 28 October 2001), and there was an obituary in the *Guardian* newspaper entitled 'Veteran Afghan Leader Seeking Post-Taliban Consensus Rule' by Lawrence Joffe (29 October 2001).

I have read a range of American commentators on the relationship between Abdul Haq and the CIA: 'First, the Bad News, Then . . . The Bad News' by Eric Margolis (*Toronto Sun*, 4 November 2001 – see also Commondreams.com); 'The Abdul Haq Fiasco' by Robert Novak (*Sierra Times*, 1 November 2001). The right-wing commentators describe a sense of grievance at the US 'abandoning' Abdul Haq, ascribing his death as partly to American 'deceit, arrogance and ignorance'.

The official US position that Haq received US assistance before his death was reported by CNN on 28 October 2001. Rumsfeld would not specify what kind of assistance Haq received, saying it was not from the US military but another branch of government.

CIA allegations that Haq was a 'cowboy' are reviewed by Barbara Slavin and Jonathan Weisman in 'Taliban Foe's Death Sparks Criticism of US Goals' (*USA Today*, 31 October 2001).

Mazar-i-Sharif: the history of the bloodiest episode of the Taliban's wars in Afghanistan is superbly covered by Ahmed Rashid on pages 72–73 of *Taliban: Islam, Oil and the New Great*

Game in Central Asia. The hanging at the shrine in Mazar is described by Liam Pleven in 'War, Death Are Their Neighbors' (*Washington Post*, 2 December 2001).

The role of the CIA in this conflict has been revealed by Bob Woodward in *Bush At War*. I read the previews serialised in the *Washington Post* on 18 November 2002 entitled 'CIA Led Way With Cash Handouts' (additional reporting by Mark Malseed).

CHAPTER TWELVE

Rob Schulteis is the author of *Night Letters: Inside Wartime Afghanistan*.

Regarding the BBC budgetary crisis, this was frequently discussed in Khoja Bahauddin by BBC staff from Moscow and London.

There is information about Afghanistan's new leader Hamed Karzai on the country's official website (afghan-info.com), but perhaps most interesting and useful is an article called 'The Lawless Frontier' by Robert D. Kaplan (*Atlantic Monthly*, September 2000). Kaplan wrote a lengthy series of articles in Afghanistan, Pakistan and Baluchistan, which included an interview with Karzai before he became Afghan leader. (Kaplan is a senior fellow at the New America Foundation, and the author of *Eastward to Tartary: Travels in the Balkans, the Middle East, and the Caucasus*.)

I have also read a series of articles by my colleagues who were in Pakistan and Afghanistan during this conflict, among them: 'Torture, Treachery and Spies – Covert War in Afghanistan' by Jason Burke in Peshawar (*Observer*, 4 November 2001); 'Who Can the Taliban Surrender To?' by Tim McGirk (*Time* magazine, 1 December 2001); 'Li'l Big Chief Has Lost His Sheep: He's the West's big hope, but the Afghan chairman has little say in his own backyard' by Rahimullah Yusufzai (*Indian e magazine*, December 2001); and 'Wondering If This Man Can Pull it Off' by Marc Kaufman (*Washington Post*, 17 February 2002).

There is a dispute over the amount of American assistance Karzai received after he was surrounded by Taliban forces. Karzai acknowledges that American troops saved him and his men, and allowed his anti-Taliban mission to continue, but in November Secretary of Defense Donald Rumsfeld reported that a US helicopter rescued Karzai and flew him to Pakistan. Karzai denied that he was ever whisked across the border, insisting that he stayed inside Afghanistan the whole time.

General Yusuf Muhammad's comments about the US bombing at Qala Qata are quoted by Levon Sevunts in his article 'Bombs Focused on the Hills' (*Montreal Gazette*, 5 November 2001).

Masood Khalili's account of his last night with Ahmed Shah Massoud is described in 'Slowly Stalking an Afghan "Lion"' by Craig Pyes and William C. Rempel.

CHAPTER THIRTEEN

John Steinbeck's perspective on men and pocketknives comes from *A Russia Journal*. NBC cameraman Tom Streithorst's perspective on Afghan men comes from his unpublished piece 'In Afghanistan'. British diplomat Mountstuart Elphinstone's nineteenth-century view comes from *An Account of the Kingdom of Caubul*.

The interview with Taliban Mullah Mohammed Hassan about the punishment for gay men is quoted in an article entitled 'With Sugared Tea and Caustic Rules, an Afghan Leader Explains Himself' by John Burns (*New York Times*, 24 November 1996).

I have read two articles by my friend Levon Sevunts as background for the advances on Mazar-i-Sharif, the battle that signalled the collapse of the Taliban: 'Afghan City Ripe: Anti-Taliban Forces Advance to Within 8 Kilometres of Mazar' (*Montreal Gazette*, 9 November 2001) and 'Bombs Focused on Hills: Northern Alliance Expected to Launch Offensive on Mazare Sharif Soon' (*Montreal Gazette*, 5 November 2001).

Information about the CIA's role in this battle, and the contribution made by direct payments to commanders come from Bob Woodward's book *Bush At War*. I read the preview serialised in the *Washington Post* on 18 November 2002 ('CIA Led Way With Cash Handouts', additional reporting by Mark Malseed). The CIA calculated that it had spent only US$70 million in direct cash outlays on the ground in Afghanistan, and some of that had been to pay for field hospitals. Woodward quotes President Bush as saying in an interview 'That's one bargain', and wondering aloud what the Soviets had spent in their disastrous war in Afghanistan that had contributed to the collapse of the Soviet Union.

The massacres at Mazar-i-Sharif are comprehensively covered by Ahmed Rashid on page 72 of *Taliban: Islam, Oil and the New Great Game in Central Asia*, and the quote about Mullah Omar giving Taliban soldiers permission to kill for two hours comes from page 73. I have also consulted the 1998 UN report by special rapporteur Paik Chong-Hyun, who investigated the deaths of the Taliban. There are also two Human Rights Watch reports: *The Massacre in Mazar-e-Sharif, 1998*, and *Afghanistan: Crisis of Impunity, 2001*.

In March 2002 the *Sydney Morning Herald* reviewed all this information, and I found that article very useful. See Paul McGeough's report on the fallout from the tit-for-tat massacres ('Too slow: UN Digs its Own Grave in Mazar', *Sydney Morning Herald*, 2 March 2002). Paul McGeough refers to a 65-page report critical of the failure of UNHCR to investigate these massacres. It was commissioned by the Afghanistan Research and Evaluation Unit, an independent humanitarian advisory body run by members from governments that donate to the Afghan relief effort and aid agencies working in the country. It was set up in 1999 in a bid to improve the humanitarian operation in Afghanistan.

In writing about Rashid Dostum I referred to Ahmed Rashid's *Taliban: Islam, Oil and the New Great Game in Central Asia*, and Patrick Cockburn's 'The Treacherous General' (*Independent*, 1 December 2001).

CHAPTER FOURTEEN

The soldiers at the front line at Qala Qata as the battle began were quoted by Levon Sevunts in 'Exchange in Trenches, Afghan Rebels Take Key City' (*Montreal Gazette*, 10 November 2001).

I have read the accounts of Paul McGeough and Levon Sevunts about the night the three journalists died. Levon went on to win an award for his article about that night, which I first read as he was writing it in the NBC house in Khoja Bahauddin: 'Journalists die, I was thinking, "We're fried" ' (Montreal Gazette, 11 November 2001).

CHAPTER SIXTEEN

Taloqan: I have read with great interest the interview with the Taliban mullah in Taloqan by my colleague Jon Lee Anderson ('The Surrender: Double agents, defectors, disaffected Taliban, and a motley army battle for Kunduz' (*New Yorker*, 10 December 2000). I also referred to 'Stallholders Selling Out of Afghanistan's New Must-have Hat' by Justin Huggler in Taloqan (*Independent*, 26 November 2001).

Crossing the Hindu Kush – once again, my experience mirrors Fitzroy MacLean's from *Eastern Approaches*. I also found that I had similar impressions of the majestic Panjshir Valley to Mohsen Makhmalbaf. The reference to the role of the mountains in defeating Afghanistan's enemies comes from page 9 of his article 'Limbs of No Body' (*see Bibliography*). Many of the images at the end of the chapter can be seen in the RAWA picture gallery – some are ghastly and extremely distressing, so be warned if you're going to look: http://rawa.fancymarketing.net/gallery.html

CHAPTER EIGHTEEN

I have read a number of accounts of visitors to Kabul from different eras, as well as my colleagues' accounts from today – including Jon Lee Anderson's 'City of Dreams' (*New Yorker*, 24 December 2001, copyright Jon lee Anderson 2001, reprinted with the permission of The Wylie Agency Inc.). His wonderful observation about comparing the layers of destruction in the city to the rings of a dead tree trunk comes from page 3 of this article.

British travel writer Robert Byron wrote of Afghanistan in the 1930s 'Here at last is Asia without an inferiority complex' (*The Road to Oxiana*). This still rings true today.

There are also interesting photos of Kabul at http://www.afghan-network.net/Photography/kabul/ This website includes some of the sad photographs that are on sale as postcards in Kabul – they show the sites as they were in their heyday, with insets of them as they are today in ruins.

The UN special investigator for Afghanistan compared Afghanistan to an 'infected wound' in an interview with Ahmed Rashid on 14 May 1998.

In addition to going to the Kabul zoo myself, I have read articles in the wire services and for MS-NBC online by producer Kevin Sites, who was in the group that crossed the Hindu Kush with me. I have also read a number of pieces on the Newspaper Zoo Wars, including Stephen Moss's piece in the *Guardian* newspaper on 29 November 2001 entitled 'Mail Mauls Rivals with Lion Coup as Tabloid War Rages'. Similarly, with the movies, I went myself and have read wire copy on the return of the cinema to Kabul, as well as 'Limbs of No Body' by Mohsen Makhmalbaf. All of Makhmalbaf's insights are fascinating, but as a film-maker who tried to work here during Taliban times, his views on Afghanistan's film culture are particularly pertinent. The Taliban minister explaining that entertainment should be limited to going to the park and watching the grass grow came from the Associated Press wire story 'Taliban Restrict Music', December 1996 (quoted on page 115 of *Taliban* by Ahmed Rashid).

The contrasting memories of Kabul in the 1970s come from Pakistani journalist and academic Javed Nazir ('A Pakistani Perspective – Afghanistan: Past, Present, Future', *Journal of the International Institute*, University of Michigan, volume 9 number 2). Javed Nazir is a Michigan Journalism Fellow from Pakistan and former editor of the *Frontier Post*, a nonconformist newspaper in Lahore. He left Pakistan after a letter published in his paper angered religious extremists, and he is writing a book about religious minorities in Pakistan.

The 'Taliban porn photos' were obtained by my friend and colleague Craig Nelson who filed for the *Sydney Morning Herald* from Afghanistan. I am indebted to him for showing them to me, along with the talcum powder container he took from the bedroom of Mullah Omar's favourite wife – wife number three – in Kandahar. Definitely a memento to rival bin Laden's birdcage! I am also indebted to him and my friend Margaret Coker for all their assistance and support in the writing of this book.

The atrocities in Mazar during this conflict have been widely covered. I referred to Andrea Catherwood's report for ITN (16 November 2001), as well as the Associated Press report of 22 November 2001 ('600 Bodies Discovered in Mazar-i-Sharif: ICRC'). The spokesman quoted is Mohammed Muhahaiq, from the Hizb-i-Wahdat militia, fighting with the Northern Alliance.

After my own visit to the al-Qaeda training camp at Rishkor I read 'For Taliban, Many Losses' by Scott Peterson in *Christian Science Monitor* (26 November 2001). There are presently reports that al-Qaeda is returning to Afghanistan and re-establishing bases there.

I am indebted to Chris Stephen for all his help on the chemical weapons plant story when we were in Kabul. He is knowledgeable, and always generous about sharing what he knows. I have also read the following articles: 'Kabul Paper Trail Damns al-Qaeda' by Jason Burke in Jalalabad, Tim Judah in Kabul and Peter Beaumont (*Observer*, 18 November 2001); 'Arrest of Second Pakistan Expert Exposes Jehadi Bomb Trail' (HTC and Agencies, Islamabad/Moscow, October 25); 'Pakistani Nuclear Scientists Questioned Over Chemical Weapons', Rory McCarthy (*Guardian*, 29 November 2001); 'UN Orders Sanctions On Pak Group' (Associated Press, 27 December 2001); 'U.S. Pinpointed Al-Qaeda Chemical/Biological Sites', Phil Brennan (NewsMax.com, 12 November 2001).

The extent of al-Qaeda chemical and nuclear weapons capability has also been widely covered. *The Times* reported in the second week in November that it had discovered partially burned documents in an abandoned al-Qaeda safe house in Kabul, used by Taliban leaders, foreign fighters and reportedly by bin Laden himself. The notes, written in Arabic, German, Urdu and English, had graphic designs for missiles, bombs and nuclear weapons. One set of notes, written on headed notepaper from the Hotel Grand in Peshawar and dated 26 April 1998, said: 'Naturally, the explosive liquid has a very high mechanical energy, which is translated into destructive force. But it can be tamed, controlled and can be used as a useful propulsive fuel if certain methods are applied to it.' Other documents included descriptions of how the detonation of TNT compresses plutonium to a critical mass, sparking a chain reaction, and ultimately a thermonuclear reaction. The design suggested bin Laden might be working on a fission device, similar to Fat Man, the bomb dropped on Nagasaki. However, it must be emphasised that it is extremely difficult to build a viable warhead.

Information relating to the issue of al-Qaeda chemical and nuclear weapons capability continued to emerge after I had left Afghanistan, including the following fascinating reports: 'Terrorist Group Placed Heavy Emphasis on Developing Nuclear Device' by

Mike Boettcher and Ingrid Arnesen, additional reporting by Sheila McVicar (CNN, 25 January 2002); 'Tapes Shed New Light on Bin Laden's Network' by Nic Robertson (CNN, 18 August 2002).

A large archive of al-Qaeda videotapes obtained by CNN in Afghanistan shed new light on Osama bin Laden's terror network, revealing images of chemical gas experiments on dogs, lessons on making explosives, terrorist training tactics and previously unseen images of bin Laden and his top aides. The archive includes 64 videotapes that span more than a decade – but it is the puppy being killed with nerve gas that is the most memorable image.

CHAPTER NINETEEN
Some statistics on women's health were provided for me at the Robia Balkh Women's Hospital in Kabul by Dr Rahima Zafar Stanekzai. I also consulted 'Women's Health and Human Rights in Afghanistan' by Zohra Rasekh, MPH; Heidi M. Bauer, MD, MPH, MS; M. Michele Manos, PhD, MPH; Vincent Iacopino, MD, PhD. See the *Journal of the American Medical Association*, Vol. 280, pp. 449–455, 5 August 1998.

UNDP country development indicators for 1995 are quoted in Chapter eight of *Taliban: Islam, Oil and the New Great Game in Central Asia* by Ahmed Rashid. Mullah Wakil's explanation that the Taliban were trying to recreate the times of the Prophet more than 1000 years ago is quoted on page 43 of Rashid's book.

I heard and saw John Simpson's coverage of the fall of Kabul, and it is on the BBC website (14 November 2001). As it became a *cause célèbre*, there was also much written about it, and he appeared on the BBC's 'Parkinson' program to explain his stance. Reports include 'Media Monkey: Simpson liberates Kabul single handedly' by Jessica Hodgson (*Guardian*, 13 November 2001); 'Simpson Sorry for "Liberating" Kabul', Lucy Ward (*Guardian*, 19 November 2001). The BBC news team, including Simpson, went on to win an Emmy for their coverage of the war in Afghanistan, and especially the fall of Kabul.

The deaths of the four journalists driving in to Afghanistan from Pakistan were widely covered. In Kabul, I interviewed some journalists who were caught up in the same attack and survived. I have read wire copy, including from the Associated Press and Reuters – who lost two of their people in this tragic incident. Pamela Constable wrote two excellent pieces for the *Washington Post*: 'On Perilous Road to Kabul, Gunmen Kill 4 Journalists' (20 November 2001); and a follow-up on the next day (21 November 2001).

CHAPTER TWENTY

I am indebted to Chris Stephen for his assistance in Kabul on this story of Osama bin Laden narrowly avoiding a US air strike. I have since read the feature piece about this incident in the *Observer* ('The Chase: He can run – but can he hide?', Chris Stephen and Tim Judah in Kabul, Ed Vulliamy in Washington, Paul Harris in Quetta, James Astill in Mogadishu and Peter Beaumont in London, 25 November 2001).

The al-Qaeda training camps at Khost were first visited by Jason Burke, who told me about them in Kabul. I have since read his piece in the *Observer* ('Bin Laden's "varsity of terror" uncovered', 25 November 2001).

I have discussed the al-Qaeda computer find with *Wall Street Journal* correspondent Alan Cullison in Moscow. I have also read widely, including articles that he and his colleague Andy Higgins wrote, such as 'PC Apparently Used by Al Qaeda Leaders Reveals Details of Four Years of Terrorism' by Alan Cullison and Andrew Higgins (*Wall Street Journal*, Kabul, 31 December 2001). Other useful articles were 'Kabul Computer Reveals Files of Top Al Qaeda Officials' by D. Ian Hopper, Associated Press, 31 December 2001; 'Al Qaeda Computer Found – Contains No Mention Of 911 Plot' by Reed Irvine (*Accuracy In Media*, 1 January 2002, based on Reuters report AFP REPORT 2 January 2002); 'How the *Journal* Got Al Qaeda's Computers' by Dan Kennedy (Boston e-mag the phoenix.com, 3 January 2002). I have also read all the reporting about the shoe bomber Richard Reid, as I was in London when his attempt to blow up a plane was foiled.

I went to the hairdresser in Kabul and read about the Taliban's restrictions on women in 'City of Secrets' by Carla Power (*Newsweek*, 13 July 1998) and Chapter 8 of Ahmed Rashid's book, *Taliban*, especially pages 113–115. Mohsen Makhmalbaf's thoughts about women wearing make-up under their burqas is on page 24 of 'Limbs of No Body' (*see Bibliography*).

I have been heavily reliant on the work of my colleagues who were in Mazar-i-Sharif at the time of the siege at the fortress: 'CIA agent possibly dead in Mazar-i-Sharif revolt' by Jim Wolf (26 November, Washington – Reuters); 'Allies Direct the Death Rites of Trapped Taliban Fighters', Luke Harding in Mazar-i-Sharif (*Guardian*, 27 November 2001); 'A Tank Roared In. It Fired Four Rounds. Then There Was Silence in the Fort', Luke Harding in Mazar-i-Sharif on the last stand of the Taliban (*Guardian*, 28 November 2001); 'Dead lie crushed or shot, in the dust, in ditches, amid the willows', Luke Harding (*Guardian*, 29 November 2001); 'The Castle of Death' by Justin Huggler (*Independent*, 30 November 2001); 'Errors revealed in siege of Afghan fort',

Luke Harding, Nicholas Watt, and Ewen Macaskill (*Guardian*, 1 December 2001); 'Smoke-blackened and Wounded, Yet Lucky to be Alive, the Survivors of Qalai Janghi Emerge', Justin Huggler (*Independent*, 3 December 2001); 'Inside the Battle at Qala-i-Jangi' by Alex Perry (*Time* magazine, 10 December 2001, Volume 158, No. 23, © 2001 TIME Inc., reprinted by permission); 'SAS Role in Fort Deaths Questioned' by Richard Norton-Taylor (*Guardian*, 15 December 2001); 'Captured Taliban Suffocated on Trip to Jail', Carlotta Gall (*New York Times*, 12 December 2001).

Nine months after the siege, *Newsweek* detailed the findings of a Physicians for Human Rights inquiry into the deaths of Taliban soldiers transported by containers from Kunduz to Sheberghan prison. See 'The Death Convoy of Afghanistan' by Babak Dehghan-pisheh, John Barry and Roy Gutman (*Newsweek*, 26 August 2002). More than 1000 men are alleged to have died of asphyxiation. The forces allegedly responsible were under General Dostum's command. General Dostum's spokesperson, Faizullah Zaki, conceded to *Newsweek* that many people did die of suffocation, but he put the total at 'between 100 and 120 people, a few from each container'. He added that some of them 'were seriously injured and died en route'. He suggested that the uprising at Qala-i-Jangi prison, just three days earlier, might have affected their treatment. 'If the incident at Qala-Jangi hadn't happened, it's possible that the prisoners would have been transferred more peacefully. There would have been less irreg-ularities,' he said, adding: "They suffocated. Died, not killed. Nobody killed anybody." Zaki also said that General Dostum was not there when the prisoners were loaded into containers. 'The tech-nical details of the transfer were left to lower-level commanders.' He added that 'there was a handful of American soldiers that didn't leave [Dostum's] side' during the period in question.

The US response to criticism of its role in Mazar came from Kenton Keith at a daily US press briefing in Pakistan, quoted in *Karachi News*, 1 December 2001. Paul McGeough's article in the *Sydney Morning Herald* ('Too slow: UN digs its own grave in Mazar', 2 March 2002) details the failure of earlier UN investiga-tions into the tit-for-tat massacres around Mazar.

The Emergency hospital for the treatment of victims of war has a website containing information about their hospitals in Afghanistan and throughout the world:

http://www.emergency.it/eng/index.html.

Statistics about land mines were provided by the UN De-mining Agency in a series of interviews I conducted in Kabul. I also referred to Ahmed Rashid's *Taliban* (Chapter 9, p. 126), and to Mohsen Makhmalbaf's 'Limbs of No Body' (p. 1, *see Bibliography*).

CHAPTER TWENTY-ONE

I reported from the Russian embassy and also referred to wire copy, which made me realise that the Russians returned to their embassy on the same day that the first movie was screened in Kabul. See the Associated Press report of 19 November 2001: 'Russia to Open Embassy in Afghanistan' by Arun Mohanty in Moscow.

With UN support, refugees from the Russian embassy compound did start returning to the Shomali plains from the end of December and rebuilding their villages and their lives. See 'The Long March Home Begins' by Rory Carroll (*Guardian*, 29 December 2001). However, the UN said it would take several months before the bulk of the Shomali's 200,000 refugees returned: 'The major obstacle is the presence of mines. Mine clearance is very time consuming and the place is basically now a desert.'

Catching the elusive Osama bin Laden: the quote from the CIA counter-terrorism chief about wanting bin Laden's head in a box, and the agent's response are both from *Bush At War*, by Bob Woodward. I read the preview serialised in the *Washington Post* entitled 'CIA Led Way With Cash Handouts' (18 November 2002, additional reporting by Mark Malseed).

Bibliography

Anderson, Jon Lee, *The Lion's Grave*, Grove Press, 2002

Byron, Robert, *The Road to Oxiana*, Jonathan Cape, December, 1966

Cooley, John, *Unholy Wars – Afghanistan, America and International Terrorism*, Pluto Press, London, 2002

Elphinstone, Mountstuart, *An Account of the Kingdom of Caubul*, London, Longman Hurst and Murray, 1815

Hopkirk, Kathleen, *A Central Asian Companion*, John Murray Publishers Ltd, London, 1993

Hopkirk, Peter, *The Great Game – On Secret Service in High Asia*, Oxford University Press, 2001

Kapuscinski, Ryszard, *Imperium*, Granta Books, London, 1998

MacLean, Fitzroy, *Eastern Approaches*, Jonathan Cape, London, 1949

Makhmalbaf, Mohsen, 'Limbs of No Body: World's Indifference to the Afghan Tragedy', *The Iranian* magazine, 20 June 2001. Also available on his website: www.makhmalbaf.com

Rashid, Ahmed, *Taliban: Islam, Oil and the New Great Game in Central Asia*, I.B. Tauris & Co, London, 2000

Schulteis, Rob, *Night Letters: Inside Wartime Afghanistan*, Orion Books, New York, 1992

Steinbeck, John, *A Russia Journal*, Penguin Books, 1999; first published in the US by Viking, 1948

Thubron, Colin, *In Siberia*, Penguin Books, London, 2000

Woodward, Bob, *Bush At War*, Simon & Schuster, 2002

Yousaf, Mohammed, *The Bear Trap: Afghanistan's Untold Story*, Pen & Sword Books/Leo Cooper, 1992